D1298322

An official publication of
THE AMERICAN SOCIOLOGICAL ASSOCIATION
WILLIAM D'ANTONIO, *Executive Officer*

APPLIED SOCIOLOGY

*Roles and Activities
of Sociologists
in Diverse Settings*

Howard E. Freeman
Russell R. Dynes
Peter H. Rossi
William Foote Whyte
Editors

APPLIED
SOCIOLOGY

Jossey-Bass Publishers
San Francisco • Washington • London • 1983

APPLIED SOCIOLOGY
Roles and Activities of Sociologists in Diverse Settings
by Howard E. Freeman, Russell R. Dynes, Peter H. Rossi,
and William Foote Whyte, Editors

Copyright © 1983 by: Jossey-Bass Inc., Publishers
433 California Street
San Francisco, California 94104
&
Jossey-Bass Limited
28 Banner Street
London EC1Y 8QE

Library of Congress Cataloging in Publication Data
Main entry under title:

Applied sociology.

Includes bibliographies and index.
1. Sociology. 2. Sociologists—Employment.
3. Sociology—Study and teaching. I. Freeman, Howard E.
HM51.A66   1983   301   82-49035
ISBN 0-87589-563-8

Manufactured in the United States of America

The paper in this book meets the guidelines for
permanence and durability of the Committee on
Production Guidelines for Book Longevity of the
Council on Library Resources.

JACKET DESIGN BY WILLI BAUM

FIRST EDITION

Code 8307

The Jossey-Bass
Social and Behavioral Science Series

PREFACE

Should there be an increased emphasis on applied sociology in the discipline? What are the implications for conventional undergraduate and graduate training of developing applied sociology programs? Will the growth of applied sociology seriously hinder theory building and basic research? What does sociology have to offer persons interested in nonacademic careers? Are ample and diverse positions really available for sociologists outside academia? Will sociology lose its respectability within the university if it encourages applied work? To what extent must applied sociologists compromise personal values? Can applied sociologists really help the groups and organizations that employ them successfully achieve their goals?

These and similar questions have been argued persistently in the published literature, at national and regional conventions, in graduate and undergraduate seminars, and in nearly every setting in which sociologists convene to discuss informally their discipline and careers. But interest in applied sociology in the 1980s represents more than just a continuation of the arguments and soul searching of the past. Rather, because sociology approaches maturity at a time when academic employment opportunities, basic research support, and public appreciation for the enterprise are declining, the discipline is confronted with answering for itself the question of its future robustness, if not its viability.

For a significant number in the discipline, developing applied sociology programs and fostering nonacademic work opportunities offer the only sensible solution to present and projected declines in recruits, resources, and recognition. These advocates represent an unusual alliance: some are scholars of distinction whose contributions have received extensive peer recognition; some are long-time workers in the field of applied sociology; others are "born-again" applied sociologists whose conversions are comparatively recent; and still others are part of the growing contingent of relatively young sociologists who see their futures tied to the growth of applied sociology. All are represented among the authors of chapters in this book.

Although clearly partisan, this book is much more than an effort to market applied sociology. The various contributors—based on their own experiences as students and academics and on their full-time and part-time involvements in nonacademic settings—are properly chary about the applied side of sociology. They are concerned and thoughtful about the ramifications, for our discipline and for the academy, of promoting applied sociology.

The first part of this volume examines the present status of applied sociology. Its chapters delineate applied and conventional work, consider the role of theory in applied sociology, and assess the present and future supply and demand for persons with sociology degrees.

The second part, devoted to the work of applied sociology, includes chapters on a range of applied roles and on the expertise these roles require. The chapters indicate the broad range of activities available to persons with sociological training—in fact, the areas discussed do not begin to exhaust the opportunities available. Persons inside academia need increased awareness of these roles; persons outside academia in positions to facilitate careers for sociologists require increased knowledge of the strengths and outlooks we can bring to other fields of endeavor.

The third part of this volume is an in-depth consideration of the academic preparation of applied sociologists. The chapters in this section examine the educational implications of promoting applied tracks at both undergraduate and graduate levels, the pedagogical issues in training applied sociologists, and the research skills required. Further, they describe current undergraduate, graduate, and postdoctoral programs and review past, present, and future educational support for sociological training. The book's final chapter places applied sociology in its historical context and speculates on its future growth and development.

This book is not a definitive exploration of applied sociology—it does not fully represent what sociologists do outside of academia, does not consider all the educational requirements, and does not emphasize the ideological and professional outlooks of those who are committed to clinical practice. Parts of the volume will be seen as controversial or opinionated, parts as less scholarly and more autobiographical than readers typically encounter in our publications. These features may be regarded by some readers as limitations, but perhaps this volume is a start toward remodeling and expanding our discipline in ways that enable us to enhance opportunities for applying sociology, to build a rapprochement between sociologists inside and outside the academy, and that thereby strengthen and further the entire sociological enterprise.

CONTENTS

CONTRIBUTORS

Richard A. Berk, professor, Department of Sociology, University of California, Santa Barbara

Joseph R. Blasi, lecturer in social studies, Harvard University, Cambridge, Massachusetts

Francis G. Caro, director, Institute for Social Welfare Research, Community Service Society of New York, New York City

David B. Chandler, associate professor, Department of Sociology, University of Hawaii, Honolulu

O. Andrew Collver, associate professor, Department of Sociology, State University of New York, Stony Brook

Herbert L. Costner, professor, Department of Sociology, University of Washington, Seattle

Robert A. Dentler, senior sociologist, Abt Associates, Inc., Cambridge, Massachusetts

Irwin Deutscher, professor, Department of Sociology, University of Akron, Akron, Ohio

L. Carroll DeWeese III, staff research scientist, General Motors Research Laboratories, Detroit, Michigan

Russell R. Dynes, professor, Department of Sociology, University of Delaware, Newark

Howard E. Freeman, professor, Department of Sociology, University of California, Los Angeles

Geoffrey Gibson, professor, Department of Health Care Management, Baruch College/Mount Sinai School of Medicine, New York City

Jean Giles-Sims, assistant professor, Department of Sociology, Texas Christian University, Fort Worth

Albert E. Gollin, vice-president and associate director of research, Newspaper Advertising Bureau, Inc., New York City

Mathew Greenwald, director of social research, American Council of Life Insurance, Washington, D.C.

Oscar Grusky, professor, Department of Sociology, University of California, Los Angeles

Lawrence D. Haber, programs adviser, Bureau of the Census, Washington, D.C.

Carla B. Howery, executive office, American Sociological Association, Takoma Park, Maryland

Paul L. Johnson, research associate, Maxwell Health Studies Program, Syracuse University, Syracuse, New York

William Kornblum, professor of sociology, Graduate School and University Center of the City University of New York, New York

Kenneth G. Lutterman, associate director, Mental Health Services Planning Research and Research Training, Division of Biometry and Epidemiology, National Institute of Mental Health, Rockville, Maryland

Ronald W. Manderscheid, acting chief, Survey and Systems Research Branch, National Institute of Mental Health, Rockville, Maryland

Hans O. Mauksch, professor of sociology and of family and community medicine, University of Missouri, Columbia

Paul D. Reynolds, professor of sociology and coordinator, Applied Graduate Programs, University of Minnesota, Minneapolis

Peter H. Rossi, director of research, Social and Demographic Research Institute, University of Massachusetts, Amherst

David R. Segal, professor of sociology and of government and politics, University of Maryland, College Park Woods

A. Emerson Smith, director of research, Metromark Market Research, Inc., Columbia, South Carolina

Robert C. Sorensen, president, Sorensen Marketing Management Corporation, New York City, and professor of marketing, Rider College, Lawrenceville, New Jersey

Daphne Spain, contributing editor, International Demographics/American Demographics, Ithaca, New York

Gordon F. Streib, graduate research professor, Department of Sociology, University of Florida, Gainesville

Seymour Sudman, professor, Department of Sociology, University of Illinois, Urbana-Champaign

Barry S. Tuchfeld, director, Center for Organizational Research and Evaluation Studies, Texas Christian University, Fort Worth

William Foote Whyte, professor emeritus of industrial and labor relations and of sociology, Cornell University, Ithaca, New York

Rosemary Yancik, special assistant for program and liaison activities, Division of Resources, Centers, and Community Activities, National Cancer Institute, National Institutes of Health, Bethesda, Maryland

INTRODUCTION

This volume reflects the interest in applied work of a significant number of sociologists, as well as the increased responsiveness to this constituency by the American Sociological Association (ASA). Most of the chapters were first prepared as papers for an applied sociology workshop held in late 1981 in Washington, D.C.; subsequently, they were revised for this book. The workshop was organized with the advice of the Committee on Professional Opportunities in Applied Sociology of the American Sociological Association, which I chaired for three years. (Committee members and participants in the workshop are listed in the appendix to this volume.) The activities of the committee and the conduct of the workshop received strong support from ASA presidents Peter H. Rossi and William Foote Whyte—both of whom identify themselves as applied sociologists—and from Russell R. Dynes and his staff at the ASA executive office. The continued collaboration of Dynes, Rossi, and Whyte should be clear from their participation as coeditors of this volume.

The workshop was well attended—in fact, oversubscribed—and the discussions over the three days of meetings were spirited, thoughtful, and valuable to authors in revising their manuscripts. A number of motives inspired the workshop, including my own need for closure after three years of committee meetings and numerous telephone calls and correspondence with committee members and others in our discipline. The overt reason for the workshop was to learn from each other about teaching applied sociology, and the conference did explore in detail both undergraduate and graduate educational programs for training applied sociologists. Perhaps the critical point learned, as Rossi and Whyte observe, is that the house of applied sociology has many rooms. The varieties of work roles and the diversity of training styles are numerous indeed, and the workshop affirmed that there is no simple approach for preparing applied sociologists.

Despite the diversity of participants—who ranged from clinical sociologists to quantitative researchers, from those with corporate positions to grassroots organizers—they shared the deep conviction that applied sociologists are the lowest persons on the sociological totem pole. This view was shared by ex-presidents Rossi and Whyte, as well as by those who were underemployed or unemployed and by those bored with conventional academic work and looking for applied sociology opportunities. Whatever else might be said about the workshop, its participants were closely bound by a sense of subdued outrage over unfair treatment by their more occupationally conventional peers and by feelings of exclusion from imagined centers of power and prestige within the discipline.

But this book is much more than the proceedings of a successful workshop, and I hope readers will not peruse individual chapters solely for their content. Rather, I believe that these chapters provide clear documentation that many in our discipline are doing more than teaching undergraduates, training their future faculty replacements, and contributing by their writing and research to an understanding of social phenomena.

As a discipline, we have generally not encouraged our applied side. We have failed to provide appropriate educational experiences for students, to develop networks that promote nonacademic career opportunities, and to provide recognition for and acknowledgment of the legitimacy of nonacademic work and even of applied research. Working in commerce and industry or for community organizations or even in a professional school has, to some degree, been regarded as disreputable.

The antagonism of conventional sociologists to applied sociology is difficult to understand fully. I am aware of many of the claims: applied work lures persons away from scholarship; liberal arts graduate schools are not meant to train professionals and practitioners; applied work requires selling out to the establishment; an emphasis on applied sociology would contaminate our values, diffuse our norms, and diminish our stature in academia.

There are counterarguments to each of these claims. Any listing of our culture heroes of the past would certainly include a significant number of persons with applied interests; other social science disciplines—economics is a fine example—have not suffered in academic stature because of their applied activities; and, since sociologists are hardly homogeneous, either ideologically or intellectually, applied sociology is not likely to have a disproportionately large impact on the norms and values of our discipline. Perhaps most telling is the case Rossi and Whyte make in their chapter in this volume—and they are hardly out of the same intellectual and research molds—that applied-side sociology is essential to the discipline for idea development, substantive hypothesis testing, and methodological advancement. Yet, at best, applied sociology has been tolerated until now, and to continue this posture will further alienate those who do applied sociology. Further, failure to be responsive to applied work and to encourage its growth is highly risky in these times.

At the risk of offending colleagues and with an awareness that I am making sweeping generalizations that are challengeable by reference to particular experiences and events in our discipline's history, I want to convey my perspective on why it is deceptive to dismiss current interest in and concern with applied sociology as simply a continuation of what has happened before. True, the applied sociology effort has continuity, as Albert Gollin informs us in detail in his chapter in the last part of this volume. However, the current trend is unique in two ways: first, many with training in our discipline no longer identify with sociology or perceive and describe themselves as sociologists, although they are doing sociological work; second, a growing number of persons with training in other social sciences and in the professions—for example, public administration, health services, social planning, and management—are engaged in work that, from a craft-union perspective, should be undertaken by a sociologist.

Admittedly, numerical estimates are not possible. Given the heterogeneity and diversity of the activities carried on under the rubric of sociology, it is senseless to ruminate on the boundaries of applied sociology; thus, numerical counts are not possible. Besides, until now, it made little difference. From World War II until the last few years, most card-carrying sociologists were kept busy within academia. Our undergraduate enrollments were high, the number of our graduate students continued to increase, research funds were easily obtainable, sociology departments continued to expand, publication outlets were abundant, and we achieved some degree of recognition, even notoriety, from persons in positions of power and influence and from the lay public. Certainly not all sociologists benefited equally from the millenium, and few became well-to-do or achieved real social power and standing. But, given the reality, or at least the aura, of plenty, there was only passing concern with persons divorcing themselves from the discipline or with individuals outside sociology encroaching on our turf. Even if it was intellectually and pragmatically in our long-term self-interests, there was little impetus in academia or among our association leadership to encourage the growth of applied sociology.

But how times have changed! In part, the discipline is a victim of the country's demography, of the economy, of increased political and ideological conservatism, and of our very weak power base in the political world. Rightly or wrongly, much of our work is not highly valued on the broader scene, and we have not generally been sensitive or astute about defending our "space." It is not worthwhile to dwell on whether it is their fault or ours—the fact is that the discipline is in trouble. In their chapter in this book, Ronald Manderscheid and Mathew Greenwald provide pessimistic but, unfortunately, rather clear evidence of the current and future supply-and-demand problem for sociologists, and our newspapers and the ASA *Footnotes* document declining public support for both our training and our research.

The consequences of our current situation are not merely a slightly reduced cadre of sociologists, diminished economic rewards, fewer trips, an ASA with less resources, and fewer trappings of the good life. For those of us who are secure in tenured positions, the impact is minimal. Others, willing to sacrifice personal life-style, will find a way to do their work for a while. But, in the long term, the life of sociology as an academic discipline is threatened. If we cannot promise graduate students reasonable career opportunities, we will certainly suffer in the quantity and quality of students that come to us. The decline in graduate enrollments affects not only the full-time-equivalent students that are allocated to our departments but also the extent to which we will continue to be challenged intellectually and to work at the frontiers of our field. If we cannot convince undergraduate students that sociology has relevance to their careers, our classes will become smaller, and we will face more severe reductions in faculty appointments and therefore reductions in the major means of support for our ranks and the chance to be conceptualizers, synthesizers, and empirical analysts. As for those in the discipline, whatever their motives, who want to apply sociology, failure to maintain and expand the scope of opportunities defined as "sociological" will further diminish the numbers of those who identify themselves as sociologists. These circumstances are not of passing significance; their impact may spell doom for the discipline. Sociology is indeed at a crossroads.

In the times of plenty I wistfully described, it was easy for colleagues to maintain a purist posture, opposing any educational innovations that might distract from what they perceived as the heart of the scholarly enterprise and remaining aloof from encounters and activities not regarded as intellectually relevant. Even then, many of us were aware that applied and basic research are frequently indistinguishable, that reorganizing graduate educational programs in order to increase the range and flexibility of career opportunities will not damage either our creativity or our standing, and that providing relevant undergraduate preparation need not cheapen the discipline. Now it is urgent to act, essential to the continued robustness of the discipline and perhaps to its very survival.

These remarks are addressed largely to academic sociologists, an appeal to our self-interests in order that we survive as a discipline within the academy of arts and sciences. But more is at stake than whether or not sociology departments will continue to have students, budgets, and research funds. The encouragement of applied interests and their incorporation into the discipline will bring the study of a broader range of problems and foster new paradigms and methods, forcing closer attention to existing institutions and practices; as a consequence, we will know more about how the world currently operates. This is not the "relevance" of the sixties but the more pragmatic outlook required for the eighties and beyond.

Los Angeles, California
January 1983

Howard E. Freeman

APPLIED SOCIOLOGY

Roles and Activities
of Sociologists
in Diverse Settings

Part One:
Current Status
· of Applied Sociology

INTRODUCTION

Howard E. Freeman

The unique, characteristic features of sociologists are impossible to delineate. The research problems we work on are also frequently proper areas of inquiry for other social scientists; our methods are often the same as those used by other social researchers; our activities sometimes overlap with persons in the so-called practicing professions; and a significant number of persons who publish in our journals and belong to the American Sociological Association (ASA) have been trained in other fields. Similar ambiguity and diffuseness characterize the applied sociologist. What one sociologist perceives as applied work may be viewed by another as the heart of the basic sociological enterprise.

Yet the distinction between applied and basic sociology persists. Those who either regard themselves or are identified by their conventional peers as being on the applied side are viewed as different and sometimes as marginal to the discipline. The social realities that groups construct for themselves are always strange and sometimes incomprehensible, but must be contended with none-

1

theless; witness the many discussions and documents that consider the special nature of applied sociology.

The three chapters in the first part of this volume deal with the social reality of applied sociology, albeit in different ways. In the opening chapter, Peter Rossi and William Whyte provide a general contemporary examination of the applied side of sociology. They observe that the low standing that sociology accords applied work is found in other scientific disciplines as well and that the current high level of interest in applied sociology is a response to the "sorry times" of the discipline, a point made in the introduction to this volume. Rossi and Whyte distinguish between explicitly sociological applied work and applied work that exploits sociology's theories, methods, and substantive knowledge. Further, they offer a three-way classification of applied work—social research, social engineering, and clinical practice—and discuss each of these three types of activities in considerable detail.

They also examine the differences between applied and academic research. To their minds, the key difference between applied sociology and basic sociology is that the former is sponsored and hence includes in its audience clients as well as peers. Relating to clients requires special competencies, according to Rossi and Whyte, including a capacity to communicate nontechnically, both orally and in writing. They further note the increasing numbers of nonacademic work sites and describe the ways participation in applied work impacts on the work commitments and careers of persons on this side of sociology.

Rossi and Whyte examine the meaning and implications of "policy-relevant" research and deal with the issue of political constraints on applied work. They also note that participation in interdisciplinary activities, which demands flexibility of attitude, is frequently required. In the last sections, Rossi and Whyte examine both the generic knowledge and the specialized competencies required of applied sociologists. Some of their observations reinforce the views of applied sociology already pervasive in the discipline; others provide new insights and wisdom reflecting these authors' varied and extensive experiences in the applied side of sociology.

In the second chapter, Giles-Sims and Tuchfeld discuss the role of theory in applied research as well as the role of applied research in the development of sociological theory. The first section of their chapter traces the historical development of the schism between what they term discipline-oriented and program- or action-oriented sociologists. They argue that the "theory gap" between conventional and applied sociology is the result of a long history of differing viewpoints within the discipline on the goals of research. Coupled with these differing aspirations has been the relatively higher prestige accorded persons in academia, which has hindered theory-based social programs, evaluations of which would contribute to theory in various areas of the disciplines. To illustrate their "theory gap" position, they cite a number of examples in which, contrary to the general rule, theory and action have been integrated.

Next, Giles-Sims and Tuchfeld offer two models of applied work. By the "disciplinary perspective," they mean applied work rooted in theory central to the academic discipline, such as organizational style in relation to productivity. By the "programmers' perspective," they refer to what usually goes by the name of evaluation research. As they appropriately observe, this model has given theory development lower priority. They do, however, provide examples of theoretical contributions that can be made under both of these models. Finally, a model is provided to illustrate how the schism between theory and applied research might be bridged. This model articulates the roles of academic theorists, programmers, on-line researchers, and consultants. Giles-Sims and Tuchfeld conclude that both theoretical development and the quality of sociological information available to programmers and policy makers would be enhanced by integration of these two orientations.

In the third chapter, Ronald Manderscheid and Mathew Greenwald project the supply and demand for sociologists and confirm that, in terms of future demand for persons with graduate training, sociology is indeed in trouble. Human resources projections are always risky; the authors are careful to cite their assumptions and are properly cautious in their estimates, but they would have to be very much in error before our complacency would be warranted. By 1990, the existence of about 22,500 positions and about 26,500 M.A. and Ph.D. sociologists will result in well over a 10 percent unemployment rate. The applied side of the discipline offers the only promise of growth, with an increase from less than 30 percent to somewhat over 40 percent of all sociologists in the next decade. At the same time, positions in academia will remain stable in number.

Two important inferences can be drawn from their work. First, applied sociologists, while still a minority in 1990, will constitute a more substantial percentage of the total number of sociologists. Second, academic positions show little chance of increasing, but the market for applied sociologists could possibly be expanded either by creating an increased demand or by "stealing" nonacademic positions now held by other social scientists and by persons with professional degrees.

The final section of this chapter offers recommendations on how sociologists and the ASA might provide better and more useful information on the supply-and-demand problem. Physicians, it has been observed, rarely seek preventive health care, and lawyers often do not have wills. But a kindred stance toward supply-and-demand data does not serve the self-interests of sociologists.

Taken together, these first three chapters provide considerable amplification of the remarks made in the preface and in the general introduction of this volume. In addition, they present many themes that are reiterated and elaborated in subsequent parts of this volume.

1

THE APPLIED SIDE
OF SOCIOLOGY

Peter H. Rossi

William Foote Whyte

Sociology does not stand alone among the scientific disciplines in displaying ambivalence to its applied side. Applied work is accorded low status in every academic discipline, even though the discipline's potential applications provide a major part of the rationale advanced for public support. In good times, when jobs and funds are plentiful, pure science rides high; in sorrier times, we are often confronted with pure scientists parading the accomplishments of the applied side of their science as reasons for continued support.

We are, unfortunately, in sorry times. A detailed recitation of sociology's current woes would range from dropping undergraduate enrollments to plummeting political support. In such times, applied-side sociology attracts more interest. Suddenly, our colleagues want to know how to tell the difference between a grant

5

and a contract or how to use their sociological training to construct more sensible social policy. Departments throughout the country are attempting to develop programs in applied sociology, newly minted Ph.D.s are applying for positions they would have bypassed a few years ago, and the American Sociological Association held a conference on applied sociology.

This is not the place to analyze why applied sociology ranks low in our profession. The fact that the applied sides of so many fields suffer similar disfavor suggests that the phenomenon is not peculiar to sociology and hence deserves the attention of the sociology of science. It is enough here to note that this low status exists despite the difficulty of drawing the line between applied and pure, or basic, sociology. As one of us (Rossi, 1980) has observed, the line is so fuzzy that applied research is often redefined by the passage of time, emerging as basic sociology in the disciplinary literature. That sociological work can be and is redefined from applied to basic (and vice versa) illustrates that the one is not easily distinguished from the other, especially in published material. This lack of clear definition applies particularly to perspectives, content, and method.

Whatever differences exist relate mainly to the organization of work. Whereas applied-side sociology has as its primary audience clients who ordinarily finance applied work in the hope that outcomes will be of value to them, the audience for basic work is diffuse, consisting of the discipline as a whole or some specialty within it, an audience that has not commissioned the work or held expectations about some specific outcome. Articles in professional journals and monographs are the way to reach the audience for basic work, whereas limited-edition reports or oral presentations are the mode for reporting applied work. Special skills and knowledge are called into play to meet the social relations and task demands of applied-side sociology, a topic we will discuss in detail later in this chapter.

Applied-side sociology consists of a variety of activities, each of which makes different demands on the sociologists involved. We will devote some of this chapter to distinguishing among major models of applied-side sociology.

Finally, this chapter reviews the prospects for applied sociology as a professional role. Both of us are optimistic about applied sociology because we believe that the social and organizational issues that we as sociologists are prepared to deal with will be with us for decades to come.

If we had written separate chapters following the same general outline, we would have differed somewhat on matters of emphasis, but we are pleased to find ourselves aligned on all matters of substance. On major points, we share the same beliefs and sentiments. First and foremost, we believe that the applied side is as important as the basic side to the intellectual growth of sociology, and we deplore the inferior status accorded it within the discipline. Second, we are convinced that applied-side sociological work can contribute to the betterment of human society. Finally, we share the belief that the fortunes of our discipline are bound up with the ability of sociologists to develop a strong and flourishing applied side.

Varieties of Applied Work

In sorting out the varieties of applied work, it may be useful to divide the territory first into two major parts: the roles played by the sociologist on a given project in which he or she is explicitly functioning as a sociologist and the roles of persons playing other official roles but making use of sociological theory, methods, and substantive knowledge. Possible examples of the latter category would be labor relations mediators, supervisors or managers, and elected or appointed public officials. We will concentrate on the first set of roles, in which the actor's primary identification is as an applied sociologist.

The house of applied side sociology has many rooms. In fact, we believe that professionally trained sociologists can be found in virtually all major occupational niches. The wide range, however, obscures the fact that many professionally trained sociologists hold organizational positions that allow only incidental use of their sociological skills; we will discuss later the uses of sociology for persons in this category. The heterogeneity of the remaining positions can be reduced by noting three broadly conceived styles of applied-side sociology—applied social research, social engineering, and clinical sociology—each of which will be delineated in this chapter. A few words of caution are necessary, however.

First, we are using these names in what may be unfamiliar ways. For example, we have included all types of consultation work, not simply consultation work involving individuals or families, under the category of clinical sociology. Second, almost all classifications are heuristic and hence have vague boundaries. Individual cases often do not fit neatly into only one of the classes, a fact of life that makes the coder's work difficult but does not necessarily make classification useless.

Applied Social Research

Applied social research, the nearest relative to basic sociological work (and hence the most likely to become confused with it) consists of the application of sociological knowledge and research skills to the acquisition of empirically based knowledge of applied issues. The research methods used are not distinctly different from those used in basic research, but the sociological knowledge employed is often different in special ways, to be described in greater detail later in this section.

There are several kinds of applied social research. The simplest applied research task is a descriptive study, in which the researcher attempts to provide empirically based information on the level and distribution of some social problem. Thus, victimization studies were developed by sociologists to provide more valid estimates of crime and victimization differentials between social groups. Business firms have used sociologists to estimate levels of worker morale or to map the social positions of the firm's customers or the preferences of consumers for various products. Needs assessment for public agencies might be regarded as the analogue of consumer market research for the public sector; such studies are often undertaken by sociologists for, say, community mental health centers. Descriptive studies may cover any one of a variety of topics, from political preferences to detailed nutritional intakes.

The border between descriptive and analytical applied social research is not clear-cut. Good descriptive studies often become analytical, like Coleman's highly publicized study of educational opportunity (Coleman and others, 1966). Coleman's research began in response to a request from Congress for a study of how educational opportunities (conceived as school physical plants, trained teachers, curricular opportunities, and so on) were distributed by race and ethnicity. However, Coleman turned the study into an analysis that modeled the determinants of student achievement.

Analytical studies attempt to empirically model social phenomena. Thus, an analytical study of voter preferences might attempt to understand support for candidates in terms of social group membership, party identification, socioeconomic position, and exposure to the messages of the electoral campaign. Although analytical applied social research closely resembles basic research conducted on the same topic, important differences exist in the kinds of variables used in the models constructed. Applied studies emphasize variables that are of interest to the client, presumably because the client might be able to manipulate such variables in order to achieve desired outcomes. Thus, in a voting study, the policy variable of interest to the client may be the campaign, alterations in which might improve the candidate-client's prospects at the polls. As we point out later, one characteristic of applied work is attention to the client's needs, which analytical applied social research translates into special attention to policy variables.

A third major variety of applied social research is evaluation, systematic attempts to estimate the effects of purposive social action, such as a social program or a new management style in a business firm. Evaluation research gives special attention to the extent to which changes purposefully introduced into a social situation achieve their intended effects. Although evaluations of a more or less systematic sort have always been undertaken by policy makers, the distinguishing characteristics of evaluation research rest on the recognition that social scientists are specially equipped to make definitive assessments of effects.

Evaluation research has become a minor industry in the United States since the 1960s, with an estimated annual volume of between two and three billion dollars. This research is mainly conducted under contract by private firms, most of which employ at least some professionally trained sociologists. Although sociologists are probably not the largest contingent of social scientists employed as evaluation researchers, this market is certainly a major one for persons interested in the applied side of sociology, and sociologists have played a prominent role in defining the field through their published work.

Social Engineering

In applied social research, the role of the sociologist is primarily technical—taking problems as defined by policy makers and translating those problems into research designs. In contrast, social engineering consists of attempts to use the body of sociological knowledge in the design of policies or institutions to accomplish some purpose. However, applied social research always has close organizational ties to policy, whereas social engineering may or may not have such ties. Applied social research requires resources from sources that are usually intimately engaged in policy. In contrast, social engineering can be accomplished for a mission-oriented agency or for some group opposed to the existing organizational structure, or it may be undertaken separately from either. Social engineering is often inexpensive and hence can be conducted in a variety of contexts. When conducted close to the policy-making centers, it is often termed social policy analysis, the devising and presenting of alternative social policies and their anticipated costs and benefits. When practiced by groups in opposition to current regimes, social engineering becomes social criticism.

When the social criticism is simply addressed to a general reading public, as in articles in the *New York Times* magazine section, it can hardly be called applied sociology, since the sociologist is not explicitly linked to an organization that might use the study's conclusions. Not that we can do applied sociology only in the service of an establishment organization. Social engineering can be done for a labor union, an Indian tribe, a community organization—in fact, for any nonestablishment or antiestablishment organization that seeks the help of the sociologist. (Of course, it is generally more difficult to find funds for projects designed to serve the interests of organizations claiming to represent the poor and the powerless; however, such practical distinctions should not obscure the similarities in the roles and activities of sociologists involved in social engineering projects designed to serve establishment and antiestablishment organizations.)

Social engineering may be closely mixed with applied social research. The Ford Foundation–funded Mobilization for Youth, for example, was a demonstration of a new approach to the reduction of juvenile delinquency through the restructuring of opportunities for disadvantaged youth using the instrumentality of community organization; at the same time, the project incorporated research on the effectiveness of the new approach. Similarly, Fairweather and Tornatzky's (1977) decade-long series of small-scale experiments with a community approach to the assimilation of deinstitutionalized mental patients combined rigorous social research with a new way of handling the problem of assimilation through the construction of specially devised living arrangements.

Current efforts to promote worker participation in the planning and management of business enterprises constitute another example of social engineering. The construction and testing of structural forms and social processes that would increase worker participation and, at the same time, increase industrial productivity offer increasing opportunities for the blending of research and social engineering (Whyte, 1982).

As social policy analysts, sociologists have been employed in the planning units of government agencies and on the management level of private enterprises. As the designers and demonstrators of new social forms, our colleagues have run new social programs as demonstrations and designed and carried through field experiments.

Clinical Sociology

By clinical sociology, we mean the use of sociological knowledge and the sociological perspective in providing consultation and technical assistance to social units ranging in size from individuals to large-scale organizations. At times, of course, it is difficult to distinguish clearly between social engineering and clinical practice, the main difference being the extent to which the sociologist actively seeks to change or redesign the institution in question. Thus, it would be social engineering to propose a new form of marriage contract and clinical sociology to advise a married couple on how to work out a division of labor in child rearing. Similarly, a social engineer might propose a new form of work group in an assembly plant, whereas the clinical (that is, consulting) sociologist might work with General Motors on improving worker morale. Social engineers are concerned with institutional arrangements and design; clinicians are more concerned with the specific problems of concrete social entities.

To be effective, each of these professionals must recognize the potential complementarity of the two approaches. The clinician will often encounter structural factors that must be changed before the clinical treatment can produce the hoped-for results. Similarly, the social engineer must recognize that the implementation of a major structural change in an organization may be greatly facilitated by a skillful clinician.

The skills involved in clinical practice extend considerably beyond those imparted in traditional undergraduate or graduate training programs. The translation of sociological knowledge into clinical practice cannot be accomplished well without the help of our sister social sciences. A family clinician needs to know a great deal about human development and individual psychology. A sociological business consultant certainly should know something about accounting, marketing, and production technology. In addition, sensitivity to the particular circumstances of the individual client is called for, a skill that academic departments of sociology are largely incompetent to impart.

With academic sociology, applied sociology shares common knowledge, theory, and method bases. In addition, applied sociology generates new knowledge, theory, and methods that influence academic, or basic, sociology. Indeed, we claim that applied social research has contributed a very significant part (if not the major part) of our current repertoire of research skills. Whether this claim is accurate is not at issue here; the point is that knowledge, theory, and methods acquired in one realm are appropriated and used by the other, so that the ultimate origins are often obscured with time (Rossi, 1980).

Distinctive Features of Applied Sociology

The three varieties of applied sociology described thus far are distinguished from basic (or academic) sociology and from each other by a number of features that carry implications for the main issues to be discussed in this book—how to enter applied work, how to obtain the necessary training, and how to derive satisfaction from such work. These distinctive features, which are outlined in this section, speak, we believe, to both the difficulties involved and the rewards to be gained in properly accomplishing such work.

Organizational Context of Applied Work

For a variety of reasons—some obvious and others obscure—the groves of academe have not been the primary location for applied work. Applied work within the university confines has generally been segregated into institutes and centers and clearly differentiated thereby from university departments. In addition, university departments have been largely inept at competing for applied contracts and completing applied tasks. In large part, this segregation has occurred because the time demands of applied work fit so poorly into the fixed academic rhythms of semesters, quarters, and summer vacations. In addition, applied work on any scale of organizational complexity beyond the model of the solo scholar and his or her graduate students fits poorly into an academic structure that has no pronounced hierarchy of authority and hence can scarcely sustain a prolonged division of labor.

Because of the university's organizational incapacity, most applied work takes place off campus. Consultants and clinicians set up organizational forms resembling those employed by professions that have strong clinical and consultative activities, or they join the clinical or consultative components of organizations. Thus, a sociologist might become a member of a policy and planning unit of a government agency or a part of the marketing section of a consumer products firm.

Applied social research is increasingly undertaken by firms specifically created for that purpose; the funding available over the past decade has been sufficient to support the establishment and growth of hundreds of applied research firms, among which are a small handful that are large enough to employ more Ph.D. social scientist–researchers than most university social science divisions.

The consequences for the individual social scientist of such organizational contexts are considerable, especially in contrast to academic locations. For one thing, permanent tenure is not ordinarily available, although, with the continued good performance and prosperity of the firm, one may count on long-term employment. Partially to compensate for less job security, applied work commands higher average salaries—for example, beginning applied social researchers earn salaries close to the upper level of the associate professor ranks.

University work is essentially solo practice, with little or no supervision exercised over teaching or research. Applied work within an organizational context usually implies close supervision, imposed deadlines, and considerable meshing with the activities of others. In short, if you cannot tolerate meetings, prefer to work alone, and grow restive under the discipline of supervision and deadlines, applied work within organizations will not suit you.

Clinical or consultative work may follow more closely the solo practitioner model with little or no supervision. But dealing with others is an integral part of such activity, and those who have no patience for listening (or for meandering talk) may not find this work suitable either.

Clients, Patients, and Audiences

As discussed earlier, one of the distinguishing features of applied work is that its results often have a very specific audience. A client employs an applied sociologist to deliver a product in the form of a report, a recommendation, or a new design for an organization—in short, some specific outcome is expected. In addition, a client may wish the applied sociologist to address other audiences as well. Thus, a client may be primarily interested in a report in order to pass it on to others: a government agency might want a report they can send on to Congress, or the plans of a social engineer might be addressed both to policy makers and to the general public.

In order to address the claims of audiences and clients, the applied sociologist has to be able to communicate effectively with nonsociological audiences. This important characteristic of applied sociology cannot be emphasized too strongly. Every applied sociologist has occasionally complained about how difficult it has been to get some message across to a client. And, when the applied sociological work is of considerable technical complexity, the difficulties are compounded. Fortunately, as sociology has become more and more entrenched in the undergraduate curriculum and has even infiltrated the professional schools—especially schools of business and law—it has become easier to reach policy makers within government and business. For example, the courts in the past two decades have come to accept social science research as evidence, in contrast to an earlier period where it was rejected as hearsay.

Communication with nonsociological audiences, no matter how well educated and intelligent, requires special speaking and writing skills, including the ability to translate technical sociological terms and concepts into language that can be easily understood and the ability to be concise and direct. Monographs may be important currency for the purchase of tenure, but, in applied work, they will often languish unread while short summative statements using a nearly telegraphic style are reaching more of the intended audience.

The speaking and writing skills needed for applied work are not innate—they can be acquired through training. Although graduate departments of sociology appear to be unlikely places to receive such training, other parts of the university may be ready to provide it. Perhaps most applied sociologists learn these skills on the job; in any case, the acquisition of such skills, in whatever fashion, is a prerequisite for a successful career in applied sociological work.

Constraints of Policy Relevance

In all applied sociological work, attention is understandably focused on the manipulable elements of the substantive phenomena. This emphasis constitutes a fundamental difference between applied and basic work. For example, it is more than enough in basic work to know that academic achievement is heavily dominated by family characteristics. This information by itself is not useful in applied work since (fortunately or unfortunately) very little can be done to affect family structure through changes in social policy or through clinical work with specific families. Applied work on academic achievement therefore has to be focused on elements that can be changed through policy changes or through the individual efforts of families. Applied work in this area would be more useful if focused on how schools contribute to academic achievement or on how parents can be persuaded to change their behavior to affect the academic achievement of their children.

This orientation to policy relevance is very different from the orientation of the basic researcher. Indeed, many of the variables that play an important role in applied work tend to be neglected in basic work primarily because policy variables usually play very minor roles in social phenomena. For example, age, sex, and socioeconomic status are all important variables in understanding crime, but none is a policy variable. Rather, those who are concerned with crime on a practical level focus their attention on matters that the current system can alter—sentencing practices, parole qualifications, living arrangements in prison, and the like. However, these variables are not going to be important in understanding crime.

To phrase it another way, basic concerns are with explaining as much as possible of the variance in the phenomena under study, whereas policy concerns are with that amount of variance that can be changed by modifications of policy or established routines. This principle applies not only to the orientation of applied versus basic researchers but also to social engineers and clinician-consultants. The social engineer must conceive of his or her new designs as ones that the society can adopt. A design for a new criminal justice system will have to emphasize changes in mutable elements—for example, sentencing and court procedures—and not simply recognize the roles played by less mutable factors, such as age and sex. Similarly, a clinician advising a family on how to keep children out of trouble is foolish to advise the parents simply to have patience while their children grow older (and hence outgrow their trouble making). Rather, the focus of the clinician should be on meeting the needs of children as they are at the moment or on altering the exercise of parental authority.

The training of applied sociologists will have to differ from that of academic sociologists at least to the extent of identifying the different substantive interests of applied and basic sociology. Note that this is not a change in emphasis but a supplementation of basic training. The elements of interest in basic research are also of interest in applied research, if only because main effects have to be held constant in the study of policy-relevant effects, but training in the identification of policy-relevant variables must supplement the basic training. Similar kinds of supplementary training must accompany the training of social engineers and clinician-consultants.

Perhaps the most important effect of this emphasis on policy relevance on the orientation of applied workers is the constraints imposed on the issues to be dealt with. Plans calling for major changes in the distant future are unlikely to be of interest to policy makers, nor are items that are currently viewed as politically infeasible. The policy spaces of governments, firms, or smaller units—defined as the range of policies that are within the limits of acceptability—set the boundaries within which it is useful to work. Thus, policy space constrains the applied sociologist. Applied work is not for radicals to the right or left of the ruling elite but for those who are willing to work for gradual change, whatever their own views.

This close tie between applied work and the political status quo is the source of much criticism of applied sociology, especially applied social research and clinical work. The criticism is well taken. However, it is directed at the consequence of the usual sources of financial support for applied work. It is not aimed at intrinsic features of applied work. That is, the current sources for the support of work in applied sociology are concerned with what they conceive to be their policy spaces. Alternative sources might conceive of different policy spaces and, if demand were to arise from such sources, one might see applied sociology in support of, say, labor and socialist movements as well as of public bureaucracies and current political regimes. Why the labor and socialist movements have not been strong customers for applied sociology is too complicated a question to answer in detail here (in other words, we do not know the answers), but, despite the fact that many sociologists strongly sympathize with such movements, those movements have not been customers for applied sociology.

Interdisciplinary Problems

The problems to which applied sociologists address themselves rarely fall entirely within the substantive concerns of our discipline. Those who work in the public policy arena are quickly brought to realize that, whatever the problem involved, other disciplines have knowledge, theory, and research methods to contribute. At a minimum, the applied sociologist should know enough about public administration to understand the limits and limitations of public bureaucracies. For social engineers, skillful work involves knowing some economics and the mysteries of cost-benefit calculations. Clinicians and consultants have to know something about individual psychology as well as, possibly, about business administration and social welfare, and the applied sociologist has to know enough about economics, political science, psychology, education, and social work to be able to query the relevant literature. But, most of all, since much applied work is organizational work, the applied sociologist must be able to deal with specialists from other disciplines, to understand what each can contribute, and to use the special knowledge and skills involved. Although the polemical stance toward other social science fields may be attractive when displayed on the pages of a sociological journal and may even be useful to one's career, it is decidedly dysfunctional within the context of organized applied work.

The applied sociologist's needs for interdisciplinary knowledge may extend far beyond the social sciences. For example, the sociologist working with an agricultural research-and-development organization must gain enough knowledge of the plant and animal sciences to avoid trying to implement plans that appear socially attractive but are technically infeasible. Not that the sociologist must take formal instruction in the plant and animal sciences—if the sociologist recognizes the importance of these disciplines, he or she can acquire the needed knowledge through conversation with specialists and through relatively nontechnical background reading.

The same point holds for the sociologist working in the field of medicine and health or law and judicial processes. Although sociology can be usefully focused on any field of human activity, the applied sociologist will only be effective insofar as he or she seeks to understand the specialists practicing in the particular field selected for study. Studies focused exclusively on patients, clients, or farmers are unlikely to result in changes being introduced by policy makers in health, law, or agriculture.

With few exceptions, and then for relatively short periods of time, academic sociology departments hardly support interdisciplinary training. Indeed, given interdepartmental rivalries over increasingly scarce resources, it seems unlikely that such departments will change much in the future. Hence, an acquaintance with the literature of other fields will remain the responsibility of individual would-be applied sociologists.

Quality Standards

Different considerations enter into the issue of how rigorous and precise research and scholarly endeavours should be—differences that are especially marked between basic and applied work. As usual, one of the main issues is whether Type I or Type II errors dominate, that is, whether false positives are harder to live with than false negatives. In basic or disciplinary work, where good ideas are hard to come by, false positives appear to be less threatening than false negatives. That is, it is considered worse to reject an idea when it is really true (false negative) than to accept an idea when it is really false (false positive). The result is that many articles appearing in scholarly journals are based on flimsy evidence and employ research designs that are not very powerful.

The opposite circumstance obtains in applied work. The harm that might result from accepting as true a good idea that is really false is ordinarily more serious than the harm that might result from rejecting a good idea that is really true. Thus, a program that might cost billions of dollars should not be put into place until it is fairly certain to yield its intended benefits. Similarly, in clinical work, a consultant who recommends a change that might cause harm to a family or an organization may be doing more damage than one who recommends rejection of a change that might do some good.

Indeed, in some areas, these priorities have been well accepted. Applied work that measures the monthly labor force employs an expensive and powerful sample design incorporating more than 60,000 households in a rotating panel. For political reasons, it is important to be able to reliably detect very small month-to-month changes in the unemployment rate. In addition, continual work on measurement problems has refined the instruments used in the Current Population Survey to reduce measurement error. Similarly, social engineering plans to transform our criminal justice system ought to be subjected to painstaking policy analysis to determine the risks to society and to individuals of any changes proposed.

In contrast, since very few practical consequences follow from basic, or academic, sociological work, standards of internal and external validity can be relaxed (and often are). Thus, studies published in professional journals are still based on students in introductory sociology courses and carelessly generalized beyond the populations studied. Needless to say, much applied work is also quite sloppy, but there are some circumstances in which the risks of Type I errors are minimal. In marketing, where good ideas are at a premium and the consequence of adopting a bad idea is often slight (as in the case of advertising copy tests), applied work can be, and often is, quite makeshift. The best applied work, however, is accompanied by higher levels of concern for internal and external validity than comparable basic work. As a consequencee, some kinds of applied work are even more challenging than ordinary academic work. In fact, the best applied work, far from being routine or prosaic, requires technical and creative skills that would challenge the best sociologists.

Generic and Special Knowledge for Applied Work

Earlier, we stressed that applied work is often interdisciplinary—if not organizationally, then at least in terms of the knowledge and skills needed. In addition, certain special kinds of sociological knowledge are useful and in some cases essential to the pursuit of applied work. This special knowledge can be classified into two types: generic knowledge that is usually needed no matter what specific applied work one enters upon and specialized knowledge that is specific to the particular kind of applied work engaged in. We will describe first the generic knowledge and then some of the specific types of knowledge needed for the major types of applied work. Obviously, this discussion will have strong implications for the kinds of training that should be offered in university departments.

Generic Knowledge. All applied sociologists necessarily have to deal with the concrete world of organizations and social forms outside academia. Hence, all applied sociologists should be trained in methods of field interviewing and observation. That these methods are commonly referred to as qualitative seems somewhat misleading (to Whyte), since they can be (and have been) used to gather data on the incomes of peasant farmers, on the frequency of member attendance at meetings, on the frequency of speaking in such meetings, and so on. *Flexibly structured field methods* seems (to Whyte) a more accurate (but also more cumbersome) rubric for this style of research. The sociologist goes into the field without a rigidly prestructured research instrument. Beginning field work is of an exploratory nature, designed to provide understanding of the lay of the land and of the cast of characters in the field of study and to build rapport with key people who may help to gain local acceptance for the project and who can be enormously helpful as informal or formal collaborators. The methodology becomes more structured as the sociologist moves beyond the exploratory stage and focuses on particular problems. With this methodology, indeed, most of the data gathered will not be reducible to numbers, but the sociologist can use it to indicate some types of quantitative data. Furthermore, the sociologist will often find it useful to combine qualitatively oriented field studies with questionnaires or surveys.

We emphasize the "flexibly structured" aspects of these field methods because the methods provide the student with the kind of field experience that develops skills in relating to persons of widely varied social backgrounds and in a variety of organizational or community situations. Even those who prefer to work primarily with quantitative data should have the skills involved in qualitative field work in order to attain and maintain productive relations with clients and other persons with whom they may be involved, such as research subjects, antagonists (in the case of consultation on court cases), and so on. The sociologist who does not know how to talk to workers and management, ordinary citizens and members of the power structure, social workers and their clients, members of Congress and their constituents—in short, the wide range of potential clients and subjects—should not go into applied work, at least not before remedying those training defects. Note that we take a stance here that asserts that such skills are not ascribed but are achieved. We believe that anyone not suffering from a major character defect can learn to be at least an acceptable qualitative field worker.

We also believe that applied sociologists, especially those in applied social research or policy analysis, should be familiar with the current state of the art in quantitative methods. To be able to read and comprehend much of the interdisciplinary literature in the relevant substantive areas requires an intimate acquaintance with at least the full range of statistical methods currently taught in the typical graduate sociology curriculum. Whether the applied sociologist will employ such methods, however, is a function of preference, substantive issues that arise out of the task in question, and other variables. Especially those intending to go into applied social research must refine their quantitative skills to a high technical level, if only to compete successfully with social scientists from other fields where quantitative traditions are stronger. (See Berk's chapter in this book for a review of the necessary skills.)

Aside from independent practitioner-sociologists who provide clinical services to individuals and families, all applied work takes place within an organizational context. Clients are rarely, if ever, individuals but are more likely to be fairly large-scale bureaucratic organizations. The objects of study also tend to be formal organizations of some size and complexity. Hence, substantive knowledge about the functioning of formal organizations in general is useful in applied work.

Specialized Knowledge. Earlier, in emphasizing the interdisciplinary nature of applied sociology, we pointed out that those interdisciplinary aspects are not limited to the social science disciplines. To work effectively in the field of law, for example, the sociologist requires some familiarity with the knowledge base used by lawyers and judges. The same point applies to applied work in medicine and health, agricultural development, or any field of study and action. Since the sociologist may do applied work in a wide variety of fields, it would be fruitless to list the types of knowledge needed for sociological work in every field that sociologists might enter. Yet specialized areas of knowledge particular to rather broad classes of applied work can be emphasized, especially since specialties entered upon may be more a matter of demand current at the time of entry than the outcome of deliberate choice.

For those entering upon applied work relating to public policy, a good understanding of the functioning of public bureaucracies and of American legislative bodies is clearly appropriate. At the present time, perhaps the most serious issue in the design and evaluation of social programs is the extent to which programs are delivered as designed to their beneficiaries. We have gradually learned that public bureaucracies are notoriously subversive in small ways and quite often change the character of program services in the process of delivering them. The welfare laws and regulations as promulgated are not the laws and regulations actually administered by human services departments at the local level. Hence, in designing an effective program, the social engineer must conceive of one that can be delivered more or less as designed.

Perhaps even less is systematically known about how legislatures function. Researchers and social engineers oriented toward serving or affecting policy-making processes know extraordinarily little about how best to proceed. Although political scientists and public-choice economists have both produced literature that is relevant to this issue, they do not seem to have gone very far beyond the collection of anecdotes (in the case of the political scientists) or the construction of abstract models that do not appear to mirror the real world (in the case of the public-choice economists). Nevertheless, policy-oriented applied sociologists should be acquainted with the relevant political science and economics literature and take courses in those departments while undergoing training.

The potential applied sociologist who might one day wish to work with one or another of the now rapidly expanding programs to stimulate worker participation in shop-floor decision making in industry or government would be well advised to acquire some background in the literature of organizational behavior (or complex organizations, or industrial sociology, as the subfield is variously called).

Those expecting to engage in clinical practice with individuals, groups, or organizations need to become aware of the "dependency trap" often encountered in consulting relationships. The beginning consultant is likely to measure success in terms of the number of recommendations he or she gets clients to accept. Success along this line tends to build a dependency relationship in which the client continues to look to the consultant for stimulation and guidance instead of developing the skills and insights for diagnosing problems and initiating changes independently. To be sure, such a relationship may offer material rewards to the consultant, at least in the short run. Some consultants are thought to foster a dependency relationship in order to keep the consultation fees flowing. However, apart from its deficiencies in terms of client welfare, such a strategy may boomerang as the client or members of the client organization come to recognize the dependency relationship and decide to declare their independence by dismissing the consultant.

Recognizing these problems, students of clinical practice have been seeking to define a new role in which the clinician serves primarily as a facilitator rather than as an advice giver and problem solver. The facilitator minimizes offerings of advice on what the client should do to solve particular problems and instead concentrates on helping the client (or client organization) to develop a structure and social process designed to enhance client abilities to diagnose problems, to gather relevant information and ideas, and to develop a more effective system of decision making.

Sociology departments have offered little formal instruction regarding the clinician or consultant role, and no coherent body of literature on the topic has as yet developed. Thus, we can only advise potential clinicians to become aware of the "dependency trap" and to look for guidance from experienced practitioners and from publications not yet included in many sociology course syllabi.

Doing Good

One of the attractions of applied work is the possibility of using sociological knowledge, theory, and research methods to do good for society or for some subgroup within the society with which one has a sympathetic bond. We were attracted to applied work out of the hope that life could be made more tolerable (and, we hope, richer in many respects) for the poor and oppressed in our society. Our successes in doing good have been modest. Peter Rossi has concentrated on applied research, an activity in which the sociologist furnishes the client with information and ideas but generally has little influence over what the client does with the findings. Early in his career, William Whyte was engaged in one social engineering project (Whyte and Hamilton, 1965) and, in more recent years, has been playing more of a facilitator role in programs to stimulate worker participation in decision making in labor–management committees in private industry and in employee-owned firms. This action-research has led to his involvement with the employee ownership movement and to working with Congress to draft and enact legislation fostering employee ownership and worker participation.

Although Whyte has had some success in these applied efforts, his individual contribution should not be overestimated. Along with such better-known exponents of these views as Douglas Macgregor, Rensis Likert, and Chris Argyris, Whyte has been writing about the practical advantages of worker participation since the 1940s, but those ideas only received lip service in management circles until the Japanese challenge suddenly made them urgent topics for study and action. Similarly, not until the 1970s, when employees and community people staved off plant shutdowns here and there by buying the plant, did worker ownership suddenly move beyond academic discourse to become a subject of widespread public concern and interest.

This experience suggests to us that social forces provide both limitations and opportunities to the applied sociologist. We cannot expect that the sheer brilliance of our ideas, the scientific weight of our data, or the charisma of our personalities will overcome social forces moving in a direction contrary to our values. On the other hand, if we understand social trends and diagnose needs and opportunities arising out of changing conditions, we can make small but significant contributions to human welfare.

Furthermore, we do not believe that our efforts to "do good" have been at the expense of advancing a science of sociology. Rossi believes his major scientific contributions have arisen out of applied projects. Whyte has found that his efforts to help persons solve problems in the field have made him aware of important variables and interactions among variables that would have escaped his attention if he had confined himself to pure sociology.

Finally, we argue that the attempt to apply some aspect of social theory to a practical problem provides a much more challenging test of theory than critiques of our colleagues in academic journals.

Prospects for Applied Sociology

To a large degree, the increased interest in applied sociology stems from the fact that the academy appears to be heading for, if not actually experiencing, hard times. Only a few departments continue to be buyers on the job market, and many are shrinking as positions vacated through retirement and resignation are not being filled. Harder times appear to be ahead of us, as state legislatures become even less generous in their support and as the federal government cuts back more and more on the sources of "soft money" that we had come to depend on over the past two decades.

Hard times mean that we have to justify our existence and provide a rationale for our support that goes beyond simple expressions of self-interest. Hence, applied sociology and its products help to justify public investment in our field. We are also faced with the problem of what to do about our students who will enter the labor force and about our colleagues who may lose their jobs in retrenchments. Here again, applied work appears to be more and more attractive as an alternative. But how much of an opportunity does applied work present?

First, we have to understand that some of the same trends that restrict the future of academia also impinge negatively on applied work. The budgets of federal, state, and local agencies are not as lush as they once were. Federal agencies that would not think twice about funding large demonstration projects in the hope of hitting upon some new effective social program for the future will now fund only literature reviews evaluating and summarizing existing knowledge. Sociologists employed in Washington, D.C., are quietly searching for alternative employment, anticipating that they may be subject to a reduction in force.

In addition, sociology has lost favor in the federal government. Although sociology has never been the favorite discipline of any administration, we were at least tolerated as benign, and at times even afforded a moderate status, by all the administrations since Kennedy's. The reduction that was initially made in the National Science Foundation sociology program budget and the excision of applied social research programs within the National Institute of Mental Health are clear indications that some in high government positions dislike sociology strongly enough to pick on us specifically.

Ironically, just when academic sociologists have become more interested in applied work, funding for such work is diminishing. One is tempted to ask in dismay of our colleagues who show today a new interest in applied work, "Where were you from 1965 through 1975, when we had more opportunities than we could take advantage of?"

Of course, not all applied work is funded with federal dollars or with state and local funds. Clinical and consultative practice are only very indirectly connected to federal funding, as are projects that are funded by private-sector organizations. Probably the private sector will never expand enough to replace the demand for personnel once commanded by federal dollars, but more of a market may currently exist than existed in the past. Sociologists have not been very aggressive in finding varieties of applied work in businesses and private associations. Scratch a sociologist, so the saying goes, and you make a liberal bleed. Perhaps our political liberalism, with an accompanying distaste for the values and attitudes of businesses and the business community, has kept us from trying to enter the business world at all. For example, consider the burgeoning of the movement known as the quality of working life (QWL) (an umbrella term covering a wide variety of projects involving sociotechnical changes in industry and emphasizing worker participation). As *Business Week* (September 21, 1981) reported: "In 1972, the first international conference on improving the quality of work life met at Harriman, N.Y., and included only 50 advocates, mainly academics, with no union officials and few managers. The second international conference, which ended September 3, attracted more than 1,500 delegates to Toronto, and the 200 unionists and 750 management people—the real practitioners—far outnumbered the academics, consultants, and government officials."

The rapid growth of QWL programs in industry is creating a growing demand for persons skilled in designing and administering projects in this field. Companies often hire consultants to help them get started but then expect to fill their major personnel needs through internal recruitment and training. This trend means expanding opportunities for sociologists as external consultants and as internal trainers and facilitators within personnel departments.

Of course, ours is not the only discipline in trouble and not the only discipline with applied interests. The fact that the problems in question demand an interdisciplinary approach means that other skills compete with ours for funds, jobs, and public attention. Indeed, some of these other disciplines are explicitly oriented toward applied work—for example, social work and educational psychology. Others, such as economics and psychology, have stronger traditions of applied work. As a consequence, in the field of applied social research, sociologists appear to be underrepresented in comparison to our total size, with psychologists and economists probably doing more applied policy-related work than sociologists.

If we are going to succeed in obtaining applied positions, we will have to show that there is something special about applied sociological work that can demand a respected place. Becoming more interdisciplinary in our orientation will help. Certainly, the argument that sociologists are better in some indeterminate way will not carry the day. We will probably do best to show that the organizational component in most applied problems demands the specialization that sociologists have developed in encountering similar issues. Another way of putting this point is that it would be fruitless to become second rate economists, psychologists, or educators; we will make more of an impression if we can show that the special knowledge and theory commanded by sociologists are needed in solving the problems in question.

Nor is the situation entirely gloomy in the public sector. With ideological zeal, the current administration disdains our discipline, and the activities with which we have been intimately connected in the past are shrinking in number and size. But the problems to which those programs were directed will not go away. Poverty will still be with us, as will crime, community disorganization, mistakes in the delivery of health care, low productivity, and so on. Sooner or later, this new administration will understand that they also need us. In fact, they have already begun to recognize the need for the criminologists among us. Either the administration does not accept that criminology is largely a sociological specialty, or they realize that our help is needed and hence are willing to allow funds to go to sociologists from the National Institute of Justice.

We will be needed to design new programs—within a new policy space defined by the administration, of course—to address those stubborn and persistent social problems that we have addressed in the past. We will also be needed to evaluate existing programs and the new ones that will be instituted. Indeed, evaluation, as we all know, is a sword with edges enough to cut all parties, including evaluators. We will be needed to provide advice and counsel to the courts, to public officials, to the legislative branch of government, and to the many agencies and organizations that are funded indirectly out of the federal budget.

Sociology for Those Practicing Other Primary Roles

Up to this point, we have concentrated on the uses of applied sociology for the person who is performing in the primary role of sociologist in research or practice. Let us also recognize that growing numbers of persons are applying sociological methods or theory in jobs not specifically designed for sociologists. The person with a graduate degree in sociology, or even the person with no more than an undergraduate major, may serve as an administrator of a social agency, as a labor mediator, as an industrial manager, or even as the director of public works in a local community. (The practical uses of sociology for a labor mediator or a director of public works are illustrated in detail in the appendix to the latest edition of *Street Corner Society* [Whyte, 1981].)

We believe the downward trend in numbers of undergraduate majors is accounted for in part by students' inability to see any direct link between an undergraduate degree in sociology and post-college employment, a problem not shared by students of business administration, prelaw, premedical, or engineering programs.

To what jobs does an undergraduate degree in sociology lead? We cannot answer that question precisely because few college recruiters for industry or government are specifically looking for sociology majors. To the extent that they are open to candidates with a liberal arts background—and many firms and agencies are—in addition to the academic record and extracurricular activities, recruiters are interested in what the student has learned and can do that would fit the needs of the employer. Since the fact that the student has majored in sociology will not answer such questions for the recruiter, the student must be especially enterprising in describing interests and skills.

For example, if a student has studied some aspects of quality of working life and has a special interest in this field, he or she should stress this interest in talking to a recruiter from a firm with a QWL program. This approach would probably not lead quickly to a major role in such a program but might provide the new employee with experience and with opportunities to advance with the program. Then, as the former student gains experience in applying a sociological eye to the dynamics of the organization, he or she may gain a more strategic role. By "sociological eye," we mean an orientation toward group processes and problems of organizational structure.

American culture, with its emphasis on individualism, tends to bias people toward individualistic explanations of social and economic problems. If a manager in industry appears to be doing a poor job, or if a program in industry or government seems to be breaking down, we see a widespread tendency to jump to individualistic explanations: the manager is a poor leader, those administering the program are incompetent or corrupt, and so on. Whoever can look beyond these individualistic blinders can make especially valuable contributions to improving the performance of the organization.

Finally, the most obvious point: we live in a society ever more dependent on computers and computer data processing. Therefore, whatever training in statistics and data processing the undergraduate student can obtain will improve his or her value to the organization and to society.

Conclusion

The issue before us is how best to prepare ourselves and the young people we train for the various opportunities in applied work that will emerge in the next few years. Applied work is not the same as basic work, although their products are often indistinguishable. Applied work requires special sensitivities and skills, and we hope that, by combining our experience and wisdom as shared in volumes like this one, we will be better able to do the job that lies ahead.

References

COLEMAN, J. S., CAMPBELL, E. Q., HOBSON, C. J., McPARTLAND, J., MOOD, A., WEINFELD, F. D., AND YORK, R. L.

    1966   *Equality of Educational Opportunity.* Washington, D.C.: U.S. Government Printing Office.

FAIRWEATHER, G. W., AND TORNATZKY, L.

    1977   *Experimental Methods for Social Policy Research.* Elmsford, N.Y.: Pergamon Press.

ROSSI, P. H.

    1980   "The presidential address: The challenge and opportunities of applied social research." *American Sociological Review* 45(6):889–904.

WHYTE, W. F.

    1981   *Street Corner Society.* (3rd ed.) Chicago: University of Chicago Press.

    1982   "Social inventions for solving human problems." *American Sociological Review* 47(1):1–13.

WHYTE, W. F., AND HAMILTON, E. L.

    1965   *Action Research for Management.* Homewood, Ill.: Irwin.

❧ 2 ❧

ROLE OF THEORY
IN APPLIED SOCIOLOGY

Jean Giles-Sims
Barry Tuchfeld

The role of theory is one of the fundamental issues in the ambivalent and often conflictual relationship between basic and applied social researchers. The controversy has three major themes. First, traditional academic sociologists often criticize applied sociologists for treating theoretical issues as superfluous. Second, applied sociologists and policy makers retort that theory is often superfluous because it lacks direct utility in their efforts to design, carry out, and evaluate social programs. Finally, in addition to these long-standing concerns about the relationship between traditional sociology and applied sociology, a new question has arisen about the use of empirical knowledge accumulated from applied sociology in the further development of theory.

These two orientations toward the role of theory differ significantly, and both the accumulation of knowledge and the resolution of social problems may be retarded because of this "theory gap." In contrast to sociology, other social sciences have emphasized that, without appropriate theoretical models, many applied problems cannot be adequately addressed. In addition, future funding for all social science research may depend on how well researchers can address pressing social problems. For instance, one statement explaining reductions in the National Science Foundation basic research program in the social and behavioral sciences accused social scientists of "being off in the cloudy heights of theory and speculation and not attending to the very real needs of our society" (Rossi, 1980, p. 889).

The purpose of this chapter is: first, to evaluate and trace the historical development of the debate between traditional sociology and applied sociology concerning the role of theory, and, second, to suggest a tentative model to encourage both the integration of theory in applied sociology and the synthesis of accumulated knowledge into further theory building. Specific issues include: What is the nature and history of the "theory gap"? What contributions have been made to theory by good applied research? How could the gap between theory and applied research be reduced? And, perhaps most important, who is going to reduce it, and how?

Brief History of the Theory Gap

The brief historical interpretation of the development of a "theory gap" presented here is grossly oversimplified for the sake of providing an introduction to the contemporary debate concerning the role of theory in the various subdivisions of the discipline. We recognize that the interpretation of the relationship between the subdivisions of the discipline is itself a focus for continuing debate.

Although sociology has been defined and accepted as the systematic study of social interaction, debate continues about the ultimate goal. Is knowledge the ultimate goal? Or is it the application of this knowledge to help direct social change?

In 1895, Albion Small warned "that the relations of man to man are not what they should be" and that "something must be done directly, systematically, and on a large scale to right these wrongs" (Small, 1895, p. 3). This action orientation within sociology never completely disappeared, but over time controversy about the ultimate goals of sociological research and debate over the role of theory in research created two major subdivisions of the discipline: traditional basic sociology and client-oriented, applied sociology, with many gradations of emphasis between.

The development of the discipline of sociology during the twentieth century can be divided roughly into three periods. The period from the late 1800s to 1920 was dominated by an urgent concern with social problems and reform. Gradually, however, it became clear that more knowledge was needed about the conditions and characteristics of the social environment in order to make solid recommendations for reform. A new research orientation arose out of these concerns, and the period from 1920 to approximately 1950 was dominated by scientific, empirical study. Since the early 1950s a widening gap has developed between basic sociological research and applied research. During this period, systematic development of theory has increasingly become the major emphasis within academia, and the branch of sociology interested in reform, social action, and program evaluation has increasingly based itself outside the academic world. During this period, both of these divisions of the discipline have grown stronger, and the relationship between them has become one of considerable ambivalence (Rossi, 1980). "Our ambivalence consists in believing—at one and the same time—that applied work is not worth our best efforts and our best minds and that an important reason for our existence is that sociology will lead to important practical applications" (Rossi, 1980, p. 889).

An understanding of the contemporary relationship between the two major divisions of the discipline depends in part on an appreciation of the development of each division's orientation toward the role of theory in its work. During the early orientation toward problem and reform, little attention was focused on theory as a set of interrelated, empirical generalizations extracted through deductive processes. Theory during this early period was characterized by philosophical discourse about the discrepancies between what ought to be and what actually occurred.

This period also saw the application of sociology to social reform through the individual participation of sociologists in community projects. For example, Albion Small served in the Civic Federation of Chicago, W. I. Thomas in the Chicago Vice Commission, and Robert Park in the Chicago Urban League (Carey, 1975). These early efforts by sociologists to become involved in social action reflected their personal commitments and their concern about the role of sociology in social action. These early attempts at policy making also led to the development of empirically based studies.

Following World War I, from 1920 to approximately 1950, a major emphasis within the discipline focused on scientific empirical study, which represented a shift away from philosophically based theory development and towards the accumulation of empirically based generalizations. The major emphasis within this new empirical orientation, which was identified at first primarily with the Chicago School of sociology, became the search for factors in the social environment related to social problems. For example, Ernest Burgess searched for social factors that predicted marital adjustment, and Charles Horton Cooley focused on individual personality adjustment under different social conditions. Martindale (1960) characterized the theoretical themes of this period as social behaviorism.

Although by 1920 social reform was not the dominant concern within sociology (Rhoades, 1980, p. 1), the social action orientation of early sociology never completely disappeared. The question continued to be raised about how to use the accumulating scientific knowledge by such books as Lynd's *Knowledge for What* (1939) and Lundberg's *Can Science Save Us?* (1947). Lundberg was an extreme positivist who regarded sociology as a science whose subject matter was adjustment by individuals and groups to each other and to the environment.

As the empirically oriented focus of the discipline became more prominent, sociologists developed more sophisticated research techniques and increasingly relied on specialists in methodology and statistics. Academia provided both the most convenient and most prestigious place to work. Increasingly, only those who could not find academic employment went to work for government and private organizations. This development over time contributed to the prestige of traditional academic sociology and the lesser prestige of applied work.

Despite the gradual divergence of traditional academy-based sociology and the client-oriented applied sociology, many sociologists during this period actively engaged in research projects that had direct implications for social policy. Often these studies provided both knowledge for direct application and major contributions to further development of theory in a specific area. Several major research projects, originally carried out as applied research, became known primarily for their contributions to basic knowledge. These include Stouffer's study *The American Soldier* (1949), originally designed to find ways to help military personnel cope with conditions of the battlefield, which made major contributions to the study of group formation and group cohesion, and the Lynds' first Middletown study (Lynd and Lynd, 1929), funded by a private foundation and designed to study how social change had affected the moral life of Americans (Rossi, 1980).

Tremendous gains were made during this period in sociological methods, sociological definitions, and theory development in substantive areas of human behavior. By the late 1950s, however, despite those gains, this orientation was being challenged. Many prominent sociologists questioned this incremental approach to sociological analysis (Martindale, 1960).

The ascendency of functionalism and conflict theory during the 1950s and 1960s (Dahrendorf, 1959; Coser, 1967) ushered the academic ranks of the discipline into an era in which theory construction was considered the most important activity. Both of these theoretical orientations took the total system as the primary level of analysis. This level of analysis contributed further to the gap between theory and social action, because system level variables are often not manipulable without widespread social and political change. For example, Gans (1971) illustrated how poverty was a consequence of our basic social system and how it served the interests of powerful socioeconomic groups within the social system, but his explanation did not provide information that social reformers could easily use, since most social reform programs focus on incremental change rather than on change in the basic structure of group relations. This problem of application contributed to the criticism of traditional academic sociology for being discipline-oriented rather than policy-oriented (Scott and Shore, 1979).

Increasingly, two separate branches formed within sociology based on two contrasting emphases. On the one hand were sociologists who sought to generalize and formalize sociological laws, and on the other hand were empirically oriented researchers who reported verifiable social facts but often did not explain them theoretically. This increasing schism led Merton to write about the bearing of sociological theory on empirical research, the bearing of empirical research on sociological theory, and the importance of mid-range theories (Merton, 1957).

When we consider mid-range rather than macro-level theoretical orientations, application of theoretical ideas to social program developments has proved more feasible. For example, Mobilization for Youth and the Ford Foundation's Gray Areas Projects drew on Merton's theory of anomie (Rossi, personal communication). With the social protest movements of the late 1960s and early 1970s, sociology as a discipline was pressured to become more "relevant," and some sociologists actively participated both in protests and reform movements. Shostak (1974) presents several case studies of attempts by sociologists to apply the ideas and theoretical implications of sociology in community action programs.

Many traditional sociologists, in contrast, paid less attention to the combination of theory and practice during this period. One notable exception to this generalization is a book by Zetterberg (1962) called *Social Theory and Social Practice,* in which he emphasizes both the importance of theory to inform social practice and the importance of testing theoretical hypotheses in natural settings.

Despite the innovative ideas of Merton, Zetterberg and others, however, the discipline of sociology has continued to separate theory and social practice. When a specific piece of research is designed by a sociologist to test a theoretical idea, it is referred to as basic research. When empirical research is conducted to test the outcomes of specific programs of a client, it is called applied research.

The respective work environments and demands of academic and applied researchers often dictate different work styles (Tuchfeld, 1976). Academic work is judged for its elegance and simplicity in the presentation of theories of social life. Standards for publications in discipline-oriented journals reward abstraction and methodological sophistication.

In contrast, the applied researcher has to balance the complexity of the problem with the level of sophistication of the client. Clients quite appropriately determine both the area of research and the audience. Most often, applied researchers must focus on specific problems and report directly to the programmer who hired them, not to the scientific community (Gibbs, 1979). Within the world of applied research, only secondary emphasis is placed on the accumulation and integration of empirical research findings. Priority must be given to the client's incremental puzzles, puzzles that demand a solution. In addition, limited edition reports of evaluative research do not generally refer to the basic theoretical paradigms that guided the research project. These differences further inhibit the integration of theoretical work and program-oriented applied research.

In summary, the "theory gap" between traditional sociology and applied sociology is the product of a long history of debate within the profession concerning the ultimate goals of the research endeavor, and the emergence of two distinct subdivisions of sociology with largely different focuses and different audiences. This gap has inhibited both the development of programs based on theoretical paradigms and the evaluation of direct outcomes of program implementation for theoretical refinement.

Two Models of Applied Sociology

One question sociologists often ask themselves and each other is, Where do you stand with respect to applied social research? Our own awareness of numerous discussions of these topics in several academic departments, at professional meetings, and at the recent ASA Conference on Applied Sociology in Washington, D.C. (December 1981) has led us to emphasize the distinction between two different models of applied sociology.

Disciplinary Perspective. The first model, the disciplinary perspective, focuses on how policy implications can be derived from theoretically relevant work that is central to the academic discipline of sociology. This view is akin to the view of Scott and

Shore (1979) but recognizes that there is more to the issue than the question of target audience (that is, peers versus clients).

Theories of deviance, social change, race relations, social stratification, and organizational structure and dynamics, among others, can provide knowledge applicable to social planning. Major findings in theoretically based research often indicate relationships between social problems and such variables as age, race, religion, and family background. Unfortunately, many of these variables are not easily manipulable; hence, implications for social change derived from this group of studies are often not applicable to specific program development.

Some research that is strictly disciplinary, however, has yielded findings with direct application—for example, studies that focus on organizational structure or management style in relation to worker satisfaction and productivity or studies on the effect of racial and ethnic matching between students and teachers on the academic achievement of minority students.

This model of applied sociology is consistent with the early emphasis within the discipline of sociology on the use of knowledge to help solve social problems. It is also potentially consistent with the "action school" of sociology, which is interested in putting sociology to work in actual social amelioration programs.

This model, however, does not demand either specific policy recommendations or plans for incremental programs. Its audience is either peers or discipline-oriented planners who are already well informed in this field.

A continuum exists within this model as a function of the amount of emphasis placed on application. At one end of the continuum, researchers suggest possible implications for policy in the discussions of their research appearing in disciplinary journals. At the other end of the continuum, discipline-oriented researchers seek actual programs that can be used as sites to apply the theoretically derived implications. Rossi and Whyte (1981) argue that this application is the most challenging test of theoretical ideas.

An additional benefit may be derived from the application of some aspect of social theory to an actual attempt to solve problems. Often these attempts make the researcher aware of "important variables and interactions among variables that would have escaped his attention if he had confined himself to 'pure' sociology" (Rossi and Whyte, 1981, p. 29).

Programmer's Perspective. The second model of applied sociology, the programmer's perspective, is somewhat analogous to Scott and Shore's (1979) policy-oriented model. Whether or not it is based on theory, an established social program needs information on its functioning and on its effects. From this perspective, research should begin with the program description and program goals. This approach is the traditional evaluation research model. If theory is at all a part of this model, the theory to be tested is the theory of the program, or the causal model on which the program is based (Patton, 1978, p. 181): "By way of contrast to logical, deductive theory construction, a utilization-focused approach to theory construction is inductive, pragmatic, and highly concrete. The evaluator's task is to delineate and test the theory or theories held by identified decision makers and information users. The causal model to be tested is the causal model upon which program activities are based."

The evaluation model discussed by Patton is the predominant, but not the sole, model in evaluation research today. From this perspective, the first task of an evaluator is to define and assess the problem. This stage emphasizes a description of the goals and objectives of the program. Next, the basic design and objectives of the research are spelled out, followed by the actual data gathering, which leads to analysis that in turn provides a basis for evaluation. When data are analyzed, the outcomes are evaluated in light of the program goals. Finally, results are reported to the client whose program is being evaluated. Where appropriate, process data are collected and may be used as independent sources of information or as intervening variables in the outcome analyses.

We have included this outline of the stages of the evaluation research process to illustrate that an attempt is rarely made to put the specific problem within a larger context of theoretical issues; that, when the results are analyzed, they are rarely integrated with other material to provide theoretically based explanations; and that information is usually presented only to the programmer. In actual practice, some of these research reports appear in public reports or monographs, but these reports are not as readily available as professional journals. The empirical research findings from evaluation research, therefore, are not readily accessible to students and researchers to use as sources on which to base further theory development.

From the programmer's perspective, further theory development has a much lower priority than immediate program concerns. Given the professional ethics of program-based applied researchers, this decision is indeed appropriate.

Studies that Successfully Bridge the Theory Gap

In the preceding section, we have emphasized the gap between discipline-oriented sociology and program-oriented research. Although our discussion has emphasized the atheoretical propensity of program-oriented research, three types of research do successfully bridge the "theory gap":

- Theoretically based empirical studies with policy implications. Examples of this type of research emphasize both theory and empirical investigation. An explicit objective is to provide knowledge that either could be applied or leads to specific implications for action. Examples of this type of research are Murray Straus and his colleagues' work on family violence (Straus, Gelles, and Steinmetz, 1980) and Robert Straus's work on alcoholism (Straus, 1974). From this perspective, the basic orientation, design, and methods of traditional and applied research differ little, if at all. The difference lies in drawing policy implications from research findings.
- Policy analysis reflecting the creative use of empirical and theoretical literature. A recent example is the role played by William Foote Whyte and Joseph Blasi as consultants to the federal government concerning worker ownership of industrial plants (Blasi, 1981, p. 4): "Creative social policy work can be defined as a process of study, research, and the creation of legislative options. This involves extensive reading and research, contacting experts, visiting actual settings around the country, and analysis of what tools and legislative strategy are likely to most quickly educate the Congress about the problem."
- Evaluation projects associated with large-scale social experi-

ments and based on a theoretical framework. An example is the evaluation of the negative income tax programs. Guaranteed cash income to poor families could create a more rational welfare system, if the income guarantees did not reduce worker incentive. The evaluation of outcomes from the negative income tax experiment provided both policy recommendations for possible implementation and an empirical test of some basic theoretical ideas (Pechman and Timpane, 1975).

Another good example of the application of theory in a large-scale social experiment is the work of Rossi, Berk, and Lenihan (1980) on income support for released prisoners, in which the actual program drew on sociological theory as well as theory from occupations, criminology, and microeconomics.

Each of these categories of studies that bridge the "theory gap" provides suggestions about the role of theory in applied research. The problem now is to provide an integrated model that indicates how disciplinary and programmatic concerns can both be furthered, given their separate emphases and the importance of their retaining their primary objectives and exclusive domains.

Potential Logic of an Applied Social Science

Science is a cumulative process, but rarely a linear one. The process of science can best be modeled as a circular diagram or flowchart that contains the components, the directions of influence, and the transformations that lead to the solution of problems and the accumulation of knowledge.

The case for employing theory in applied research has been presented elsewhere. Therefore, we will focus here on the issue of the use of empirical research findings for further theory development.

Clark Abt of Abt Associates in Boston recently presented a discussion of the "theory gap" from the point of view of the applied researcher. His major assumption is the importance of theory. With the retrenchment in sociological departments and the lack of money for basic research, he foresees the possible drying up of theory sources. Without theory, Abt acknowledges, research becomes raw empiricism. One of his major concerns is that social theorists are increasingly unaware of the vast accumulation of empirical knowledge and are therefore not using this knowledge in theory construction. The large-scale social experiments in poverty, medical care, income supports, unemployment, and education are examples of research where empirical findings could feed into theory in a synthesis of induction and classical theory construction. Abt (1979, p. 5) suggests: "The best kind of progress that we can probably make on the theory gap is to continually push ourselves to draw the theoretical implications and try to apply our empirical results to the integrations with theory or reformation of theory and first-order analyses across the different disciplinary lines."

Abt goes on to make the critical point that this is very difficult to do, both in universities and independent research institutes, because of the reward structures. For long-range payoffs in both areas, however, integration is a desirable goal.

A Modest Proposal for Synthesis

In principle, few social scientists would argue against the value of theory. To do so would be akin to proposing a ban on God, mother, and apple pie. The issue at hand is, in effect, how to facilitate mutually beneficial relationships among the practioner-researcher, the program administrator or policy maker, and the social scientist committed to the accumulation of theoretically relevant knowledge. Convenient though it might be to assume that each participant in applied research is equally committed to the objectives of the other participants, this assumption is unrealistic, in our view. The social scientist must recognize that the context of most applied research activities requires a priority on information for incremental decision making. Abstract theory building is a luxury, except in those organizations that have experienced the utility of research guided by the theories of social science.

We suggest a model that incorporates academics, program administrators, on-line evaluation or policy researchers, and consultants in an effort to synthesize knowledge and make it usable. These components and the basic transformations are presented in Figure 1. This figure is designed to present a concise model approximating the complexity of the relationship between traditional and applied social research. The objective of this model is to

Figure 1. A Proposal for Synthesizing Social Theory and Applied Research.

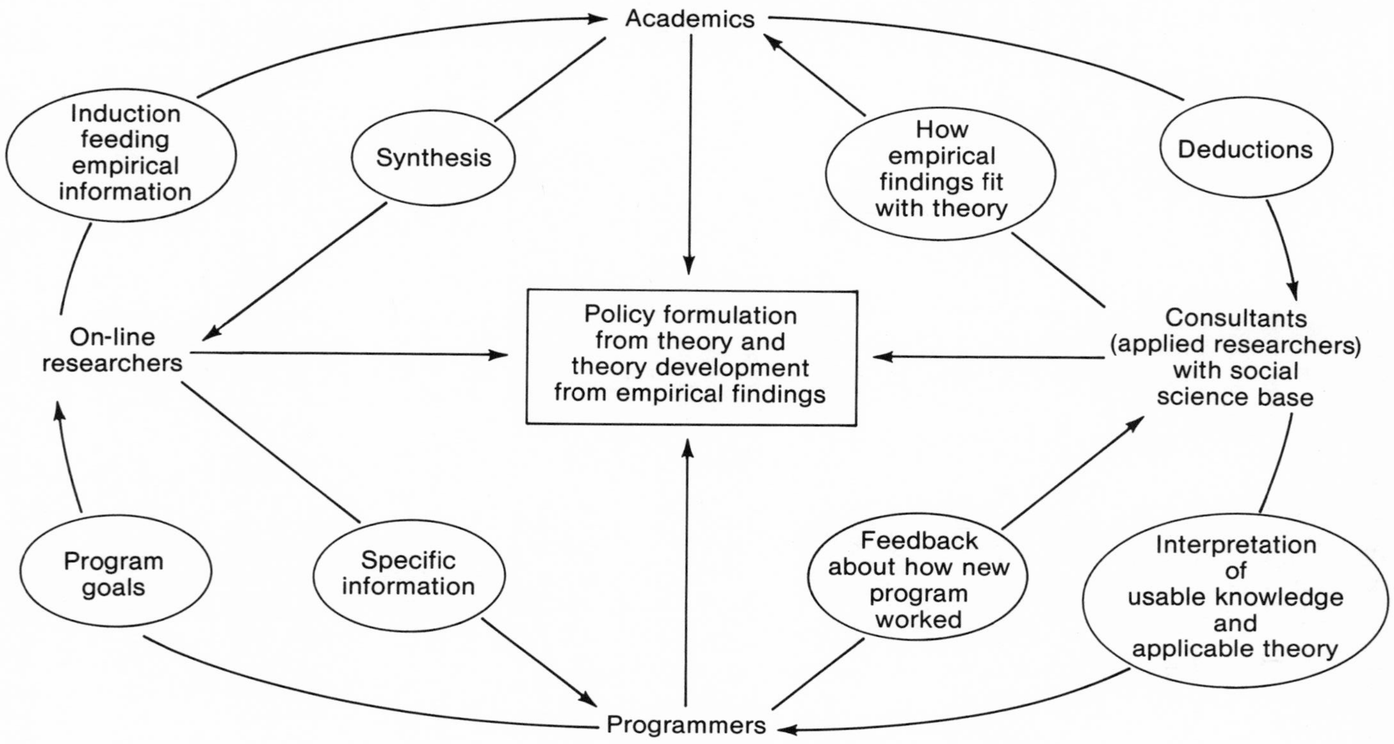

join theory and empiricism. In brief, Figure 1 suggests realistic cooperation between program administrators, researchers, academics, and consultants in the development both of theoretically supported policies and of sound sociological theory that incorporates the findings of empirical research.

The components—program administrators, on-line researchers, academics, and consultants—each have a role to play in this overall process. The role of each component and its critical interactions with the other components will be discussed separately.

Programmers. Individual programs are highly specific, problem-oriented, and essentially concerned with unique situations. The individuals who administer these programs must be the prime policy makers—after all, they are the ones who are accountable for mistakes. They also orchestrate the interplay between the goals of the program and the realities of finance and actual day-to-day activities.

To make their decisions, they often need expert advice from two sources: their own or hired on-line researchers and professional consultants. Because we believe that the consultants should come first in the process, we will discuss their role next.

Professional Consultants. In our model, professional consultants provide the interpretation of basic science knowledge and applicable theory that the program administrator can use to make policy decisions. Often program administrators can invest a few thousand dollars in a consultant instead of instituting their own needs assessment or other research. The professional consultant is familiar with the theoretical knowledge relevant to the specific problem and can make theoretically derived program suggestions. A consultant can also tell a programmer about the results of past research in this area. Taken together, this information can bring order and perspective to the specific problems and help the programmer weigh the alternatives and their likely consequences.

Consultants can potentially influence the shape of social policy more than on-line evaluation researchers because they draw from a broader perspective. In the actual program situation, however, the roles of consultant and researcher are sometimes combined, which is problematic for two reasons: the consultant should be more familiar with the theoretical and empirical knowledge of the social sciences than on-line researchers in order for the pro-

gram to have theoretical relevance; and on-line researchers emphasize methodology, and their role is to provide program administrators with specific information about how programs work.

The consultant's role as we have discussed it has two disadvantages. First, the consultant is limited by what is available in the
body of accumulated social science knowledge. Social science has
often not focused on applied problems, which may prove to be a
serious limitation. Second, the consultant may not have enough influence on the development of specific on-line research projects to
assure that the information that is gathered in these projects is theoretically relevant.

It is as important for the theorist to use the available empirical information as it is for the program administrator to use the
available theoretical information. The actual research done should
therefore reflect theoretical designs. We suggest that, for this to
happen, consultants must act as a bridge back to the academic the-
oretician and must influence on-line researchers in the design of
research projects.

On-Line Researchers. On-line researchers have the role we
traditionally associate with the applied social researcher. Their research is always specialized but, as we have said, should have theoretical relevance. The on-line researcher translates program goals
into a few specific outcome variables to be measured and provides
the programmer with specific information about those variables.
This researcher knows those specific variables better than anyone,
and program administrators often put considerable weight on the
outcomes of this type of research.

This type of research presents two problems, however, from
the program administrator's point of view: these few variables are
only part of the picture, and the researcher is only one voice
among many. The administrator must take many social and ideological factors into account when planning the program.

There are also problems from the theoretical point of view.
The theoretical solutions received from consultants may not be
feasible to implement in their entirety. Therefore, research which
evaluates the outcomes of programs that have partially implemented a theoretically based program may prove inadequate either
to prove or modify the theory on which it was based.

Despite all these possible problems, applied researchers play an important role in the link between theory and applied research or policy development. As Thomas (1981, p. 32) has commented: "The social scientists have a long way to go to catch up, but they may be up to the most important scientific business of all, if and when they finally get down to the right questions."

Academic Theorists. Although the burden of synthesis rests primarily with the theorist, the theorist does not bear total responsibility. According to the model proposed in Figure 1, each of the components in the process plays a contributing role in the synthesis of theory and applied research.

The role of the theorist is threefold: to provide the theoretical framework for basic research from which consultants can provide usable knowledge to program administrators; to listen to the applied researchers, particularly when the program being studied has a theoretical basis; and, in some cases, to integrate and synthesize theory and research to provide direct policy recommendations.

These recommendations challenge the theorist to take a more active role in policy making and applied research. Anytime that new demands are made, however, we must take into account the context in which the theorist works. The primary concern is whether academic theorists will be rewarded if they take on this new responsibility. We raise this issue here because universities and professional societies have traditionally rewarded this work less than pure research or theory building. Nevertheless, we maintain that the impetus for change lies within the academy, not within task-oriented organizations that pursue survival on a day-to-day, incremental basis.

Conclusion

Discussions and debates about the role of theory in programmatic research are not new, but what has been absent is a practical model available to academicians, program personnel, policy makers, and on-line researchers. The model we propose can be utilized to achieve multiple objectives. Decisions must be made at the program level, to be sure, but the dynamics of the decision-making process are not in themselves antithetical to the objectives of the social scientist. Social scientists must accommodate themselves to the reality of the situation while recognizing opportunities for new inputs into the theory-building process. In time, decision makers may seek theoretical guidance, even if such input is not labeled theory. In the meantime, the discipline should not completely default to the current incremental trend in applied research, although intrinsic accommodation should not be dismissed offhandedly.

There is perhaps a larger issue, in some ways previously addressed by Cronbach (1975). The prestige hierarchy in sociology has traditionally placed large-scale, nationally focused research at its pinnacle. Most applied research is conducted at a more modest, local level. To accommodate this reality, the sociologist will have to legitimate intensive local efforts directed toward incremental decision making and recognize the utility of such efforts as grist for the theoretical mill.

To summarize: theoretical efforts that have utility for decision making will be sustained because both science and social programs benefit. In this process, it is incumbent on social scientists not to let themselves become superfluous and to further the goals of theory building by recognizing the utility of applied sociology.

References

ABT, C. C.
    1979   "The theory gap in social policy research." Presidential address, Council on Applied Social Research, Washington, D.C.

BLASI, J. R.
    1981   "Legislative consultation." Paper presented at the ASA Workshop on Directions in Applied Sociology, Washington, D.C.

CAREY, J. T.
    1975   *Sociology and Public Affairs: The Chicago School.* Beverly Hills, Calif.: Sage.

COSER, L. A.
    1967   *Continuities in the Study of Social Conflict.* New York: Free Press.

CRONBACH, L. J.
    1975   "Beyond the two disciplines of scientific psychology." *American Psychologist* 30:116–127.

DAHRENDORF, R.
    1959   *Class and Class Conflict in Industrial Society.* Stanford,
            Calif.: Stanford University Press.
GANS, H. J.
    1971   "The uses of poverty: The poor pay all." *Social Policy*
            2:20-24.
GIBBS, J. P.
    1979   "The elites can do without us." *American Sociologist*
            14:79-85.
LAZARSFELD, P. F., AND REITZ, J. G.
    1975   *An Introduction to Applied Sociology.* New York:
            Elsevier.
LUNDBERG, G.
    1947   *Can Science Save Us?* New York: Longman.
LYND, R. S.
    1939   *Knowledge For What?* Princeton, N.J.: Princeton Uni-
            versity Press.
LYND, R. S., AND LYND, H.
    1929   *Middletown: A Study in American Culture.* New York:
            Harcourt Brace Jovanovich.
MARTINDALE, D.
    1960   *The Nature and Types of Sociological Theory.* Boston:
            Houghton Mifflin.
MERTON, R. K.
    1957   *Social Theory and Social Structure.* New York: Free
            Press.
PATTON, M. Q.
    1978   *Utilization-Focused Evaluation.* Beverly Hills, Calif.:
            Sage.
PECHMAN, J. A., AND TIMPANE, P. M.
    1975   *Work Incentives and Income Guarantees.* Washington,
            D.C.: Brookings Institution.
RHOADES, L. J.
    1980   "Society grows in size and complexity in first 25
            years." *ASA Footnotes* 8:1.
ROSSI, P. H.
    1980   "The presidential address: The challenge and opportu-
            nities of social research." *American Sociological Re-
            view* 45:889-904.

ROSSI, P. H., BERK, R. A., AND LENIHAN, K.
   1980   *Money, Work, and Crime: Experimental Evidence.*
          New York: Academic Press.
ROSSI, P. H., AND WHYTE, W. F.
   1981   "Applied-side sociology." Paper presented at the ASA
          Workshop on Directions in Applied Sociology, Wash-
          ington, D.C.
SCOTT, R. A., AND SHORE, A. R.
   1979   *Why Sociology Does Not Apply: A Study of the Use
          of Sociology in Public Policy.* New York: Elsevier.
SHOSTAK, A. B.
   1974   *Putting Sociology to Work.* New York: McKay.
SMALL, A.
   1895   "The era of sociology." *American Journal of Sociology*
          1:1-15.
STOUFFER, S. A.
   1949   *The American Soldier.* Vols. 1 and 2. Princeton, N.J.:
          Princeton University Press.
STRAUS, M. A., GELLES, R. J., AND STEINMETZ, S. K.
   1980   *Behind Closed Doors: Violence in the American Fam-
          ily.* Garden City, N.J.: Doubleday/Anchor.
STRAUS, R.
   1974   *Escape from Custody.* New York: Harper & Row.
THOMAS, L.
   1981   "Science may be a gamble, but it's the only game in
          town." *Princeton Alumni Weekly,* December, p. 32.
TUCHFELD, B.
   1976   "Putting sociology to work: An insider's view." *Ameri-
          can Sociologist* 11(4):188.
ZETTERBERG, H. L.
   1962   *Social Theory and Social Practice.* New York: Bed-
          minster Press.

🦢 3 🦢

TRENDS IN EMPLOYMENT
OF SOCIOLOGISTS

Ronald W. Manderscheid
Mathew Greenwald

Incongruity between the supply of sociologists and the number of employment opportunities has been a concern at various times in the history of the profession in the United States. During the 1930s, for example, F. Stuart Chapin (1934), while president of the American Sociological Society, expressed the view that the number of sociologists being trained was almost double the number needed to fill available jobs. In 1968, Abbott Ferriss called for at least a 67 percent increase in the production of sociologists to meet the "surging" demand. However, five years later, McGinnis and Solomon (1973, p. 58) found "a dismal picture of future employment prospects for sociologists."

Opinions vary as to how the profession should react to the job market of the 1980s. In an interesting exchange, Irwin Deutscher

(1981) argued that a civilized society should encourage all those who feel a calling to sociology to study it, while Beverly Porter (1981, p. 174) stated that projections of demand are useful to the field and that students "deserve . . . to know about both need and demand."

Recently, a growing disparity has been apparent between the supply of sociologists and the number of positions available to professionals who obtain terminal master's or doctoral degrees in sociology. Recent reports by Doris Wilkinson (1980) in *Footnotes,* the informal evaluation of the 1979 Job Placement Center at the Eastern Sociological Society meeting by Manderscheid and Manderscheid (1979), and hallway comments at national and regional meetings all support this inference. Kurt Finsterbush, after a 1981 analysis of admission patterns in sociology graduate programs, concluded that, despite good long-term prospects, the outlook for the short-term demand for sociologists was weak (1981).

In the early fall of 1980, a subcommittee was formed from the ASA Ad Hoc Committee on Expanding Professional Opportunities in Applied Sociology to investigate supply-and-demand issues within the profession. The subcommittee was charged with the following tasks: compilation of available data on the current and projected number of sociologists in the United States in relation to the current and projected number of professional positions available in academia, government, and industry; preparation of a report to the committee on the results of the investigation; and development of recommendations in regard to future data collection efforts. The findings and recommendations are incorporated into the present chapter.

Methods

The primary source of labor-force projections in the United States is the Bureau of Labor Statistics (BLS), whose most recent estimates are based on the Occupational Employment Statistics Surveys. The data are collected through questionnaires mailed directly to work establishments. The questionnaires are tailored to specific industries, each of which was surveyed triennially during the 1970s. Each survey instrument lists up to 200 occupations, and employers are asked to identify significant new categories of occupations. This information is supplemented by data collected on private household employment and agricultural industries through the Census Bureau Current Population Surveys (CPS). Counts of self-employed workers and unpaid family workers are also collected through the CPS.

With this information on employment as a base, the BLS formulated three projections of changes in employment over a twelve-year period (to 1990). Common to these projections are analyses of historical trends for each job category and a variety of factors influencing potential change. Then projections were developed assuming: a decline in labor force expansion, high inflation, and modest increases in production and productivity; large increases in gross national product and high labor-force growth; and large increases in gross national product with labor-force growth restrained by increases in productivity (Carey, 1981).

As the most conservative approach, we averaged these projections based on the best available data in order to derive the anticipated number of applied sociologists in 1990. The BLS did not project the number of academic sociologists as part of their efforts. However, BLS staff—using data from the National Science Foundation Manpower Report for Scientific Activities at Universities and Colleges and from the Projections of Education Statistics to 1988-1989 developed by the National Center for Education Statistics—projected employment in academic sociology to 1990. These projections are based on student enrollment patterns, past employment trends, degrees granted, and other variables (Wilkinson, 1980).

We define the projected employment of sociologists, applied and academic, as the demand for sociologists. The tentative nature of projections of this type, as well as the ability of the profession to react to and redirect these trends, is clearly recognized. However, we argue that the extensive nature of the data collection by BLS—through large national surveys—and their effort and experience in labor-force projections make the results of their efforts worthy of consideration. In addition, once the BLS makes a projection, the figure has a widespread impact on various institutions and on supply and demand itself.

The supply data were more difficult to project. The current count of sociologists and accurate data for the past decade are readily available from the National Science Foundation and the BLS. The Digest of Education Statistics provides good information on the number of B.A., M.A., and Ph.D. degrees granted in sociology since 1972. To project the supply of sociologists in 1990, we made a series of assumptions that will be listed. In every case, an effort was made to estimate growth in supply very conservatively. Therefore, we feel very comfortable in forecasting that the supply figures listed are the absolute minimum that will be produced during the 1980s.

To estimate supply in 1981, we started with an estimate for 1980 of 21,225—the 20,911 employed sociologists plus an estimated 314 temporarily unemployed sociologists. For professions like sociology, it is commonly assumed that 1.5 percent of the number of employed are unemployed. This number was adjusted by adding the number of persons granted M.A.s and Ph.D.s in sociology minus an estimate of the number of persons granted M.A.s who continued in graduate school and therefore did not join the supply. The number was further adjusted by subtracting the estimated number of sociologists who left the field due to death or retirement. This number was estimated to be 500 per year (Hecker, 1981). Finally, the number was adjusted by subtracting the number of sociologists who permanently left the field—estimated, based on similar professions, to be 1 percent of employed sociologists. The result of these calculations was the estimated supply of sociologists at the start of 1981 (see Table 1).

This process was repeated for each year to derive an estimate of the supply of sociologists in 1990 (see Table 2). To make these calculations, it was necessary, of course, to estimate the number of M.A.s and Ph.D.s awarded through the 1980s. Since federal organizations do not make these projections, we made our own estimates by assuming the average of two assumptions. The first assumption is that the production of degrees will fall by the same amount from 1980 to 1990 as occurred between 1972 and 1980. The second assumption is that production will remain at the 1980 level during the 1980-1990 period. These two approaches were used to derive separate estimates, which were subsequently averaged to derive the final estimates.

The authors are aware of the dangers of these assumptions and projections. However, we feel that the projections are reason-

Table 1. College and University Employment of Sociologists and Production of B.A., M.A., and Ph.D. Degrees, 1972–1980, with Projections for 1990.

Year	Academic Sociologists[a]	Number of Degrees in Sociology[b]		
		B.A.	M.A.	Ph.D.
1972	—[c]	35,216	1,944	636
1973	12,483	35,436	1,923	583
1974	13,016	35,491	2,196	632
1975	14,234	31,488	2,112	693
1976	15,182	27,634	2,009	729
1977	15,535	24,713	1,830	714
1978	15,403	22,750	1,611	599
1979	15,084	20,285	1,415	612
1980	14,529	18,782[e]	1,345[e]	584[e]
1990	14,750[d]	10,565[f]	1,046[f]	558[f]

[a] From National Science Foundation (1981), p. 5.

[b] From U.S. Department of Education, National Center for Education Statistics (1981), table 110.

[c] Data not available.

[d] Based on a personal communication from Hall Dillon, Bureau of Labor Statistics.

[e] Projected data.

[f] Projection = $((N_{1980} - N_{1972-1980}) + N_{1980})/2$. This figure represents the average of two assumptions: production will fall by the same amount during 1980–1990 as during 1972–1980, and production during 1980–1990 will remain constant at 1980 levels.

able and based on the best available data. Further, we tried to be as cautious as possible in estimating the growth of supply. Therefore, the excess of supply over demand predicted in this chapter is conservative. If anything, we underestimated the problem of excess supply.

Results

In this section, we present data on supply and demand and anticipated changes in these variables. *Supply* refers to the estimated number of sociologists who hold M.A.s or Ph.D.s in sociology. *Demand* is defined as the estimated number of positions in academic and applied settings that are typically filled by professionals labeled sociologists. The term *applied* is used instead of the more pejorative label *nonacademic* to refer to all sociologists employed in government and private-sector settings. However, we

Table 2. Expected Changes in Employment Patterns of M.A. and Ph.D. Sociologists, 1980–1990.

| | Demand | | | | | |
| | 1980 | | 1990 | | Change | |
	N	Percent	N	Percent	N	Percent
Academic						
Total	14,529	69.5	14,570	64.8	+41	0.3
Full-Time	10,877	52.0				
Part-Time	3,652	17.5				
Applied						
Total	6,382[a]	30.5	7,675[b]		+1,293	
			7,946[b]		+1,564	
			8,130[b]		+1,748	
			7,917($\overline{x}$)	35.2	+1,535	24.1
Total	20,911	100.0	22,487	100.0	+1,576	7.5
	Supply					
Total	21,225	100.0	26,483[c]	100.0	+5,258	24.8
	(Supply–Demand)					
Total Un-employment	314[g]	1.5[d]	3,996	15.1[e]	+3,682	1,172.6

[a]Occupational Employment Statistics Survey, Bureau of Labor Statistics (unpublished). This recent survey was comprised of a count of jobs (as reported in the Current Population Surveys) formerly used by the Bureau of Labor Statistics.

[b]The Bureau of Labor Statistics developed three projections of economic growth to project employment in various occupations, as described in the text.

[c]The methodology used to estimate supply figures is described in the text.

[d]Assumes an unemployment rate of 1.5 percent (based on a personal communication from Albert Gollin).

[e]Unemployment as a percentage of supply.

should point out that not all of those employed in applied settings are engaged in applied work.

The first part of this section describes employment and production trends in academic settings. These two intercorrelated variables are essential factors with respect to future supply. The second part of this section compares trends in supply and demand. Since the composition of demand is expected to change in favor of applied positions between 1980 and 1990, the third part of this section presents a more detailed analysis of demand in applied settings and describes future trends in such settings.

Employment and Production Trends in Academic Settings.
Table 1 shows the numbers of sociologists employed in colleges
and universities, as well as the number of B.A., M.A., and Ph.D.
degrees granted in sociology, for the period 1972–1980, with corresponding projections for 1990. (See Panian and Defleur [n.d.]
for estimates between 1956 and 1972.) Academic employment of
sociologists reached a maximum of 15,535 in 1977 and has declined since that time to a total of 14,529 in 1980. (It should also
be noted that, of the 12,483 sociologists employed in academic
settings in 1973, 2,797 (22.4 percent) were employed part-time.
By 1980, the number employed part-time had increased to 3,652
sociologists or 25.1 percent of the 14,529 academically employed
sociologists.) The projection of 14,570 academic sociologists in
1990 is only slightly higher than the 1980 level.

For all academic levels, the number of degree recipients
reached a maximum near the middle of the decade and has since
been declining steadily. B.A. production reached a maximum of
35,491 in 1974 and had declined to 18,782 by 1980; M.A. production reached a maximum of 2,196 in the same year and had
declined to 1,345 by 1980; Ph.D. production reached a maximum
of 729 in 1976 and had declined to 584 by 1980. Projections for
1990 reflect a continuation of these trends. Based on the methodology employed in the absence of any published projections (see
Table 1, footnote f), we would anticipate that the following numbers of degrees will be awarded in 1990: B.A.s, 19,565; M.A.s,
1,046; Ph.D.s, 558. Obviously, these numbers are speculative and
subject to relatively large error. However, we feel that the methodology is reasonable, given past performance.

Comparison of Trends in Supply and Demand. Table 2
shows supply-and-demand figures for M.A. and Ph.D. sociologists
at two points in time, 1980 and 1990. The table also presents an
analysis of anticipated changes in demand and supply, as well as a
comparative analysis of the two at each point in time.

In 1980, about 14,529 sociologists (69.5 percent) were employed in colleges and universities. The remaining 6,832 (30.5 percent) were employed in applied settings. Hence, total demand consisted of about 20,911 positions. These figures do not represent
full-time equivalents, however, since 3,652 sociologists (17.5 percent) were employed part-time by colleges and universities. Estimates of part-time employment in applied settings are unknown.

By 1990, demand is expected to increase by about 1,576 positions to 22,487. The composition of the discipline will have changed somewhat, with applied positions representing about 35 percent of the total, a new increase of about 5 percentage points. The number of academic positions is expected to increase by about 4 per year, a ten-year growth rate of less than 1 percent; the number of applied positions is expected to grow by about 154 positions per year, a ten-year growth rate approaching 25 percent.

On the supply side, we have assumed a conservative unemployment rate of 1.5 percent in 1980. As a result, we estimate that there were approximately 21,225 M.A. and Ph.D. sociologists in the United States during 1980. By 1990, this number is expected to increase to 26,483, a ten-year growth rate of 24.8 percent, or an annual increase of about 526 new M.A. and Ph.D. sociologists.

Based on these supply-and-demand projections, it can be inferred that, by 1990, 3,996 M.A. and Ph.D. sociologists, or 15.1 percent of all sociologists, will not be able to find either academic or applied positions in this discipline. Stated differently, if present expectations hold, the supply of sociologists will increase at somewhat more than three times the rate at which positions become available between 1980 and 1990. However, if one assumes that a 1.5 percent unemployment rate is normal for the discipline, the projected number of trained sociologists who have little or no chance of finding academic or applied sociological positions will be approximately 3,659 individuals.

Employment Trends in Applied Settings. As noted earlier, employment of sociologists in applied settings will grow at a considerably faster rate than academic employment. Table 3 provides an analysis of trends in specific areas of employment between 1980 and 1990.

In 1980, applied employment in the public sector comprised about 1,806 positions, or 28.3 percent of all applied positions. This number is expected to grow to 3,267 positions, or 41.3 percent of all applied positions, by 1990. Employment of sociologists by the federal government will decrease appreciably, and employment by local governments will increase at a moderate rate. The greatest growth in applied employment of sociologists in the public sector will occur in state government, where the number of positions is expected to increase by 1,542, a growth rate of more than 225 percent.

Table 3. Growth in Applied Employment of M.A. and Ph.D. Sociologists, 1980-1990.

	1980		1990		Change	
	N^a	Percent[b]	N	Percent[c]	N	Percent
All Applied	6,382	100.00	7,917	100.00	+1,535	24.05
Government	1,806	28.30	3,267	41.26	+1,461	80.90
Federal	533	8.36	340	4.29	− 193	− 36.21
State	676	10.59	2,218	28.01	+1,542	228.11
Local	597	9.35	709	8.96	+ 112	18.76
Services and Industry	4,576	71.70	4,650	58.74	+ 74	1.62
Educational Services	1,855	29.07	1,533	19.36	− 322	− 17.36
Miscellaneous Professional Services	722	11.31	925	11.69	+ 203	28.12
Medical/Health Services	702	11.00	1,111	14.03	+ 409	58.26
Nonprofit Organizations	676	10.59	607	7.67	− 69	− 10.21
Business Management	293	4.59	400	5.06	+ 107	36.52
Other Services	87	1.36	73	0.92	− 14	− 16.09
Miscellaneous Industry	241	3.78	1	0.01	− 240	− 99.59

[a]Summary figure based on Bureau of Labor Statistics Current Employment Surveys and Occupational Employment Statistics Survey. Data for sociologists unpublished.

[b]U.S. Department of Labor, Bureau of Labor Statistics (1981), pp. 81–82. Note: 1978 distribution applied to 1980 data.

[c]Average of three projections (see text).

In the private sector, employment in medical/health services is anticipated to grow by more than 50 percent, an increase of more than 400 positions. Growth is also expected in the areas of business management and miscellaneous professional services. Other areas are expected to show a pattern of contraction. The most precipitous decreases are expected in educational services and miscellaneous industries.

Discussion of Trends

A number of the trends described in the previous section deserve further comment. Trends in employment and production within academic settings are disturbing in terms of the future viability of the discipline. Productivity of all types of degrees has decreased steadily since the middle of the last decade and is expected to decrease further over the next decade. Although this decrease will serve to reduce the supply–demand differential, it will also further erode the future strength and vitality of sociology. Yet should students be advised to go into sociology without full knowledge of the bleak prospects in academic and applied job markets?

Employment trends in the academic setting are also disturbing. Academic employment of sociologists is expected to remain relatively constant over the next ten years. However, this pattern does not consider the increase in the percentage of academic sociologists who are employed part-time. Such part-time employment is likely to create further stress in the applied job market. In addition, as the number of degrees declines, particularly undergraduate majors, the academic job market is likely to erode even more. Should we continue to socialize the majority of advanced degree recipients to desire to become college and university teachers?

Trends in supply and demand between 1980 and 1990 are also unsettling. If one assumes that the projections are generally valid, even if somewhat inaccurate, about 15 percent of all sociologists will not be able to find employment in either academic or applied settings in 1990. However, the projected trends for applied settings present a considerably brighter picture. Demand in applied settings is expected to show a growth rate approaching 25 percent between 1980 and 1990. Should we continue to view sociology as basically an academic profession?

Employment trends in applied settings offer some indication of the type of training that will be required for future sociologists. In the government sector, demand is expected to increase most at the state level. One can infer that evaluation, research, and administrative skills will be desirable (Manderscheid, 1978). In the private sector, demand is expected to increase in medical/health services, business management, and miscellaneous professional services. Again, one can infer that evaluation, research (particularly skills in large-scale market surveys, cost–benefit analysis, and organizational productivity), and administrative skills will be required. Should we continue to train sociologists as we have done in the past?

Taken as a whole, the data presented in this paper suggest one of two courses of action: (1) contract supply—this could be accomplished by further reducing the number of degree recipients or by developing programs that lead to earlier retirement and replacement; (2) expand demand—this option will require a bold effort to restructure training, build effective liaison with government and industry, and create new roles that do not currently exist.

Obviously, we favor the option of expanding demand. The American Sociological Association Workshop on Directions in Applied Sociology held in 1981 in Washington, D.C., was an excellent first step in defining pertinent issues. The enthusiasm expressed at this conference indicates that grass-roots support is growing and that changes in the nature and scope of the discipline are likely to occur in the short-term future. This issue must be given high priority by the ASA and members of the profession.

Recommendations for Future Data Collection Activities

The subcommittee was somewhat frustrated in its work by the sparseness of the available data, as evidenced by the number of assumptions required. There is clearly a need for better, more detailed data that is collected routinely. Obviously, future programs are difficult to plan when one has estimates and projections based on tenuous assumptions and unknown validity.

Due to the potential gravity of the supply-and-demand problem, the subcommittee recommends that the ASA acquire the necessary resources to conduct detailed studies of supply-and-demand issues within the profession.

We recommend that the following studies be instituted in the immediate future:

1. An annual survey of all graduate and undergraduate departments to monitor the production of bachelor's, master's, and doctoral degrees. This survey should include projected productivity over a five- to ten-year range.
2. A cohort study of a sample of a single year's Ph.D. recipients, initiated at five-year intervals.
3. An annual survey of ASA members conducted in conjunction with membership renewal. The survey initiated by the ASA in 1981 shows considerable promise.
4. Development of a routine system to monitor and project the numbers and types of positions available outside academia in government and industry. This area deserves special attention, since present data suggest that the greatest growth over the next ten years will occur in these sectors.

The numbers we have discussed acquire additional impact if one has witnessed the anxiety experienced by recent job seekers. Immediate action is required to develop reliable data on which future planning and action can be based.

References

CAREY, M. L.
    1981   "Occupational employment growth through 1980." *Monthly Labor Review* 104(8):42-55.
CHAPIN, F. S.
    1934   "The present state of the profession." *American Journal of Sociology* 39(4):506-508.
DEUTSCHER, I.
    1981   "Social needs vs. market demands." *Sociological Focus* 14(3):161-172.
FERRISS, A.
    1968   "Forecasting supply and demand for sociologists." *The American Sociologist* 3:225-234.
FINSTERBUSH, K.
    1981   "Employment prospects for sociologists in the 1980s." Memorandum, University of Maryland, College Park.

HECKER, D.
    1981   Personal communication. Washington, D.C.: U.S. Department of Labor, Bureau of Labor Statistics, October 1.
McGINNIS, R., AND SOLOMON, L.
    1973   "Employment prospects for Ph.D. sociologists during the seventies." *The American Sociologist* 8:58.
MANDERSCHEID, R. W.
    1978   "Recommends specific training for federal careers." *ASA Footnotes* 6:4-5.
MANDERSCHEID, R. W., AND MANDERSCHEID, F. E.
    1979   "Follow-up study of the ESS job placement center." *ESS Newsletter* Winter, pp. 3-4.
NATIONAL SCIENCE FOUNDATION
    1981   *Academic Science: Scientists and Engineers, January 1980.* Washington, D.C.: National Science Foundation.
PANIAN, S. K., AND DEFLEUR, M. L.
    n.d.   *Sociologists in Non-Academic Employment.* Washington, D.C.: American Sociological Association, Professional Information Series.
PORTER, B.
    1981   "Some comments on social needs versus market demands." *Sociological Focus* 14(1):174.
U.S. DEPARTMENT OF EDUCATION, NATIONAL CENTER FOR EDUCATION STATISTICS
    1981   *Digest of Educational Statistics.* Washington, D.C.: U.S. Department of Education, National Center for Education Statistics.
U.S. DEPARTMENT OF LABOR, BUREAU OF LABOR STATISTICS
    1980   *Occupational Projections and Training Data.* (1980 ed.) Washington, D.C.: U.S. Department of Labor, Bureau of Labor Statistics.
U.S. DEPARTMENT OF LABOR, BUREAU OF LABOR STATISTICS
    1981   *The National Industry-Occupation Employment Matrix, 1970, 1978, and Projected 1990.* Vol. 2. Washington, D.C.: U.S. Department of Labor, Bureau of Labor Statistics.
WILKINSON, D. Y.
    1980   "A synopsis: Projections for the profession in the 1980s." *ASA Footnotes* 8(4):6-7.

Part Two: Sociologists in Diverse Settings

INTRODUCTION

Herbert L. Costner

Applied and basic sociology have long lived in uneasy alliance, even though the distinction between the two has never been as sharp as the terminology suggests. To early academic sociology struggling for recognition as a scholarly discipline, the reformist zeal of "do good" sociology was a status threat, and applied interests were muffled and underplayed, even though they were persistently present. Once firmly established in American colleges and universities, academic sociology, like other scholarly disciplines, developed a momentum of its own, and most of those who moved into the world of practical affairs found themselves defined as outsiders. Nonacademic employment carried some stigma during the great expansion of higher education in the 1960s, when sociologists who made their living in other settings were commonly perceived as the rejects of academia. The recent revitalization of applied sociology suggests that the tide is now flowing in another direction. While academic sociologists find themselves threatened by the eroding financial base of higher education and diminishing federal support for basic research, fresh talent pours as never before into positions calling for the application of knowledge.

Although the old stereotypes may persist, the terms of the uneasy alliance have changed. Applied sociology, once viewed as a reformist challenge to the status quo, now shamelessly serves the governmental and corporate establishment. Academic sociologists, still privileged in selecting the focus of their own research, now cast an envious eye on those who work in other settings with no teaching responsibilities and with research assistance and resources that frequently exceed those available even in the most affluent universities. Applied sociologists, who typically work in interdisciplinary teams, seem better informed about neighboring disciplines than their academic counterparts, who tenaciously maintain disciplinary boundaries and seem reluctant to cross them. And, while applied sociologists strive to show that their work measures up to the methodological standards of academic sociology, enthusiasts for basic social science strive to show that the results of basic social research are, after all, useful to the larger society. (Adams, Smelser, and Treiman, 1982).

In the following chapters, sixteen sociologists, most of them employed in nonacademic settings, describe the applied work they do, outline the skills required, and comment on their satisfactions and frustrations. Their tasks vary greatly, but these chapters attest to a common (but far from universal) function of applied sociologists that I will call reconnaissance sociology. Like the reconnaissance function in a military unit, reconnaissance sociology gathers and reports information that may have a bearing on the choice among alternative courses of action. The reconnaissance function is not the only conceivable role for applied sociologists, as some of the following chapters make clear, and it represents a departure from an older tradition in applied sociology. But it is evidently the most common current conception of what an applied sociologist does. Not surprisingly, then, a fundamental theme runs through those skills seen as requisite by applied sociologists themselves. The most commonly emphasized skills are research methodology and the communication skills necessary to report effectively to nonsociologists. Although these skills are appropriate for reconnaissance sociology, alternative roles would require alternative skills, and it is a commentary on the state of the discipline that research methodology, not sociological theory, constitutes the stock-in-trade of most applied sociologists.

The satisfactions experienced by these applied sociologists are not always explicitly stated, but one readily infers that most applied sociologists find their work stimulating and feel it to be worthwhile, although some express doubts about the influence of their work on policy formulation and important decisions. Common sources of frustration are isolation from disciplinary colleagues and a pervasive unease about the standing of applied sociology as a vocation. The common assumption seems to be that academic sociologists have an unwarranted bias against applied sociology built on old stereotypes and inadequate understanding. I will suggest, on the contrary, that a venerable and respected tradition of applied sociology exists in the discipline but that contemporary applied sociologists work largely outside that tradition. At least some of these chapters also maintain that the term *sociology* does not have a very clear image or enjoy high esteem among nonsociologist colleagues in nonacademic settings. The common assumption here seems to be that the lack of support for and emphasis on applied sociology in the discipline as a whole puts sociologists in nonacademic settings at a disadvantage. Although this may well be the case, the lack of a clear image and high esteem for the job title "sociologist" in nonacademic settings may also derive from the peculiarities of reconnaissance sociology as commonly practiced.

What Is Applied in Applied Sociology?

Except for the familiar assumption that applied sociologists are concerned primarily with practical affairs rather than theoretical understanding, the chapters that follow may not seem at first glance to have much in common. They range over many settings and a great variety of substantive and methodological specialties and styles. But, whatever the substantive focus of their work, applied sociologists seem to have been cast most typically into the role of social data specialist or reconnaissance sociologist, as many of the chapters in this part indicate. Francis Caro highlights the variety of data collection and analysis skills used in evaluation research. Discussing careers in survey research, Seymour Sudman focuses on the style of data collection and analysis characteristic of that specialty. Paul Johnson emphasizes the importance of social indicator data for human services planning, while also suggesting the utility of social theory as background. Daphne Spain discusses her work and the work of other applied sociologists in demographic analysis and suggests that sociologists are valued in applied settings primarily for their skills in quantitative analysis. Lawrence Haber indicates that sociologists in government agencies are hired for their methodological skills, even though other skills are necessary as well. Carroll DeWeese, describing his role as a sociologist in industry, emphasizes a number of skills, including quantitative methodology, but suggests that substantive sociological knowledge is not a prerequisite for successful performance in that role. Robert Sorensen highlights the uses of survey research in marketing, litigation, and corporate merger decisions, and Emerson Smith concentrates on the use of survey research in consumer and advertising research.

Other authors describe their applied work in some of the social problem areas of sociology: crime, health, the military, education, aging, and housing. The emphasis on research methodology and data analysis as requisite skills is less explicit in these social problem chapters than in most of the preceding chapters, although David Chandler, writing on applied work in law and criminal justice, and Robert Dentler, commenting on applied sociologists in educational research, again point to the data specialist role of applied sociologists. Chapters by Geoffrey Gibson on health services, Gordon Streib on aging, and David Segal on military research are distinctive in focusing primarily on the background of substantive research in their respective areas rather than emphasizing the data specialist role. The earlier chapters by Joseph Blasi on legislative consultation and Rosemary Yancik on governmental administration are still more distinctive in that they concentrate not on the research role of applied sociologists but on their role as links between researchers and legislators and between funding agencies and researchers. Thus, the data specialist function of applied sociologists is not universally stressed in these chapters, and even those chapters that do highlight that role do not focus on it exclusively. But the collection and analysis of data emerge clearly in these chapters as the predominant way that applied sociologists make their contributions to the firms or agencies that employ them.

Many sociologists, both academic and nonacademic, will undoubtedly find satisfaction in the pervasive emphasis on research skills in these descriptions of applied sociologists' roles and activities. A research-oriented discipline, one might reason, should have an applied branch that is no less research-oriented. But there is something strange about our use of the language when we refer to problem-oriented research as applied sociology. Gathering and reporting information about social life, whether as background information for practical decision making or for other, less immediately practical purposes, would seem to be properly called applied methodology, not applied sociology. To apply sociology is to apply the substantive ideas of sociology, not its research methodology. The application of substantive sociological ideas entails anticipating the human and social consequences of changes in institutional arrangements, public policies, and social practices. If sociological theory is conceived as distilled knowledge about the processes by which changes in the organization of social life have effects on people and their social arrangements, then sociological theory would serve as a guide for anticipating the consequences of change. In this view, sociological theory and applied sociology are intimately related, and applied sociology would be, in effect, applied sociological theory, not applied research methodology.

Many applied sociologists, including those engaged in reconnaissance sociology, may object to the characterization of their craft as applied research methodology. Substantive sociological insights are required, of course, in deciding what information will be useful, how the analysis might be framed to be maximally informative, and how results might be interpreted to enlighten the decision maker. But reconnaissance sociology focuses on gathering, analyzing, and interpreting information, not on designing feasible courses of action and anticipating their likely impacts. To return to the military analogy, reconnaissance provides essential information, and considerable judgment is required to make it useful, but it is the military strategist who decides what will work best to achieve given goals by anticipating the likely effects of alternative strategies.

Reconnaissance sociology currently seems to be the role

most in demand among sociologists in nonacademic settings—perhaps because sociologists themselves have moved into nonacademic settings with that role in mind. It is difficult to argue with success, and reconnaissance sociology—whether it is called applied sociology or applied social research methodology—should be recognized as useful in providing background information for policy formulation and decision making. At the same time, we should recognize that another applied sociology tradition exists and that a merger of the two might have benefits for sociologists in nonacademic settings and for the discipline as a whole.

Tradition of Applied Sociology

Applied sociology—although not exactly in its present form —is as old as the discipline itself. In attempting to outline the theoretical requirements for applied social science, Gouldner (1957) evidently did not have reconnaissance sociology in mind when he drew from a long tradition of applied work in sociology oriented to the application of theory rather than research methodology. According to Gouldner, Emile Durkheim is readily identified as an applied sociologist. As evidence in support of this identification, Gouldner points to the concluding chapter of *Suicide*, "Practical Consequences," and to Durkheim's proposal of a remedy for anomie in the *Division of Labor* (Gouldner, 1957). But Gouldner also quotes from Durkheim's volume *The Rules of Sociological Method*: "Why strive for knowledge of reality, if this knowledge cannot aid us in life? Social science can provide us with rules of action for the future" (Gouldner, 1957, p. 94). Although Durkheim's optimism about "rules of action" derived from social science may be viewed with some skepticism, the more modest goal of anticipating with reasonable accuracy the consequences of alternative courses of action—consequences that can then be assessed in the light of important values—seems more readily achievable.

But the roots of an applied sociology tradition antedate Durkheim. When Alexis de Tocqueville came to the United States in 1831 to begin the tour that culminated in his classic study *Democracy in America* (de Tocqueville, 1864, 1900), he was sent by the government of France to study the prisons of this country. As a minor functionary in the French government, de Tocqueville was undoubtedly expected to submit a report that would describe the new penal practices in America and thereby allow the appropriate minister to seem well-informed about the latest trends in prison architecture and operation. If there is a de Tocqueville report on American prisons, I have never heard of it. But de Tocqueville's two volume work on the pervasive influence of equality in American life has become a sociological classic, even though de Tocqueville's compatriot Auguste Comte was just "fathering" the field at about the time that de Tocqueville wrote. The long-term trend of human history, de Tocqueville asserted, is toward increasing equality in human affairs, and he sought to discern what France might be like when democracy there had reached the same stage as American democracy and how the French might encourage its positive features and guard against its weaknesses. Thus, his was an applied purpose; he states: "It is not, then, merely to satisfy a legitimate curiosity that I have examined America; my wish has been to find there instruction by which we may ourselves profit" (de Tocqueville, 1864, p. 15). One might take de Tocqueville's words as an approximate statement of the purpose of applied social science.

Evidently, de Tocqueville could not apply the sociological theory of his predecessors and contemporaries in achieving his purpose; he found it necessary to create the theory he sought to apply. That will undoubtedly be the task of contemporary applied sociologists who would apply theory to their task. As Gouldner (1957, p. 96) suggests, the inadequacies of current theory for application may put applied sociologists "under pressure to design their own formal theories." Although this imposes a heavy burden on applied sociologists who follow this tradition, it may prove a boon to the discipline at large. Theoretical formulations geared to public policy and social action will probably turn out to be not only more useful but also more satisfying intellectually than theory divorced from practical affairs. It will certainly contribute more to the development of the discipline than the scholasticism that sometimes masquerades as sociological theory. And the practical problems of effecting social change should provide fertile inspiration for theoretical development.

Specialists in the history of sociology could undoubtedly provide additional instances of sociological classics that are applied in the sense that they attempt to show the practical implications of theoretical formulations. But additional illustrations are unnecessary to make the points I wish to emphasize here. First, sociology boasts a venerable tradition of applied work that is widely respected in the discipline. Indeed, such works are often cited as classics of sociology rather than of a subdiscipline called applied sociology, and their applied orientation is often overlooked. Second, these classics of applied sociology are not venerated so much for the reconnaissance they report as for the theoretical ideas they develop in the attempt to cope with applied problems. Third, applied sociologists working in this tradition rarely have found existing theory adequate for their applied purposes but have had to become theorists in order to be applied sociologists.

Applied Sociology as a Vocation

In an information-oriented society, it is perhaps inevitable that sociologists in nonacademic settings be cast in the role of social data specialists. But the absence of a distinctive theoretical perspective or substantive focus in the data specialist role has certain consequences for the way nonacademic sociologists are perceived by their academic counterparts and by their nonsociologist colleagues. First, the specifically sociological aspects of the role remain obscure, if they are seen to exist at all. The role of social data specialist may be fulfilled also by political scientists, psychologists, economists, or even statisticians. A social data specialist trained as a sociologist will, to be sure, be attentive to different kinds of data, will analyze data in a somewhat different way, and will have interpretive insights that stem from a different perspective on social institutions and social behavior. But, to non–social scientists, these are likely to be subtle distinctions that are all but imperceptible because they are overshadowed by the data specialist role itself. In the chapters that follow, some authors comment on the vague connotations of the title "sociologist" among their nonsociologist colleagues. Those colleagues know what a survey researcher does, how a demographic analyst works, and what can be expected of a specialist in statistical analysis—all aspects of the role of sociologist as data specialist. But "sociologist" as a title remains hazy at best and amorphously negative at worst, presumably because the substantive contributions of the sociologist remain obscure.

The data specialist role of sociologists in nonacademic settings also implies that other kinds of potential contributions of applied sociologists may never come into play, since they are not a part of the role expectations of the data specialist. Whatever the problem and whatever the setting, the crucial matter in deciding on policies and actions is to lay out the feasible alternatives and to anticipate the likely consequences of each—intended and unintended, direct and indirect, programmatic and political. But such consequences are almost always yet to be realized and hence are not contained in the data drawn out by the data specialist. Rather, they have to be anticipated on the basis of some conception of how things work. Sociological training provides such a conception and therefore provides a foundation for anticipating the likely consequences of alternative courses of action. But the sociologist as data specialist—the reconnaissance sociologist—is identified as one who can use data to describe, not as one who can use insight or theoretical understanding to anticipate. Hence, the role of sociologist as data specialist does not draw on the full range of talent and skill that a well-trained sociologist brings to the applied setting.

A third consequence of the data specialist role bears on the standing of applied sociologists in the discipline and on the progress of the discipline itself. Cast in the role of data specialist, the applied sociologist runs the risk of thinking about the data in a nontheoretical way. If the demands of the role are for descriptive data, the inclination is to think about producing descriptive data rather than about the relevance of those data to a general understanding of how things work, how effects come about, or how change in one aspect of a system ramifies into other aspects. Descriptive data localized in time and place are like yesterday's television newscast; it has served an immediate information function and then lost its timeliness and relevance. In contrast, data used to shed light on how things work serve a more lasting intellectual function; the general ideas they confirm or modify persist even when the data themselves are no longer timely. Although social data are crucially important for sociology, now, as always, the discipline is hungry for ideas. The data specialist role of sociologists in nonacademic settings limits their contributions to the flow of ideas that sustain the discipline and thus limits the standing of reconnaissance sociologists. This feature of the data specialist role is especially unfortunate for the discipline because of the potentially rich data resources and the problem-oriented stance of many nonacademic sociologists.

Conclusion

I will conclude this commentary with an irony and a paradox. The irony is that those contemporary applied sociologists who are most widely known are disproportionately academic sociologists rather than sociologists in nonacademic settings. Peter Rossi and William Whyte come readily to mind as illustrations. Several reasons for this circumstance can easily be conceived, and, as is commonly the case, the alternatives are not inherently contradictory. Nonacademic sociologists might suggest that the criteria applied by the major journals are biased against the work of nonacademic sociologists. If a bias against reconnaissance sociology is implied this hypothesis is probably true and seems likely to remain true. Some academic sociologists might suggest that the differential selection of individuals for academic and nonacademic positions over the past thirty years has favored the rise of applied academic as compared to nonacademic sociologists. Such selective processes may have favored academic sociologists in the past, but such selectivity seems to have ended and seems unlikely to resume again in the foreseeable future. A role theorist might suggest that the pressures and limitations built into the roles of academic and nonacademic sociologists, including differential access to stimulating sociological colleagues and the incentives created by making academic as opposed to nonacademic advancement dependent on publications, puts nonacademic sociologists at a disadvantage in achieving visibility in the discipline.

Although these hypotheses may have some validity, reconnaissance sociology without a theoretical focus seems likely to remain an unpromising avenue for achieving visibility in the discipline, whether the sociologist in question works in an academic or a nonacademic setting. Unless the data specialist role is supplemented by a focus on theoretical ideas, nonacademic sociologists are likely to remain disadvantaged. If data analysis and theoretical ideas can be successfully fused, the advantage seems likely to shift in favor of nonacademic sociologists, both because of their data resources and their problem orientation, which constitutes a valuable stimulus for the development of useful and insightful theory.

The paradox is that moving toward the ostensibly apolitical role of data specialist has—probably unwittingly—created a special political role for the applied sociologist. Unlike sociologists working in the older tradition of applied sociology, contemporary applied sociologists rarely lay out a theoretically-based agenda for political implementation. As suggested by the comments of a few of the authors in the following chapters, this lack of a political agenda does not mean that reconnaissance sociologists serve no political function. Data have come to be used as a political weapon—to justify and support actions already decided on, to draw attention to a problem, to persuade the uncommitted. This use of social science data is also indicated by the results of surveys, recently summarized by Demartini (1982), of policy makers and their perceptions of the utility of such data. Although policy makers and other officials have not been inclined to acknowledge publicly this use of social data, that reluctance seems to be waning; witness a recent statement calling on researchers to provide data that will justify preselected changes in policy and that will "demonstrate and convince" others to support a particular kind of political agenda (Gerson, 1982, p. 19). Paradoxically, then, in becoming apolitical, applied sociology has become political in a different way. The implication is not that applied sociologists are thereby diminished but that applied sociologists may want to reconsider the political import of their work, especially when it is used to support programs and policies that are unenlightened by substantive sociological knowledge.

References

ADAMS, R. M., SMELSER, N. J., AND TREIMAN, D. J. (EDS.)
  1982   *Behavioral and Social Science Research: A National Resource.* Washington, D.C.: National Academy Press.
DEMARTINI, J. R.
  1982   "Basic and applied sociological work: Divergence, convergence, or peaceful coexistence?" *The Journal of Applied Behavioral Science* 18(2): 203-215.
DE TOCQUEVILLE, A.
  1864   *Democracy in America.* Vol. 1. (H. Reeve, Trans.) Cambridge, England: Sever & Francis. (Originally published in French in 1835.)

1900   *Democracy in America.* Vol. 2. (H. Reeve, Trans.) London: Colonial Press. (Originally published in French in 1840.)

GERSON, M. D.
    1982   "Western research on women in Third World criticized at meeting." *Chronicle of Higher Education* 25(2):19.

GOULDNER, A. W.
    1957   "Theoretical requirements of the applied social sciences." *American Sociological Review* 22(1):92-102.

🍂 4 🍂

PROGRAM EVALUATION

Francis G. Caro

In the past two decades, evaluation research has emerged as a major form of applied social research. Evaluation has come to be recognized as a distinct and often critical element in rational program and policy development, and social scientists have focused on evaluation research as one of the major ways that they as professionals can make a productive social contribution. At the same time, the evaluation field has grown into an important source of employment for social researchers.

Intended as a brief introduction to evaluation research, this chapter will describe the field, giving attention both to its role in directed social change efforts and to its central methodological concerns. The chapter will suggest the flavor of actual evaluation work, discuss the pertinence of sociology as a disciplinary resource for evaluation research, and offer speculation about the future of the evaluation field.

Those interested in more than an overview are encouraged to draw on the substantial and rapidly growing evaluation literature. Texts, journals, and edited collections provide good introductions to the field. Several general textbooks have been published, including recent volumes by Franklin and Thrasher (1976) and Rossi and Freeman (1982). The journals *Evaluation Review* and *Evaluation and Program Planning* focus on evaluation research. Edited volumes on evaluation research include Guttentag and Struening (1975), Caro (1977), Attkisson and others (1978), and Hyde and Shafritz (1979). In addition, Sage Publications issues an edited collection each year, *Evaluation Studies Review Annual.*

Defining Evaluation Research

Evaluation is a judgmental process; it seeks to reach conclusions regarding the worth of an effort. Evaluation research flows from attempts to deal rationally with human affairs and assumes that human activity is (or should be) purposeful, that is, a means to one or more ends. From this perspective, activities are not intrinsically meritorious; their worth lies in what they accomplish. Because the consequences of human actions are often uncertain, it is not sufficient to judge their value on intended or desired results. Rather, the rational perspective dictates that evaluations be based on what actually happens as a result of activity.

Evaluation is an aspect of everyday life. Inevitably, much of this evaluation is informal. Only when the consequences of purposeful action involve both importance and substantial doubt do formal evaluation procedures come into play. Evaluation research is one of several formal evaluation traditions; accreditation and licensing are others. Evaluation research is an appropriate formal evaluation methodology when doubt about the consequences of a program necessitates more than an umpire and .scorekeeper. An evaluation research approach should be considered when its distinctive social research methodology promises to yield evidence substantially more credible than the evidence offered by other, simpler approaches.

Orderly program development involves three major phases: planning, implementation, and evaluation. In the most basic formulation, evaluation follows implementation, providing information on the degree to which the objectives articulated in the planning phase have been attained. Evaluation can be used as a basis for summary judgments regarding an intervention, or it can be used to guide those who must decide whether an endeavor should be continued or a pilot program replicated. Evaluation can also be conceived as a resource for program refinement. Program development can be thought of as a succession of planning, implementation, and evaluation cycles. Evaluation results that show imperfect goal attainment can provide the impetus for renewed planning, which leads, in turn, to a refined intervention.

In some cases, evaluation efforts address potential rather than actual consequences. To what extent is a program conducted in a way that makes the attainment of objectives likely? This question invites an empirical examination of program operations and a projection of their probable consequences. Thus, monitoring to determine how program operations are being carried out is an aspect of program evaluation. To what extent does a program's structure facilitate the realization of objectives? To answer this question, the design of a program may be examined for its plausibility even before the program is implemented. Such anticipatory evaluation is particularly important in instances when an intervention is costly, cannot be readily modified once introduced, and offers possibilities for major negative consequences.

Even needs assessment can be considered an aspect of program evaluation. If a proposed program is to address needs as they exist in a target population, data on problem scope are required. Survey research is sometimes required to establish a sufficiently accurate estimate of the number of persons who might use a program. Data on extent of need are useful in preimplementation evaluation of the adequacy of projected program capacity.

Although evaluation is usually concerned directly or indirectly with the extent to which intended results have been attained or are likely to be attained, evaluation efforts should not be narrowly guided by announced objectives. Deutscher (1977), for example, argues that, by studying actual program operations, evaluators may discover guiding purposes that are not officially recognized. The need to include attention to potential harm inadvertently caused by programs also illustrates the importance of going beyond official objectives. In environmental impact studies, for example, anticipation of negative consequences is a major concern. Wholey (1979) also points to the need to analyze official objectives when he observes that many public programs are so loosely formulated that they defy evaluation. He advocates what he calls evaluability assessment as a device to prod managers to clearly articulate objectives and program logic and to anticipate what they would do with evaluation findings.

Comprehensive program evaluation includes concern not only for results but also for efficiency. Cost-effectiveness or cost–benefit analyses that address the relationships between costs and outcomes are important forms of evaluation. Sophisticated contemporary evaluation, then, involves the convergence of social science disciplines concerned with program effects and another set of disciplines concerned with cost measurement and analysis (see, for example, Stokey and Zeckhauser, 1978, and Thompson, 1980).

The evaluation field can therefore be conceived as embracing a wide variety of activities, all concerned with the consequences of programs. In some instances, evaluation is directly concerned with actual program outcomes. In other instances, questions are asked about program structure, program operations, the client population, and costs because of their implications for program outcomes.

Evaluation research is best seen as a resource for decision making rather than as a disinterested search for truth. Its purpose is to reduce the uncertainty that confronts those who make decisions regarding programs. Those who sponsor evaluation research should regard the process as an investment. Evaluation deserves resources in proportion to the likelihood that it will provide information of practical importance. The merit of evaluation research is not to be judged entirely on the strength of its methodology. Sometimes evaluation studies make important contributions because they yield data that, although imperfect, are timely and substantially better than the data otherwise available.

Dimensions of Evaluation Research

Evaluation research studies were conducted in a number of fields during the first half of this century. Among sociologists, F. Stuart Chapin is particularly conspicuous for his early evaluation research on programs designed to ameliorate the effects of the Depression (see, for example, Chapin, 1977). In the 1960s, the federal domestic assistance programs provided impetus for the emergence of program evaluation as a major applied research enterprise. Not only has the federal government been the primary sponsor of evaluation research, but the federal emphasis on evaluation has stimulated interest in the field at other levels of government, in the private sector, and in the academic world.

In principle, evaluation research can be addressed to any purposeful activity; in practice, it has been conducted on a variety of interventions. Evaluation research activities can be found in all of the human and public services fields and lend themselves to varied uses in the commercial world as well. The enterprises studied by evaluation research also vary enormously in scale. Evaluation research is done on highly specific clinical treatment modalities involving small numbers of cases, as well as on massive interventions involving large numbers of persons in many sites. During the 1970s, the federal government conducted large-scale formal experiments with strong evaluation research components concerned with such matters as income maintenance (Kershaw and Fair, 1976), housing allowances (Kennedy, 1980; Struyk and Bendick, 1981), and aid to released prisoners (Rossi, Berk, and Lenihan, 1980). Most often, evaluation studies are conducted on programs, that is, on relatively specific sets of activities carried out by formal organizations. In other cases, evaluation research addresses itself to the effects of legislation or regulatory changes that are not implemented in a program context. Evaluation research has been conducted, for example, on the effects of legislation seeking to limit the use of firearms (Deutsch and Alt, 1977) and legislation mandating the wearing of helmets by motorcyclists (Hyde and Schervish, 1979).

The degree to which evaluation research is central to the interventions studied also varies greatly. Occasionally, the evaluation research agenda is at the core of an intervention effort. In such cases, programs are often implemented within the framework of a formal experiment. More commonly, evaluation research is only one of many secondary aspects of a program. In these instances, the weaker evaluation research designs employed necessarily reflect the greater importance attached to other agendas.

Evaluation Research Methodology

The issues of methodology central to evaluation research can be roughly divided into questions of measurement and questions of inference. Evaluation studies characteristically involve measures of outcome variables, costs, characteristics of program participants, and aspects of service transactions. The applicable measurement methodology is the one used in social research generally. Many of the data for evaluation studies, for example, are collected through conventional survey research (see the chapter in this volume on survey research). A number of measurement issues, however, tend to be specific to evaluation research. In principle, selection of variables in evaluation research should largely follow from program objectives. Anticipation of what can feasibly be measured, however, often influences the manner in which program objectives are formulated. When researchers play an aggressive role in negotiating specific, measurable objectives, they are open to criticism for encroaching on the policy domain. Yet when evaluators, instead of pressing for specificity, work within an ambiguous configuration of objectives, evaluation findings may ultimately be set aside as peripheral to major policy concerns. Similarly, evaluation researchers are never able to address thoroughly all the pertinent process and outcome questions. Further, not all the variables included in an evaluation study can be measured with precision. The decisions made about allocation of measurement resources should reflect a strong sensitivity to both policy and technical measurement concerns.

Another important set of measurement issues in evaluation research arises from reactivity of program participants to research variables and measures. Those who carry out programs tend to have strong personal and professional interests in evaluation results. When such persons know how their efforts and program outcomes are to be measured, they may seek to manipulate records or distort the intervention itself to achieve favorable evaluation findings. Evaluators, then, are challenged to find measurement strategies that minimize the risk of corruption.

In addressing problems of causal inference, evaluators are influenced extensively by the tradition of formal experimentation, which originated with physics and was later adapted by agricultural researchers and experimental psychologists. In evaluation research, the randomized experimental design is strongly preferred as a basis for addressing issues of causal inference. Evaluation researchers, of course, frequently find that they cannot employ an experimental design. Donald Campbell has made a particularly useful contribution in identifying some of the quasi-experimental options evaluators might employ (Campbell and Stanley, 1966; Cook and Campbell, 1979).

Extensive quantitative analysis is characteristically a major ingredient of evaluation studies. Evaluators must be prepared to draw on a wide range of descriptive and inferential statistical techniques. In many instances, evaluators are simply able to draw on the conventional statistical techniques developed for analysis of experimental data. In other instances, evaluators use specialized statistical techniques developed to address the problems peculiar to quasi-experimental designs (see, for example, the chapter in this volume on quantitative training).

Although evaluation research is dominated by quantitative analysis, qualitative methods can also play an important role in evaluation. Particularly in the case of complex interventions that tend to unfold in unanticipated ways, qualitative methods are useful for addressing questions about the implementation of programs and in exploring subtle ways that both practitioners and clients respond to a program approach in their interactions with one another. Qualitative methods, however, cannot be expected to produce the authoritative data needed to resolve controversies regarding program effects. For an extensive treatment of the role of qualitative methods in program evaluation, see Patton (1980). Also pertinent is the chapter in this volume on qualitative training.

Organizational Considerations

Beyond matters of methodology, it is important to be sensitive to evaluation as an organized enterprise, including questions of how evaluations are initiated and of what happens to the results of evaluations. Characteristically, evaluation is a sponsored activity initiated by parties with administrative or policy responsibilities. Frequently evaluations are sponsored by funding agencies; sometimes they are initiated by agencies conducting programs; and oc-

casionally they are introduced by another party. Sometimes evaluations are conducted by units that are part of the organizations
conducting the programs. Perhaps more frequently, evaluation
studies are conducted by outsiders. (The evaluation literature includes debates on the relative merits of internal and external evaluations.) In seeking evaluations of the programs it sponsors, the
federal government has developed a strong preference for contracting with third parties who specialize in applied research. As indicated earlier, the interaction leading to decisions about the variables to be measured—and sometimes the program options to be
tested—is a key aspect of the overall evaluation process. Similarly,
the articulation of program and policy implications of evaluation research findings and the dissemination of research results are
important aspects of the process. Rarely, if ever, does a single evaluation study have immediate and decisive impact on an important
policy or professional practice issue. Lack of use of evaluation results is a widespread concern among evaluation researchers. The
utilization issue has stimulated attention to communication strategies that can be used to enhance the impact of evaluation findings.
The issue has also led some to argue that evaluator expectations
about the use of results have been unrealistic and that evaluation
research should not be expected to make more than modest contributions to policy development (see, for example, Weiss, 1977,
and Cronbach, 1980).

The flavor of evaluation work varies from one endeavor to
another and is strongly influenced by the scale of the effort. Two
hypothetical cases will illustrate the point. In the first case, the
evaluation concerns a relatively small program operated in a single
setting. The evaluation is initiated by administrative personnel in
the operating agency. The level of evaluation effort is to be modest; the agency draws on its own resources to finance the evaluation. The process of selecting an evaluator is likely to be simple: if
there is an internal evaluation unit, it will probably take on the assignment; if not, a potential evaluator will probably be located
through an informal contact network. In this instance, the evaluator is likely to be extensively involved in shaping the evaluation
agenda. Characteristically, at the outset, the administrator will
articulate only a few broad evaluation concerns. Through direct interaction with the administrator and exchanges of memorandums,

the evaluation director then negotiates a specific evaluation approach. In their communication, they may cover such themes as the relative importance of various evaluation questions; the date by which evaluation results are required; the degree to which hard evaluation research findings are necessary; the feasibility of using a randomized experimental design; potential data sources; and costs. The evaluation group will then have responsibility for fleshing out the evaluation design. A small group of perhaps two or three persons will perform all the research tasks, including literature review, instrument design, data collection, coding, data processing, analysis, and writing. While the technical work is being done, the evaluators may continue to have considerable face-to-face contact with their administrative client to negotiate such matters as access to data, modifications in the research design, delays in completion of the research, and perhaps the reporting of interim findings. If a service delivery program is at issue, evaluators may also have a great deal of day-to-day contact with practitioners—perhaps about implementation of an experimental design or about data on client characteristics, service transactions, and outcomes. In this instance, the evaluation group is likely to carry responsibility for interpretation and dissemination of their findings. Their efforts in fostering utilization will include face-to-face discussions with administrators and practitioners to outline findings and interpret their implications.

The second hypothetical case is a comprehensive evaluation of a large federally sponsored demonstration program involving services delivered at a number of sites throughout the country. A large-scale evaluation effort is required, costing in excess of one million dollars. The evaluation is initiated by the federal agency with oversight responsibility for the program. Their major rationale for the evaluation is to inform Congress about the program's accomplishments. The evaluation is not legislatively mandated, but some questions about the program's effectiveness have surfaced in hearings, and others have been transmitted informally by staff members of the congressional committees with oversight responsibility.

In this instance, an evaluation strategy is developed by evaluation research specialists on the staff of the federal agency. They may solicit the advice of external evaluation experts in developing the design. Eventually, the evaluation strategy is written up as a request for proposal (RFP). Before the RFP is issued, it is likely to be reviewed thoroughly not only by agency personnel with policy and budget concerns but also by those with procurement responsibilities.

The process of competing for the contract looms large as a task for potential evaluation contractors. In some cases, potential bidders learn informally that an RFP is to be issued. Others learn of the project only by reading the notice in the *Commerce and Business Daily*. The RFP will provide all or nearly all the clues available to bidders. It will identify the issues to be employed, outline the methods to be used, indicate the time frame for the project and the anticipated level of effort, and list the criteria to be used in reviewing bids. Very little, if any, clarifying information will be available from federal personnel.

Within a very tight time frame (perhaps four to eight weeks), bidders will be expected to prepare a substantial document that includes an informed discussion of the substantive issues, an elaborate and sophisticated methodological approach, the organizational capacity to carry out the project, and a detailed, defensible budget. Preparation of the proposal is a major effort requiring skillful orchestration of a variety of specialized talents. Because of the expense, expertise, and organizational capability required to prepare a competitive bid, only large research organizations are likely to be serious bidders.

The proposal review process itself is a complex matter involving panels of experts who give separate attention to technical and business aspects of proposals. In the late stages of the review process, the finalists may be asked to participate in an oral review and respond in writing to questions or requests for elaboration.

Extensive oral discussion between the federal agency and the contractor usually takes place only after the successful bidder has been selected, and the substance of the work may be substantially altered at this stage. In this process, the federal staff plays a crucial role. Although they do not conduct the research, federal staff members establish the evaluation issues, outline the evaluation design, determine the level of effort, and have the option of providing very close supervision throughout.

Beyond the technical issues involved in the evaluation research, a project of this kind will pose challenging administrative problems for the contractor. An elaborate division of labor is likely, with the project director calling on specialists each one of whom performs a relatively narrow set of tasks. Separate individuals or groups may be assigned such tasks as sample design, questionnaire development, survey administration, data management, and quantitative analysis. If a substudy is to be conducted on implementation questions, still another group may be involved. Critical for the project manager are careful scheduling of project activities and monitoring of productivity and expenditures. The project manager will also be responsible for submitting to the federal project officer a steady stream of documents that will provide assurance that the work is progressing as projected and is consistent with contract requirements. Some of the specialists who contribute to the project are likely to be involved simultaneously with several projects. All of the professionals involved will intermittently work on responses to new RFPs.

For the organization doing the research, participation in the evaluation process usually ends with submission of a final report. Formal responsibility for dissemination of findings will rest with the federal agency sponsor. In some instances, the federal agency will simply distribute in its own name the summary of findings and recommendations prepared by the contractor. In other instances, federal staff may prepare its own summary and recommendations. Alternately, still another organization may be retained to repackage the findings and recommendations and help with dissemination. The federal agency will be interested, of course, in orchestrating any reporting done directly to Congress.

Clearly, the two cases indicate important differences in the work experiences of the evaluation researchers involved. Differences in the degree of specialization and division of labor are most conspicuous. In the first case, the evaluation researchers are involved in all technical aspects of the research and participate extensively in shaping the evaluation issues and in interpreting and communicating findings. In the second case, most of the researchers participate on a much more segmented basis. For some, participation is on a narrow technical level; the fact that the research involves evaluation may be irrelevant to their role. For others, participation may be largely managerial; their major concern may be that a complex set of tasks is completed on schedule and at an acceptable cost. The two situations are likely to differ also in the allocation of overall effort. The organization that does federal contract research probably invests a rather high proportion of its overall professional resources in the preparation of proposals. If it is successful on no more than 10 to 20 percent of its proposals, such an organization must bid frequently to survive. If it is fortunate, the smaller evaluation group will establish its working relationship quickly and use more of its resources for the evaluation process itself. In both cases, the evaluators will spend a good deal of their energy on external relationships. In the small-scale evaluation effort, informal, face-to-face exchanges with administrators and practitioners will be of greatest importance in establishing, sustaining, and strengthening relationships. In the second case, much more emphasis will be placed on preparation of written documents, and more energy will be invested in preparation of fully documented proposals, progress reports, contracts, and memorandums of understandings.

To thrive in the small-scale evaluation research setting, the evaluation researcher needs broad technical skills, a strong grasp of the evaluation process as a whole, and skill in face-to-face interactions with administrators and practitioners. In the large-scale setting, it may be sufficient for a researcher to be highly proficient in a specific technical area. The capacity to work quickly, predictably, and with thorough documentation is likely to be of particular importance. Sensitivity to the nuances of evaluation purposes or the uses of evaluation results is not likely to be crucial. For others involved in large-scale evaluation, managerial skills will be of greatest importance. Some technical background may be needed, but the most critical day-to-day skills will be in the areas of coordination, scheduling, budgeting, and monitoring.

Sociology and Evaluation Research

Sociological training can be useful for evaluation researchers. Because it has some substantive concern with every major institutional sector, sociology can offer an evaluation researcher a perspective for understanding the potential contribution of a wide range of intervention efforts. Further, the rigorous training in empirical research methods offered in many sociology programs is directly pertinent to evaluation research.

Sociology, however, is not alone among the academic disciplines in providing a useful background for evaluation research. In fact, in important respects, other disciplines may provide stronger training. The basic and applied social and behavioral sciences share the same basic research technology. In some universities, disciplines other than sociology may provide training in that technology at least as strong as the training offered in sociology departments. Further, professional training programs directly linked to applied fields such as health administration, social work, and educational psychology provide students with a substantive orientation directly pertinent to that specific applied field. As the evaluation research fields grows, it is becoming more specialized, and evaluation researchers who are also trained in a particular applied field will be at a distinct advantage over those who are subject-area generalists. Not only may those tied to applied fields benefit from their substantive knowledge, but they may benefit from professional loyalties in competing for jobs and contracts.

Further, certain possible limitations to sociology as a background for evaluation researchers should be recognized. Most conventional sociology programs do not offer training in some skills that are important for evaluation research—sociologists do not conventionally give attention to cost analysis, for example. Sociological perspectives on large-scale organization are useful for evaluators in understanding the politics of evaluation research and the increasingly bureaucratized nature of evaluation research, but sociology programs do not usually include prescriptive preparation for managerial or entrepreneurial roles.

On a more positive note, sociologists tend to be particularly well equipped to address certain aspects of a comprehensive evaluation research agenda, such as the importance of the cultural, political, and organizational context in which an intervention is introduced. The way that an intervention is interpreted by the professionals and organizations administering it and by the target population to be affected by it contributes significantly to the eventual impact and shape of the intervention. Qualitative research methods—better appreciated by sociologists than by most other social scientists—are particularly useful in examining this contribution. If sociologists were more aggressive in pursuing this theme, they would gain the greater attention they deserve in the evaluation research field.

The implication of these thoughts for graduate training is that interdisciplinary preparation for evaluation research is highly desirable. Interdisciplinary programs that include such academic disciplines as sociology, psychology, and economics and such professional fields as accounting, public administration, and educational psychology can provide students with strong preparation for evaluation research. In the absence of such formal programs, students will do well to put together their own programs drawing on a variety of disciplines.

Future Developments

Evaluation research is showing signs of becoming more than an occupational specialty drawing from a variety of other disciplines. Rather, it appears to have entered the early stages of professionalism in its own right. It now has a number of national, regional, and state associations, and, as indicated at the outset, journals, textbooks, and readers have appeared in substantial numbers. To date, the communication among evaluation researchers at meetings and through publications has been largely technical, the associations are playing a limited role in job placement, and there is modest interest in such matters as standards, ethics, accreditation, and licensing of evaluation researchers. Eventually, evaluation research may develop a distinct, single identity embracing all areas of application. Alternately evaluation professionalism might be fragmented, that is, organized within such traditional applied fields as education and mental health. To the extent that professionalism in evaluation research may eventually involve certification or licensing, it will have implications not only for evaluation research practitioners but also for educators. Conceivably, not only may the skills required of evaluation researchers be prescribed, but the training and acceptable sources of training may be specified as well.

Reasonable arguments can be set forth for projecting either contraction or continued growth of the field. The present massive shift in federal domestic assistance policy will almost certainly lead to a short-term decline in evaluation research activity, and, in an era of cost-consciousness, questions will increasingly be raised regarding the payoff of investments in evaluation research. Broadly speaking, evaluation research, like other forms of social research, is often expensive, clumsy to administer, and crude in its results. As indicated earlier, even when evaluation research is done carefully, results tend to be only a modest consideration in policy formulation. If rigorous, narrowly conceived cost-effectiveness projections were to be applied more often in devising evaluation research strategies, the evaluation studies authorized in some sectors would be fewer in number.

The dramatic growth of evaluation research resulted from efforts to rationalize and justify the federal human services programs of the 1960s and 1970s. The federal government has been the single most important sponsor of evaluation research. To the extent that human needs are withdrawn from the federal agenda, federal sponsorship of evaluation research concerned with the impact of social programs is likely to diminish. The extent to which other units of government, reflecting their increased responsibility for financing and management of social programs, will accelerate their sponsorship of evaluation research is a matter of speculation.

Alternatively, it can be argued that the evaluation research rationale and technology have been sufficiently developed and disseminated to enable the field to persist and grow in the long run. Belief in the efficacy of rational problem-solving methods and the inclination to intervene to affect the direction of human affairs are strong trends in our culture. Although somewhat new and less than fully established, evaluation will endure because it is a modest and sensible extension of conventional problem-solving methods. Formal organizations have learned that the methods of science are useful, if not in guiding decision making, at least in justifying their actions. In addition, evaluation research skills have been widely enough disseminated to assure not only that evaluation researchers can be found when needed but also that practitioners will energetically pursue new areas of application. All of this points to a solid future for evaluation research.

References

ATTKISSON, C. C., HARGREAVES, W. A., HOROWITZ, M. J., AND SORENSEN, J. E.
    1978 *Evaluation of Human Service Programs.* New York: Academic Press.

CAMPBELL, D. T., AND STANLEY, J. C.
    1966   *Experimental and Quasi-Experimental Designs for Research*. Chicago: Rand McNally.
CARO, F. G. (ED.).
    1977   *Readings in Evaluation Research*. New York: Russell Sage Foundation.
CHAPIN, F. S.
    1977   "An experiment in the social effects of good housing." In F. G. Caro (Ed.), *Readings in Evaluation Research*. New York: Russell Sage Foundation.
COOK, T. D., AND CAMPBELL, D. T.
    1979   *Quasi-Experimentation: Design and Analysis Issues for Field Settings*. Chicago: Rand McNally.
CRONBACH, L. J., AND OTHERS.
    1980   *Toward Reform of Program Evaluation*. San Francisco: Jossey-Bass.
DEUTSCH, S. J., AND ALT, F. B.
    1977   "The effect of Massachusetts' gun control law on gun-related crimes in the city of Boston." *Evaluation Quarterly* 1(4):543-568.
DEUTSCHER, I.
    1977   "Toward avoiding the goal-trap in evaluation research." In F. G. Caro (Ed.) *Readings in Evaluation Research*. (2nd ed.) New York: Russell Sage Foundation.
FRANKLIN, J. L., AND THRASHER, J. H.
    1976   *An Introduction to Program Evaluation*. New York: Wiley-Interscience.
FREEMAN, H. E., AND SOLOMON, M. A.
    1981   *Evaluation Studies Review Annual*. Vol. 6. Beverly Hills, Calif.: Sage.
GUTTENTAG, M., AND STRUENING, E. L. (EDS.).
    1975   *Handbook of Evaluation Research*. Beverly Hills, Calif.: Sage.
HYDE, A. C., AND SHAFRITZ, J. M. (EDS.).
    1979   *Program Evaluation in the Public Sector*. New York: Praeger.
HYDE, A. C., AND SCHERVISH, P. H.
    1979   "The problem with motorcycle helmets: An evaluation of Indiana's experience." In A. C. Hyde and J. M. Sha-

fritz (Eds.), *Program Evaluation in the Public Sector.* New York: Praeger.

KENNEDY, S. D.

1980 *Final Report of the Housing Allowance Demand Experiment.* Cambridge, Mass.: Abt Associates.

KERSHAW, D., AND FAIR, J.

1976 *The New Jersey Income Maintenance Experiments.* Vol. 1: *Operations, Surveys, and Administration.* New York: Academic Press.

PATTON, M. Q.

1980 *Qualitative Evaluation Methods.* Beverly Hills, Calif.: Sage.

REIN, M., AND SCHON, D. A.

1977 "Problem setting in policy research." In C. H. Weiss (Ed.), *Using Social Research in Public Policy Making.* Lexington, Mass.: Heath.

ROSSI, P. H., BERK, R. A., AND LENIHAN, K. J.

1980 *Money, Work, and Crime: Experimental Evidence.* New York: Academic Press.

ROSSI, P. H., AND FREEMAN, H. E.

1982 *Evaluation: A Systematic Approach.* (2nd ed.) Beverly Hills, Calif.: Sage.

STOKEY, E., AND ZECKHAUSER, R.

1978 *A Primer for Policy Analysis.* New York: Norton.

STRUYK, R. J., AND BENDICK, M., JR. (EDS.).

1981 *Housing Vouchers for the Poor: Lessons from a National Experiment.* Washington, D.C.: Urban Institute.

THOMPSON, M.

1980 *Benefit-Cost Analysis for Program Evaluation.* Beverly Hills, Calif.: Sage.

WEISS, C. H. (ED.).

1977 *Using Social Research in Public Policy Making.* Lexington, Mass.: Heath.

WHOLEY, J. S.

1979 *Evaluation: Promise and Performance.* Washington, D.C.: Urban Institute.

❦ 5 ❦

SURVEY RESEARCH

Seymour Sudman

In recent years, the demand for qualified survey researchers has exceeded the supply of trained professionals. Although this demand will decline in some sectors in the immediate future as a result of actions by the current administration, the long-range outlook for careers in survey research remains positive, in part because of the wide variety of activities conducted by survey researchers and places where survey research is conducted.

A survey researcher may be defined as anyone who designs, gathers, or analyzes survey data. This definition overlaps several other categories. Omitting strictly academic careers, an analysis of membership in the American Association for Public Opinion Research (the broadest organization of survey researchers) includes the following types of employers: market and advertising research firms; opinion organizations; government agencies; businesses; television and print media; nonprofit institutions (for example, health agencies); and universities (nonteaching applications).

Sociologists should realize, however, that their education

and background represent only one of the ways in which survey researchers may be trained. Other academic fields that may also lead to careers in survey research include survey statistics, political science, economics, social psychology, and marketing research.

Role of Survey Research in Different Organizations

Market and advertising research firms are suppliers of information about consumer needs, attitudes, and behavior primarily for manufacturers, but also for advertising agencies and the media. Services may be supplied on a syndicated basis, where multiple clients share the costs and information of a standard data collection method, or on a custom basis, where a special survey is designed to solve a particular client problem. The largest companies, such as the A. C. Nielsen Company, IMS, and SAMI, all provide syndicated services that report grocery and drug purchasing and television viewing.

Opinion organizations tend to concentrate on measuring public opinion and behavior usually unrelated to consumption. Their chief clients are government and nonprofit organizations and the media. Although the distinction between market and opinion research is ambiguous, with some organizations involved in both, one distinction is useful: most opinion research is in the public domain, its major purpose being to inform or persuade, whereas most market research is proprietary and is intended only for the use of the firms that commission it. Market research firms are clearly intended to be profit-making organizations; opinion organizations may be either profit-making or nonprofit. Large organizations of both types exist.

Government agencies are primarily users of survey research. The outstanding exception is the U.S. Bureau of the Census, which is the major data-gathering agency for the federal government. In addition to the Decennial Census of Population and Housing, the Bureau conducts periodic censuses of business, government, and agriculture, the Current Population Survey, the National Health Interview, and many other special surveys. Since not all government data gathering can be conducted by the Census Bureau, however, other government agencies frequently purchase services from outside survey organizations. Survey staff members in these agencies remain responsible for data analysis and report preparation and participate extensively in research design.

Businesses will typically have market research and public relations staffs but will seldom collect their own survey data. Generally, the staffs will design the survey, select a supplier firm, analyze the data, and prepare written and oral presentations to management. Research is used in business largely in developing new products and in aiding firms that are considering mergers.

Television and print media are heavy users of survey data for news purposes. Although the print media have been long-term users of poll data from the Gallup, Harris, and other polls, television news use of polls has grown rapidly in the past decade. Not only do the networks all have continuing polls, but also many local television stations poll their areas periodically. In addition, the media use surveys of listenership and readership to generate advertising revenues.

Nonprofit institutions such as health agencies, hospitals, libraries, park districts, and symphony orchestras use survey data in the same way as businesses—to determine the characteristics of their potential markets as well as the effectiveness of their current programs. Most nonprofit organizations do not have and cannot afford a full-time survey researcher; instead, this role is combined with another role in the organization.

University nonteaching applications of survey research are not unique, except for the setting. Many universities now have survey research organizations either as free-standing units or as parts of social research organizations. Other research units on campus, such as agriculture experiment stations, medical research groups, and environmental and business research groups, may also conduct survey research. Finally, the university itself may use survey research to obtain the views of students, faculty, alumni, and other important audiences.

Number of Professional Jobs in Survey Research

Census data are not specific enough to allow a precise estimate of the number of professional jobs in survey research. However, crude estimates can be made by examining the membership directories of major professional organizations that have some connection with survey research. Based on these directories, I estimate at least 25,000 professional jobs in survey research, with the profit sector—including market research firms, other businesses, advertising agencies, and the print and television media—accounting for two thirds of these jobs. The remaining third are with government, academic, and other nonprofit survey organizations. Although the field is not large in comparison to some professions, it is larger than the total current membership of the American Sociological Association.

The Surveys of Science Resources conducted by the National Science Foundation (NSF) (1978) estimated the number of employed statisticians, sociologists, and other social scientists whose major activities were surveys, forecasting, and statistical analysis to be 27,400 in 1978. This number includes some persons who do only forecasts and statistical analysis and excludes persons who are primarily administrators of survey research activities. Thus, the NSF results appear to yield the same approximate estimate of at least 25,000 professional jobs.

The importance of the various project director tasks will differ substantially, depending on the client and the job setting. Proposal writing is an important part of the project director's task if the client is a government or nonprofit agency, since contracts are awarded competitively on the basis of the judged merit of the proposal. Commercial clients, on the other hand, are likely to choose a survey organization on the basis of previous satisfactory performance.

Work Roles in Survey Research

A typical survey organization has the following units or work roles: project direction/coordination, sampling/statistics, field operations, data processing/data reduction, and administration. Not all organizations have all these roles, since they may subcontract or purchase services from other organizations.

Sampling, field operations, and data processing staffs typically work on several projects simultaneously and never more than a few months on any project. The project director, on the other hand, may spend several years on a project from its inception until the data are analyzed and the report is written. Even project directors, however, may work on more than one project simultaneously, unless they are involved in a very large study.

We will now consider each of these work roles in turn, discussing the tasks involved and the academic background and personal skills required.

Project Direction and Coordination. Depending on its size, an organization may have many project directors. These positions are sometimes grouped into levels, such as program director, senior study director, study director, and associate study director.

The main tasks of this role are writing proposals; meeting with clients or granting sources; designing studies; overseeing progress on projects and controlling expenditures; analyzing (unless done by client); and writing reports and making oral presentations.

If a proposal is required, a substantial part of the task of designing the study will need to be done in advance. Although many projects will utilize standard designs, others will require ingenuity and creativity. In this respect, a project director is very much like an architect. It is important that a project director enjoy the design aspects of a study, since, typically, only a minority of proposals will be funded and conducted.

Once a project is under way, the project director's role becomes more administrative. Time schedules must be watched and adjusted if unexpected events require changes in methodology, and budgets must be adjusted to mirror these changes. Since these administrative activities are full-time only for the largest projects, a project director will work on other projects as well.

When the data have been collected and cleaned, the analysis and report writing begin. Depending on the project requirements and on the advance planning that has been done, the analysis will be straightforward, requiring only a short time to complete, or lengthy and complex, requiring months or sometimes years. For large-scale projects, the analysis may be divided among several people, and the project coordinator will have the additional task of integrating these efforts into a unified report.

The project director is a social science generalist who must have a strong background in all aspects of survey research. Project directors usually have one or more substantive specialties as well, such as higher education, epidemiology, or manpower planning. Over time, project directors will tend to work on projects in their areas of specialization because they will have a better knowledge of the important problems in those areas, the sources of funds, and methods that are especially appropriate.

In addition to their basic courses in sociological methods and theory, with heavy concentration on quantitative procedures, project directors will normally have been exposed to specific courses in survey methods, including questionnaire design and sampling. From my perspective, the most effective training in survey methods has been through hands-on experience gained in a practicum. Practicums such as those at the universities of Michigan, Illinois, Indiana, and Chicago give students real-world experience in questionnaire construction, interviewing, and data analysis.

Specialized courses in multivariate analysis are a must for anyone who wishes to analyze complex survey data. These courses provide the theoretical underpinnings and make clear the assumptions underlying alternative procedures. Again, however, hands-on experience is essential if one is to be comfortable with these procedures.

The project director must have strong skills and be familiar with both writing and quantitative procedures. Writing ability is essential, both at the beginning of the project, when a proposal must be prepared, and at the end, when the report must be written. What is necessary is not great literary skill but simply the ability to express oneself clearly and to write with sufficient speed and facility to meet deadlines. Lack of writing skills is probably the single most important reason why some otherwise well-qualified persons fail as project directors. However, clear writing cannot rescue fuzzy thinking in survey design, and not all proposed problem-solving designs are equally powerful and imaginative.

Another important skill for project directors is the ability to present numerical data to readers in clear, understandable form. Obviously, to be able to do this, the presenters must themselves be comfortable with numerical data and statistical procedures—one cannot explain to others what one does not understand. Sensitivity to the audience is also crucial—certainly, one should not present data in the same way in a report to the president of an organization and in a paper in the *American Sociological Review*.

Finally, since project directors deal continuously with large numbers of persons both inside and outside their organizations, they need good interpersonal skills. As a group enterprise, survey research is not an ideal career for the brilliant loner.

Sampling/Statistics. The main responsibilities of a sampler include designing samples in conjunction with the client and project director, selecting samples, computing sample variances, and preparing sampling reports, including cooperation rates. A wide range of sampling procedures exists, and, from among the numerous alternatives, the sampler must recommend the optimum design —the one that yields the most accurate information for a specified level of funding. Samples of special populations for which lists are not available require considerable creativity by samplers.

Once a design is agreed on, the actual sample selection may be done by computer or by clerical workers, whichever approach is more efficient. When the study is fielded, it is frequently necessary to adjust sampling rates if the cooperation rate or the fraction eligible is too high or too low or if unexpected growth has occurred in some areas.

The sampler is usually responsible for the preparation of the sampling methodology report, including cooperation rates and sampling errors. The computation of cooperation rates may require complex estimation methods if screening is required. Sampling error computations are done by computer, but the sampler must select the methods and programs to be used and ensure that the data are processed in a manner that permits efficient computation.

The sampler deals with all units in a survey organization but most intensively with the field unit, since interviewers cannot be selected or interviews conducted until the sample is ready. The sampler must also be able to communicate with clients and project directors.

The sampler or sampling statistician will usually have a strong background in mathematical statistics, with one or more courses in sampling. In addition, as with other staff roles in a survey organization, a sampler will usually have served an apprenticeship under the supervision of a more experienced person. During this apprenticeship, samplers learn about the wide range of census materials, lists, and other sources used for sample selection and about the packaged programs available for sample selection and for sampling variance computation.

In addition to considerable quantitative skills, samplers require reasonable writing skills as well. Samplers must have a good understanding of interviewing, since they must design samples that not only are theoretically sound but also can be made operational in the field, and they must have the ability to deal harmoniously with a wide range of clients, project directors, and field personnel.

Field Operations. The main responsibilities of the field operations staff are designing the questionnaire in conjunction with the client and project director, preparing interviewer instructions, hiring and training interviewers, interviewing respondents, supervising interviewer quality and budgets, and debriefing interviewers.

The typical field unit consists of a group of field supervisors and a much larger group of interviewers who usually work part-time as needed. Field supervisors are responsible for preparing the final draft of a questionnaire in consultation with the client and project director. Normally, the client is responsible for determining the information required, but field supervisors revise wording, order, and format to make the questionnaire easier for respondents and interviewers. Field supervisors are also responsible for preparing written instructions and developing training materials for interviewer use.

The other major task of field supervisors is the hiring and training of interviewers. When hiring face-to-face interviewers, field supervisors often spend substantial time away from home traveling. After interviewers are hired, they usually receive initial training from the field supervisors who hired them.

Since telephone interviewers are most often hired to work in one central location or in a few locations, the hiring and training of telephone interviewers does not require substantial travel. Supervision of telephone interviewers after they begin to work is facilitated by the use of monitoring equipment within the central office. The major task of interviewers is to obtain cooperation from respondents, conduct the interview as instructed, and record responses accurately. Interviewers must also probe for additional information without influencing respondents' answers.

Usually field supervisors do not accompany interviewers on face-to-face interviews, except during training. Supervisors do check all, or at least a sample, of completed interviews to ensure that they have been recorded correctly. Supervisors are also in constant touch during the interviewing to ensure that the work is being done on schedule and within budget and that any interviewer problems are resolved. When interviewing is completed, interviewers report—either in writing or in debriefing sessions conducted by supervisors—any problems that they or the respondents had with the questionnaire.

The field operations staff is the group within a survey organization that requires the least formal educational background. Interviewers require only intelligence and the ability to interact well with respondents. Formal interviewer training is conducted by the survey organization after the interviewer is hired. College training is not required, but most successful interviewers have college backgrounds, many in sociology or other social sciences. Interviewer instructions may be complex and require the kinds of skills developed in college. Ultimately, however, a desire to achieve and enjoyment in talking with respondents seems to distinguish the successful interviewer.

Field supervisors are persons with strong executive skills who usually, although not always, come from among the ranks of interviewers. They are initially given supervision over a small group of interviewers and are then given greater and greater responsibility as they become more experienced. Field supervisors must understand the fundamental principles of sampling, since they interpret sampling instructions to interviewers, and they must also be sensitive to data-processing issues in order to ensure that the questionnaires are sufficiently complete and accurate for processing.

Field supervisors do not need strong quantitative skills, but they must have strong verbal skills. They must be able to write clear instructions for interviewers and communicate effectively in training sessions and in subsequent supervisory contacts.

Data Processing/Data Reduction. The main responsibilities of this unit are advising on data-processing aspects of a questionnaire, handling the data after the interview is completed, and providing the required tabulations. The tasks include coding and data entry; cleaning (correction of respondent and data entry errors); maintaining data files; writing special computer programs as required; and using packaged programs, such as the SPSS.

If the questionnaire is carefully constructed, only open

questions (such as occupation) need be coded. To ensure that coding is reliable requires the preparation of coding instructions and the supervision of coders by a coding supervisor. The supervisor hires coders as well, usually on a part-time basis. If coders discover questionnaires with substantially incomplete or obviously incorrect data, these questionnaires are returned to the field for a reinterview or a decision to discard the questionnaire.

After coding, the data must be entered into machine-readable form, usually on floppy disks or directly onto tape. This may be done by a separate data entry staff, by the coders, or by the interviewer using computer-assisted telephone interviewing (CATI).

The next stage is data cleaning, based on specifications prepared by the client and project director and involving the correction of impossible data caused by respondent or data entry errors. Data cleaning is usually done jointly by coders and data-processing staff. The latter are responsible for establishing and maintaining project data files and formatting the data so that packaged programs can be used. Data processors must also write special computer programs as needed.

Data coders require no formal training but must have the ability to follow complex instructions. Data processors, however, require formal computer courses. In addition, skills in handling data and using the packaged programs are obtained under the same apprenticeship system that is used by the other operating units. The skills needed here are primarily quantitative; however, strong verbal skills for communicating with the project director are also desirable, although data processors who communicate well with others are sometimes difficult to find.

The supervisor of data processing/data reduction must have very strong executive, quantitative, and verbal skills and must be able to evaluate the technical proficiency of programmers and deal with project directors, clients, and the field operations staff.

Administration. As in all organizations, the following administrators are essential: manager or director and staff, personnel administrator, and financial administrator. Administrative roles in a survey organization are most similar to those in other research organizations and not similar to the administrative roles of either academic departments or manufacturing companies. The accounting systems of a survey organization have special features that distinguish them from the systems of other organizations, even other research organizations. A very large part of the budget of a survey is consumed during a short field period, and field costs must be readily available if budget control is to be possible. To be effective, accountants in survey research organizations must have a thorough understanding of the tasks of all the groups in the organization—an understanding that can only be obtained through on-the-job training and experience.

Entry into Survey Research

Initial jobs in survey research are obtained in several ways. One route is to take part-time work as either an interviewer or a coder. As I pointed out, neither of these jobs requires previous experience. My first job in survey research was as a part-time coder, and, shortly thereafter, while still in graduate school, I was doing interviewing for a commercial market research company. Although I have not coded or interviewed for quite a long time, I have always found that experience useful. A variant on this approach is to do voluntary political polling for a candidate before an election.

A second route is to work as a programmer or as a research assistant with a survey organization or a user of survey data. The research assistant route has probably been the one most commonly taken by those who ultimately become project directors. All these routes tend to involve part-time work for relatively low pay, but they provide experience that leads to better employment and allows beginners an opportunity to decide whether survey research appeals to them as a possible career.

Yet another route, although less common, is to acquire expertise in a substantive area. For example, a person might specialize in labor economics and become involved with survey research as a method for obtaining data.

Learning More

One easy way to learn about the kinds of work done in survey research is to read past issues of the *Public Opinion Quarterly,* the journal of the American Association for Public Opinion Research (AAPOR). A better way is to join AAPOR and attend its annual conference. Still another alternative is to talk with survey researchers about their work; most of us would be glad to share this information, as time permits. In my experience, most survey researchers enjoy their work—it is challenging and diversified, requires hard thinking and creativity, and produces an end result that is socially useful.

Reference

U.S. NATIONAL SCIENCE FOUNDATION.
    1978   *U.S. Scientists and Engineers 1978.* Surveys of Science
        Resources Series 80-304. Washington, D.C.: National
        Science Foundation.

❦ 6 ❦

HUMAN SERVICES PLANNING

Paul L. Johnson

The idea that sociologists should be actively contributing theory and method to the everyday tasks of human services planners and community organizers is found in essays scattered throughout the history of American sociology. In the early 1920s, Park and Burgess were asked by directors of community centers to apply their Chicago area studies to the development of a scientific approach to neighborhood work (Shenton, 1927). In the 1940s, Merton (1949) argued for the contributions that an applied social science could make to sensitizing agencies to new achievable goals and to more effective means for establishing those goals. And, in the 1960s, Gans (1967), lamenting their limited role, also encouraged an expanded role for his fellow sociologists in the social planning projects and community action programs associated with the War on Poverty.

This chapter illustrates the contribution, both historical and current, of sociology's various specialities to the major tasks of human services planning. The importance of sociological theory to planning and the issue of values and scientific objectivity in social planning are also discussed.

Sociology in Human Services Planning

The tasks of human services planning can be roughly divided into five areas: needs assessment, resources analysis, resources allocation and decision making, citizen participation, and services design and implementation. If a sociologist were to examine closely the bibliographies and suggested reading lists of the various planning texts and articles that discuss any of these five areas, he or she would be pleasantly surprised by the number and variety of citations from both sociology classics and recent works on theory and method. Without a thorough sociology of knowledge, it is impossible to speculate on whether the applied influence of individual sociologists was intentional or was, like most sharing and dissemination of knowledge, simply fortuitous and circumstantial.

Needs Assessment. A major component of any human services plan, either city, county, regional or state, documents the number of persons in the community forecasted to be in need of services for a specified time period. The techniques employed for these estimates vary from relatively inexpensive interviews with community services experts to very costly citizen surveys and statistical analyses of secondary data sources.

Overall, needs assessments have benefited from sociology's contributions to developments in survey design and sampling; more specifically, planners have been able to estimate needs by adapting classical analytical schemes from sociology and human ecology, such as social area analysis and ecological distribution mapping. Interestingly, the original work of Shevky and Williams (1949) in mapping the "social areas" of Los Angeles according to combinations of socioeconomic status, family characteristics, and ethnic group affiliation is cited twenty years later in planning literature as a useful analytical approach for gaining a better understanding of community populations and their selective use of human services. This understanding by planners can lead to suggested changes for more effective community services delivery systems (Struening, 1975; Kay, 1978). Others at the National Institute of

Mental Health (NIMH) (Redick, Goldsmith, and Unger, 1971) have demonstrated the applicability of the social area analysis concept for planners in community mental health centers who must assess needs according to ecological concentrations of known target groups for specific kinds of services. NIMH (1979) has also provided mental health centers with a data base capability for conducting a local social area analysis with its National Mental Health Demographic Profile System (MHDPS). This computer-stored data resource consists of 1970 and 1980 demographic and socioeconomic characteristics of the population of center catchment areas in units of census tracts and other aggregated units. It also has the capability of integrating MHDPS data with other catchment area data on vital, public health, crime, and services utilization statistics.

The more common needs assessment approach of analyzing social indicator data draws on the work of early human ecologists and urban sociologists. In mental health particularly, methodological discussions of the social indicators approach (Bell and others, 1978) credit the sociologists (such as Faris and Dunham, Hollingshead and Redlich, and Srole and associates) who studied the individual and ecological correlations between socioeconomic status and physical or mental illness. These early sociological studies are viewed as the precursors of contemporary social epidemiology. The planners who are analyzing prevalence and incidence rates of mental illness in order to forecast services needs are looking to these early works for theoretical propositions to support their own etiological models.

Resources Analysis. A second task of social planners is the continuous process of keeping abreast of changing resources in the community human services network. This task involves constant updating of inventories of service resources in order to know which agencies have the capability of providing what service and at what capacity. The method of resources analysis often goes beyond a simple, mechanical inventory-file maintenance. Not only do service and target-group definitions vary considerably across agencies, but, more significantly, interagency competition for clients and conflict over services strategies and treatment approaches make resources analysis a subtle and complex political process. Not surprisingly, then, planning textbooks include discussions of resources analysis (Lauffer, 1978) that focus on the concept of organizational environments. This concept offers the planner a broad perspective for understanding the turbulent environment of any single agency in the community and how it must adapt or must plan actions to shape that environment. The recent sociological works of Aldrich (1979), Meyer and others (1978), and Pfeffer and Salancik (1978) represent a new applied knowledge base for the planner's understanding and method of resources analysis.

Another related sociological knowledge base that is relevant to resources analysis is interorganizational relations and network theory. The practical application of knowledge in this area addresses the planner's problem of establishing and maintaining interagency linkages and his or her task of planning for better services coordination. Seymour Sarason and his associates (1977) provide an excellent example in the planning literature of applying network theory not only to the understanding of services networks but also to the practice of organizing and leading them toward coordinated objectives. Combined with the studies of Turk (1973) on interorganizational relations in War on Poverty programs and Aiken and his associates (1975) on coordinating human services, these works provide a practical course in the analysis of human services resources.

Resources Allocation and Decision Making. Perhaps the most difficult task of planners is to determine how to engage themselves in the decision-making process of budgeting and allocating human services funds to either internal agency service programs or interagency purchase-of-service contracts. As Rein (1970) points out, the legitimate role of the planner in this process is rarely clearly defined by the community at large. The disinterested planner who looks for only the areas of broadest community consensus to apply the tools of the trade is no less immune to criticism than the rational planner who strategically explicates a plan from the vague goals of divergent interest groups or the advocacy planner who champions the cause of rejected or excluded groups.

This distinction is emphasized here because each type of planner can draw from different areas of sociology for practical knowledge on decision making. First, the community development planner focuses on the local neighborhood or community self-help project. The sociological theory and research on urban neighborhoods and the classical community studies represent a knowledge base of considerable scope and depth for the theory and practice of this approach. Second, the social planner who looks at the larger metropolitan or regional level of human services concentrates on manipulating large bureaucratic organizations. In this case, the planning literature draws examples from the community power studies of the 1950s and 1960s to guide planners in decision making. And, third, the social action planner approaches planning from the standpoint of representing and mobilizing disadvantaged segments of the population, such as ethnic and racial minorities or socially and economically oppressed groups. The sociological literature of ethnic and racial minorities and the sociology of social movements and collective behavior is a valuable resource for this application of planning.

Citizen Participation. Although most state and local human services planning processes are mandated by their enabling legislation to obtain citizen input and document the methods used, the planning profession values citizen participation as an ongoing and integral part of services delivery systems. The participation techniques of conducting citizen surveys, organizing community forums, interviewing key services agency experts, and holding public hearings are the primary mechanisms for documenting citizen needs and priorities, involving the public in evaluation and review of plans and programs, incorporating public sentiments and perspectives into services decision making, and disseminating services information to the public. Overall, citizen participation generates support for both planning and operation of community services delivery systems.

For the most part, planning textbooks offer techniques for involving citizens during the formulation stages of a plan and during the final stages of plan review and public comment. Suggestions are provided on how to form and help structure the activities of advisory boards and how to minimize political confrontations that could undermine the entire planning process. However, one planning text (Gates, 1980) shows the indirect contribution of political sociology as a basic knowledge resource for understanding the dynamics of citizen participation. The planner's theoretical understanding of variation in participatory behavior draws on conclusions from Lipset's theory of democracy and political institutions and from Almond and Verba's research on political attitudes and socialization.

Services Design and Implementation. What logically follows any human services plan of goals and objectives for different programs is an implementation or procedural plan that contains the means—an organized set of activities, guidelines, operating procedures, reporting requirements, or any other administrative mechanisms—required for carrying out the original goals and objectives. The success of any agency plan and, in the long run, of the planning process will depend on the planner's skill in designing program implementation strategies that fit realistically with the agency's subtle and complex organizational structure and processes.

Planners acquire these design skills largely from on-the-job training, but planning texts on this subject show that the profession is turning to the organizational development literature for pragmatic methods of program implementation. Although sociology's general contribution of organizational theory to the practice of organizational development is clear, more important are the sociological studies of public bureaucracies. These studies offer planning students not only organizational theory but also more substantive insights into the kinds of bureaucracies in which they must design programs.

The social networks literature of sociology is also being applied to the design of human services programs. Basic research on social friendship networks has contributed to new strategies of social work intervention, such as the emphasis on helping networks of friends, relatives, and neighbors who can aid individuals in achieving economic self-sufficiency, in obtaining support in coping with acute or chronic problems, or in avoiding institutionalization (Collins and Pancoast, 1976).

One might easily conclude, after reading this review, that the only specialty of sociology that has not contributed to planning is the sociology of sport. But is it surprising that American sociology—with its historical roots in the Chicago School, which sought to study urban social problems, and in the later functionalist schools of Parsons and Merton, which sought understanding of the nature of social systems—would be so broadly applied by social planners to the task of designing human services to ameliorate social problems and enhance the quality of life in social systems?

The evidence of broad application should not be interpreted to mean that no problems have arisen in the past regarding utilization of sociological knowledge in the area of planning. For example, Schuman (1977, p. 137), in a historical review of the Detroit Area Survey (DAS), remarks: "In the early years of DAS some effort was made to connect parts of the program to the more practical needs of the Detroit metropolitan area and especially to produce occasional publications (called "Profiles of Detroit") that presented selected DAS findings in a form useful to community organizations. For a variety of reasons this type of service never achieved very high priority, as compared to graduate training and theoretically oriented research goals."

The potential of university-based community surveys for serving both academic sociology and community planners is illustrated by the recent example of the sociology department at the University of Nebraska and its annual social indicators survey (Booth and others, 1980). The department reports that nine public agencies who bought time on the survey found the results useful for preparing statewide plans and federal reports and for providing background information to support new policies and funding allocations. More partnerships of this type between sociology departments and human services agencies will move us further away from the traditional separation of basic and applied sociology.

Applied Sociology of Planning

The role that sociologists should play in the various tasks of social planning is concisely formulated by Gans (1967, p. 443). He suggests that planners need sociologists in four respects: "for the development of a theoretical scheme to guide the planner, for goals determination, for means of program development, and for the evaluation of action programs." The first three, concerning theory, goals, and means, are germane to current discussions on the future of applied sociology.

The importance of sociological theory to planning is easily underestimated if one views planners largely as technicians who apply rational techniques to organizing human and physical resources to accomplish someone else's goals. Yet what is often overlooked is the responsibility, either sole or shared, of planners to articulate the rationale for spending public or private funds in the pursuit of a social goal. In a human services plan, the needs assessment is not just a presentation of descriptive statistics but also a clear definition of the social or individual problems that have caused certain persons to require a service. The written statements of goals in a plan are more than mindless copying of the rhetoric of political leaders or social reformists. As well, the specifications of objectives and activities in a plan often require a theoretical rationale, in terms of organizational structure and processes, as to why one implementation plan for a program is more likely to be cost-effective and efficient than another. Thus, planners, whether or not they come from a sociology background, require a basic understanding of theory in social problems, social deviance, social stratification, psychological needs, social change, and organizational systems.

The importance of sociological theory to planning is also well stated by Merton (1949) and Foote (1974), who argue that the sociological perspective itself, although vaguely defined, represents a unique viewpoint from which applied problems, such as social needs or program effectiveness, are defined or formulated. The planner who appreciates the sociological imagination will likely conceptualize problems of human services delivery differently than others. Merton (1957) illustrates this point with a hypothetical case. Two analysts, one an intellectual and the other a bureaucrat, are studying the problem of low worker morale and output among blacks in a segregated factory; white resistance to desegregation is also in evidence. In formulating a policy and program to address the situation, the bureaucrat might set a goal of making segregation more palatable to blacks and thus design a program of propaganda to heighten morale despite continuing segregation. The intellectual, on the other hand, might choose a policy of desegregation and pursue an integration program that would not significantly lower the morale of white workers. Merton's example is not intended to argue that one definition and solution to the problem is more valid than another but that each definition serves a different purpose. He writes: "The crucial point is to recognize the value-implications entailed by the very choice and definition of the problem itself and that the choice will be in part fixed by the intellectual's position within the social structure" (1957, p. 218). His point here leads to a concluding discussion on the classical issue in applied sociology of the relationship between values and scientific objectivity.

Problem of Values and Objectivity in Planning

Sociologists no longer seriously argue about the Weberian notion that ethical neutrality or a value-free sociology is maintained by sticking to basic research and the university campus; attention has now turned to questions of how all sociologists, basic and applied, must relate to the organizations that support their research. What value commitments are made by involvement or association with a particular sponsor? What uses or abuses may result from the outcomes of research?

It is easy to label social planning as social engineering par excellence, the valueless technology of "liberal practicality" or "abstracted empiricism" best characterized by Mills (1959); however, to do so would be an oversimplification of the importance of both values and objectivity in planning. As Rein (1970, p. 214) aptly puts it: "Social policy is all about social objectives and the values that embody the choice of social programs. These are precisely the problems that touch the limits of social science and raise the spectre of that ancient but still inadequately explored terrain where facts and values merge." The important question is how planners are able to face a value dilemma that might lead to a compromise in the objectivity of any method employed.

Value conflicts between planners and agency directors can take several forms. Values may differ on the significance attached to various planning activities, the particular uses of planning information obtained, the fairness of decisions made on the basis of planning information, and the necessity of following through on basic principles of rational planning. Planners faced with these conflicts might accommodate their values to the agency, seek to alter the prevailing policies of the agency, or dissociate and thus fall back into the role of pure technician. Resignation from the agency is certainly a possible response, but not a solution to value conflicts in the long run.

Among these responses, the one of assuming the role of technician is most problematic. Over time, it is likely to result in feelings of alienation or, more specifically, a sense of powerlessness in controlling one's professional responsibilities. Sometimes the planner's agency benefits from this role of technician by obtaining greater loyalty and cooperation from the planner in carrying out agency objectives. The agency can assume by default the largest share of the total organizational life of the planner.

However, we know from sociological research that membership in work-related associations is inversely related to expressed feelings of powerlessness on the job (Neal and Seeman, 1964). The hypothesis tested here is whether organizations such as unions or professional societies represent a potential buffer, or mediating association, for individuals in relating to the demands placed on them by their agency of employment.

Applying this hypothesis to potential value conflicts between planners and their agencies, the question becomes: Do professional planning associations serve to buffer or mediate value conflicts between planners and their agencies? Does the mediation process serve to help planners clarify value conflicts and offer them alternative responses to agency demands?

The corollary question for sociologists is whether its professional associations should actively pursue roles of mediators or buffer organizations for future applied sociologists who are likely to enter the profession of human services planning. Should the national and regional associations of sociologists bring together the professional value concerns of human services planners and the applied interests of sociologists? Such an exchange would enhance the professionalism of planners and sociologists and diminish the stereotype of planners as valueless technicians.

References

AIKEN, M., AND OTHERS.
  1975   *Coordinating Human Services.* San Francisco: Jossey-Bass.
ALDRICH, H. A.
  1979   *Organizations and Environments.* Englewood Cliffs, N.J.: Prentice-Hall.
BELL, R. A., AND OTHERS.
  1978   "Service utilization, social indicator, and citizen survey approaches to human service needs assessment." In C. C. Attkisson, W. A. Hargreaves, M. J. Horowitz, and J. E. Sorensen (Eds.), *Evaluation of Human Service Programs.* New York: Academic Press.

BOOTH, A., AND OTHERS.
  1980 "Combining contracts and sociological research: The Nebraska Annual Social Indicators Survey." *American Sociologist* 15:226-232.
CAREY, L., AND MAPES, R.
  1972 *The Sociology of Planning.* London: Batesford.
COLLINS, A. J., AND PANCOAST, D. L.
  1976 *Natural Helping Networks.* New York: National Association of Social Workers.
FOOTE, N. N.
  1974 "Putting sociologists to work." *American Sociologist* 9:125-134.
GANS, H. J.
  1967 "Urban poverty and social planning." In P. F. Lazarsfeld, W. H. Sewell, and J. L. Wilensky (Eds.), *The Uses of Sociology.* New York: Basic Books.
GATES, B. L.
  1980 *Social Program Administration.* Englewood Cliffs, N.J.: Prentice-Hall.
KAY, F. D., JR.
  1978 "Applications of social area analysis to program planning and evaluation." *Journal of Evaluation and Program Planning* 1:65-78.
LAUFFER, A.
  1978 *Social Planning at the Community Level.* Englewood Cliffs, N.J.: Prentice-Hall.
MERTON, R. K.
  1949 "The role of applied social science in the formation of policy." *Philosophy of Science* 16:161-181.
  1957 *Social Theory and Social Structure.* New York: Free Press.
MEYER, M. W., AND ASSOCIATES.
  1978 *Environments and Organizations.* San Francisco: Jossey-Bass.
MILLS, C. W.
  1959 *The Sociological Imagination.* New York: Oxford University Press.
NATIONAL INSTITUTE OF MENTAL HEALTH.
  1979 *Mental Health Demographic System Description.* Washington, D.C.: U.S. Government Printing Office.

NEAL, A. C., AND SEEMAN, M.
    1964   "Organizations and powerlessness: A test of the media-
            tion hypothesis." *American Sociological Review* 29:
            216-226.
PFEFFER, J., AND SALANCIK, G. R.
    1978   *The External Control of Organizations.* New York:
            Harper & Row.
REDICK, R. W., GOLDSMITH, H. F., AND UNGER, E. L.
    1971   *1970 Census Data Used to Indicate Areas with Differ-
            ent Potentials for Mental Health and Related Problems.*
            DHEW Publication No. HSM 72-9051. Rockville, Md.:
            National Institute of Mental Health.
REIN, M.
    1970   *Social Policy.* New York: Random House.
SARASON, S. B., AND OTHERS.
    1977   *Human Services and Resource Networks.* San Fran-
            cisco: Jossey-Bass.
SCHUMAN, H.
    1977   "The Detroit area study after 25 years." *American So-
            ciologist* 12:130-137.
SHENTON, H. N.
    1927   *The Practical Application of Sociology.* New York:
            Columbia University Press.
SHEVKY, E., AND WILLIAMS, M.
    1949   *The Social Areas of Los Angeles.* Berkeley: University
            of California Press.
STRUENING, E. L.
    1975   "Social area analysis as a method of evaluation." In
            E. L. Struening and M. Guttentag (Eds.), *Handbook of
            Evaluation Research.* Beverly Hills, Calif.: Sage.
TURK, H.
    1973   *Interorganizational Activation in Urban Communities.*
            Washington, D.C.: American Sociological Association.

7

SOCIAL AND DEMOGRAPHIC ANALYSIS

Daphne Spain

Social and demographic analysis can be considered subsets of the field of sociology. Social analysis is a broad term that could encompass much of sociology, whereas demography deals specifically with population issues. For the purposes of this chapter, social analysis is defined as the study of social trends and can include anything from analyzing racial changes in socioeconomic status to assessing rates of political participation. Demographic analysis deals with the basic processes of fertility, mortality, and migration.

Just as theoretical concepts are operationalized for easier measurement, academic social and demographic analyses can be operationalized through their applied versions. A social analyst

Note: Although this manuscript was written by the author during the time of her employment at the U.S. Bureau of the Census, the views expressed here are entirely her own.

conducting purely academic research might concentrate on methods of measuring differences in socioeconomic status between blacks and whites. An applied approach might result in a report on the income gap between whites and blacks working for the same company. An academic study of political participation might revolve around historical shifts in party identification by sex, whereas the applied social analysis might be a national survey of women's voting patterns for the League of Women Voters.

An academic demographer may conduct studies on the effects of rapid industrialization on the birth rate of a hypothetical cohort of women. The applied demographer is more likely to be in a third-world country studying the extent of knowledge of birth control techniques among women of child-bearing age. Academic studies of migration might predict the amount of migration induced by war or a bad economy, whereas applied migration research would report to the local school board on the number of families with school-age children who moved from central cities to suburbs.

Whether research is ultimately academic or applied, similar skills are used in its execution. Knowledge of methodology and statistics and the ability to summarize results clearly are essential tools for both academic and applied sociologists. However, the sociologist with quantitative skills appears to have an edge in the nonacademic market over the sociologist with only qualitative skills. Since demographers have obvious quantitative expertise, their opportunities in applied work may be greater than those of social analysts.

Demographers may also be perceived as able to help a client earn or save money through correct population estimates and forecasting. For example, demographic techniques can be used in marketing research to target consumers by age, sex, and income, data on which profits are made. In contrast, social analysis is often perceived as costing money. When sociologists conduct a study of school desegregation, worker safety, or discrimination in the housing market, it can result in policy decisions with a high cost to government or private industry.

The term *applied* is often used interchangeably with the term *nonacademic*—not necessarily an appropriate identification, considering that sociologists in academic institutions often apply their skills to specific issues and many sociologists employed by federal or private agencies contribute to the body of academic research. Rossi (1980) points out that applied research is often indistinguishable from basic research due to changes made by researchers, clients, or the passage of time.

The applied researchers described in this chapter are sociologists who use their skills in nonacademic settings to perform specific tasks for their organizations. Those tasks may be assigned by the organization or initiated by the individual. In the case of a privately-owned consulting firm, the individual is the organization. Reviewing the skills used in nonacademic employment helps identify the types of applied opportunities available outside teaching institutions.

Specific Work Roles

A short questionnaire was sent to a nonrandomly selected sample of sociologists employed outside academia in an attempt to portray as many work roles as possible. The sample was quite small ($N = 25$), with a response rate of 60 percent. It was intended to collect job descriptions from people conducting social and demographic research in several different settings. Employers include private business, nonprofit organizations, and federal agencies.

Social Analysis in the Federal Government. One sociologist with a federal agency is the editor of an annual report to Congress. He is responsible for developing social indicators of all aspects of his subject and presenting trend data in a readable form. The job requires statistical and analytical skills and the ability to work with representatives from other agencies. Another sociologist with a federal agency is a statistician whose specialty is epidemiology. The agency publishes an annual report on health statistics, to which she is a contributor. Her primary duties include statistical analysis of national data sets, methodological design of research projects, and some computer programming.

Social Analysis in Private Business. As an account executive, one respondent from a large marketing firm works as a sales and research consultant to major consumer and industrial marketing corporations. This individual's background was in marketing and sociology; he uses the research skills he developed in both areas and notes that the business community could benefit from more knowledge of sociological concepts. Another sociologist who taught for seven years is now the vice-president of a private firm that works on government contracts. His skills include research design, statistical analysis, report preparation, and management of a research staff.

Social Analysis in Nonprofit Organizations. A sociologist for a multidisciplinary research corporation is responsible for every aspect of grants funded by the federal government. She responds to the requests for proposals, designs the project, oversees data collection and analysis, writes the report, and presents the results at in-house seminars and professional meetings. She also has the task of consulting on the social science aspects of non–social science projects. A sociologist with a health insurance agency is in charge of policy evaluation for the organization. Her duties include managing data collection and writing final reports and will eventually involve evaluating various components of the health delivery system (such as nursing standards and appointment systems).

A sociologist who does not fit clearly into any of these three categories works for a major religious denomination. He uses theoretical knowledge from the sociology of religion but also depends extensively on such research training skills as computer programming and data analysis. He conducts his own research and supervises contracts outside the organization.

Demographic Analysis in the Federal Government. My own work involves research design, analysis of national data sets, a knowledge of statistical techniques, and report preparation and publication. Contract work sometimes requires collaboration with other agencies. The skill used most frequently, aside from data analysis, is writing. Research results are prepared for publication in an agency series or an academic journal. Other demographers in the same agency review population estimates and challenges to agency programs. They conduct surveys, develop estimation procedures, and prepare reports on substantive topics.

Demographic Analysis in Private Business. The largest number of respondents fall into this category, with skills ranging from market research to the more academic work sometimes possible with federal contracts. Members of a private consulting firm are also included. The most applied job is one in which the individual conducts market analysis relating promotions to returns, analyzes penetration rates for advertising, and develops new products for private industry. Another sociologist doing market-related work manages a marketing group with a large company. He also evaluates requests for proposals and organizes research projects into market areas. On the more academic end of the spectrum, one demographer uses skills similar to those used in academic settings. A great deal of his time is spent writing proposals for contract work and preparing final reports for presentation to the funding agency. Finally, the private consultants conduct a broad range of research projects for a variety of clients. Their jobs include some market research, some basic research for city governments, and some work for private foundations.

Demographic Analysis in Nonprofit Organizations. The demographer in this category is responsible for overseeing other researchers, conducting his own research, and preparing funding proposals for the organization. The organization produces a series of nationally distributed reports every year, to which he and other sociologists on the staff contribute.

Review of Skills. Almost without exception, the job descriptions listed include research design, data analysis, and report preparation. In order to perform their jobs well, applied sociologists must use the same skills used by academic sociologists—methodological, statistical, and writing. Although academic research is more likely to appear in professional journals, applied sociologists often do more writing than academics. Their writing is generally addressed to a less sophisticated audience, is sometimes done under greater time pressure, and does not get the same circulation as journal articles. However, the results of applied social and demographic reports can be more tangible. Marketing techniques, for example, succeed or fail on the basis of demographic reports. If a product is fielded for a specific consumer population and that population does not exist or does not respond, the results are evident immediately.

In sum, although the audiences are different and the consequences sometimes greater for applied research, the necessary skills can be gained from graduate programs geared toward academic research. Quantitative skills are paramount, closely followed in importance by writing skills. The ability to present research results clearly is central to both social and demographic analysis.

Solitary Sociologists

Applied sociologists are often faced with being the only sociologist in the organization. Faculty in all but the smallest schools have several colleagues in the same discipline, but, in a nonacademic setting, sociologists may be the token in their field and may not have a peer group, as their academic counterparts do. Two thirds of the respondents were the only sociologists in their immediate work groups. When asked how often they worked with another sociologist, the majority responded "seldom or never" or "once or twice a week." Few applied sociologists work with other sociologists on a weekly or daily basis.

This situation produces certain working conditions not experienced by academic sociologists. First, the sociologist must recognize that not everyone shares the sociological imagination; in many instances, no one else will even have a social science mentality. Therefore, the nonacademic sociologist is challenged to effectively represent the sociological perspective to colleagues or clients who have never thought in those terms. For example, a social analyst working on a defense contract may be able to point out loopholes in military strategy caused by potential failures in social organization due to a breakdown in the chain of command. Military personnel may be so intent on the mechanical aspects of the plan that they neglect the social component.

Or a demographic consultant may be presenting data to persons who have no knowledge of existing research on their particular problem. An expert witness on a school desegregation case reported talking with a judge who believed racial segregation was due entirely to income differences between blacks and whites. The demographer explained the noneconomic origins of nationally high levels of residential segregation and, in the process, educated the judge to the sociological perspective (Farley, 1981).

These examples contrast with the ivory tower of the academic sociology department, where one assumes a shared knowledge of social organization and basic demography, to the extent that one seldom comments on obvious issues like the disproportionate impact of welfare cuts on female-headed households. Yet many professionals in policy-making positions are not aware of the social ramifications of economic policy. The sociological perspective is greatly needed in these situations.

A second condition specific to nonacademic work is that a job opening may not be for a sociologist per se. Universities and colleges recruit specifically for sociologists, but one seldom sees advertisements from private business for a sociologist. The federal government employed only 100 people as "sociologists" in 1979, although there were approximately 3,000 "social science analysts" (Dotzler, 1981). Many sociologists enter line positions as "statisticians." This paucity of slots indicates that nonacademic employers do not recognize a need for sociology. In order to get in the door, the sociologist must advertise one set of skills (usually quantitative) and then hopefully apply the full range of sociological expertise to the task at hand.

Applied Sociology and the
American Sociological Association

The work-place separation from other sociologists described in the previous section means that nonacademic sociologists may feel isolated from other sociologists and from the American Sociological Association. The association is unquestionably oriented toward academic sociology. A review of the slates for ASA elective offices over the past five years shows that 95 percent of the candidates were affiliated with universities or colleges. Only 5 percent held nonacademic jobs at the time of the elections. The history of the discipline and employment opportunities in the past have allowed that orientation to go unchallenged. But now the organization needs to refocus on a broader definition of sociological employment—not to do so risks losing a growing number of sociologists. The ASA estimates that approximately 11 percent of its members are working in nonacademic settings. This figure is probably an undercount of all nonacademic sociologists, since they are less likely than their academic counterparts to maintain their ASA memberships. Several issues of concern to nonacademic sociologists are discussed in the following paragraphs.

Does one stop being a sociologist after several years outside academia? This concern springs from the perception that "being a sociologist" means publishing in the *American Sociological Review* (*ASR*) and presenting papers at annual meetings. If this definition reflects the association's criteria, it is almost certain to mean that they risk losing their sociological credentials. Many applied researchers cannot compete in publishing with their academic counterparts because the reward structure in nonacademic positions is totally different than in universities. One's job security is not determined by how many articles and books one publishes but by how well the organization profits from one's contribution.

A familiar scenario recurs at every national meeting. People are catching up on the progress of old friends and acquaintances, and someone inquires about Susan, who has left academia. "Oh, she's working for the government now, and you never hear from her anymore"—in other words, her name is no longer on the cover of *ASR* and the *American Journal of Sociology* (*AJS*). The sentiment is that Susan has left the fold and is no longer a real sociologist. Those at the gathering silently vow that it will never happen to them. The reason Susan has dropped out of sight is that there are no institutionalized forms of recognition for nonacademic sociologists. No nonacademic forum is comparable to the "Teaching" and "New Programs" columns in *Footnotes. The ASA needs to acknowledge and encourage alternative criteria for measuring success in the discipline.*

Academic sociologists appear to assume that everyone wants an academic job and that those who can not get one have to settle for applied work. This is probably the most aggravating of all attitudes. Contrary to popular belief, not everyone wants to be a college professor. Many sociologists who have done both find applied work more interesting and challenging than teaching. Some people even enter graduate school never intending to become teachers. The way most departments are currently run, however, makes it difficult to enter a nonacademic career. Most of one's professors only have contacts in the academic network, and the employment bulletins and professional meetings are dominated by academic recruiting. The student who wants to prepare a résumé instead of a curriculum vita finds no models to copy. *The ASA should promote nonacademic employment as actively as it promotes academic employment.*

The annual meetings are dominated by academic sociology. With only a few exceptions, session organizers and discussants are academics; a large source of program participation from the nonacademic sphere is excluded. The majority of topics are not aimed at an applied audience. Over half the nonacademic sociologists who responded to the brief questionnaire do not attend the annual meeting. Without comparable information for academic sociologists, it is not possible to know if this attendance rate is high or low. However, several respondents expressed the opinion that the meetings are totally irrelevant to their work. For one consultant, other types of conferences (for example, on public data use or computer software systems) were of more direct use to his business than the ASA meetings. *The ASA should incorporate applied sociology into the annual meetings.*

Summary

Applied social and demographic analysis, then, encompass a wide range of skills similar to those used by academic sociologists. Applied work can take place in both academic and nonacademic settings, although this chapter has concentrated on the nonacademic realm. The concerns of demographers and social analysts conducting applied research are similar to those of other nonacademic sociologists. Isolation from the discipline is a problem experienced by many nonacademic sociologists. The ASA can help address their needs by recognizing alternative criteria of success, promoting nonacademic employment, and incorporating applied sociology into the annual meetings. Some of these measures are being initiated now. The benefit to the discipline could be a greater involvement of nonacademic sociologists in the ASA at a time when academic employment is becoming increasingly scarce.

References

DOTZLER, R. J.
    1981   "A Master's program in applied social research? Some issues and information." Unpublished manuscript, Department of Sociology, George Washington University.
FARLEY, R.
    1981   Comments prepared as a participant in the panel "The new demographic practitioner: Broadened opportuni-

ties for employment" at the 1981 annual meeting of the Population Association of America, Washington, D.C.

ROSSI, P. H.
1980   "The presidential address: The challenge and opportunities of applied social research." *American Sociological Review* 45:889–904.

GOVERNMENT POLICY RESEARCH

Lawrence D. Haber

A few years ago I was introduced to a man who was described as a biophysicist. When I asked him what a biophysicist did, he explained that a biophysicist talked physics to biologists and biology to physicists. In a similar vein, I would describe sociologists engaged in policy and program research as people who talk policy to researchers, research to policy people and sociology mainly to themselves. However, if they are capable analysts who believe that what they know about society and social organization is relevant, they will incorporate a sociological perspective into their research and relate it to the programs and policies for which they have a research and statistical responsibility. Hopefully, they will also develop the ability to entertain apparently contradictory

Note: The opinions expressed are entirely those of the author and are not intended to reflect the policy or position of the Bureau of the Census or any federal agency.

notions. On the one hand, the client, manager, or policy official has little or no interest in the sociological implications of the data; on the other hand, the researcher has a professional responsibility to introduce sociological concepts, approaches, and findings that are relevant to his or her work and to point out their implications for program and policy issues.

Of course, the client or manager is concerned with his or her own questions, program, and policy issues. To the extent that the intellectual framework of the policy and program research sociologist is technically and politically creditable, intelligible, and feasible, most managers will be interested. They will listen and may incorporate sociological ideas or findings as one more element in the array of conditions, factors, and constraints which enter into a program or policy development.

What does this description of the position of the sociologist in policy research imply for the development of applied sociology? In my view, it suggests that there is a meaningful and useful role for sociologists in program and policy research situations within the federal government. These situations permit sociologists to do sociological research within a set of modest expectations and to the extent that they recognize that sociological research is not their function but their set of tools. The "pay off" of sociological research in a policy or program setting is the application of sociological methods and concepts to policy problems. From the sponsoring agency's perspective, the value of the research is a function of its contribution to an understanding of policy options and outcomes, regardless of its merits for broader social analysis.

Context of Policy Research

Sociologists bring a particular grab bag of skills, orientations, concepts, and preconceptions to their work or to their search for employment. In many areas of the federal government, they will find that they are competing against other professionals with similar or related skills but with somewhat different concepts and orientations—for example, statisticians, economists, and public administration specialists. Competition exists not only among those seeking employment but also among those already employed—in the definition of the problem, the design of the research, the analysis of the data, and the interpretation of findings. In many areas, of course, where a problem is complex and the budget is large enough, interdisciplinary groups may include sociologists, statisticians, and economists.

At times, the competition of ideas may also lead to complementarity and the interplay of ideas, resulting in a new approach and a different perspective than either one alone would have arrived at. Despite the differences in conceptual approach and training that become apparent when sociologists, economists, and statisticians work together, they have more in common with one another, as social scientists and policy researchers, than they have with administrators, managers, and other clients. As one research journal pointed out:

> The gap between research person and program administrator is wider than that between one researcher and another. People who administer programs operate on different circuits than researchers—they attend different professional meetings, they read and publish in different journals, and, most important, they have different concerns. The program administrator is almost wholly concerned with process variables: How many people are being served? What is the per capita cost of providing the service? . . . Are the clients happy with the service? Research persons are concerned with different types of problems: What is the hypothesis to be tested? What is the population to be sampled? What data are to be collected? How are the data going to be analyzed?
>
> Research workers are analytically oriented. They want to know what the question is and what methods and techniques are available to try and answer the question. Program administrators want to know what the answers are. They are so answer-oriented that often they pose their questions in the form of answers [Halpert, 1973, pp. 377-378].

Job Skills, Attitudes, and Expectations

I have worked in several agencies in the federal government under a variety of titles, primarily as a social science research analyst and research supervisor. I have been classified as a survey statistician and even, for a brief period, as an economist. After several years in market research, I came to the Office of Research and Statistics of the Social Security Administration, where I developed a research program of economic and social surveys on aging, retirement, and disability. I spent a brief period with the National Center for Education Statistics and several years with the Office of Management and Budget and the Office of Federal Statistical Policy and Standards, evaluating, reviewing, and coordinating statistical activities. Currently I am a social science analyst and programs adviser in the Population Division of the Bureau of the Census.

From my experience, I would consider the major functions or roles of a sociologist in government to be educational and archival. The important personality traits include a reasonable tolerance for ambiguity, a moderate amount of professional self-appreciation, and an enormous amount of humility. This includes an understanding of the complexities of policy and program decision making and the limitations of the role of social research in contributing to this process; it presumes an appropriate respect for the competence of program managers and policy people, who have the task of developing and carrying out the policies, and for the difficulties of separating fact from myth in determining a reasonable approximation of what the world is really like.

The social scientist should bring a unique, disciplined disinterest to the examination of social phenomena as well as an array of conceptual approaches and questions as to how or why certain forms of behavior occur. Although it is primarily his technical and methodological skills that are of interest to the administrator, the substantive questions of his disciplinary training provide a framework through which the researcher can look at program phenomena as a naturalistic inquiry. Where the economist might be concerned with the effect of the participation rates on the costs of a program, the sociologist might be more oriented toward questions relating to why people do or do not participate in a program or to how participation is affected by program conditions or requirements. Where the economist might be interested in the effect of program benefits as disincentives to work, the sociologist might ask through what pathways the claimant became involved with the program and how clients are selected. The structuring of the problem poses different questions and may lead to different kinds of answers or illuminate different aspects of policy.

Within an organization, there are organizational, administrative, and political pressures to support particular policies, procedures, or programs. The training of the sociologist in scientific method and objectivity provides him with some basis to resist these organizational pressures as part of a disciplined approach to the definition of the problem and the evaluation of the data. In this sense, the line between sociologist as advocate and sociologist as researcher must be clearly drawn.

In terms of skills, one should come to the job with a reasonable background in sampling and sampling statistics, programming and computer systems, analytical methods and methodology, questionnaire design, and other data collection techniques. These are largely the fungibles of social research, the common currency shared among statisticians, sociologists, economists, and other social and policy researchers. There is, however, no substitute for a thorough and complete understanding of the program. The legislative history, organizational structure, and specific provisions, including the minutiae of acronyms, titles, and subsection citations, provide the background and the basic language in which policies and programs are discussed.

The federal agencies with which I am familiar have usually had competent statisticians to deal with sampling problems and designs. Most federal agencies have computer programming staffs who take responsibility for the actual systems and program work. A variety of statistical and survey personnel are generally available, within the agency and in collegial organizations such as the Bureau of the Census, to undertake the management and operation of large-scale surveys and other data collection and processing operations. Program knowledgeability and problem definition are, however, largely inseparable and indispensable.

A thorough knowledge of the program is usually needed for an adequate definition of the research problem. Program knowledge, however, is even more necessary for establishing credibility with program managers, for understanding the language they speak and the way that they think about problems. When a researcher reveals an obvious or persistent ignorance of the details of the program, the administrator asks himself or herself, "How can he understand the problem if he doesn't know the program?" The question is one of credibility.

Intramural and Extramural Research

The need for familiarity with program requirements and personnel also has a bearing on the relative advantages of the in-house social researcher, as a member of the permanent staff of the agency, versus the outside consultant or contractor. In terms of knowledge of the program and legislative and political limitations and constraints, the in-house staff member is usually in a better position to understand the dimensions of the problem and to deal with management.

Continuity of purpose and of personnel are also major considerations in the development of an agency research unit (Merriam, 1972). Effective program and policy research involves a sustained building process; it requires the continuing attention of a core staff that can stay with the job and maintain and transmit an institutional memory. Not least among these considerations is a familiarity with the operating and policy personnel in the program agency. The opportunity to develop close working relationships with management facilitates planning, the exchange of information, and a mutual understanding of program and research objectives.

Extramural research has an important place in government policy research functions. It can provide specialized skills or resources not available to the agency staff. University and private contractors usually have more flexibility in staffing, budgeting, and planning. For some projects, an outside organization may be needed to provide objective evaluation or a critical overview. The development of a productive extramural research program, however, requires a strong in-house staff. The agency research group is in a better position to determine what projects have relevance for the policy process and to monitor and collaborate with the extramural research projects in assuring that policy objectives are met. In my view, extramural research programs are effective only in partnership with a competent intramural staff.

Policy Guidance and the Limitations of Social Research

While a great deal of lip service is paid to the need for guidance from policy and program people, the fact is that policy people are in fact rarely able to specify their concerns in a way that is directly useful for the research process. Policy and program people tend to be tied up with the concerns of the moment and to look at problems in a different way than researchers. Administrators turning to social research for answers usually want the answers to last week's problems today. Given adequate time for development, data collection, data processing, and analysis, a study commissioned to answer a specific and pressing concern rarely fulfills its immediate purpose—possibly one of the major causes of the apparently widespread disappointment with social science research so extensively noted in the literature (Weiss, 1980).

Some analysts believe that the findings of social science seem to come after, rather than before, changes in policy. Henry Aaron suggests that political events may influence scholars more than research influences policy (Weiss, 1980). Weiss (1980, p. 15) also points out the intrinsically political nature of public policy and the simplistic standards used in judging the impact of research on policy: "They expect research to be authoritative and potent enough to alter the direction of specific decisions in obvious ways, and they expect it to supersede the play of political forces and partisan interests in the bargaining over decisions. The implicit image is decision maker as fresh blotter: the decision maker is expected to soak up all relevant research. An even better metaphor might be decision maker as fresh stencil. Social science research imprints its message, and the decision maker is expected to transfer it to the stack of blank pages awaiting his action."

In fact, rarely is a single official solely responsible for any major decision, and rarely is a decision made quickly and unilaterally. Decision making in major program and policy areas is an elephantine process involving interactions among agencies, within agencies, across departments, between departments and the executive office, and among the departments, executive office, and legislative staffs. Decisions in a policy or program setting can be said to accrete like pearls, rather than to be made. The social scientist has an opportunity to add one more set of factors or constraints to the gradually accumulating layers of language, opinions, views, and politics.

The purpose for which a social research study is undertaken may also be different for the policy maker than for the researcher.

The policy maker may use research for a variety of purposes: to reinforce commitment to a decision; to reduce uncertainties; to persuade or neutralize critics; to bolster supporters; to shift responsibility for a decision elsewhere; or to legitimate decisions already made on other grounds (Weiss, 1980). Research studies, like the programs they support, may also have latent as well as manifest functions.

Discounting some of the criticism of social science research by attributing it to unrealistic expectations still leaves one with "the nagging suspicion that, even with more reasonable expectations, research is not being used as widely or as well as it might profitably be" (Weiss, 1980, p. 15).

Education and Anticipation as Policy Research Functions

As I mentioned earlier, I would consider the two major functions of sociologists to be educational and archival. First, they try to introduce a mode of thinking, a vocabulary, and an analytical approach to the definition of the research problem. Through the exchange of information and expertise, they seek to understand the concerns, constraints, and limitations under which the program and policy people work and to communicate interpretations or definitions of the problem.

Second, the archival function of policy research involves anticipating policy questions rather than simply responding to problems as they are raised. To be effective in a policy setting, the findings or data should be available or accessible at the early stages of policy formulation. Facts or findings known at the start of policy review can help to set the universe of discourse and the boundaries of consideration. Findings produced as a result of policy process are more likely to focus on specification and refinement of the question.

Moynihan (1980, p. 1) cites a comment by Walter Lippmann that is illustrative of the use of statistics in determining social perceptions of need: "The printing of comparative statistics of infant mortality is often followed by a reduction of the death rates of babies. Municipal officials and voters did not have, before publication, a place in their picture of the environment for those babies. The statistics made them visible, as visible as if the babies had elected an alderman to air their grievances." Often the most valuable function that policy studies can perform is to point out the existence of a problem or a nonproblem or to place upper and lower limits on the size or scope of a recognized problem. For example, no more than x or less than y million people would be affected by a particular action or benefit. Or, under one of two given sets of circumstances, more people are likely to do this than to do that, to be eligible, to apply, or to use a benefit or service. Answers to questions of how, why, and what if may or may not be available from existing research. The data that are available are more likely to enter into the thinking, planning, and basic policy development than into the research developed in response to the policy questions. Rarely is a new research undertaking available in time to answer the kinds of policy and program questions posed for immediate action. Fortunately or unfortunately, major policy questions tend to be enduring themes in the development of major government programs and policies. The research developed for one period of policy review becomes part of the archive for the next cycle of consideration.

Organizational Relationships

From my own perspective, I have always tried to view the work role of the social analyst in a policy setting as a form of contractual relationship with a client. This contractual relationship has three components: "paying the rent," "earning your pay," and "having some fun." "Paying the rent" consists of giving the client what was asked for, within the limits of feasibility. The concerns tend to be the narrowest and most immediate. "Earning your pay" includes a redefinition of the problem to encompass not only the immediate questions raised but also more basic policy questions and considerations. I regard this redefinition as the basic professional responsibility of the policy researcher. "Having some fun" is both a form of play and a payback to the discipline of the social sciences as a by-product of the research. This component attempts to relate policy research to the field of sociology by setting up an interaction between practical concerns and sociological concepts and issues. It assists the researcher in maintaining intellectual contact with areas of interest and can provide a lively mixture of survival, professional responsibility, and personal involvement.

Summary

In conclusion, I will repeat my earlier statement that, with all its limitations and ambiguities, there is a useful and meaningful role for sociologists in policy research within federal agencies. There are certainly problems and conflicts about the role, and there is no standard on what a reasonable level of expectation is for the social sciences. Archimedes said, "Give me a place to stand and I will move the earth." Where we stand, as sociologists, is not a firm enough place to move the earth. It may, however, be solid enough to dislodge rocks and uproot stumps. I am sufficiently optimistic about the future of the social sciences to anticipate that there will be improvements in sociological theory and methodology that could enhance the utility of sociology for policy research.

References

HALPERT, H. H.
  1973 "Research utilization, a problem in goal-setting: What is the question?" *American Journal of Public Health* 63(5):377-378.

MERRIAM, I. C.
  1972 "Social security research: The relation of research and policy planning in a government agency." *Journal of Social Policy* 1(4):289-303.

MOYNIHAN, D. P.
  1980 "Introduction to the statistical abstract centennial." In U.S. Bureau of the Census, *Reflections of America.* Washington, D.C.: U.S. Government Printing Office.

WEISS, C. H.
  1980 *Social Science Research and Decision Making.* New York: Columbia University Press.

❧ 9 ❧

LEGISLATIVE CONSULTATION

Joseph R. Blasi

The purpose of this chapter is to describe one work role of an applied sociologist in the U.S. Congress. Hopefully, through a more detailed understanding of individual roles, applied sociologists can become more comfortable with practicing sociology in nonacademic settings. A recipe, a theory, a general model, is not suggested. The role of the applied sociologist in the Congress is too new, too innovative, and too dependent on factors that have not yet been institutionalized to allow recipe knowledge to be of much assistance.

A theory is not applicable at this time for several reasons. No conceptual framework seems to be at work here other than the one that guides us generally in understanding the role of a helping outsider in a large, complex organization. I am not eager to generalize from one case or to recap theories of process consultation and organizational change agents. A general model is also inappropriate because it might suggest the existence of factors whose interaction is predictable. The most powerful generalization I can offer from this experience is that the chemistry of personality between individuals, the cooperative style of collaboration in a group, and the degree of trust between team members are of paramount importance in ensuring a successful consultation role once agreement is reached on the sphere or topic of influence. Successful consultants would prefer to describe their behavior, view their successes and failures, and then universalize the implications of their actions by ascribing them to formal aspects of organizations, the power of their ideas, and grand theories of intervention rather than risk diminishing their egocentric view and their status among others by simply admitting the role of personal chemistry, chance, styles of cooperative collaboration, and feelings of trust. Explanations that professionals often do not like can account for the role of the applied sociologist.

Setting for Legislative Consultation

For four years, from 1976 to 1980, I served as an adviser on social policy for a young congressman. The congressman's constituency was conservative on fiscal issues and fairly liberal on foreign policy questions and human rights. During this period, I spent two days to one week per month in Washington, while maintaining research duties at Harvard. It was a part-time position, and legislative and administrative assistants on the congressman's staff did not perceive the position as a threat to their own.

The task was limited to certain topics: legislative education and encouragement of worker ownership of businesses as a job preservation and job creation strategy in both new and declining communities through federal enabling legislation.

A regular legislative aide is a generalist who must deal with many complex issues at the same time, usually under the strain of the congressional calendar, political pressures from the congressperson's district and from national pressure groups, and the unpredictable press of national public opinion. The media creates magical issues that, for reasons of intercongressperson competition and the illusion of responding to such so-called citizen interests, must eat up an aide's time.

In the office of a young congressperson, this problem is intensified. Because the member at the beginning of his or her career has unimportant junior committee assignments (which do not entitle him or her to a committee staff), the member's regular staff must do scheduling, press and political relations, casework with constituents, research, management of events and legislation on the floor of the Congress or in committee, office organization, personal advising to the member, and relations with other offices on the Hill and in the Executive Office. A congressperson who is "young" in his or her term may therefore have only two to four real legislative aides who do creative work. The rest mainly answer mail, do press work, and do casework with constituents. Given the pressures of a permanent campaign, very little creative social policy work actually takes place.

One can distinguish careful research and study from what passes as serious social policy work in many members' offices. Instead of careful research and study, the following are examples of social policy work undertaken with less than serious consideration: generalists who are superficially fast on their feet, knowing and, in cursory fashion, following the major issues and developments of a topic; staff members serving as conduits (at almost every step of the social policy process I have described) for political supporters and pressure groups or (in media-created situations) as passive pipelines for others' work; and the determination of the least risky stand likely to maximize short-term political gain on an issue deemed urgent by external forces (this process is called politics by reaction).

Aspects of Legislative Consultation and Stages of Involvement

The story has been told elsewhere (Whyte and Blasi, 1980) of how William Foote Whyte, Corey Rosen, and I, from 1976 to 1979, attempted to get legislation passed on employee ownership of companies in order to bring this issue to the attention of Congress and the country. In the early 1970s, Senator Russell Long proposed and passed several laws to encourage employee stock ownership of companies (ESOPs), utilizing the ideas of Louis Kelso and Norman Kurland. The new worker ownership initiative was unique in its emphasis on majority worker-owned firms, job creation and job preservation, community economic development,

the union role in employee ownership, and the importance of research on worker participation and the quality of working life
(QWL) for the success of such firms. Other key actors in this continuing initiative were Long's aides Jack Curtis and Jeff Gates. The
Whyte and Blasi article just mentioned was written shortly before
the Small Business Employee Ownership Act of 1980 (Title V of
the Small Business Development Act of 1980, Public Law 96–302)
became law, and the testing of democratic models of worker ownership has continued (see Whyte and Blasi, 1981; Blasi and Whyte,
1981; Blasi, Mehrling, and Whyte, 1982). Political scientist Corey
Rosen, who staffed the Senate Small Business Committee, was responsible for the Senate initiatives; since then, he has created the
National Center for Employee Ownership in Arlington, Virginia, a
major resource center and research organization that shares the
policy field with the ESOP Association of Washington, D.C., the
Industrial Cooperative Association of Somerville, Massachusetts,
and the Philadelphia Association for Cooperative Enterprise
(PACE).

In describing legislative consultation, the following stages
will be considered: liaison and liaison maintenance, entry and the
work itself, and exit and follow-up. Several aspects of legislative
consultation will prove helpful in clarifying problems at each stage:
formal versus informal processes; a cooperative network approach
versus an executive-individual approach; substance versus process;
inside Congress versus outside Congress (and the coordination of
the congressional work flow with consultant assistance); and research versus politics. Admitting the tensions in each of these aspects of legislative consultation and learning to manage them was
an important part of this process at every stage.

Liaison and Liaison Maintenance

A network of friends, contacts, and associates is helpful in
unblocking critical barriers in a social science career. Unfortunately, except in rare moments, people are not willing to admit the influence of such fortuitous events and personal contacts on their career. Consultants must prove that they were brought in because of
their brilliance, superior skill, inherent value, or the power of their
ideas. In fact, the greater the influence of events that are really

network-based and about which the public could have little knowledge, the more the consultant feels the need to prove or explain those events with more lofty explanations. The most successful consultants—especially social scientists who desperately need more status than a teaching and journal publication career can deliver—engage in this game of delusion with their comrades and colleagues, pretending that their work is all substance and no process. In fact, this may at least partly explain why so few social scientists break into applied work. Successful applied sociologists become an upper class of the profession who mystify knowledge of how they got there.

Liaison maintenance and liaison work have value for creating options for entry into the applied field. A scholar first needs to regularly review newspapers and information sources on national and state legislatures to learn about the special interests of legislators and committees and about press-created and real public opinion. Time must be invested to meet legislators and staffs. Volunteering to be an issues manager early in someone's campaign is an easy way to gain early access. A scholar should keep an up-to-date mailing list of all such contacts and their interests and regularly send papers, idea pieces, exploratory letters, bright suggestions, and so on.

One should have the *National Directory of Addresses and Telephone Numbers* (Nichols Publishing Company, 1977), which, among other things, includes all major and minor newspaper, TV, radio, and magazine addresses and phone numbers and similar information on federal, state, and local government agencies. When an issue arises in which one has competence, one can effectively use the telephone to talk to the involved parties and, using the *National Directory* and one's university press office, issue a press release to national and appropriate local press agencies. One should have a copy of the *Congressional Directory,* the *White House Staff Book,* and a directory of the federal agencies most appropriate to one's interests, such as the annual *Government Directory* available to the congressional staffs. In addition, one should have the *State Legislative Directory,* the *Governor's Office Directory,* and relevant state agency information books. A copy of the *Almanac of American Politics* (Gambit Inc. Publishers, 1974) is also very useful, along with a complete list of the staff members of one's congressional representative and senators. With these resources, if one has an idea, it can be quickly directed to the appropriate persons.

The American Sociological Association should help sociologists obtain these resources, and *ASA Footnotes* should regularly carry cut-out resource sheets on key national legislative, executive, and media contacts in particular areas of sociological interest.

More important, however, is developing personal connections and acquaintances. Legislatures, especially of a national scope, are time-scarce settings, and people rely on very small amounts of time to conduct business that is large in importance, quantity, and intensity and often depends on a sense of rapport. When a scholar finds that a legislator needs help on a certain topic, personal chemistry with that person's staff member may be more important than the quality of the relationship with the legislator.

Making one's work available to national associations and task forces as well as to interested members of the press is quite important and requires time and attention to detail to find, for example, which reporters are most interested in juvenile delinquency or which tend to cover such stories for major news outlets. One should have ready at all times, on xeroxed address labels, the addresses of the top fifty U.S. newspapers, so that ideas, pieces, or completed analyses of research can be quickly sent to the editors of opinion and editorial sections. To be sure, such aspects of liaison maintenance and liaison are time-consuming and do not jibe with the solitary days of statistical analysis, reading, teaching, and creative thought of many scholars. Scholars do waste a lot of time, and an occasional venture outside the ivory tower can be quite beneficial. A secretary is often required if one is to take advantage of most opportunities to establish and maintain legislative liaison.

Therefore, the social scientist interested in public involvement considers an informal contact to a legislator more valuable than many public policy seminars and mailing lists. A fortuitous "in" can replace months of such leg work. Remember, legislators and their staffs are short on time to reach out to anyone, yet they too are looking for ways to meet people and to find talents and ideas without endlessly reading mail and sifting through journals. (Nevertheless, smart aides realize that only the tip of the iceberg of quality ideas and research ever arrives at their desk, and they develop a healthy curiosity.) One can call almost any state or federal government agency or reporter and request that they call back on an available WATTS line.

Sociologists are not taught the skills to engage in such behavior and may have few role models. They focus on publications that seldom reach legislators because of the irrelevant style of scientific sociology and its lack of concern for clear writing about its complex methodologies. One of the best ways to gain access to a series of good contacts is to methodically share contacts and experiences with a network of colleagues. Sociologists, however, may focus on an executive-individual approach to knowledge generation, where each person's finished product competes in the marketplace. Concern with the substance of one's ideas divorced from a concern with the process by which ideas get disseminated, used, evaluated, and applied is responsible for the serious suffering of some who feel they must leave academia in order to be relevant. Sociology departments aid and abet irrelevance and generally do not include in their course of studies information on the social policy apparatus surrounding each facet of society. I am now working on a specific plan for individual sociology departments and the ASA to stimulate the approach to social policy and legislative consultation discussed in this chapter. It differs from the traditional impressions (mentioned earlier) of social policy work in assumptions, practice (especially in the emphasis on theoretical grounding, which I view as paramount), and my wariness of the loss of objectivity and the opportunism of full-time, "hired gun" sociologists.

Entry and the Work Itself

I entered the congressional office through contact with an old high school friend who had also been a political colleague of a family member in later years. When the congressman got elected, he and his administrative assistant expected to create great legislative achievements. After nine months of work, they began to realize that their office was mired in the routine described earlier in this chapter, and they decided to ask for some proposals on social policy initiatives. The process of negotiation was difficult because members of congress seek short-term projects that have immediate media or political advantage. Usually they are interested in the serious work of a scholar only if it helps them buttress a point or win an argument.

Despite the personal connections, there was an extensive initial process in which I submitted legislative ideas and suggested topics for research. It took six months to negotiate a position because I insisted on having enough lead time to prepare a serious project. Members of Congress want proposals more than they want research; they want something they can introduce on the floor of Congress in a speech, write a press release about, or connect to a major issue. Entry was successful because of the time spent exploring the congressman's real political needs. One should independently assess whether such needs can be met by the various topics of substance one submits and whether they overlap with one's real interests. Opportunism is a cancer for seriousness. It is best to make this assessment process explicit in negotiations and in reporting one's progress in ripening an idea for a member of Congress.

One can readily see that the informal process of ongoing conversation with other members of the staff, namely, taking the time to really get acquainted, is the only way for the consultant to discover what real political "sets of accounts" surround his or her issue. This process is time-consuming, but it is important to get to know—and hopefully like—members of a congressperson's office and somehow take one's place in the association that exists there. Most of the important decisions in the worker ownership initiative were taken as asides to social occasions or general banter. The traditional social policy consultant usually leaves the setting before this process begins. This chapter, however, distinguishes between a legislative consulting role that only gives information and one that is actually involved in the ongoing "stages of action" of formulating a new social policy. In response to the high pressure in Congress, people like to conduct serious business in the least formal way, as a safety valve.

In entering the office and developing all phases of the action on the worker ownership issue and bills, I used a collaborative-network approach, which is the normal operating procedure learned from William Foote Whyte. Whyte worked as an orchestrator of research and contacts in the academic network around the country. He paid attention to these contacts, which dovetailed with his consultant role. In turn, his consultant role made him pay attention to the series of actions that had to be taken in Congress, to the required work of substance and how it was to be formulated, communicated, and phrased, as well as to the kinds of crucial questions that arose and the way that a research process could provide answers to those questions.

A major advantage of the style we developed was the coordination of our initiatives with the work flow of the congressman's office. As the inside staff adviser, I always knew the pulse of the office and the precise stage of the initiative. I could judge which actions by Whyte and others in the network were likely to be most helpful, influential, and timely. This contrasts with the vague, hopeless, coincidental approach of many sociologists, who drop in for a chat or testify at hearings without any sense of the significance or insignificance of their actions. Perhaps the team of an inside adviser and an outside consultant, a senior sociologist and a junior sociologist, best copes with this problem.

Both researchers voluntarily gave regular biweekly (if not weekly) progress reports to interested persons. Members of the congressman's staff and other congressional aides who were part of the informal team as well as interested academics and citizens were regularly invited to provide evidence, plans, and criticism of ideas. The technology of the modern congressional office, with WATS and federal government telephone lines, facilitated this interaction.

Within the congressman's office, collaborative reporting by the consultant (especially of when and how we would move from one "stage of action" to the next and of what had been accomplished in the previous phase) was important to maintain office support of the initiative and allow those with varied experience on the congressman's staff to sense problems and act as early-warning aids.

One may wonder about the congressperson's role in this welter of activity. He or she is formally viewed as the executive of the office; however, so much goes on that the congressperson becomes rather a chairperson who monitors the process for serious problems or disagreements with his or her basic political philosophy or needs.

The legislative consultant should insist on a direct relationship with the member of Congress—that is, on not having to go through aides to approach the member of Congress, while at the same time working collegially with those aides and learning to take up the congressperson's time only when absolutely necessary. The applied sociologists in Congress are really the tutors of the members of Congress. However, the member must first be interested enough to have a tutor and committed enough to go through with all phases of the initiative.

The collaborative approach—in contrast to the executive-individual approach—means that, to tutor a member of Congress, one must, because of office politics and the degree of decentralization in such offices, tutor the whole office. This role is not what the sociologist may dream of as consulting, but it is significant. One dreams of pearls of wisdom falling on adoring subjects, with no need for leg work, acquaintanceship, persuasion, or dirty details. Several factors influence one's capacity to retain commitment from the member of Congress, and one should work hard to pay simultaneous attention to these factors: personal rapport and ongoing tutoring; collaboration with the staff; the perceived thoroughness of one's ability to approach the subject of the study and the initiative and the care taken in planning each "stage of action"; the degree of attention given by the press and by persons whose opinion and status the member of Congress respects; and the connection between the issue and constituency politics. One should avoid the politicization of research or rank corruption and subjective manipulation of a scholarly perspective by the following means: write as many speeches on the subject as possible, and work hard at communicating the complexity of the topic and the evidence and interpretations the research will reveal (in understandable English); see hearings not as beauty shows but as research interviews—prepare hard questions and encourage a wide range of witnesses; rely on the less involved, corrective perspective of a colleague in the academy (in this case, William Foote Whyte) who does not work for the office as a paid adviser but can be an essential and more distant participant in the project; and rely on the academic network for support and criticism and on feedback from a group of advisers to other Congresspersons with whom you are collaborating. The close connection with an outside colleague provides checks and balances against the possible compromising of an applied sociologist.

Two aspects of the role do not fit neatly into this outline:

personal processing and the redefinition of the consultant's role. At critical moments, I found myself talking out personal differences, airing feelings, setting relationships aright, paying attention to hurt individuals, and so on. Many consultants take for granted the basis of fellowship and sense of honest human relationship that is an elemental foundation of successful consultation. Those who are more willing to engage in this kind of personal processing in business and work settings may be aware of its ability to change the nature of both the research and the political process. If you respect people (or try to), they are more willing to search for answers and collaborate in a decision-making process. The legislative consultant, to be successful, must have the skills of a therapist and conflict resolver.

The consultant's role in this setting is unique. I was not a full-time or permanent staff member. I was responsible for one issue only, but my responsibilities transcended the traditional approach of "You ask me questions, I give you answers, and then you apply it." A departure from this role was necessary for several reasons. First, congresspersons have no lack of information, but, as pointed out earlier, their offices have an inherent inability to organize information coherently and carefully. Second, it is of little value for a member of Congress to pay for information only, since he or she can usually get it free from agencies, eager liaison offices, or the Library of Congress's Congressional Research Service (CRS). They prefer a package that includes the research, an analysis of how it relates to their political philosophy, to their constituents, to other politicians, and to their image in the press; and a plan to take it through the phases of legislative initiative. This package is something the applied sociologist can offer that is hard to obtain elsewhere, especially on a congressperson's staff, which may be unable to deal with a certain issue.

A third reason for departing from the traditional role is that members of Congress use academics and then deride them after taking their services in spot situations. In contrast, they develop respect when an academic is willing to share the burden of the political process. The "stages of action" enumerated require a continuous research process throughout and benefit from ongoing scholarly input. In the worker ownership initiative, research questions were raised continuously in each phase. Students and colleagues in an already formed network on worker ownership fed material to the office at no cost in overhead funds or administrative complication. The legislative consultant presents himself or herself as likely to have a multiplier effect in bringing resources to bear on a problem. As research budgets are squeezed, this factor may become more important to both parties.

Fourth, modern communication technology allows one to broaden one's role while working only a few days per month. While I was in Washington, the use of a WATS line and the highly automated congressional office made networking easy. While at the university, I was able to call any office on the Hill using an FTS telephone line, which allowed for occasional consultation in lieu of travel to Washington.

The applied sociologist role is for the still-functioning university sociologist, for one who has part-time employment, or for one who is in the process of leaving the academy. Congressional offices cannot afford to pay high consulting fees to long-term advisers. If one charges the Congress only for Washington-based time and really mounts an aggressive initiative, the offer of a consulting role can be very beneficial to a legislative office. One final note: it is best to choose a consulting topic that you already work with extensively and not expect the kinds of consulting fees big industry pays.

Exit and Follow-up

Abundant resources are available to an ongoing adviser on a congressperson's staff, including opportunities for acquiring understanding, data, academic contacts, sources, useful materials, possibilities to visit important sites of the idea under study, and material for later writing and research projects. In fact, one does not realize that the process of consulting, when combined with significant time for further reflection and reading at a later period, can itself represent a major stage in researching a topic.

The people, documents, information, case studies, evaluation procedures, and opportunities for implementation that were available to me in my work on the issue of worker ownership firms have provided a significant contribution to my teaching, my work with students, and my research—a contribution that represents far more resources than I could have mustered in twice the time and effort as an isolated, nonapplied sociologist.

Exit and follow-up mean digesting the experience away from ever-present political considerations and practical decisions about "stages of action" and creating a new research agenda. In some instances, one finds evidence that objectivity has been lost and that one has gone beyond the best sources and analyses. For me, that discovery served as the basis of renewed questioning and analysis. For sociologists who do not have an academic home or teaching position and therefore view this advisory role as a permanent job, objectivity will be difficult indeed, and those who become full-time legislative assistants will be slowly socialized by the maddening pace in Congress. Sociology departments should be encouraged to purposely develop part-time positions called public service lecturers that would allow for the mix described in this chapter.

One aspect of follow-up which can be enjoyable is the role of commentator. Members of Congress, the press, government agencies, and others can use the reflections of applied sociologists who have returned to a quieter life of reflection.

Conclusion

The advisory role described in this chapter is suitable for increasing the congressional standing of sociologists who are not well known enough nationally to be called on to testify. Those who do testify at hearings and give formal advice on specific occasions really accomplish little. I support an involvement of sociologists in all "stages of action" of social policy in the legislative branch. The applied sociologist in Congress will encounter a more collegial approach to research than in the university. The itinerant scholar will see the sociology of knowledge firsthand and will be hard pressed to maintain rigorous rules of analysis while the political agendas and constructions of social reality continually try to interfere.

In a large lecture or even a medium-size seminar, a teacher cannot see how the students' illogical dispositions, psychological problems, and inordinate needs are constantly interfering with the search for truth. In a tutorial, these forces are available for all to see and must be actively engaged, for they share the room with the tutor and the student. This is also the challenge of legislative consultation, and, like good teaching when the substance of ideas and research methodology can be taken for granted, it is mainly a matter of how much personal effort and sensitivity the imperfect teacher can muster and how carefully thought out are his or her strategies for enlightening others.

I am now developing a list of recommendations for departments of sociology on how to use this model, as well as a curriculum that uses the worker ownership initiative archives as a teaching case study. The worker ownership initiative was based on an analysis of the American government—namely, that there is a need to innovate decentralized, self-reliant, cooperative models of job creation—and on a clear set of values—extending democracy into the work place, favoring local control over economic development, and building work places which have the potential for improving work life. This analysis and these values interacted with the political needs of the congressperson's office and with what the Congress in general and the public in particular were willing to tolerate, given the signs of the times.

References

BLASI, J. R., MEHRLING, P., AND WHYTE, W. F.
    1982   "The politics of worker ownership in the United States."
            In *The International Yearbook of Organizational Democracy for Participation, Cooperation, and Power.*
            New York: Wiley.
BLASI, J. R., AND WHYTE, W. F.
    1981   "Employee ownership and self-management in legislation and social policy." Paper presented to the social policy seminar in Toronto, Canada.
GAMBIT INC. PUBLISHERS.
    1974   *Almanac of American Politics.* Ipswich, Mass.: Gambit.
NICHOLS PUBLISHING COMPANY.
    1977   *National Directory of Addresses and Telephone Numbers.* New York: Nichols.
WHYTE, W. F., AND BLASI, J. R.
    1980   "From research to legislation in respect to employee ownership firms." *Economic and Industrial Democracy* 1(3):395–416.
    1981   "Worker ownership participation and control: Toward a theoretical model." *Policy Sciences,* December.

🎜 10 🎜

HEALTH SERVICE
ADMINISTRATION
IN GOVERNMENT

Rosemary Yancik

As an administrator and extramural research program director, I work in the Division of Resources, Centers, and Community
Activities (DRCCA), one of five divisions in the National Cancer
Institute, which, in turn, is one of the eleven institutes of the National Institutes of Health. As a sociologist in this work setting, I
have been primarily concerned with projects that involve: problems of emotional stress and coping behavior of cancer patients,
their families, and health care providers; terminal care; the effects
of old age on cancer prevention and treatment; health behavior
and illness behavior; and technology transfer.

Generalizations about the role of sociologist as government

Note: The views expressed in this paper are solely those of the author,
who, at the time of the workshop, was a program director in DRCCA. She is
now a special assistant to the director of DRCCA, NCI. This paper was written for the purpose of describing the role of an applied sociologist in a federal
agency to colleagues in the discipline of sociology. No official support or endorsement by DRCCA is intended or should be inferred.

152

executive are difficult to make. My work experience is not necessarily identical with the experiences of other sociologists who work in other federal agencies, and my assigned responsibilities and duties also differ from those of other persons in my discipline in different areas of the Department of Health and Human Services (DHHS), in other institutes, or even within NCI. However, those of us who are program or research administrators commonly perform our work in an interdisciplinary setting and share the fundamental objective of government-sponsored health research— to maintain a tradition of excellence in scientific research through peer review.

In this chapter, I describe my work as a government projects manager in the extramural program in the NIH. My perspective is that of a medical sociologist interested in applying social science principles and techniques to efforts to improve health. I briefly discuss the NIH context and the NIH staff role in general and then define my work role in a particular division in the National Cancer Institute, with reference to my specific substantive interests in cancer prevention and treatment. After making some final remarks on the multidisciplinary nature of the work performed, I provide some comments on the attraction of an applied work setting.

NIH Work Context

NIH is a biomedical research establishment devoted to acquiring new knowledge to help prevent, detect, diagnose, and treat disease. NIH supports extramural research in universities, medical schools, hospitals, and research institutions in this country and abroad and conducts intramural research in its own laboratories and clinics. NIH also seeks to apply research findings to the care of patients and to transferring such advances to the health care system by way of technology transfer (for example, consensus conferences and demonstration projects).

As an organizational entity, NIH is a component of the Public Health Service, and it is one of several agencies responsible to the assistant secretary for health in the Department of Health and Human Services (DHHS) (see Figure 1). A unique health research system with a diversified program in major disease categories, NIH is the largest basic and clinical research facility in the world and is

Figure 1. Organizational Structure of DHHS.

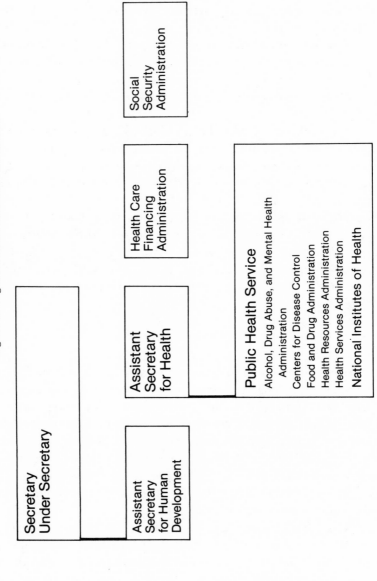

comprised of eleven research institutes as well as additional research support components (see Figure 2).

In general, all institutes are similarly organized into an extramural and an intramural program. Each institute supports extramural research projects with grants and contracts mechanisms. Intramural research, both laboratory studies and clinical investigations, are conducted directly within the institute. Figure 3 shows the major component programs of a typical institute.

In Figure 4, the separate but equally important work roles of review, program, and grants and contracts management staff are identified. As a member of the DRCCA program staff, I perform in what I have labeled work role B, developing program initiatives related to increasing the effectiveness of cancer control activities on a national scale.

A program director is the predominant person in the triad of roles when scientific content is concerned. Review staff members ensure that the research applications are evaluated for scientific and technical merit, and grants and contracts management staff members handle business considerations and evaluations.

Division of Resources, Centers, and Community Activities

NCI's Division of Resources, Centers, and Community Activities (DRCCA) has a technology transfer mandate to ensure that cancer research results are translated into use. DRCCA's cancer control mandate includes the responsibility to identify, field-test, evaluate, demonstrate, and promote the widespread application of available and new methods for reducing the mortality from cancer, as well as the disease's incidence and morbidity. Primary and secondary prevention, diagnosis, pretreatment evaluation, treatment, rehabilitation, and continuing care activities are included. The research and knowledge bases of the biomedical, clinical, behavioral, and social sciences and of epidemiology are utilized in conducting cancer control activities and research.

Work Roles in DRCCA

I joined NCI in November 1978 as part of a unit then called the Treatment, Rehabilitation, and Continuing Care Branch (TRCCB) of the Division of Cancer Control and Rehabilitation

Figure 2. Organizational Structure of NIH.

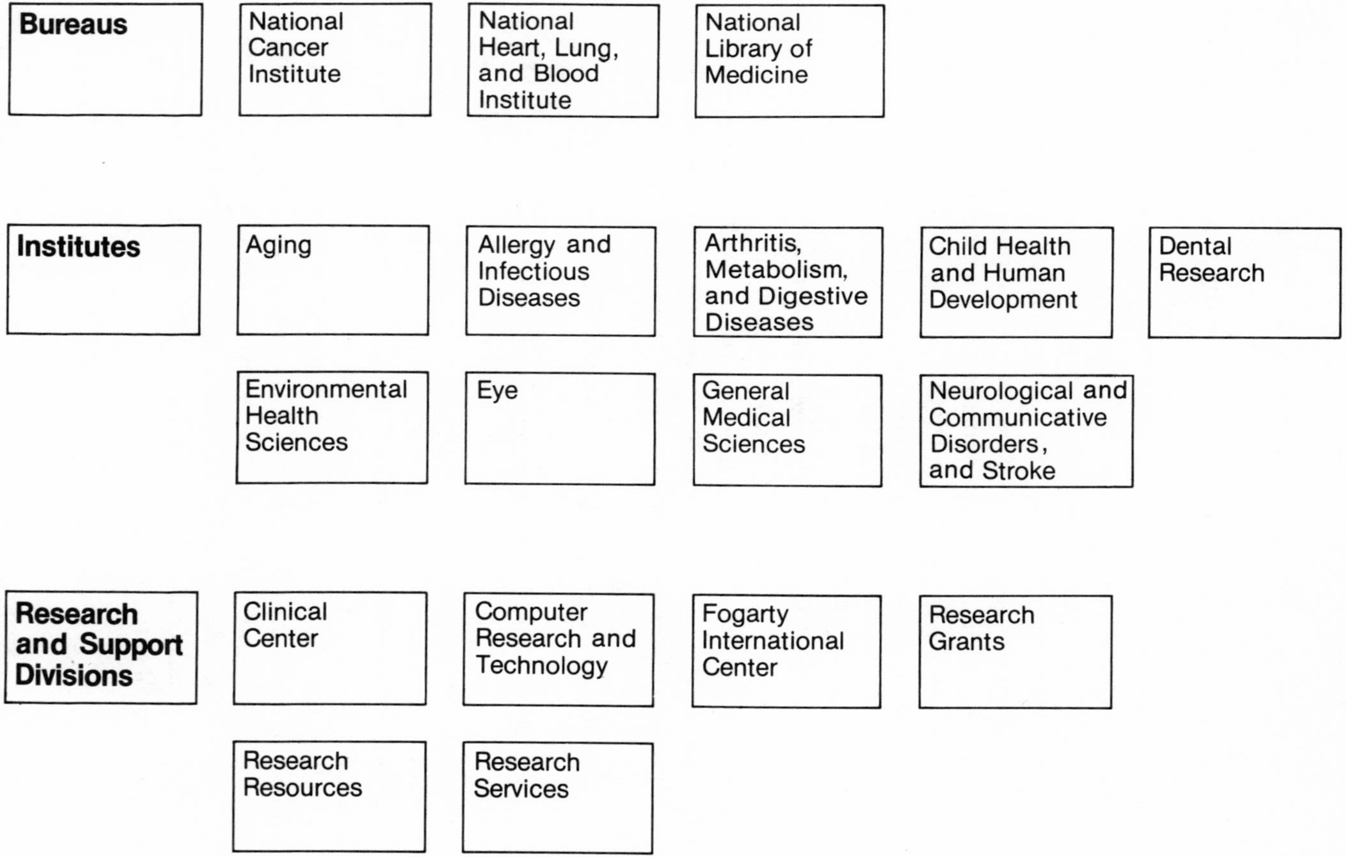

Bureaus

| National Cancer Institute | National Heart, Lung, and Blood Institute | National Library of Medicine | | Dental Research |

Institutes

| Aging | Allergy and Infectious Diseases | Arthritis, Metabolism, and Digestive Diseases | Child Health and Human Development |
| Environmental Health Sciences | Eye | General Medical Sciences | Neurological and Communicative Disorders, and Stroke |

Research and Support Divisions

| Clinical Center | Computer Research and Technology | Fogarty International Center | Research Grants |
| Research Resources | Research Services | | |

Source: U.S. Department of Health and Human Services (1980).

Figure 3. Program Activities of a Typical Institute.

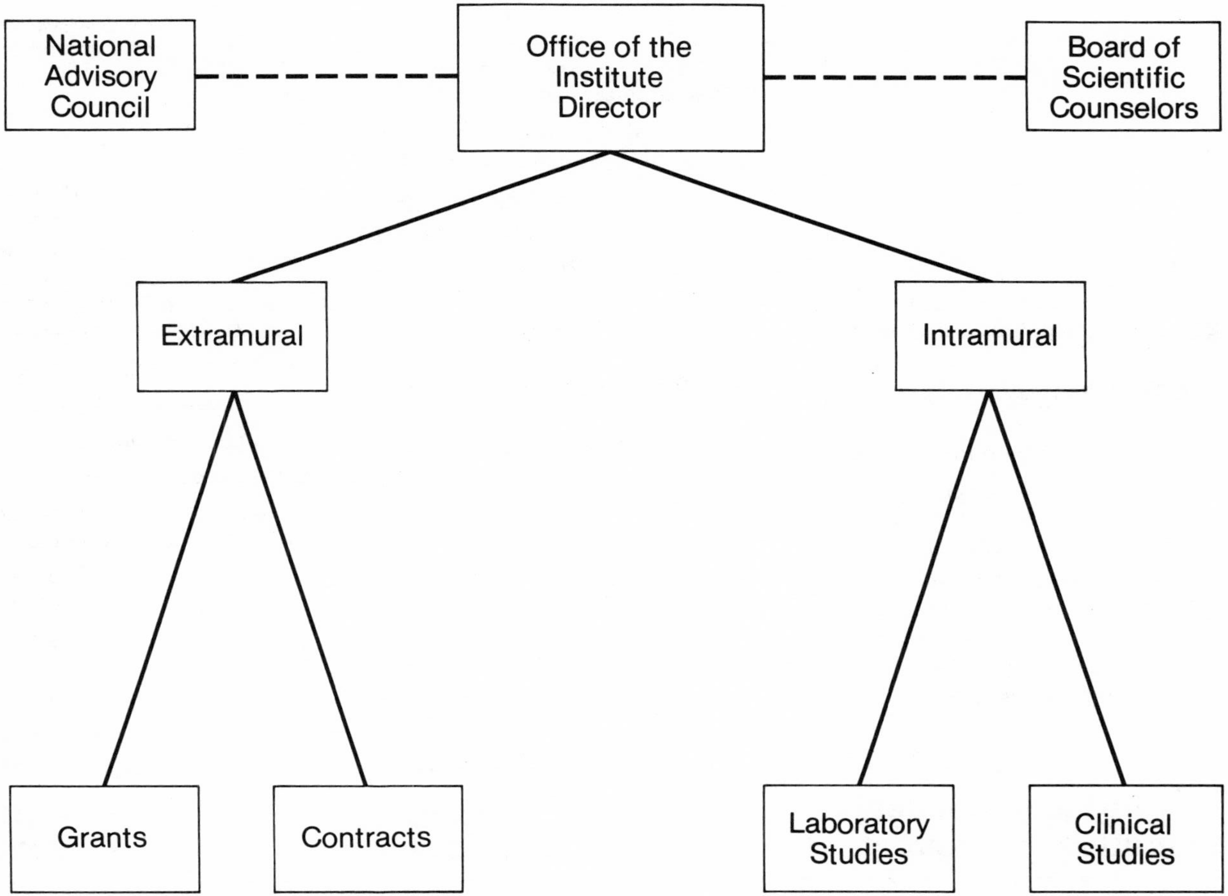

Source: U.S. Department of Health and Human Services (1980).

Figure 4. Essential Work Roles and Responsibilities of NIH Staff in Extramural Programs.

Review Staff	Program Staff	Grants and Contracts Management Staff
Work Role "A"	Work Role "B"	Work Role "C"
■ Nominate SRG members	■ Develop program initiatives	■ Provide business guidance to applicants and reviewers as necessary
■ Select ad hoc reviewers and site visitors	■ Provide guidance and assistance to applicants	■ Participate with program staff in budget negotiations prior to and following awards
■ Provide orientation for SRG members	■ Interpret program policy and guidelines for reviewers	■ Attend SRG meetings as resource person(s)
■ Explain and interpret NIH review policies and procedures	■ Attend scientific review group meetings as program resource person(s)	■ Maintain official grant and contract files
■ Assign review responsibilities	■ Present SRG recommendations to Council	■ Assist in developing program policy
■ Manage project site visits	■ Communicate results of review to applicants	■ Provide fiscal management of grants and contracts
■ Manage SRG meetings	■ Make award decisions	
■ Prepare summary statements	■ Participate in identifying prospective SRG and Council nominees	
■ Attend Council meetings to provide requested information in support of committee recommendations	■ Evaluate programs	
■ Communicate with program staff on review matters	■ Communicate with review staff on program matters	
	■ Monitor research progress during the award period	

*Scientific Review Group

Source: U.S. Department of Health and Human Services (1980).

(DCCR). My duties and responsibilities as program director for social science projects included addressing the psychosocial aspects of cancer as they contribute to more effective treatment, rehabilitation, and continuing care of the cancer patient and dealing with technology transfer concerns. Indeed, I was initially attracted to sociology because of a special interest in transferring medical research results into clinical practice, stemming from my early career days as a health professional.

The attraction of the NCI work setting for me was the opportunity to apply social-psychological concepts to cancer problems in prevention and treatment and to encourage acceptance of their relevance to clinical medicine. Social and psychological factors are believed to affect the occurrence and outcome of disease conditions; therefore, we must try to understand health behavior and illness behavior in relation to social structure and social processes. Clearly, I look at cancer prevention and care through a sociological filter. If we agree with David Mechanic (1972, p. 128) that the principal tasks of medicine are "to understand how symptoms and disease entities arise and occur in individuals or among groups of individuals; to recognize and cure these or to shorten their course and minimize any residual impairment; and to promote living conditions in human populations which eliminate hazards to health and thus prevent the occurrence of disease," then all medical activities require an understanding of the processes of human behavior that contribute to the efficacy of health and medical care.

Many general questions may be raised from the sociological perspective regarding health care and the prevention and treatment of disease. For example, what influences or prompts persons to protect their health; recognize that they need medical advice; seek care after discovering certain signs and symptoms; cooperate with medical regimens; remain in contact with the health care system; and adjust to the disease condition. The goal, with respect to cancer, is to determine how various social, cultural, and psychological factors enhance or attenuate the effects of cancer prevention, treatment, and care. More specifically, in treatment and care matters, adjusting to the strain of living with cancer and the various phases of the illness, adjusting to the side effects of treatment in terms of functional recovery and the quality of life, and dealing with the social and economic costs of the disease are of primary importance. From the standpoint of cancer prevention, how can we successfully modify certain behaviors known to be associated with the disease condition (for example, lung cancer and smoking) or increase the effectiveness of the health-monitoring behavior of individuals (for example, breast self-examination or other methods for perceiving the signs and symptoms of cancer)? And how can the practicing physician make effective contributions to the health promotion efforts of the client population?

Then, too, one or more family members (spouse, child, parent, or sibling) usually bear the stress of illness with the cancer patient. Pratt (1976) has pointed out that the role of the family in mobilizing health behavior, affecting the decision-making process, and providing health care has not been extensively explored. How does the structure of the professional medical care system incorporate efforts of the family to provide for their members' health care needs? I too think the family role in health promotion and health care has been largely ignored with regard to its potential for positive intervention. However, the hospice movement, with its philosophical orientation of responding to both patient and family needs, is beginning to provide some insights into the implications of including family members as part of the terminal care team (Yancik, 1980).

Other social science concepts in relation to cancer care and treatment may also be explored—life-styles; beliefs and attitudes about cancer, health, treatment, and medical care; social support; personality factors; work and occupational history; community contexts (that is, social structure); coping behavior in response to stress; and physician behavior in relation to patient outcome. These concepts are illustrative of the many processes that can be examined at the sociomedical interface to carry out our division's mission.

Multidisciplinary Functioning of NIH Staff

As far as I can determine, no community of sociologists exists within NIH or, for that matter, within the federal system, although, as sociologists, we do share common values and a common language. Work at NIH requires a multidisciplinary approach.

Boundaries between disciplines and professions are blurred by identification with the federal agency's organizational goal and mission established by congressional mandate and the suborganizational units created to accomplish them. The strongest sense of identity is shared with members of other disciplines and professions who work in the same context. The ideal of service to the agency, which clearly transcends disciplinary and professional boundaries, can present a problem to those of us who do not wish to lose touch with our own discipline. We must make a concerted effort to continue to be associated with our original field.

The subject matter of the work at NIH also promotes a multidisciplinary approach. For example, I have been working on a program initiative that will solicit research designed to improve delivery of care to patients who are in advanced stages of cancer. In addition to drawing on my knowledge of terminal care and hospice principles, I have chosen to consult with program staff physicians and nurses as well as several individuals working in the NIH Clinical Center. I will also utilize the recommendations of an interagency committee on terminal care and will feel free to seek assistance from any of the health professionals who once served on the committee. Quite possibly, no other sociologist will be asked to contribute to this work effort.

Another example, again from my own work experience, involved organizing a two-institute, cross-disciplinary, multiprofessional conference. September 21–23, 1981, the National Cancer Institute and the National Institute on Aging jointly sponsored a working conference entitled "Perspectives on Prevention and Treatment of Cancer in the Elderly." The meeting brought together geriatricians, oncologists, epidemiologists, and social scientists who work in the fields of cancer and aging. The goal was to explore the ways in which geriatric physicians and oncologists can make contributions toward resolving the problems of the elderly. Although the idea for this successful conference came from a sociologist who recognized the importance of looking at the impact of old age on cancer patient management (because over 50 percent of cancers occur in individuals aged sixty-five years and older), the dialogue was primarily between geriatric generalists and clinical oncology specialists. Both groups had to be initially convinced that the conference was a good idea. The next step was to get these busy professionals to make a commitment to write a paper and then attend the two-and-one-half day meeting. A great deal of creative persuasion was involved.

This experience illustrates an important point: to function as an applied sociologist, one must know one's work territory, whether it be science or industry; one must know its language and culture; and one must be able to communicate with the persons who work in that environment.

My world of work as a sociologist has always been in medicine. I entered sociology from a health professional background, I am comfortable in the medical sector, and, as I progress through my career, I continued to learn the language and substance of this field. Sometimes, my selections for education and training are extremely challenging. For example, two summers ago, I spent a week at the W. Alton Jones Science Center in Lake Placid, New York, learning about the histopathobiology of neoplasia. After the first day of looking through the microscope, I realized that one of my prime achievements by the end of the week would be to distinguish pathological and normal cell structures from an artifact of preparation of the slide. Recently I chose a more mainstream type of educational experience—I enrolled in an epidemiology course, since my work requires that I know about such things as hemoccult tests, mammography screening, staging for breast cancer, and the toxicity of some drugs in chemotherapy. Of course, every now and then, it is absolutely necessary to *bring sociology back in.*

Socialization Within NIH

The process of socialization and the notion of reference group, two central concepts in sociology, are applicable to this discussion. In the process of becoming an NIH employee, socialization is both explicit and intentional and, like all socialization, has both positive and negative consequences. For example, one may acquire in-depth knowledge of certain fields but lose contact with one's chosen discipline. In the process of socialization, one must adhere to certain rules and regulations and take certain special courses. Competent performance in the job requires learning the ways of the organization, as well as the substantive scientific content. Selective acquisition of the language, values, interests, knowledge, attitudes, and skills of the organization is both necessary and wise. Course work, communication and interaction with one's colleagues, and the demands of the work role all serve to transmit the professional culture of NIH.

The reference group of NIH colleagues serves a normative function in the sense described by Kelley (1952). That is, NIH sets and enforces standards and norms for behavior of program directors. There are formal guidelines for how one interacts with the outside research community and with NIH personnel in review and contracting positions. The NIH reference group also provides the perspective for how one perceives and functions in the work context in a more general sense (Hyman, 1942)—maintaining acceptance, judging one's growth and development in the position, and successfully learning the job requirements.

Medical Sociology as a Career Choice

It has never been a dilemma for me, as a medical sociologist, to move within the confines of the medical world, either in the present position at NIH or in previous positions at the Association of American Medical Colleges and the Gerontological Society of America (where the job involved working with the biologists and physicians of the society's biology and clinical medicine sections). I went into sociology as a health professional seeking a discipline that would give me the knowledge, theory, and methods to consolidate and organize for general use the information contained in medical records. From this concern evolved my interest in technology transfer and my involvement with NIH, NCI, and DRCCA.

Minor adjustments must be made to these various medical work environments, of course. Robert Straus (1957) described these adjustments as chameleonlike. Perhaps it is true that the survival of medical sociology in the medical care system depends on the ability of medical sociologists to change their outward appearance. I make my adaptation readily, for I must confess to harboring some rather lofty ideas about the prominence of our discipline —ideas that date back to Auguste Comte. I do not assume, like the first sociologist, that all knowledge must find practical application in society (even though I have chosen to focus my own work there). But, in concert with Comte, I do have rather high aspirations for the sociological consciousness or imagination to provide insights and understanding on health and medical issues where no other disciplines can.

References

HYMAN, H. H.
  1942   "The psychology of status." *Archives of Psychology* 38:15.
KELLEY, H. H.
  1952   "Two functions of reference groups." In T. Newcomb and others (Eds.), *Readings in Social Psychology*. New York: Holt, Rinehart and Winston.
MECHANIC, D.
  1972   "Response factors in illness: The study of illness behavior." In E. G. Jaco (Ed.), *Patients Physicians and Illness*. New York: Free Press.
PRATT, L.
  1976   *Family Structure and Effective Health Behavior: The Energized Family*. Boston: Houghton Mifflin.
STRAUS, R.
  1957   "The nature and status of medical sociology." *American Sociological Review* 22:200-204.
U.S. DEPARTMENT OF HEALTH AND HUMAN SERVICES
  1980   *Orientation Handbook for Members of Scientific Review Groups*. Washington, D.C.: National Institutes of Health.
YANCIK, R.
  1980   "Family stress and terminal illness in the hospice context." Paper presented at the annual meeting of the Gerontological Society of America, San Diego, Calif.

❦ 11 ❦

SOCIAL RESEARCH IN INDUSTRY

L. Carroll DeWeese III

I am employed as a staff research scientist in the Societal Analysis Department of General Motors Research Laboratories. In this chapter, I describe my general work environment as well as some of the characteristics needed by successful researchers in the Societal Analysis Department. In addition, I note opportunities available for researchers in the department.

Research Objectives

The General Motors Research Laboratories, a division of General Motors (GM), has the following objectives: (1) to generate new technical knowledge of commercial interest to GM; (2) to evaluate outside technical advances for possible application to GM products and processes; (3) to anticipate future technological needs and develop the expertise required to meet those needs; (4) to provide information for corporate priorities, policies, and operating programs; and (5) to contribute to the solution of problems that require the Laboratories' specialized facilities and personnel.

The job of the Research Laboratories is to insure that GM is not taken by technological surprise. Although the Research Laboratories sometimes handles short-term projects dealing with immediate, pressing technical problems, its primary emphasis is on long-range applied research that will provide a solid, scientific base for GM products, processes, and operations in the future.

The Laboratories is staffed by approximately 1500 persons —about 550 of whom are professionals in research and development. Over half those professionals have Ph.D.s, about three quarters are engineers, and only 5 percent are in the social sciences. Currently the Laboratories has four Ph.D.-level sociologists. Projects in the Laboratories include mechanical engineers working on specific car problems, biologists working on the effects of noxious emissions on rats, and theoretical mathematicians developing mathematical models for other researchers.

The professionals are backed up by over 800 technical and administrative services personnel who can supply almost any type of in-depth assistance. For example, anything from ultraclean rooms to first-of-a-kind instruments can be built for research projects at the self-sufficient fabrication facilities of the Laboratories. Computer facilities are virtually unlimited, and researchers are encouraged to use consultants, if necessary, and receive funding to attend conventions and academic courses that are relevant to their work. Many live or videotape courses in statistics, mathematics, communications, and technical subjects are offered in-house. Seminars are frequently provided to inform researchers about what is going on in other parts of the Laboratories and of GM.

Scope of Activities

Research done at General Motors Research Laboratories is "hard money" research, which means that researchers do not have to spend time trying to obtain grant money. Once projects are approved, the necessary financial support and facilities are available and approval is usually not too difficult to get. However, a person must be able to convince peers and management that a project is worthwhile. Research activities in the laboratories are reviewed regularly by a science advisory committee consisting of renowned scientists from the academic world who have meaningful input into the directions and quality of work performed at the Laboratories.

Salaries are on a par with academic salaries and include health, insurance, retirement, stock-sharing, and product discount benefits. Researchers are typically hired for career positions; no tenure decisions exist. Turnover is usually more a function of a researcher's desire to leave than of a decision by GM to let the researcher go.

Located in a campuslike complex just north of Detroit, the GM Research Laboratories is divided into about twenty departments organized by research area. Departments are grouped under a set of technical directors who are in turn grouped under an executive director reporting to the vice-president for research.

The mission of the Societal Analysis Department is to develop concepts and methodologies for quantifying the impact of GM on society as well as society's impact on GM. The department is very interdisciplinary—for example, I lead a group of Ph.D.s in applied math, economics, operations research, psychology, and sociology. The department also has a group of computer programmers and a third group led by a chemical engineer. The assistant department head is an economist, the department head is a physicist, and his superiors are a physicist, a chemical engineer, and a mechanical engineer.

Research in the Societal Analysis Department is generally interdisciplinary, problem-oriented, and quantitative. Research projects vary from those with short-range impacts to those with long-range effects. Researchers work to quantify the benefits, costs, and risks of air pollution, auto safety, diesel odor, and other areas of public concern. Some researchers develop methods to analyze the supply and demand of energy and materials in order to anticipate the effects of shortages on a changing society. Psychologists and others, through laboratory testing, field surveys, and computer modeling, have quantitatively determined the relationship between subjective noise annoyance and noise levels where people live, with emphasis on traffic noise. Also in progress are studies to identify and develop social indicators or measures of social change. One project, for example, demonstrated the technological feasibility of using large-scale computer content analysis techniques to monitor day-old newspapers and systematically identify and assess emerging public concerns. Other topics being studied include automotive service, customer satisfaction, international exchange rates, seat-belt usage, suicidal motor-vehicle fatalities, and so forth.

Researchers are responsible for all phases of research—from initiation through implementation to follow-up. Their customers are staffs and divisions of General Motors. For example, in the past three years, I have directly assisted twenty different staffs and divisions of GM on various projects and studies. The members of the societal analysis department are tool builders—we develop concepts and methodologies for others to use.

I should note that I have chosen all the projects I have worked on at GM—no one has told me what I should do or how I should do it, although the input of managers and colleagues has been important. My superiors are primarily concerned with providing the resources necessary for me to accomplish my objectives and with helping me communicate my results to others. Time and resources are specifically available for researchers to explore and test ideas without having to justify them at an early stage of development. To the extent that one demonstrates the potential usefulness of one's efforts, the work becomes formalized as a project. I have more freedom to do research than the academic sociologists I know, and I do not have to worry about tenure decisions or about teaching classes, doing committee work, raising money for research, limiting myself to sociological problems, or many of the other constraints faced by my academic colleagues.

Attributes of the Successful Researcher

In this section, I discuss the characteristics of the researcher who, in my observation, is successful in our environment. I have not empirically tested these factors, nor do I list them in order of their importance.

First, such persons are primarily problem-oriented rather than discipline-oriented. They are flexible and able to handle ambiguity, pragmatic rather than ideological, and primarily interested in doing whatever is necessary to solve a problem. They are persons looking for tools to solve problems rather than persons with some particular tool looking for problems to solve. They have a tolerance, appreciation, and recognition of the contributions of other disciplines and perspectives and know how to work with others with backgrounds different from their own.

Second, the successful person is able to communicate. Such a person is rewarded for simplifying the complex, not for elaborating the simple, and is able to excite and interest others. Researchers must know how to write and express themselves orally, with brevity as a virtue. When necessary, after a year's work, a researcher should be able to convince a decision maker of the importance of the problem studied and of the results found on either a single sheet of paper or within five minutes of oral conversation.

Third, a successful person knows how to identify and solve critical problems. The more critical the problem, the more attention practical results will receive. Successful persons tend to become experts in areas in which GM needs expertise.

Fourth, successful persons are perceived as team players. They know how to gain credibility and secure the cooperation and support of others.

Fifth, successful persons, in my observation, are persistent. They are self-starters, can go a long time without positive feedback, and can carry a project from beginning to end, knowing how to keep it alive until it bears fruit. Some of the most successful research projects I have encountered were not totally supported by management at first but were kept alive by researchers who believed in the importance of their work. These researchers knew how to overcome all obstacles until their ideas were used by others and how to take risks to provide what was actually needed, not just what others originally thought they needed.

Sixth, a successful person has quantitative ability and qualitative flexibility. Our job is to quantify the quantifiable without overlooking the qualitative dimensions of a problem. Methodology is the bag of tricks for unlocking the secrets of problems, the means of technical communication between scientists of diverse backgrounds. A person is expected to maintain or add to their methodological skills to the degree necessary to solve the problems they are working on.

Since it is taken for granted that a person will acquire the substantive knowledge necessary to solve a given problem, my list does not include this characteristic. However, sociological imagination—the recalling, manipulation, reorganization, and recombination of ideas, images and situations to form new patterns—is critical to our mission. Sociologists use their perspective to build the concepts and methodologies necessary to study the relationship between General Motors and society.

Conclusion

I have given a view of the Research Laboratories as a whole, of my department, and of the factors that I consider necessary for success in this context. For those readers who want more insight into what industry is like for a social scientist, I have provided a selected list of references at the end of this chapter.

Some readers may wonder, "What if I don't like industry? What alternatives do I have?" Of course, each job, each position, is different and must be viewed on its own merits. However, experience in our department has opened up a greater variety of opportunities than most academic jobs. Members of our department have left for positions in universities, private consulting firms, other research laboratories, government, other industries, and other parts of GM. A psychologist in our department recently took a leave of absence to teach and, when finished, resumed his responsibilities with us. Risks are involved in taking a job in industry, but rewards and opportunities exist that, in my view, can offset those risks.

References

FOOTE, N. N.
    1973   "Putting sociologists to work." *The American Sociologist* 9:125-134.
GLASER, B. G.
    1964   *Organizational Scientists: Their Professional Careers.* New York: Bobbs-Merrill.
KLEIN, L.
    1976   *A Social Scientist in Industry.* New York: Wiley.
LEVENTMAN, P. G., AND BAKER, S. H.
    1979   "Sociologists at work: Satisfactions and dissatisfac-

tions." Paper presented at 28th annual meeting of the Society for the Study of Social Problems, Boston.

MORRISSEY, J. P., AND STEADMAN, H. J.

1977 "Practice and perish? Some overlooked career contingencies for sociologists in nonacademic settings." *The American Sociologist* 12:154–162.

RADOM, M.

1970 *The Social Scientist in American Industry: Self-Perception of Role, Motivation, and Career.* New Brunswick, N.J.: Rutgers University Press.

SHEPARD, H. A.

1956 "Nine dilemmas in industrial research." *Administrative Science Quarterly* 1:295–309.

VAN DeVALL, M., BOLAS, C., and KANG, T. S.

1976 "Applied social research in industrial organizations: An evaluation of functions, theory, and methods." *The Journal of Applied Behavioral Science* 12:158–177.

❦ 12 ❧

CORPORATE MARKETING

Robert C. Sorensen

This chapter is based not on empirical research but on experience and participant observation and trial-and-error learning in the business and public affairs communities during the past thirty-five years. As an applied sociologist (although I have never once served under that title), I have applied sociological concepts, analytical techniques, and research methods to a variety of problems and have developed certain concepts and methods of my own that I have described in various writings through the years and that have been embodied in research designs, questionnaires, reports, and expert testimony.

From time to time, I have utilized these applications in various lecturing and teaching assignments, including those at the University of Nebraska College of Law, at the New York University College of Law, Practicing Law Institute, and, since September 1981, at Rider College. In this business school professional capacity, I teach consumer behavior, marketing management problems, and social/legal issues in marketing—all courses in which applied sociology plays a prominent role.

Marketing: A Corporate Proving Ground

Marketing is the corporate proving ground, the process whereby information is generated and put to use in persuading people to purchase and consume a corporation's products and services. Indeed, a corporation is organized for one sole purpose: to earn a profit as a consequence of selling its products and services for a higher price than it invested in their making. A corporation that lacks this ability for very long loses its reason for being or becomes a nonprofit organization, which, by definition, pays nothing to it owners.

Every company markets its products and services, but companies define and implement their marketing functions in many different ways (Kotler, 1980). Marketing departments in the larger corporations are often gargantuan centers of information and persuasion, reaching out to their target markets throughout the country through sales forces, mass media, and retail establishments while exerting strong influence inside the corporation on its manufacturing and financial policies. Other marketing departments function more as staff advisory services than as operating departments, their function being to plan, research, and record and then to report to those who are charged with the sales and promotional functions. Still other companies pay little heed to research and planning but concern themselves entirely with selling.

Consumer Behavior and Values Exchange. Consumer behavior has become a popular branch of marketing thanks to the increasing importance of competition: competition for consumer attention and, of course, competition for the consumer's purchasing dollars and the loyalties that go with them (DeLozier, 1979). Fifty years ago, many companies used marketing simply as a device to inform the public of what the company had to offer and then to sell it to the public regardless of its reaction. Today, even despite certain "demarketing" procedures whereby consumers must be discouraged in the use of certain products (for example, energy), marketing is the feedback medium whereby corporate management is apprised of what consumers want, what they reject, and why they make the choices they make (Sorensen, 1980). At stake in the buy/sell transaction are not only the goods or services and the dollars exchanged between company and consumer but also the multitude of items also exchanged between seller and buyer that must also concern marketing—for example, credit information, modes of delivery, models and colors, varieties of packaging, and so on (Sorensen, 1981).

The sale of a product or service is not always a direct transaction involving broad categories of people. The purchaser of goods or services is often a member of a highly segmented group that may be working in the interstices between many buying and selling groups—for example, a distributor that buys and sells for repurchase. Or the consumers may be the purchasing agents of a very small group of companies that use the purchased products in the manufacture of their own products, which they then sell to others.

Marketing must take into consideration: the behavior of human beings segmented in numberless ways according to their wants and needs; particular products and services made (or in the making) to service particular wants and needs; and the seemingly infinite value exchanges that take place in millions of annual buy/ sell transactions. The symbols of groups and the characteristics they provide those who identify with them, the channels of personal influence, the signals groups give to their own members and to others, the ways in which they influence their members and can be used to influence their members' purchasing behavior, human nature's susceptibility to appeals to brand loyalty and its perception of sales appeals—all involve what many sociologists have given their lives to studying and researching.

Marketing Functions of the Applied Sociologist. Five basic marketing functions are carried out in American companies that manufacture, and usually have ultimate responsibility for selling, their products; in marketing organizations that are in business to plan and promote the selling of the products and services of others (for example, advertising agencies); and in nonprofit organizations (cause and affinity groups) that market membership and a wide variety of services to their members as well as lobby implementations of well-defined values in behalf of their members. Although the marketing function in any organization specifically includes sales, sales promotion, and fund raising, these three functions usually do not attract the trained sociologist.

The five major functions in which applied sociologists function effectively are:

1. Market planning—jobs in which individuals generate and acquire information that they then implement in identifying new product needs, new uses for existing products, and sales projections.
2. Market research—jobs in which individuals design primary research and utilize secondary research techniques to obtain information about consumer behavior and decision making, advertising effectiveness, and the structure of industries.
3. Media buying—jobs in which individuals carry out research and implement plans for purchasing advertising media (print, radio and television broadcasting, billboards, magazines, newspapers) in behalf of advertisers in ways intended to provide maximum cost-effectiveness to their clients.
4. Evaluation and communications research—jobs in which individuals monitor and evaluate the effectiveness of marketing efforts, including their advertising campaigns.
5. Marketing counsel—jobs in which individuals provide specialized forms of counsel—combining market planning, research counsel, and expert testimony—to corporate management, law firms, and sometimes their own employers.

The remainder of this chapter deals with five aspects of the role of the applied sociologist in the marketing of services in the corporate setting: what company managers perceive is sociological about the person they employ; how the applied sociologist perceives and identifies the sociologist in himself within the corporate marketing situation; major distinctive accomplishments of the applied sociologist in corporate marketing; the major functions pursued by the applied sociologist in the corporate marketing setting; and the future of sociology as a marketing specialty or discipline in the business arena.

Corporate Management Perceptions of Sociology and the Applied Sociologist

Company managements have become increasingly sophisticated about defining the positions they seek to fill and about defining the means by which persons filling these positions define and label themselves. Their awareness has increased regarding disciplinary boundaries in the social sciences and in the competencies of the applied professions, particularly psychologists and economists. Even social workers have been retained by business to fill needs that were once considered the province of private or public social welfare groups. Many positions have come into being that require the skills and talents of an applied sociologist, yet corporations seldom include a company or departmental sociologist on their rosters. Accordingly, no job definition exists for a position entitled "applied sociologist," and no survey that scans company job titles and specifications will find the words *applied sociologist* mentioned therein.

This omission is understandable. The sociologist has not been perceived as a student of business, even though his concern with the science of society has included the structure and behavior of corporate institutions. Relatively few corporations have been the subject of well-known studies by sociologists. In any event, corporate executives do not perceive the study of their institutions to be an important business topic, preferring to relegate such research to the archivist or librarian or perhaps to the director of financial or public relations. The sociologist is sometimes confused with one who is charged with responsibilities for social welfare within the company, but, for such a position, individuals with more specialized skills are preferred. A company training director is either a "personnel type" (sometimes thought to be a psychologist or someone with psychological training) or a teaching specialist in a particular occupational field.

I have spoken with corporate executives who view the applied sociologist as a person of lower status than the teacher. The teacher, the old saying goes, "can't do it, so he teaches it." The applied sociologist, in the minds of some, "can't hack it as a teacher—which is what she is supposed to be—so she pretends to be something else and applies to industry." This discussion has no bearing on entry-level positions or other appointments that sociologists receive in company departmental training programs. But, for marketing positions, sociologists are not received as sociologists, trained as sociologists, or evaluated as sociologists in decisions to promote, curtail, or terminate.

Sociology is not recognized in this context for several reasons. Corporate managements know or recall little about the definition of sociology or its practitioners. The American Sociological Association has probably never sought to educate corporate executives or recruiting management with a definition of sociology and sociologists or an assessment of what sociologists can contribute to marketing and other corporate fields.

Sociologists, as indicated later in this chapter, do not identify themselves as sociologists when they apply for positions or once they have obtained them. They describe themselves by a variety of labels, depending on the positions they are filling and the hierarchical needs of their employer. For all practical purposes, they are "passing"—not only passing as individuals whose academic credentials they fear no management will acknowledge, but they have papered over their sociology credentials with an overlay of skills and jobs titles recognizable to the job recruiter and work supervisor.

Thus, management may not hear the word *sociologist* uttered by those who would recruit that person for a particular marketing position, nor will the applicant be encouraged to characterize his professional training as sociological or to express hopes of winning a position where he can put sociology to work. The applied sociologist, for fear of alienating or somehow mystifying management by identifying his true professional discipline, only compounds management's ignorance by failing to identify himself and demonstrate the values that being a sociologist contributes to his work. Thus, the applied sociologist is not acknowledged by others as having applied for or received her job because she is a sociologist, nor are her qualifications for promotion necessarily perceived as including sociological training. Management and workers collaborate to deny the applied sociologist her professional due.

How, then, do company managements define the applied sociologist? They define him in terms of the job title he holds or to which he aspires and in terms of his characteristics as an applied sociologist without labeling him as such. Thus, he may be known in the company for his doctorate, although both person and company may obscure the fact that it is a doctorate in sociology, not in economics or psychology. Or he may be perceived for his various applied abilities—for example, to study and research consumer behavior, to undertake focused group interviews, to evaluate advertising effectiveness, or to predict how people will react to advertising in groups rather than as individuals.

Administrative and high-level management duties are awarded to persons who fulfill these and other marketing functions by executives who would not credit sociology with making any meaningful contribution to administrative capacities.

The Applied Sociologist's Perception of the Sociologist in Himself or Herself

This section is brief, foreshadowed as it is by the previous section. I do not argue that the sociologist in marketing pretends to be a nonsociologist in order to conform to the business world or that she deliberately conceals or disowns her sociology credentials. But, to a greater or lesser degree, certain conditions prevail:

1. The applied sociologist has sometimes come to perceive herself as an inferior sociologist because she is isolated on the fringes of the major profession of sociologists—teaching. Isolated, she lacks certain contacts and forms of recognition, regardless of her accomplishments as a sociologist in other arenas.
2. Instead, the sociologist in marketing seeks recognition from her company peers and from those who occupy the same or similar marketing positions—persons called not sociologists but market researchers, media planners, and so on.
3. With few exceptions, the security measures that insulate competitive companies from each other's accomplishments also hamper potential contacts with other marketing sociologists, a limitation that most hinders the scientific study of society. Yet sociologists meet with nonsociologists to compare notes on their corporate accomplishments.
4. Not surprisingly, the applied sociologist develops negative feelings toward her "real" sociologist colleagues in academia— not scorn or contempt but disinterest and apathy, which discourage communication and other forms of collegiality between the two groups.
5. In marketing, the applied sociologist seldom publicly identifies appropriate tools, resources, and means of classification as

sociological, even though she brings sociological theory and knowledge to her task both in defining and in resolving problems. Most sociologists in business know that those who are the direct beneficiaries of their sociological contributions distrust the sociology label and thus react negatively to suggestions defined as sociological. In the same vein, the applied sociologist is not committed to any single field of applied sociology in the corporate marketing milieu. She will not be perceived nor ask to be sought as an expert in social institutions, as a social psychologist, or as a working expert in the sociology of knowledge. Instead, she is an industry or content analyst or a consumer surveyor.

6. The nature of the corporate problems and their institutional structure often require that the applied sociologist in marketing fulfill the role of a systems analyst. Marketing problems in particular often have implications for the corporate organization as a whole that extend beyond the office or marketing group that initially sought to resolve the problems.

Distinctive Accomplishments of the Applied Sociologist in Corporate Marketing

What distinctive contributions can the applied sociologist make to the corporate marketing sector? Is this offering unique? Can persons who are not sociologists do every task as well as applied sociologists, and vice versa? The following are several distinctive characteristics of an applied sociologist that are of unique value in marketing.

A holistic approach to a marketing or research problem. The applied sociologist is frequently a product of education and experience that dictate a systems approach to marketing problems. He is inevitably sensitive to the potential effects of his actions, his enlistment of others' participation, and the implementation of his findings on components of the business enterprise. Admittedly he can sometimes only imagine or conceptualize this impact, but nevertheless this is often more than others can do.

An ability to differentiate between spurious correlations and cause and effect when seeking to establish the cause of a problem. The collapse of time intervals in decision making, as well as people's inability to distinguish between their own opinions and what they have heard from others, tends to cause things to mistakenly seem to happen at the same time or derive from the same origin. What is needed in such instances is the learned ability to identify root causes and sources of origin as well as their channels of influence and impact. A news broadcaster, for example, was perceived as lacking objectivity not because of his sponsors, the station that carried his broadcasts, or his own personal image— three factors to which analysts attributed the audience's reaction. Instead, a factor that had not previously been correlated with an audience reaction was found to be the source of the problem: the news broadcaster's accent, which many perceived as a sign of bias and absence of learning.

An understanding of the applications of analysis of social class, reference to group theory, and self-activating processes such as those of segregation, in accomplishing the very major marketing task of market segmentation. Without marketing segmentation— that process whereby consumers can be divided by salient characteristics into targets relevant to advertising subject matter, the media, the products and services being advertised, and key attitudes—the advertising message is uneconomical because its impact is wasted on those who are not motivated or otherwise constituted to perceive and act on the message.

Appreciation of the role of personal influence exerted by people fulfilling informal leadership roles in certain modes of consumer behavior; the role of crowd behavior in reaction to a product as opposed to mass behavior of an affinity group. The purpose and content of an advertising message inevitably determine its susceptibility to these factors and its consequent usefulness to the originator of the message. These roles need to be identified, anticipated, controlled for, and monitored in order to identify and assure their impact on the cost-effectiveness of the message.

A capacity to apply and manipulate variables in both experimental design and its implementation. If an advertising message is going to have predetermined accountability, a relationship needs to be documented among inputs (that is, message content, media reach, and frequency purchased), outputs (that is, advertising message perception, reach and frequency achieved, and communication impact) and effectiveness (that is, achievement of end purposes of leads, orders, pledges, and sales themselves).

The key to the sociologist's role in marketing is her ability to observe, evaluate, explain, and predict collective behavior. In marketing plans and media buying, it is not enough to estimate what an individual or a few people will think or do. Products are born, live, and die on the basis of what large numbers of people think and do. Mass persuasion has as its purpose the influencing of large numbers of people to react in certain ways and to activate their consumption and usage behavior. The economics of manufacturing, distribution, and return on investment require increasingly large numbers of buyers. Information must be generated that will permit the potential reactions and behavior of these populations to be rehearsed, tested, and anticipated within definable limits and at certain levels of confidence. The trained sociologist, with her theories and knowledge of group behavior plus her sampling tools, can make explanations and predictions that are projectable to entire populations. Information about the behavior of single individuals will not suffice, because no single individual or miscellaneous group of individuals represents either a model or a microcosm of the larger population whose attention or purchasing dollars are at stake.

Whether the applied sociologist is unique in the characteristics just outlined is impossible to answer with certainty. Courses in consumer behavior are becoming increasingly popular at graduate (and even undergraduate) schools of business, courses that contain substantial findings of sociologists and psychologists concerning human behavior as well as an abstract of techniques of inquiry applicable to marketing fields. The uniqueness of the applied sociologist is that he is usually not a product of the business school but has developed his business acumen experientially in the real world. Because of his *in situ* experience, he brings to his work a vocabulary, ways of reasoning, a disrespect for false deadlines and rituals, and a record of challenges met and overcome that are relevant to successful performance in the business world. I believe this real world experience is a healthy form of preparation, provided that the business novitiate is willing to present his findings and apply his techniques in the language of business rather than of sociology.

Business has borrowed much of its language from military argot—
phrases like "consumer targets," "product invasion," and "psychological warfare" are all commonplace in marketing efforts. Sociology borrows scientific terms from other disciplines (for example,
"ecology," "symbiosis") and uses its own coined terms in its effort to be exact.

Marketing Efforts of Applied Sociologists

Conflict Situations. The applied sociologist often involves
herself in an adversary situation. At issue is frequently not only
the cause but also the solution to a problem involving parties in
conflict. Conflict, unlike other forms of social interaction, involves
persons who are seeking gain at the expense of others.

The basic marketing situation embodies varying degrees of
adversary relationships between seller and buyer as well as between
sellers and sellers and between buyers and buyers. All such relationships are exchanges of values involving money, information,
time, work, and status. The buyer and the seller both want satisfaction from their mutual transaction; each will ordinarily require
assurance of a requisite reward before consenting to the terms of
the transaction. Yet each is taking a risk in the endeavor.

The buyer–seller relationship is an adversary situation in the
sense that each of the two parties is in competition with the other,
the goal being to gain as much benefit from the transaction as the
other party can be persuaded to permit.

The competition between buyer and seller is a function of
supply and demand for the seller's products and services. Typically, the market favors the buyer to the extent that the seller competes with other sellers for the buyer's attention and then with the
potential buyer himself for the buyer's time and financial commitment. The time resources are substantial; an economics of attention inevitably develops, for example, out of the billions of hours
consumed each month by Americans viewing television. Sellers use
television as one medium in which to involve potential buyers,
thus capturing their attention.

This adversary situation also has the makings of a conflict
relationship in which one party is seeking gain at the expense of
the other. The conflict relationship is no longer confined to efforts

at persuasion by each party but instead involves efforts at coercion as well—not only by one party over another but by each party seeking, by every measure (presumably within the law), to influence the behavior of prevailing political and government powers, economic agencies, and other parties who have the power to influence the terms of the transaction. Such efforts at mutual coercion frequently occur between two parties to a buy–sell transaction as an outgrowth of the transaction, or such a conflict situation may arise not between buyer and seller but between two sellers competing for the same buyer's attention and purchase.

The marketing expert is frequently utilized in the litigation of these conflict situations, in which he will offer marketing counsel, design and implement research, analyze the research of opposing parties, and testify as an expert witness in court and before administrative tribunals.

The marketer's sociological knowledge is potentially very useful in legal cases involving what lawyers refer to as "intellectual property"—for example, trademark infringement, where one trademark strongly resembles another; source confusion, where consumers are thought to confuse the source of one product with the source of another; and copyright infringement, including plagiarism. Other legal issues include deceptive or misleading advertising, where facts are distorted and comparisons confused, and unfair competition, where a variety of illegal competitive techniques are at issue. Survey research, content analysis, and institutional (industry) analysis are essential tools of the sociologist in these situations, as is the sociologist's ability to analyze the sample and questionnaire design of any research performed by experts representing opposing counsel.

Criteria have gradually emerged for the utilization of survey research in litigation. One of the earliest definitive statements on this matter, cited by the *Handbook for the Trial of Protracted Cases* used in the U.S. District Courts, was set forth by an article that I coauthored (Sorensen and Sorensen, 1953). These criteria, originally confined to measurement techniques, have expanded to include methods by which populations and markets are defined in market planning and in litigation. Indeed, in the decision handed down in *Brooks Shoe Manufacturing Company, Inc.* v. *Suave Shoe Corporation* (1981)—in which the issue was whether or not the de-

sign or pattern on the side of the Suave leisure shoe was so similar
to that of the Brooks running shoe that people seeing the Suave
shoe would believe it to be made by the Brooks firm—U.S. District
Court Judge Spellman indicated that my study in behalf of the defendant was acceptable and the plaintiff's survey was not. In finding for the defendant's survey, Judge Spellman noted that its "universe selected, households where one or more individuals had
purchased one or more pairs of athletic-type shoes within the last
twelve months, adequately represents the opinions of the class of
buyers relevant to the issue of secondary meaning in the case *sub
judice*." On the other hand, "since the (plaintiff's) survey failed to
examine the proper universe, the 71 percent recognition rate
among those interviewed must be discounted."

Acquisitions and Mergers. Fact finding is frequently at a
premium in corporate negotiations involving mergers, acquisitions,
and buyouts. A variety of types of marketing information is essential in the determination of a company's value, and no little portion of it is affected by perceptions of the impact of new technologies and social change, cycles of fashion, psychological obsolescence, and potential new uses for existing products. Sociology and
economics provide valuable professional resources for those who
seek the essential marketing facts behind the financial figures.

When buyers seeking to purchase a company can obtain
fully relevant information about such matters, they have a sound
basis for offering a higher or lower bid than they might otherwise
proffer; the price sellers seek to obtain is similarly affected. Seller
and buyer alike have often ignored these nuances, but such information can and frequently does change the course of negotiations.

The sociologist may also be useful in assessing the attitudes
of stockholders toward a merger or acquisition. Predicting popular
reactions, suggesting what should be said to stockholders as a result
of their hopes and fears for their stock, and reflecting the perceived motivations behind the offers of the participating corporations are all important functions. Knowledge of a company's customer and employee groups, its ability to mobilize its corporate
resources in bringing a new product to market, and its reputation
among distributors and retailers is also important information that
a corporate marketer might be expected to gather.

Marketing Segmentation and Advertising Effectiveness. Advertising is vital to corporate success for two reasons. First, it is a major component in marketing effectiveness, because no marketing effort can prevail if advertising fails to be cost-effective on a continuing, indefinite basis. Second, sales result in money to spend to produce the kind of advertising that will generate more sales.

The sociologist is frequently involved in evaluating the effectiveness of advertising, either as a corporate employee or as an employee of an advertising agency. To be effective, advertising must first be cost-efficient to the extent that production and media costs produce results within predictable and feasible limits. But, to be even more effective, advertising must attract attention, impress on its audience company and brand advantages, and activate consumers to purchase and use the product while reinforcing their belief in the wisdom of their purchase and the desire to purchase more.

Obviously, the process requires marketing segmentation, a professional assignment for the sociologist, who will put his knowledge of demographic characteristics, social class data, reference group theory, and census data to work in segmenting people by who they are, what they believe, and what products they buy and consume. Precision in choice and measurement are vital elements in this endeavor.

In creating and assessing advertising effectiveness, the corporation must understand the difference between what it intends to convey and what it actually conveys in its advertising messages. Without knowing what it intends to convey, a company fails to translate its marketing goals into advertising effort and has no basis for later assessing its effectiveness. In turn, this failure results in an inability to allocate advertising dollars in terms of management objectives.

Advertising management must also seek compatibility between what it promises, what others think has been promised, and what consumers have experienced with its products. The sociologist can test for compatibility between expectation and experience and can further seek to determine which customers are low risk and which are high risk with respect to complaints, utter dissatisfaction, and outright demands for refunds. Dissatisfied customers cost money—better that they are not customers at all.

Introducing New Products and Brands. I was director of research for a major advertising agency many years ago when my agency was asked to introduce a new toothpaste for its client. The new toothpaste, tortuously slow in its product development, was intended to challenge a giant competitor that had obtained the written blessing of the American Dental Association. The competitor had already proclaimed the innovative and startling endorsement for over a year and built a substantial market share as a result.

Our client challenger, much against my advice, concentrated on two factors: seeking the same professional organization's endorsement for its own toothpaste and concentrating on the criterion of recall to test the potential effectiveness of the newly prepared television commercial. Not millions but hundreds of millions of dollars were riding on the effectiveness of the television commercial to be used in introducing our client's toothpaste. Indeed, each single point of market share (the percent of total toothpaste product sold by all toothpaste manufacturers) was worth a great deal of money.

Agency and client personnel insisted on evaluating the new agency commercial in terms of consumer recall and the message's conformity to the message of the already established competitor. In contrast, I wanted a careful examination of the consumer motives as a whole, the consumer's ability to distinguish between competing advertising messages, and the impact of the message on consumer attitudes toward the newly introduced toothpaste.

As a distinct minority of one, I sought a unique entry place for the new toothpaste in the minds and lives of its potential consumers. I feared that to repeat and concentrate on the same endorsement by the same association for the client's new product—repeating, in other words, what millions of dollars had already been spent to say in behalf of the established competitor—would be largely wasted on consumers who were not searching for another such toothpaste and would probably think that this new, relatively low-budget message was repeating just another variation of the well-known endorsement. I also believed that the critical measure should have been one that would indicate how attitudes toward our client's product were changing.

In this particular instance, my counsel was vetoed. Unfortunately for our client, the consumer public also vetoed our new toothpaste. Did the commercial fail because I was correct and my nonsociologist advertising agency was not? I do not know. In the marketing arena, as in many other areas of controversy where full objective evidence is lacking, a marketing person who invents or opts for a routine is credited with having been correct if the routine succeeds and incorrect if the routine fails. I had asked, "Why not hold off this introduction for two years, until the established giant competitor with the dental association endorsement has exhausted the value of this endorsement?" But other business demands on our client prevented this delay. Of course, the effect of factors militating against the success of the new product may have been so great that, at best, my approach would only have helped the product be less unsuccessful than it actually was.

Future of Sociology as a Marketing Specialization

The ability of the sociologist to take the larger view and perceive the systemic dimensions of his organization as they relate to marketing is vital to his company's economic success. The marketing person no longer earns his keep only by how much he sells, because people will spend and consume less at various times. Profits are also to be found not simply by charging more than the cost of manufacturing but also by seeking consumer approval for less costly product variations, reducing the variety of service and model permutations, and persuading people to make new uses of existing products and services. Old concepts of psychological obsolescence, originally disguised for consumers as technological obsolescence (for example, in the automobile and appliance industries), turned out to cost the seller even more than the buyer.

Marketing needs the sociological orientation. Marketing can afford less than ever to experiment without theories of consumer behavior. Marketing can ill afford to field a project without understanding the need to define and implement demographic and attitudinal segmentation prior to asking questions and counting the results. Marketing requires increasing application of probability to the predictable behavior of masses of individuals rather than generalizations derived from the reactions of a few.

It is not sociology but the applied sociologist who will fulfill or deny any meaningful role for sociology in the corporate marketing functions of the future. The basic question is not so much

whether sociology helps to equip an individual to perform marketing functions but whether the person with training in sociology is
both able and willing to put his education to work. A further question is whether academic sociologists will perceive the tremendous
resources of applied sociology disciplines such as corporate marketing and will proceed to extract and use these resources to en-
rich our discipline as a whole.

References

DeLOZIER, M. W.
    1979   *Consumer Behavior Dynamics: A Casebook.* Colum-
            bus, Ohio: Merrill.
KOTLER, P.
    1980   *Marketing Management: Analysis, Planning, and Con-
            trol.* (4th ed.) Englewood Cliffs, N.J.: Prentice-Hall.
SORENSEN, R. C.
    1980   "Research techniques for measuring the impact of dis-
            paraging use." In U.S. Trademark Association, *1980–
            1981 Trademark Law Handbook.* New York: Board-
            man.
    1981   "Marketing information and the determination of val-
            ue." In S. J. Lee and R. D. Coleman (Eds.), *Handbook
            of Mergers, Acquisitions, and Buyouts.* Englewood
            Cliffs, N.J.: Prentice-Hall.
SORENSEN, R. C., AND SORENSEN, T. C.
    1953   "The admissibility and use of opinion research evi-
            dence." *New York University Law Review* 28(7):1213.

$\maltese$ 13 $\maltese$

CONSUMER AND ADVERTISING RESEARCH

A. Emerson Smith

Sociologists in consumer and advertising research may work in advertising agencies, public relations firms, and marketing research companies or in a marketing, strategic planning, or advertising division of a bank, an insurance company, a public utility, a manufacturer, or a grocery or department store chain.

Consumer and advertising research can be divided into two types: studies of retail markets and studies of wholesale markets. Studies of retail markets may include research into teenagers' television viewing habits, homemaker evaluation of canned tomatoes, restaurant dining preferences of males between the ages of eighteen and twenty-five, or the way that people select a checking account (see, for examples, Golden, 1979; Gorn, 1982; Kneale, 1982; Urban and Hauser, 1980). Wholesale market studies may include research into how electrical contractors decide on certain brands or types of circuit breakers, how manufacturing plant managers select janitorial supplies or cleaning solvents, or why printers buy one kind of computerized typesetter instead of another.

Marketing research, which encompasses consumer and advertising research, may involve impressionistic judgments of consumer preferences based on observation of a small group of purchasers discussing the merits and disadvantages of a product, or it may involve the systematic, quantitative study of the attitudes and behaviors of randomly selected consumers.

Marketing research may include a study of a neighborhood's social and economic characteristics, which is then used to advise a client on the sales potential of a proposed site for a hotel or fast-food franchise. Such site analysis may involve a study of pedestrian and vehicular traffic within a given mile radius of the proposed site. Members of the research staff may pose as shoppers in order to observe the verbal and behavioral patterns of the sales personnel and the physical environment of a business, or researchers may interview consumers as they leave a business establishment.

One major objective of marketing research is to describe the consumer. This description can help direct advertising messages to that segment of the market audience most likely to purchase the product or use the service. Another objective is to understand why it is that certain persons buy the product regularly while others may try the product only once or never try it at all. If a business is trying to increase its share of the market, it may want to appeal to those who rarely, if ever, try the product or to persons who match an established profile of regular users. The business may want to lure consumers away from a competitor or attract new users of a general kind of product or service.

In order to achieve these objectives, the sociologist in marketing research performs a variety of tasks, including: research design and analysis, marketing social research, time and cost control, personnel management, and the presentation of research results. In performing these tasks, the sociologist can be much more than a researcher involved with statistical models and computer terminals —he or she can also be an active participant in the marketing of goods and services.

Research Design and Analysis

Although the sociologist may be unprepared for some of the tasks of marketing research, one task he or she can be relatively well prepared for is understanding research methods and statistical analysis. Traditional sociology departments have courses in research methods, social statistics, demography, experimental design, and the use of the computer for data analysis. In most sociology departments, however, the examples of sociological research rarely involve business applications.

Nonetheless, the sociologist who finds his or her way into a business setting may have a knowledge of research methods and statistics that actually exceeds the day-to-day demands of consumer and advertising research. The sociologist may appear to be too sophisticated to the business client, and many classical research designs and statistics may be beyond the client's expertise and need.

Much of marketing research data analysis may involve running one variable against several other variables in a cross-tabulation table. It is the sociologist, more often than the client, who will want to run the data in a particular multivariate analysis, feeling perhaps that the analysis is necessary to an understanding of the research problem. The client may want a thick volume of tables as a shelf reference or as physical evidence of the sociologist's work, but the most important product the sociologist can produce is a brief report on the highlights of the findings along with unequivocal recommendations for actions to assure a successful marketing program.

Although consumer and advertising research has its own argot, sociologists will find the data-gathering methods familiar (see Joselyn, 1977). Five methods of data gathering are primarily used: telephone interviews (see Dillman, 1978), small group studies, shopping mall or in-store interviews (see Gates and Solomon, 1982), personal interviews in the home or at the respondent's office, and mail questionnaires.

Telephone interviewing using professional interviewers at a monitored bank of phones in a central telephone facility is probably the most common method for testing advertising recall or for gathering basic information either from the general public or from people in specialized markets. Commercial data banks and available computer programs make the drawing of samples from listed telephones or the use of random digit dialing precise and uncomplicated. With central telephone facilities available at marketing research companies in nearly all major cities in the United States, telephone surveys of local areas or of the whole country can be arranged on short notice.

Another popular method of getting information from consumers is called a focus group study, which involves an extended, in-depth discussion with a group of consumers (see Kanner, 1982; Seymour, 1982). The focus group study requires what is essentially a small groups laboratory: two rooms separated by a one-way mirror. One room contains a group of eight to fifteen consumers selected (not necessarily at random) on the basis of their social and economic characteristics and their use of particular goods or services. The other room contains the clients, who can see the consumers through the mirror and not be seen themselves. The consumer discussion is recorded with audio or video equipment, and consumer participants are paid for their time. The focus group is led by a moderator, who can certainly be a sociologist with background in small groups and group dynamics. The moderator focuses the discussion toward topics prearranged between the moderator and the client.

After the discussion, the moderator analyzes the recordings and prepares a report for the client. Clients often need to be cautioned that they cannot draw conclusions about the population or consumers in a particular market based on the comments of this small group. As an exploratory tool, the focus group is often used as a guide for further research using more systematic methods.

A third method commonly used in consumer and advertising research is to intercept shoppers at a single store or shopping mall. Shoppers are usually selected on the basis of a quota on sex, age, or previous use of the product under study and may be asked to taste a food product or to view rough versions of commercials. On occasion, shoppers are given a product to take home and use and then interviewed at a later date by telephone for their evaluation of the product. Various experimental designs are used in connection with shopping mall studies, with shoppers assigned at random to control and experimental groups.

Primarily due to cost constraints, the use of in-home interviews with the general population is limited to those studies requiring visual materials, such as packaging, advertising copy, or long lists of questionnaire items. However, personal in-office interviews are often used when trying to get evaluative information from such groups as physicians, dentists, and business executives.

The mail survey, although once a popular method of data gathering, is now used primarily for panel studies in which consumers are asked to report their usage of certain products each month. Although most marketing research firms can achieve high return rates on mail questionnaires, many clients still perceive the results of mail surveys as having limited validity. Clients, moreover, do not usually want to take the time necessary to conduct a full mail survey, including a series of follow-up mailings to encourage the consumer's participation.

Sociologists can provide a valued service to clients by detailing the advantages and disadvantages of various methods of data gathering—comparing costs, time constraints, the amount of information that can be gathered using each method, the relative quality of the data, and specific applications that may solve the client's problems.

An additional area of research in which sociologists can demonstrate their skills is in the use of secondary data sources. Sometimes the data that the client wants to gather may be readily available from a data bank. The data available from the U.S. Department of Commerce alone can supply information on retail sales, the production of goods, import–export trade, as well as the familiar population data from the Census Bureau. In addition to the data files directly available from the U.S. government, many computer time-sharing services provide on-line computer access to reformatted government files (see Riche, 1981). Private data banks, including such information as the characteristics of persons who read specific magazines or persons who eat in certain restaurants, are also available through a simple computer terminal in the researcher's office. Sociologists with a background in demographics can advise a client by using available census data in conjunction with surveys of selected geographic areas and on-site mapping of existing uses of land in the area.

Personnel Management

The task of personnel management may or may not be a significant part of the sociologist's role. In many advertising agencies, public relations firms, and research departments of corporations, the sociologist may be either the only member or one of three or four members of the research division. These sociologists rely on contract research suppliers, such as marketing research firms, to provide the personnel to design the specific procedures in a research project, gather the data, and provide an initial report of the findings. In a larger research department or in a marketing research firm, the sociologist may have staff members who design projects, construct questionnaires and experimental procedures, select samples, gather data, enter the data into the computer for processing, analyze the data, and write the research report.

Personnel management involves maintaining a research staff, including field supervisors, interviewers, and research assistants, hiring personnel, creating work schedules, setting pay rates and benefits, resolving problems and disputes, and training staff members in research methods. The personnel management role therefore involves the administrative duties incumbent in any organization, including employee education and quality control.

Time and Cost Control

Whether or not the sociologist has an in-house staff, both time and cost control are demanding tasks in business research. In academia, time constraints are often seen as detriments to good quality research. In the university setting, a survey may take six months to design and three months to field and may require weeks or months for data gathering, months for computer processing, and still more months for writing the final report. In the business research setting, it is not unusual for a problem—for example, a product is to be test-marketed, an old product is not selling, or the competition is introducing a new product—to arise one week, for a research assignment to be given the sociologist the next week, and for the final research report—for example, a national survey of 1500 homemakers—to be presented to the corporate marketing executives three weeks later.

Business often needs information as soon as possible, with any delays on the part of the research staff resulting in a potential loss of revenues for the client. Even if the sociologist is given abundant time, such as a two-month period to plan, conduct, and analyze a research project, deadlines and timely reports to the client remain important.

Cost control is also essential. Sometimes clients pay an

hourly rate for each work component in the project, with overall cost dependent on the number of hours required to complete the project. At other times, the research firm makes a bid to do a study at a set price, independent of the actual number of hours the project takes. In either arrangement, the researcher must keep careful records on current costs and projected costs for the duration of the project. If a bid is to be made, the researcher must know how much each phase of the project will cost and must consider not only overhead but also a reasonable profit for the firm.

Sociologists are not usually trained in time and cost control. In fact, some sociologists may complain that time and cost constraints lead to a decrease in the quality of research. However, in a business setting, sociologists are given time and cost limits and expected to produce the highest quality practical research within those limits.

Marketing Social Research

Sociologists in a marketing research firm are not just handed one research assignment after another together with the funds necessary to conduct the research. Even in a corporate setting, the sociologist will not be given research assignments by the sales or marketing department until he or she has assured decision makers in those departments that he or she can provide useful information at a reasonable cost. Nonresearchers are suspicious of sociologists and other research personnel and must be convinced that the research is necessary and will lead directly to a practical test of their products, services, or concepts. The researcher may feel that he or she is misunderstood and neither fully respected nor fully recognized as a social scientist.

The sociologist has to be a salesperson and a public relations practitioner. Skills have to be marketed. Sociologists in business who are openly identified as sociologists may, in practice, have more selling to do than sociologists who present themselves as market researchers. Business executives are more interested in whether a person can produce useful and timely marketing recommendations than in whether the researcher is a sociologist, a Ph.D., or a published scholar. In fact, these credentials may connote, from the business executive's perspective, someone who is antibusiness, esoteric, full of jargon, slow to act, and unable to make concrete recommendations.

Once a trusting relationship is developed between the sociologist and the client, the sociologist is given greater control over the research process. Certainly, the most rewarding research projects are those that the sociologist has planned in consultation with the client from problem conception to final report. One reward is to see the client successfully implement one or more of the sociologist's recommendations.

Presenting Results and Recommendations

The sociologist may be viewed by the client in one of several roles: a technician who constructs questionnaires, gathers data, and operates a computer terminal; a consultant who makes recommendations for a marketing program; or a researcher who not only conducts the research but also synthesizes research data into a form that is clear, concise, and complete, with recommendations that can be realistically applied to produce results. The technician may find that he or she is not asked for recommendations, but asked only to perform specific research tasks. The consultant who makes sweeping recommendations that are not specifically related to available data may not be taken seriously by the client for long. However, the sociologist who can combine these two roles and emerge as a researcher with specialized technical skills and the ability to present research findings in a way that explicitly suggests applications to marketing programs will be likely to succeed in marketing research.

Although sociologists are trained to do research, their research papers are often full of caveats and qualifications together with a lengthy discussion of alternative explanations and a call for more research. A business client given such a report will not read far. Clients expect that the researcher will become familiar with the client's business, make only the most necessary research measurements, and be a keen observer of what makes customers buy the client's product. The client expects that the sociologist's reports will not be an original contribution to consumer behavior research but will be blueprints for increased profits for the client.

A final and persistent problem of the sociologist in the business world involves the release of research findings to the general literature of sociology, public opinion, and marketing. When a business client buys a sociologist's time and skills, the research report is almost always designated as "proprietary" and thus cannot be published by the sociologist. The knowledge gained about consumer behavior remains the property of the client. The issue of proprietary research is more a problem for the sociologist who has a commitment to both the academic and business communities than for the sociologist who has made a career commitment to the business community alone.

Conclusion

Sociologists who become employed in corporations or research firms as consumer and advertising researchers may be equipped to perform the research task. In fact, the sociologist's skills in research methods and statistics and his or her perspective on human behavior can bring considerable refinement and other positive contributions to the field of consumer and advertising research.

However, sociologists entering this field may find themselves lacking skills for the tasks of personnel administration, time and cost control, the marketing of social research, and the presentation to the client of recommendations for action.

Sociologists in this field may also find that they must reevaluate what they believe the sociologist ought to be doing. The academic training of a sociologist stresses at least two perspectives: that sociologists should be detached, value-free observers, studying human behavior as true scientists and leaving any involvement in action to others; and that sociologists should be solving social problems and championing the cause of the poor, the worker, and the oppressed.

Many sociologists in academia say that a colleague who has become involved in business, ostensibly supports capitalism and the free-enterprise system, and champions the cause of corporations listed on the New York Stock Exchange has abandoned sociology. Sociologists who work for companies rather than for colleges or universities, nonprofit research institutes, government agencies, or social service organizations may discontinue—or not

apply for—membership in national, regional, state, and local sociological associations. They may have a degree in sociology but not
perceive themselves as sociologists.

Primarily because sociologists have traditionally found employment in academic, government-funded, and other noncom-
mercial institutions, graduate sociology students especially have
been guided by their professors into career roles in those institutions. However, as a consequence of current pressures in the marketplace and the applicability of the methods and content of sociology to the study of consumer behavior and the business community, sociology departments can offer their students a broader
view of career roles, including that of the sociologist in business
and industry.

References

DILLMAN, D. A.
     1978   *Mail and Telephone Surveys.* New York: Wiley.
GATES, R., AND SOLOMON, P.
     1982   "Changing patterns in survey research—growth of the
             mall intercept." *Journal of Data Collection* 22(1):3-8.
GOLDEN, L. A.
     1979   "Consumer reactions to explicit brand comparisons in
             advertisements." *Journal of Marketing Research* 16
             (November):517-532.
GORN, G. J.
     1982   "The effects of music in advertising on choice behav-
             ior: a classical conditioning approach." *Journal of Mar-
             keting* 46(Winter):94-101.
HERZOG, A. R., AND BACHMAN, J. G.
     1981   "Effects of questionnaire length on response quality."
             Public Opinion Quarterly 45(4):549-559.
JOSELYN, R. W.
     1977   *Designing the Marketing Research Project.* New York:
             Petrocelli/Charter.
KANNER, B.
     1982   "Through the looking glass." *New York* 15(June 21):
             16-20.

KNEALE, D.
   1982   "Stations that show only ads attract a lot of TV watchers." *The Wall Street Journal* 200(September 23):37.
RICHE, M. F.
   1981   "Choosing 1980 census data products." *American Demographics* 3(11):12–16.
SEYMOUR, D. T.
   1982   "Three-stage focus groups used to develop new bank product." *Marketing News* 16(September 17):11–15.
URBAN, G. L., AND HAUSER, J. R.
   1980   *Design and Marketing of New Products.* Englewood Cliffs, N.J.: Prentice-Hall.

ϟ 14 ϟ

LAW AND CRIMINAL JUSTICE

David B. Chandler

Although faith in the rule of law is a basic value, legal institutions in the United States are buffeted by criticism from within and without. Chief Justice Warren Burger, articulating the concerns of a conservative within the system, considers the flood of litigation reaching the Supreme Court to be intolerable. In 1981, the court's docket for the term was filled in the first three months. So-called silly suits, poorly drafted legislation, excessive appeals for criminal convictions, poorly prepared trial attorneys, and poor management of the system are some of Justice Burger's concerns (*U.S. News and World Report,* 1982). Similar criticisms are made by conservative and liberal attorneys at every level of the system.

From the outside, the criticisms are numerous and varied. Some claim that the legal system is inaccessible to ordinary people for ordinary problems (Nader, 1980). Inadequate control of crime, failure to rehabilitate criminals, and lack of coordination between police, courts, and prisons are common complaints made against the criminal justice system by the public, politicians, and the press. The radical left sees the legal system as an instrument of oppression by the privileged few, and the religious right sees it as a servant of godless humanists. As with many public institutions, costs are considered excessive. In short, the legal system is seen as having major problems and as being in need of serious change.

For sociology, legal systems have been an important object of study for generations. Close scrutiny of the details of their operations and broad historical and comparative studies are common. In fact, outside the law school, sociology knows more about legal systems than any other academic field. Sociology and sociologists are thus uniquely placed to make an important practical contribution to basic change and immediate reform.

Sociologists, like academics in many fields, are now scurrying to new careers, at once pushed by the shortage of academic opportunities and enticed by the developing needs of business and government for their talents. But these new careers have new patterns of training and entry often only partially related to traditional academic preparation. Unlike economics and psychology, which have strong nonacademic employment traditions, sociology has been primarily an academic field (MacRae, 1979), and the activities of sociologists who have worked exclusively outside the university have not been well catalogued or documented. Amorphous roles and unclear definitions of nonacademic sociological practice may account for this deficiency. Clearly, empirical research on the practice of sociology in current and potential nonacademic work places would be timely.

The first part of this chapter presents an overview of nonacademic sociology in the fields of law and criminal justice. The next session suggests areas of possible growth that may hold employment opportunities for sociologists in the future. The final section examines the academic and professional responsibilities of the applied sociologist in law and criminal justice.

Current Situation

Several problems confound a precise description of the current situation. Delimiting the legal field is difficult, since the law penetrates virtually every aspect of social life. Distinguishing between pure and applied research and disentangling the roles of so-

ciologists as members of a profession, a discipline, and a work organization are important and difficult issues (Miller, 1980).

American sociology clearly originated in concern for social
problems (Fisher and Strauss, 1978). Indeed, even with the subsequent emphasis on abstract theory and method, most current sociological research, no matter how pure, has at least some potential application. Some research is in fact designed to be applied.
The issue or dependent variable to be examined is a problem to
nonsociologists, and the factors selected for a potential causal relationship to it are more open to short-term intentional change.
Although the situation is changing (Ward, 1980), criminology is
one of the few explicitly applied subfields within sociology. Not
only is research oriented toward application to problems, but also
specialized journals and professional associations collect and dis-
seminate research information of special relevance to problems in
criminal justice. In addition, higher academic training in criminology and criminal justice programs has evolved to include professional preparation for a nonacademic work place (Cressey, 1979).

In the legal field, the most promising work place for sociologists is in postconviction criminal justice. For years, both B.A.
and M.A. sociologists and criminologists have found employment
in state corrections agencies as probation and parole officers and
administrators of programs. More recently, Ph.D.s in this field
have taken positions as planners and higher-level administrators.
Although some become computer specialists or statisticians, many
never practice their sociological research expertise. On the occasion of an annual report or grant application, they may write from
a sociological viewpoint; otherwise, however, their duties seem unrelated to sociology. They counsel clients, do presentence investigations, write bureaucratic reports, and attend committee meetings about the agency's coordination, financial, and training
problems. The urgency of these practical problems and the need
for quick solutions overshadow the contribution of a traditional
sociological perspective. These sociologically trained persons may,
however, become the contact points for the academic or consulting sociologists who periodically do evaluations and other research
work for the agency.

Use of sociologists in private-sector corrections programs
seems to be minimal. Such programs—which often contract with

state agencies to provide in-community facilities and programs for offenders, usually those with specific problems such as drug or alcohol abuse (Davis, 1980)—tend to use clinically trained personnel such as psychologists and social workers. Nor are sociologists extensively involved as regular employees in the preconviction phase of criminal justice. Sociologists are becoming more important as expert witnesses or jury selection specialists in criminal cases, but, with a few exceptions, such experts are usually academic sociologists working as volunteers.

The involvement of sociologists with the other two major sectors of the criminal justice system, the prosecution and police, has been growing but is still minimal. A few police departments hire sociologists, usually for statistical work, but much of the sociological expertise is provided by police officers subsequently trained as sociologists or criminologists. Other than in the relatively new victim-witness programs, which are often housed in prosecutors' offices and often employ some sociologists, prosecutors' offices do not seem to be using sociologically trained employees. As in corrections programs, considerable applied sociology has been conducted in these agencies, but usually by sociologists from outside the agencies, either from the university or from private consulting firms.

The legislative field offers some employment opportunities for sociologists. Currently, legislative offices employ a combination of outside, usually university-based experts in sociology, who testify or assist legislative committees to research and draft legislation, and employees of legislative committees or legislative reference bureaus, who have advanced training in sociology and are often also attorneys. Recruitment for such work is heavily politicized, and, whereas law schools seem to have routinized the informal political participation necessary to secure these positions, sociology departments have not.

Finally, the evaluation research industry employs a significant number of research sociologists. Much of the applied research conducted over the past decade on crime and corrections has been done by private nonprofit corporations and institutes in this field. As a consequence of the federal government's requirement that federally funded projects be evaluated, a specialized private research industry has developed with the resources to respond more quickly than university-based scholars and with sophisticated, cost-efficient applied research techniques.

Future Possibilities

What changes are likely in the next few years that will affect the career options of applied sociologists in the field of law? Crime-producing conditions and policies, such as high rates of unemployment among minority youth, seem unlikely to change, and, if the current political rhetoric on crime continues, even more persons will be incarcerated for longer periods of time.

The popular political wisdom opposes rehabilitation and community programs. Some states are restricting the use of parole and probation. But crowded prisons will produce many problems and necessitate alternative responses, such as probation and parole, in which sociologists have been employed (Lieber, 1981). Thus, career opportunities in postconviction criminal justice can be expected to expand—it is the only area within the legal system where some job descriptions require sociology, where specialized academic preparation is available (criminology and criminal justice studies), and where those in authority have or are familiar with sociological skills.

The opposite trend may be expected in the private research and evaluation industry. Unless federal policy changes, massive funding for criminal justice programs and for their evaluation is at an end, and the criminal justice evaluation industry will contract unless alternative activity or support is found. However, private sector demand for research and development in the field of social control may increase. The subcontracting of crime prevention and correctional programs to the private sector may be one source of continuing demand for evaluation and policy research. Another source may be the rapidly growing private security and police business. Many corporations have developed sophisticated internal policing functions which attempt to reduce employee theft, prevent industrial espionage, and protect computers. Many businesses and residential communities hire their own security forces from the private sector (Shearing, Farnell and Stenning, 1980). Further, the balance between university-based and private applied research will probably shift as the sources of funding and problems shift to the private sector. This trend would tend to favor the career opportunities of the nonacademic applied sociologist.

Another trend that may be accelerated by the current shift away from big government and big bureaucracy is toward finding alternatives to the legal system for solving problems. Two specific movements, now in their infancy, show promise: victim assistance programs and the community mediation movement (Alper and Nichols, 1981).

Many police and prosecutors' offices around the country have established victim/witness assistance programs. Although one purpose of these programs is to make the prosecution of accused persons easier by strengthening the morale and resolve of witnesses, many programs evolve primarily into service programs for victims of crime. Similarly, the specialized programs established for rape victims and for victims who are children support prosecution and provide psychological and social services to the victims (Ruch and Chandler, 1980). Also, criminal injury compensation has been established in many states to help victims of violent crime recover monetary losses and expenses. All these programs suggest that legislators and criminal justice professionals recognize the limited role of the criminal justice system in solving the problems of crime in modern society.

A second trend that points in a similar direction is the neighborhood justice center, or community mediation movement. Programs with the capacity to resolve disputes informally have been established in over one hundred American communities (McGillis and Mullen, 1977). Not only are these programs intended to divert minor disputes away from the courts, but advocates claim that the informally and voluntarily mediated resolution of interpersonal problems is more lasting and meaningful than court-imposed solutions. In addition, these programs can sometimes solve problems that would not effectively reach the formal system (Wahrhaftig, 1980)—for example, conflicts between groups, disputes that are criminalized into low-priority minor crimes, and problems that are not reported because of fear of formal authority. Thus, community-based mediation programs can expand their problem-solving capacity beyond that of the legal system at precisely the time when the legal system, overburdened and costly, has effectively restricted itself.

These two movements, the victim service movement and the dispute mediation movement, have already had sociologists involved in their birth and infancy. If the movements continue to expand, they may require the increased participation and employment of applied sociologists.

In police and prosecution, future career opportunities may depend primarily on the diffusion of technology, since sociologists regularly employed in these fields work in data management and statistical analysis. As scientific management and computer technology in police and prosecution spread from the cities to suburban and rural areas, opportunities for sociologists may expand.

Future prospects, then, are mixed and uncertain for applied sociologists in the legal field. However, since personnel account for 85 percent of criminal justice costs (Hudzik, Bynum, and Green, 1981), sociologically sound planning, organization, and management are clearly needed.

Academic and Professional Responses

Naturally, some within the discipline resist the need for sociology to become more interdisciplinary and applied. In some universities, sociology departments have not taken the lead in this evolution for a number of reasons, many of which seem plausible or unavoidable. One consequence, however, is that, within the university, other units have been established or have evolved to meet the need. Public policy studies, criminal justice studies, urban studies, social planning, and schools of management have all developed a capability in applied sociology. Many sociologists are now finding academic placement in these units, and their graduates are finding professional employment.

Research and analysis in two areas should help support academic debate and planning about the future of applied sociology in law. First, descriptions of what nonacademic sociologists actually do in the field of law are vital. A second and more difficult task is to divine what new sociological roles could and should evolve in this field. Then academic sociologists might be able to decide which areas of applied research and training ought to be strengthened and developed in sociology programs, which should be left to others, and which could have a useful collaborative relation to sociology.

Value of Field Research

Field research is the backbone of any program of applied research and training. As a method, it has earned legitimate academic credentials as a major contributor to the basic literature in the social sciences in general and in the sociology of law in particular.

But the real impact of a well-designed field research program is in its capacity to achieve many useful goals almost as a by-product of the research process. Gaining and retaining access to a field research site usually requires interpersonal skills that other research approaches do not require. This capacity to navigate a social setting or organization populated by a variety of persons performing a variety of roles is essential for the nonacademic sociologist.

The previous section indicates that, with the exception of corrections, the role of the practicing sociologist in the legal field is not well established. Thus, sociologists are now creating new roles as they enter law-related work. Field research stresses the ability to understand the needs and perspectives of organizations and their occupants, and the sociological field researcher is uniquely trained and located to identify functions that sociologically trained employees could perform.

Not only must a successful field researcher be able to establish sufficient trust and legitimacy to get important and sensitive information, but he or she must also be able to explain a sociological perspective and project to the uninitiated. Thus, two-way communication skills must also be learned and tested in a fieldwork program.

Field research may have a highly sophisticated design and require a long time to complete, but the field researcher often learns about existing data that can be made to serve in place of more ideally gathered materials. The practicing sociologist in a nonacademic setting must be able to bring usable, high-quality empirical research to those who can use it, within the serious constraints of time and cost typical of most organizations. Field research may be the best preparation for the flexible use of the sociological imagination under such circumstances.

Another unexpected value of a field research program is the impact that it can have on the academic mentor. The monitoring and advising of students in a field research situation orients and sensitizes the university sociologist to practical problems in the agencies and systems under study. In addition, the quid pro quo of entry to a field research site is often some research product of use to the agency. In this way, the natural processes of propinquity and interpersonal motivation can reorient academic curiosities and research toward applied areas.

In some cases, the connection with university personnel and resources is a considerable benefit to the agency where field research is being conducted. Volunteer student and faculty assistance with various projects and informal use of local university facilities and expertise all strengthen the applied sociologist as an employee.

Students in field research settings have an opportunity to become familiar with the ethical and political issues of a sociologist practicing in the legal field. Large sums of money in civil suits and decisions regarding guilt or innocence, long or short incarceration, even life or death, can depend on who knows what information. Traditional legal procedures concerning access to knowledge are often antithetical to the more open access norms of a university community.

The sociologist can function as an agent of progressive change in law-related institutions but needs experience in determining which actions are desirable and possible. Fieldwork not only exposes the sociologist-in-training to the political and ethical realities of the potential work place but also allows these potential dilemmas and opportunities to be brought into the academic program for clarification and debate.

Finally, students in field research have the advantage of being known to potential employers and of knowing about potential employment roles and settings.

Interdisciplinary Networks

One advantage of field research is that it exposes the potential applied practitioner to other professions and occupations; in the same way, academic sociology must incorporate increased interdisciplinary familiarity into its advanced training. An understanding of the perspectives and problems of lawyers in their various roles inside and outside the judicial system, for example, should be established early in the professional training of applied sociologists. Since the perspectives of the lawyer dominate most policy and practice in the legal field the sociologist needs to understand these perspectives. Unlike the academic sociologist, who can assert his or her orientation without compromise, the potential applied sociologist must learn the prevailing orientation as a practical exigency of potential employment. Field research and academic work would both ideally include some contact with lawyers and law students.

The second objective is for students of applied sociology to become familiar with and familiar to lawyers and law students by entering their social networks. Lawyers control many entry-level positions in the field of law. If they have sociology students in classes and work with them on projects, they will not only learn the sociological approach to a problem but also know one or more sociologists personally who will be able to implement such an approach. Opening explicit links with law schools could also familiarize the academic sociologist with the texture of problems as seen by practicing and teaching lawyers and might influence researchers to take up issues of relevance to lawyers, thus enhancing the relevance of sociology and the prospects for applied practice in the legal field.

Developing relations with clinical professions, such as social work and psychology, that have a significant presence in corrections programs and victim assistance efforts could have a similar effect on employment opportunities. Broadening the social networks into which students of applied sociology are introduced in their training not only reflects the interdisciplinary realities of the legal field but also provides a practical basis on which to compete for a broad range of entry-level positions.

Clinical Sociology

Traditional research is likely to be a minor role for most sociologists practicing in the legal field. Thus, in addition to research methods, professional preparation should include many other general practice skills as well as clinical training. Sociologists are often called on to study human relations problems in prisons, police-community contacts, juries, victims, components of the criminal justice system, and a host of other law-related areas. As practitioners, they may in fact be called on to devise new approaches and manage new programs that actually solve some of those problems. And sociologists currently working in corrections often have direct relations with clients. To anticipate this need, academic sociology should include training and experience in clinical relationships as part of programs in applied sociology.

Social Inventions

As indicated in the opening of this chapter, many serious problems face legal institutions and law-related organizations in the United States. Graduate programs can and should be modified to increase the chances of professional employment for sociologists in these fields. But few sociologists would rest content if the only goal of a shift in emphasis to applied sociology was to insinuate a few well-trained social science bureaucrats into existing institutions.

No place is better than the university to think through the analysis and design of new social organization. Social innovation and invention in legal institutions can occur when academic sociologists, working closely with their colleagues in the field, have the incentive to apply their considerable resources to the immediate solution of practical problems. Even more appropriate is a revival of utopian analysis among a new pragmatic constituency of applied sociologists. Organizational development, alternative institutional arrangements, and social change are all needed by legal institutions and are activities for which sociologists are trained and to which they are inclined.

Applied sociologists practicing in the legal field can become agents of practical and progressive change, provided they can offer new ideas that have some chance of being adopted and of succeeding. The past decade has produced promising ideas based on research sponsored by government agencies, professional associations, and private foundations, but much of this research has not been tailored to local agencies, which might be willing to innovate were expert resources available to support their efforts. Applied sociologists, field research students of applied studies, and academic sociologists in local universities could provide such resources.

Technology

Traditionally, sociologists have been employed as experts in the application of quantitative methods to legal problems—for example, in studies of the deterrent effectiveness of criminal sanctions. In addition, the management of a modern criminal justice system requires the centralization of information and the extensive use of computer technology. With the advent of small, inexpensive computer systems, the use of such technology is rapidly expanding, thereby increasing the quantity of sociolegal data available for secondary analysis by sociologists, once it has been collected and quantified for management purposes.

The rapid growth in computer technology has two implications. First, all applied sociologists should be literate in quantitative methods—methods in which academic sociology is well prepared to offer training. Second, applied sociologists need to understand and control the computer explosion as it affects social organization and work roles—a task with which the sociological establishment is far less well prepared to provide assistance. The criminal justice systems of the country will need professionals who know not only how to use the microcomputer to serve the ends of the organization but also how to anticipate and ameliorate its impact on the current system and its employees.

Politics, Ethics, and Criticism

Bureaucratic settings, where many applied sociologists will be working, often discourage criticism by employees. The lesson of criminology as a field is that special associations, journals, workshops, and conventions encourage individuals to take a critical and political stance as members of a professional group. This stance may be aided by academic colleagues in the same organizations (Cressey, 1979). Academic sociologists and their national and regional associations need to develop the capacity to protect and encourage the critical potential of their applied colleagues.

Law is at once the most powerful and the most politicized institution in a democratic society. If sociologists are going to become practitioners within it and not remain academically protected observers and researchers, serious attention must be paid to the ethical and political issues they will face. Field research has the potential to reflect these issues back into academia during the training of the applied practitioner, but academia must be prepared to treat the issues seriously, and the profession must be prepared to create structures to protect the applied practitioner's independence.

Conclusion: Need for General Practice Skills

The forgoing analysis of the prospects of applied sociology in the areas of law and criminal justice indicates that sociologists will, to a great extent, create their own careers in law-related fields. At this fluid stage in the development of applied sociology, graduate training should be quite general.

Sociologists will bring their traditional strengths—analytical skill and empirical method—to the applied situation. Identifying social and organizational problems and casting them in the larger context of social structures is of great practical value. However, sociologists may need to be trained in demystifying sociology and in making empirical research more easily appreciated before their skills can be fully appreciated.

The applied sociologist in the legal field should have skills in creating appropriate new roles; the capacity to write quickly and well, with a practical appreciation of his or her audience; verbal communication skills; and interpersonal acumen. Often the sociologically trained corrections worker is one of the few who have studied the whole system and have both valuable substantive knowledge and a unique perspective on the criminal justice system.

An emphasis on the practice of applied sociology can infuse the sociology of law and criminal justice with a new vitality and relevance. Return to a tradition of concern about social problems and participation in social change should be embraced. Such a rediscovery of the roots of American sociology is now needed to create a wider variety of career options, research topics and styles, and disciplinary viability.

References

ALPER, B. S., AND NICHOLS, L. T.
    1981   *Beyond the Courtroom: Programs in Community Justice and Conflict Resolution.* Lexington, Mass.: Lexington Books.

CRESSEY, D.
   1979   "Fifty years of criminology: From sociological theory to political control." *Pacific Sociological Review* 22 (4):457-480.

DAVIS, S.
   1980   *The Seduction of the Private Sector: Privatization in Ontario Corrections.* Ottawa: Carleton University.

FISHER, B., AND STRAUSS, A.
   1978   "The Chicago tradition and social change: Thomas, Park, and their successors." *Symbolic Interaction* 1 (2):5-23.

HUDZIK, J. K., BYNUM, T. S., AND GREEN, J. R.
   1981   *Criminal Justice Manpower Planning: An Overview.* Washington, D.C.: U.S. Law Enforcement Assistance Administration.

LIEBER, J.
   1981   "The American prison: A tinderbox." *The New York Times Magazine* (Mar. 8):26-35,56-61.

McGILLIS, D., AND MULLEN, J.
   1977   *Neighborhood Justice Centers: An Analysis of Potential Models.* Washington, D.C.: Law Enforcement Assistance Administration.

MACRAE, D.
   1979   "Changing social science to serve human welfare." *Social Science History* 3(3-4):227-241.

MILLER, G.
   1980   "Intellectual craftsmanship in sociology: An assessment of its current status." *The Wisconsin Sociologist* 17(1)-3-9; comments,9-19; reply,20-22.

NADER, L., ED.
   1980   *No Access to Law.* New York: Academic Press.

RUCH, L. O., AND CHANDLER, S. M.
   1980   "An evaluation of a center for sexual assault victims." *Women and Health* 5(1):12-22.

SHEARING, C., FARNELL, M., AND STENNING, P.
   1980   *Contract Security in Ontario.* Toronto: University of Toronto, Centre of Criminology.

U.S. NEWS AND WORLD REPORT
   1982   "Unclogging the Courts—Chief Justice Speaks Out." (Feb. 22):36-40.

WAHRHAFTIG, P.
   1980   *Grassroots Citizen Dispute Resolution Clearinghouse:
          An Overview of Community Oriented Citizen Dispute
          Resolution Programs in the United States.* Pittsburgh,
          Pa.: American Friends Service Committee.
WARD, D.
   1980   "The theft of criminology from sociology." *Contem-
          porary Sociology* 9(3):368.

15

HEALTH SERVICES RESEARCH

Geoffrey Gibson

Medical and health care settings for applied sociology are among those offering the greatest opportunity for scholarship and social action. Few settings offer easier access to data, greater possibilities for directly influencing the quality of health care, or better collaborative opportunities to work with physicians, administrators, and other social science health care researchers. However, these same settings may expose sociologists to substantial political interference as they develop their research agendas and to the interference of physician- or administrator-dominated research units that may choose to sacrifice theory for relevance, rigor for responsiveness. For every sociologist in such settings who can claim to have improved health care through his or her research, at least one will claim that his or her research was ignored or rendered ineffectual.

Nevertheless, the health care setting is likely to increase greatly as a source of employment and as a source of available data for secondary analysis. The challenge, therefore, is to identify such settings and to discover those units and strategies most likely to minimize the disadvantages and maximize the advantages. This chapter identifies general types of applied settings for health services research and assesses their desirability as places for employment for sociologists by considering a variety of issues or criteria concerning the role of research in such settings. The chapter ends by making recommendations for departments of sociology, graduate sociologists, and the applied settings themselves that are likely to make it more probable that sociologists are employed in such settings and that, once there, they can undertake rigorous scholarly research, have unconditional access to high-quality data sets, and directly influence the policies of important social institutions and individual health care providers.

Applied Settings for Health Care Research

Although this chapter is almost entirely concerned with Ph.D. sociologists undertaking health care research, nonresearch roles are available in increasing numbers. These nonresearch positions are within program areas of health associations and federal agencies where social scientists with master's degrees are attractive for their writing and analytical abilities as well as for their capacity to perform statistical and computer-based draft analyses. However, most of these positions require much more health program experience and training than M.A. sociologists are likely to have at present. For this reason, most such positions will continue to go to M.B.A.s with a health care specialty or to those with master's degrees in hospital or health administration. This situation has obvious implications for broadening the practice and applied content of, and even for introducing residency components into, master's programs in medical sociology. This issue will be dealt with at the end of this chapter.

The several major types of health care settings can be characterized in terms of the following criteria likely to be of greatest importance to Ph.D. sociologists engaged in research:

- The quality, comprehensiveness, availability, and hypothesis- or model-testing relevance of data sets at that setting
- The encouragement and rewards given by the setting for under-

taking and publishing theory-based scholarly research in peer-review journals and the setting's perceived prestige and credibility
- The availability of supportive colleagues with shared backgrounds in social sciences and/or health care research and the degree of insulation from academic sociology and its professional associations
- Academic freedom
- The ability to influence the policy of health associations and agencies and the behavior of health care providers

The major types of applied health settings are:

- Voluntary health associations (American Medical Association [AMA], American Hospital Association [AHA], Blue Cross and Blue Shield of America) at both the national and local levels
- Federal agencies (National Center for Health Services Research [NCHSR], Health Care Financing Administration [HCFA], National Institutes of Health [NIH], the Public Health Service, the Veterans Administration)
- Individual hospitals and multihospital systems (Lutheran Hospital System, Sisters of Mercy Hospital Corporation, Hospital Corporation of America)
- Foundations funding health services research and demonstration activities (Robert Wood Johnson, W. K. Kellogg, Kaiser Family Foundation)

Health Associations. Over the last ten to fifteen years, health associations have established research and policy analysis centers to undertake the following kinds of activities:

- Conduct applied research mainly on the data bases created by the association (AHA Annual Survey, AMA Physician Master File, and so on)
- Offer technical assistance to other program units within the association and within state and local affiliates as those units undertake research or, more usually, need to assess the research of others

- Secure government and foundation funding for research and evaluation and thereby generate revenue for the association
- Act as a contact point between the association and the research community, disseminating within the association research results for relevant research and informing researchers of available association data
- Undertake legislative and policy analyses of suggested initiatives and their impact on the interests of the association
- Monitor economic trends in society as they are likely to affect the work of the association
- Monitor the health services research agendas of federal and nonfederal agencies at the national level

Although these units have traditionally been staffed by economists, sociologists are becoming increasingly involved, to the extent that, of the 100 to 150 qualified Ph.D. researchers in these settings, about one third are sociologists, one half economists, and the remainder statisticians. Indeed, until recently, the directors of research at the American Medical Association, the American Hospital Association, the Blue Cross Association of America, and the American Dental Association were all sociologists. Most are medical sociologists, although some have backgrounds in organizational theory.

Health associations have certain advantages as settings for applied sociologists. First, easy access to large-scale data bases have been developed by the particular associations, providing the researcher with preferred or even exclusive access. To be able to spend three to four years at an association where one can be assured of publishing several major articles in peer-reviewed journals based on data to which no one else has access is particularly attractive for new Ph.D.s with a prior and close familiarity with the data bases as well as a clear idea of how they are to be used on a specified project. Careers can be made, national reputations launched, and tenure guaranteed by early specialization and a strategic choice of model and data, while other careers are bogged down with three sections of Sociology 101 and two of "Introductory Research Methods."

Second, such settings do not involve teaching responsibilities, and the sociologists can often be assured of spending all their time on research. This depends in part on whether the research setting is organized to protect the researchers from demands on their time to give technical assistance to program units or regional affiliates. Such demands are rapidly increasing as research projects and results are being used as a basis for policy decisions, although some associations have been more successful than others in having master's-level individuals undertake this function. Although a minimal amount of unavoidable committee work and technical assistance is involved, it is of the kind that will increase the researcher's program knowledge in his or her area of expertise and also increase contact with the external research community. In any event, much more time is available for research than at a university at a comparable stage in a sociologist's career.

The final advantage may be more apparent than real and not an advantage at all: the possibility of researchers influencing the policies of health associations at the national and local levels. Unfortunately, social scientists have made somewhat exaggerated claims as to the impact of research results on institutional policies. As with government policies, many health associations use the work of their research unit to support an already-adopted position or to justify a policy being adopted mainly for political rather than pragmatic reasons. More infrequently are research results (either intramural or extramural) actually the cause rather than the rationale for a change in policy. This characteristic is not, it should be added, unique to health associations, which, in this respect, are no different from federal agencies or from most other applied health care settings. Rather, it is a general consequence of the tendency in most health-related policy-setting organizations for the decision horizon to be too short and the decision context too unpragmatic—perhaps even for research activities to be too unresponsive, in the sense of being irrelevant to the association's day-to-day concerns. Ironically, health associations do have separate policy analysis units that influence policy, although not through research or even through analysis. This important distinction between such research and policy analysis will be examined in greater detail later in this chapter. In most health associations, this distinction confronts Ph.D. sociologists and even economists with a Faustian choice between theory and relevance and between rigor and influence.

Some of the current disadvantages of working in health associations refer to features that, until recently, were advantageous. For instance, until recently, such positions were supported by hard money and involved, in essence, lifetime tenure. For the last few years, however, the associations have been facing varying degrees of difficulty in obtaining and retaining members, have been faced with budget constraints due to revenue shortfalls from membership dues, and have emphasized representation and advocacy functions directly related (as research is not seen as being) to membership services. Research units have thus been urged and budgeted to attract external funding to help support themselves, and, in some cases, certain research positions have been abolished and incumbents let go. A major disadvantage, then, is that research units in health associations need increasingly to attract external funding, although, unlike university settings, the association will provide hard money for a substantial portion of the research budget. Health associations give more hard money research support and uninterrupted time to researchers than typical university departments of sociology and, incidentally, pay higher salaries (starting, in 1981, at about $32,000 for a new Ph.D. and increasing about 10 percent per year, with supervisory research positions available at up to $60,000).

A further disadvantage of health associations as an applied research setting is that they are perceived as having lower credibility than universities as a source of scholarly knowledge. This belief seems to be quite independent of the research quality of the papers produced, which are published in reputable peer-review journals at least as frequently per capita as those from university-based researchers. This lower credibility seems to be declining but is still a stigma to be reckoned with for the sociologist who wants to spend his or her first three to four postdoctoral years with the AMA or AHA and then wants to rejoin academia. Somehow, political goals and lobbying positions are seen as inevitably influencing the research process and product. Whether or not this influence does occur, its extent varies and is not at all inevitable or fixed, as will be shown later in this chapter.

Another related disadvantage is the explicit rather than implicit absence of the normal quality-assurance mechanisms of peer review, and promotion norms based on publication. Again, these features are not entirely absent, as directors of research in such associations are becoming more successful in developing a management acceptance of such norms using peer review as a major technique. Initial recruitment is based, for the most part, on the assessment of scholarly productivity. For instance, when I was the American Hospital Association director of research, my recruitment process was no different from that of a department of sociology: ask leading professors doing relevant hospital-related research to nominate their brightest graduate students or fellows, advertise, secure references, have the candidates' reprints peer-reviewed by an outside panel, have the candidates present a seminar and be interviewed with other staff members. Once the research staff member is recruited, his or her annual performance review is also based mainly on scholarly output, and the salary increase, which is assigned differentially, reflects research production more competitively than do similar increases at universities. Increasingly, researchers are being retained or encouraged to move on the basis of their research performance, in contrast with the situation still predominant in some associations, in which research is a sinecure for life, demanding only technical assistance based on political loyalty and descriptive reviews of association statistics for in-house publications. Even worse (from the perspective of research, though not necessarily of the individual) are the cases of promising young researchers who successfully seek promotion out of the research unit to higher management. Although this phenomenon is not unknown in academia—where associate deanships can lure the brightest and the best in addition to the less gifted normally attracted to such middle-level bureaucracy—it seems to be a particularly attractive notion in associations, with the lure based on the same questionable but widely believed equation between higher levels in the bureaucracy and greater influence on policy.

The final major disadvantage of working in health associations, which is related to the previous discussion, is the enormous managerial difficulty of defining and prioritizing the relevant clients and audiences for research. Although, as the previous discussion maintains, the research community is the primary audience and reference group for the research staff, the process is more complex at the supervisory level of research director or vice-president for research and development, particularly during the budget process, where the following questions are raised: What influence ought association policy to have—on individual researchers' preferences, theory-derived models, and so on—in constructing the research agendas of an association? In addition to journal publications, what dissemination techniques within the health care sector being served and what recommendations can an association appropriately expect of its research unit? What is an appropriate balance between theory, past studies, future policy requirements, and political values as sources of hypotheses for individual studies?

The individual researcher runs the risk of being insulated from professional reference groups (and the associated norms, values, and rewards) and having his or her professional identity and quality primarily determined by the secular norms of the health association rather than by the norms of the professional discipline. It is therefore of particular importance that the researcher and the research directors become or remain active in professional groups such as the medical sociology section of the American Sociological Association (ASA), the appropriate section of the American Public Health Association (APHA), and regional sociology societies.

In summary, then, health associations are attractive as applied research settings for sociologists in terms of preferred access to important data sets and the availability of uninterrupted research time but present problems of perceived low credibility, potential professional isolation, and political influence on the topics included on the unit's research agenda. On balance, however, it does represent a professionally productive way to spend a well-delineated three to four postdoctoral years, provided that the individual has a clear idea of the data sets he or she will be working with and agreement from the association as to the research topics he or she will be focusing on.

Federal Agencies. Federal agencies have long employed sociologists as researchers and program and project officers. At the major settings for health services research—NCHSR, HCFA, NIH, and VA—the roles for sociologists may include: research analysis of data in an intramural research division; monitoring the awarding of research grants and contracts; program management of health initiatives; and policy analysis and technical assistance to the department.

Needless to say, employment in the federal sector is not currently expanding; indeed, many sociologists are being let go. The most likely short-term prospect for a sociologist in a federal agency is as an Intergovernmental Personnel Act fellow, whereby the researcher's employer (university or other agency) is compensated by the government for salary, fringe benefits, and overhead, and the researcher works for the federal agency for a one- to two-year period on an agreed-on assignment.

The advantages (as well as the disadvantages) of working for a federal agency are similar to those of working at a health association. Preferred access is available to comprehensive and important health data sets, among which those at NCHSR, the VA, and HCFA are particularly attractive. In addition to federal data sets, federally based researchers are also able to undertake secondary analyses of data collected under grant or contract to that agency. Indeed, some system-wise researchers use the grant, the contract mechanism, and the taxpayers' dollars in exclusive support of their own professional research activities.

With regard to reward for scholarly activity, a distinction should be made between settings in intramural research units where research is the exclusive or major activity (NCHSR) and settings (HCFA) where research is incidental or at least subsidiary to project monitoring. Intramural researchers are especially encouraged to publish in peer-reviewed journals, and research products are taken into account as a major component in their annual performance review. Nevertheless, apart from encouragement, special monetary awards, and increased internal and external prestige, research output does not often lead to salary increases. Salary levels as well as promotion in most civil service jobs depend on seniority and relatively standard raises independent of merit. In addition, although staff members are encouraged to present their results at professional meetings, the unavailability of travel funds in recent years has prevented many from attending. Salaries are higher in the federal service than in the universities, fringe benefits are excellent, and job security is normally guaranteed to the point of offering no disincentives for bad or even no research. This situation is even more pronounced in federal settings other than intramural research units, in which the researcher is program or project officer and monitor of others' research, and research is a minor part of the job responsibility and of the criteria for performance review.

An important, albeit intangible, reward is professional prestige, and the perceived prestige of federal sociologists seems to be higher than that of sociologists in health associations—perhaps higher than in any other nonuniversity applied setting—and nearly comparable to the prestige of university sociologists. Of course, prestige varies across federal agencies (high in NIH and low in HCFA, for example), just as it does between universities, and individual accomplishments will certainly continue to outweigh the perceived credibility of the setting. Nevertheless, the sociologist who wants to move into academia four to five years after receiving the Ph.D. or indeed after twenty years of service will find it easier from a federal agency than from a health association. The agency's relatively high credibility appears to reflect current perceptions of federal employment as disinterested public service and of employment by health associations or individual health care providers as rather venal and politically influenced.

Federal agencies are also more likely than other settings to provide research sociologists with supportive colleagues with shared interests and backgrounds. Even compared to most departments of sociology, federal agencies represent a community of social scientists more seriously interested in interdisciplinary research and more inclined and willing to work together as colleagues.

Academic freedom in most senses of the term is guaranteed in federal agencies. As in health associations, no one tells the researcher how the research is to come out or how the results are to be written up, and he or she is free to pursue the analysis of the given topic according to the norms of scholarship. In most applied research, however, the individual, unlike the university researcher, is not free to choose any topic for which he or she can find support. Directors of research in federal agencies and health associations, in responding to staff members' requests for resources to pursue their own interests, are guided by a number of considerations in addition to technical merit, feasibility, and contribution to the literature. These considerations reflect the director's need to attract external resources from the department or Congress, to respond to his or her program's constituencies, and to build alliances with program units. Considerations also involve, among others, such factors as program relevance of the proposed project, dissemination opportunities among influential program groups, and responsiveness to policy decisions to be made. Although such concerns do not explicitly lead to political interference, they do involve nonresearch criteria in project selection and thereby may lead, without courageous resources management at the directorate level, to a dilution of academic freedom. Precisely in this worrisome context must the absence of external peer review in most intramural research activities be seen, since it contrasts so ironically with the same agencies' commitment to extramurally organized research.

The ability of research to influence policy is severely constrained by the size and complexity of the federal bureaucracy involved. Although it is important for other purposes (access to operational data, for example) to distinguish between federal agencies with operational responsibilities for providing health services (HCFA, VA) and federal agencies without these responsibilities (NCHS, NCHSR, and NIH), researchers in agencies in the first category do not necessarily have more influence on their agency's policies. In fact, there seem to be as few examples in federal settings as in health associations of research results causing a change of policy, as opposed to being supportive of a change already being made for other reasons. Indeed, despite the exaggerated claims of the health services research leadership, research results cannot reasonably be expected to have a direct, independent impact on policy. To seek direct influence over policy or to seek social relevance and responsiveness can even hinder the development and implementation of research agendas and individual projects, particularly in federal agencies, which tend to see agency rewards (increased appropriations) and individual incentives (promotion) as related to political influence rather than research rigor. The across-the-board salary increases, the relative absence of salary incentives for research quality, the lack of external peer review for intramural research, and, until recently, career-long tenure have all contributed to many young federal social science researchers doing worse and less research than they would have produced at a university or to their leaving research altogether. The same factor should, in all fairness, also make us all the more appreciative of the high quality that federal researchers have produced in the face of such disincentives.

Individual Health Care Providers. There is a widely held belief that the researcher's influence on operational policy will be greater the nearer he or she is situated to the operational program level. Although my view, articulated earlier in this piece, is that the nearer the researcher is to operations the less freedom he or she will have to do research at all (in the sense of interested, independent analysis), many hospitals and researchers have been attracted by the prior argument into joining forces. This discussion will be confined to hospitals, since very few researchers are employed by other health care providers, with the exception of local health departments, which will be dealt with in the next section. Approximately 200 to 300 hospitals have formally established research departments—that is, departments that include a full-time director with social science research training and a formal budget in excess of $50,000. In addition, substantial research and other activities likely to attract sociologists are carried on in hospital departments of planning, marketing, operations, and finance.

These hospital-based research centers—of particular interest to sociologists as sources of data, research sites, employment, and student interns as well as adjunct faculty—are usually situated in larger hospitals, particularly teaching hospitals, and in the corporate headquarters of investor-owned or nonprofit hospital chains. Such research units—which range in size from one full-time professional and a secretary/research assistant to twenty to thirty professionals with support staff—may perform the following functions: population and patient utilization projections for strategic planning purposes; patient origin and referral studies for facility planning; patient compliance studies aimed at improving the quality of health care through provider education; quality assurance studies; and applied research, whether externally or internally funded.

Typically, hospital-based research units are established because of current industry fashion, because they are mistakenly seen as generators of revenue, and, ironically, because many hospital Chief Executive Officers have come to believe the exaggerated claims of the research community that health services research can improve health services across the board. Often a relatively junior person with training in the social sciences (particularly economics and sociology) is made director, with a budget of $50,000 for his or her own salary and that of a secretary/research assistant. Typically, the research agenda is almost entirely determined by the director's unsophisticated overresponsiveness to the line managers' operational problems, at the cost of theory-derived hypotheses. When this approach fails to solve any problems or bring in many grants, hospital administrators become disillusioned with the research activity, and the center may be terminated.

This scenario is less likely to occur in large, complex hospitals where the research unit can be somewhat insulated from front-line operational pressures or where those pressures are more sophisticated and require less day-to-day problem solving. In teaching hospitals, for example, joint appointments with an academic department (social and preventive medicine, for example, or even the mainline clinical departments of pediatrics, medicine, and surgery) can attract better-qualified individuals and provide them with additional and more supportive reference groups. Similarly, the research unit situated in the corporate headquarters of a hospital chain is likely to be a more flexible environment for high-quality research responses to reasonable and better-informed expectations. In terms of the criteria already reviewed, hospital-based research units have the following specific advantages and disadvantages: access to data is likely to be excellent, although the data sets are facility-specific and do not allow population-based statements about utilization patterns; and hospital chains collect detailed data from their many hospitals and have, as a result, more comprehensive data sets, although they are less likely than individual hospitals to allow its detailed use in publicly available documents.

The rewards for external publication are few, except in teaching hospitals, and the demands for internal staff reports are many. Research is likely to be based on operational problems rather than theory, and there is little opportunity to choose the variety of study sites demanded by a particular model or hypothesis. Although the research is not usually generalizable to many settings, hospitals offer the best settings for experimental control and randomized clinical trials. Research colleagues in individual hospitals are scarce, although hospital settings allow the researcher good exposure to clinicians and administrators and the important perspectives and knowledge they represent. Academic freedom is not a relevant norm in this setting, since much of the data is regarded as proprietary and external publication is not often encouraged. Finally, this setting offers the researcher the greatest opportunity for influencing policies and services, although that influence is not always based on the quality of the research.

Foundations and Local Government. In addition to the applied settings already described are others that, although involving fewer jobs or collaborative opportunities now, are likely to be of increasing importance in the future. Foundations employ social scientists as program officers to develop and monitor program initiatives and the research and demonstration activities of others. Although foundation positions involve program management rather than research, the director of research for the foundation (Linda Aiken) is a sociologist. Her foundation, incidentally, has the largest health services research budget of any agency in the world.

Since foundations fund research and program activities by others, their own staff members have access to a variety of data sets and indeed publish their analyses of these data, with particular attention to policy implications. Foundation staff members are encouraged to publish, since this is seen as enhancing the foundation's image and influence, and publications seem to be taken into account in salary increases and promotions. Articles are likely to be policy analyses rather than research and to be based on program concerns rather than theory-derived hypotheses. Supportive colleagues are available both inside and outside the foundation. Foundation staff members do not have freedom to choose which topic to analyze but are recruited in a particular program area in which they are expected to be supportive of the program's policies—policies they have helped formulate. Policy influence is likely to be substantial because foundations see influencing policy through funding innovative demonstration activities and being able to do so without the bureaucratic and programmatic constraints of governmental agencies as their role. Foundation employment is prestigious, well rewarded, and likely to lead easily back to academia, with which it has close symbiotic ties.

In contrast, local government as an applied setting for sociologists is usually neither prestigious nor flexible. State and city agencies are increasingly likely to employ master's- or doctoral-level social scientists in such departments and functions as program evaluation of social and health programs, health planning analyses, and Medicaid population projections. Such settings can involve close access to excellent data sets that allow population-based as well as facility-specific analyses. As another civil service setting, local government is subject to the same constraints as federal agencies on rewards for research. Although local governments do not have as long a history of intramural research, there is growing interest in and encouragement of disinterested analyses and their presentation before professional audiences. Availability of supportive fellow researchers tends to be low in such settings, although social scientists are exposed to collaborative clinicians and highly experienced program managers from whom they can learn much. Academic freedom is likely to be as confined as in federal agencies, but policy and program influence can be substantial, avoiding both the parochialism of being limited to a local facility such as a hospital and the programmatic detachment of the non-operational federal agencies.

Strategies for Improvement

As the discussion in this chapter makes clear, the blessings of working in an applied research setting are mixed. In general, the researcher has preferential access to important data sets and uninterrupted time for research but few external rewards for research productivity, somewhat lower prestige than in academia, and greater isolation from professional networks. These features are summarized in Table 1. Although some of these characteristics are unalterable, some can be modified by thoughtful preparation by the three parties concerned with the involvement of graduate sociologists in applied settings: graduate departments of sociology, graduate sociologists, and the applied settings themselves. This chapter will conclude by suggesting several ameliorative strategies.

Graduate Departments of Sociology. Departments can help prepare graduates for positions in applied settings by:

- Offering courses in relevant health program areas jointly with medical departments as well as offering courses in urban studies, geography, industrial engineering, and policy analysis so that graduates can be more employable as knowledgeable program analysts with substantive skills
- Providing courses in program evaluation and grant writing

Table 1. Applied Research Settings as Employers of Research Sociologists.

| | | Applied Setting | | | | | | |
| | | Federal Agencies | | Hospitals | | | Miscellaneous | |
Criteria	Health Association	Intramural Research	Nonintramural Research	Chains	Individual	Teaching	Foundations	Local Government
1. Preferred access to valuable data sets	H	H	M	H	H	H	H	H
2. Rewards for scholarly research	M	M	L	M	L	H	H	M
3. Academic freedom	M	H	M	L	L	H	M	M
4. Macro-policy influence	M	M	H	H	L	L	M	H
5. Micro-policy influence	L	L	M	H	H	M	H	M
6. Perceived credibility and prestige	L	H	M	M	L	H	H	L
7. Encouragement of theory-based research	M	H	L	L	L	L	L	L
8. Salary and fringe benefits	H	M	M	H	L	L	H	M
9. Political interference	M	H	H	M	H	L	M	M
10. Availability of supportive colleagues with same interests	M	H	H	M	L	H	H	M

Note: H = high, M = moderate, L = low.

- Offering field placements, internships, and practicum experiences in applied research settings involving joint supervision by program managers and sociology faculty
- Developing an inventory of such settings within commuting radius and cataloguing their data sets, research interests, and senior leadership
- Inviting the setting's leadership to conferences and seminars and discussing with them their continuing education and evaluation needs, which the department may be able to meet
- Offering adjunct faculty positions to research directors from applied settings and considering joint appointments for future recruitment
- Having existing faculty consider applied settings as potential sites for research, sabbatical leave, or summer employment and their leadership as potential collaborators with whom to apply for grant funding
- Having faculty members assume responsibility within their program interest for a particular national applied setting; visit that organization's national headquarters; and invite a research sociologist from that organization to visit the department so that he or she can be an informed liaison between the organization and the department and can advise graduate students and faculty

Graduate Sociologists. Graduate sociologists can make themselves attractive largely by developing their program expertise and their familiarity with the data sets and activities of the applied settings in which they would be interested in working. Whether senior graduate students or junior faculty members, sociologists can improve their employability and, once hired, their professional productivity by:

- Visiting with agency representatives when in Chicago or Washington
- Offering to present a seminar at the agency on the topic of interest to them, perhaps involving their data or at least their mission
- Identifying, within an overall career plan, three to five years (preferably immediately after graduation) when agency employment would be attractive and developing a clear idea of

what kind of academic department or federal agency the
student would then join

- Negotiating an explicit agreement with the potential employer
  on data access; the models to be tested and the publications to
  be developed (written outlines could be usefully discussed as
  part of the initial negotiations); travel expenses to professional
  meetings; the possibility of concurrent adjunct faculty appointments; salary, salary increases, and criteria for performance review; moving expenses; responsibilities in addition to research;
  and processes for research project identification
- Once hired, maintaining or accentuating linkages with regional
  and national professional associations (ASA, APHA) and, even
  if an adjunct faculty appointment is not possible, visiting with
  the local department of sociology, attending their seminars, offering data, and accepting graduate students as part-time research assistants
- Developing an external peer group to advise on each research
  project so its nature and quality will be influenced more by an
  external professional reference group than by internal bureaucratic accountability

Applied Research Settings. If they are to attract creative,
productive researchers, applied settings must modify their behavior and expectations by:

- Not expecting that researchers will necessarily be interested in
  career-long employment and making provisions for three- to
  five-year employment contracts
- Offering TIAA/CREF so that academics are not forced to forgo
  their retirement pension provision while working for a nonuniversity setting
- Allowing increased extramural access to data sets
- Revising their expectations that research agendas can always be
  short-term, have day-to-day relevance to the agency's mission,
  and provide the basis for testimony
- Distinguishing between policy analysis and research and coming
  to appreciate the latter for its own intrinsic worth
- Involving extramural researchers on advisory committees
  throughout the agency so that the critical research perspective
  can be appreciated

- Taking research productivity into account in salary and promotion review and introducing merit awards for particularly valuable research contributions
- Providing for university-based researchers during summers or short periods at the agency's expense to analyze the data sets for a well-specified research project and providing for postdoctoral and predoctoral fellowships

Many of these suggested strategies for improvement represent radical departures from present arrangements, and some are not likely to occur in the immediate future. They all, however, represent well-justified investments by each party, not only because applied sociology will gain more data, jobs, and influence but also because applied settings themselves can benefit increasingly from greater exposure to sociology and the critical richness of its perspective.

16

MILITARY STUDIES

David R. Segal

The Department of Defense budget in the 1980s allocates tens of millions of dollars annually for research and development in the behavioral and social sciences. Although almost unnoticeable in comparison to the total defense research effort, most of which is concerned with high-technology hardware, this figure is considerable when compared to the level of research funding in the behavioral and social sciences from all other federal agencies. These funds are the main base of fiscal support for applied or policy research on the military, some of which has implications for the civilian sector as well. A considerably lower level of funding comes from other federal agencies, such as the Veterans Administration and the Department of Labor, and from private foundations that provide support for policy analyses of military issues. However, the Defense Department and the military departments, through their own research laboratories or through extramural funding, support most of the applied social science research on the military.

Much of the social science research supported by the defense establishment has been sociological, but relatively little has been done by sociologists. This situation is due in part to the overlapping substantive jurisdictions of the social science disciplines and to the traditional tendency of sociologists to seek employment in colleges and universities rather than in government laboratories or in the private-sector research-and-development firms that execute the Defense Department's research program. In addition, military sociology has been one of the smallest substantive specialties in our discipline. Economics and psychology, by contrast, have been more willing to regard the military as a legitimate object of analysis and have not treated scientists who work in nonacademic contexts as outsiders. As a result, a considerable number of scientists from these disciplines have been employed by the government and by the research-and-development industry to execute most of the Defense Department's behavioral and social science research program. Consequently, over time, the manpower, personnel, and organizational problems of the military that might lend themselves to sociological analysis have been conceptualized in terms of the basic individualistic and utilitarian assumptions of psychology and economics rather than the collectivistic and normative assumptions of sociology.

Recent years have seen a modest increase in graduate student enrollments in military sociology, and many of these students have in fact found employment in government research centers or in research-and-development corporations that do contract research for the government. In addition, academically based military sociologists have been playing an increasingly visible role in the defense policy process, serving on advisory bodies or as consultants to executive branch agencies, testifying before congressional committees and providing guidance to legislators through the activities of the Congressional Research Service, and serving as expert witnesses or contributing to amicus curiae briefs when policies are subjected to judicial review.

The number of sociologists involved in these activities is still very small, both in absolute terms and relative to the involvement of psychologists and economists. However, in proportion to its size, the impact of military sociology on applied policies and programs may be higher than for any other area of sociological inquiry.

Moreover, the arena for applied research is growing. Controversy on the success of the all-volunteer force, a possible return to military conscription, the reestablishment of G.I. Bill educational benefits in return for military service, the redefinition of appropriate roles for women in the armed forces, problems of military families, and a multitude of other issues regarding the nature of military service in a democracy have all broadened the policy agenda for which sociological analysis is appropriate. In addition, a range of social programs within the military, covering family services, drug and alcohol abuse, racial and ethnic tensions, and other social issues, are in constant need of evaluation and refinement.

Historical Overview

World War I. The utilization of social science research in support of the national defense effort began with the declaration of war in 1917. Robert M. Yerkes, then president of the American Psychological Association, encouraged his colleagues to contribute to the national defense by devising methods for screening volunteers and draftees. The results of his call were the army alpha and beta tests for the classification of literates and illiterates, respectively. The test development was performed by psychologists employed in institutions other than the military, and, with demobilization, the research effort ceased. Two important precedents, however, had been established: the discipline of psychology had legitimized participation in defense-related research, and the armed forces had adopted psychometric screening tests as a major instrument of manpower management. This latter point is particularly important, because psychometric tests have subsequently been viewed by defense policy makers as a major tool for dealing with a wide range of personnel and manpower problems, ranging from selection and classification—where, given the luxury of a favorable selection ratio, they have proven beneficial—to drug abuse and the problem of AWOL, where they have not. World War I also saw the dawning of social science interest in propaganda techniques in wartime (Lasswell, 1927). Although in some ways similar to other applications of social-psychological principles to attitudinal change, such as market research, this tradition in the military was broadened over time to cover a wider range of psychological warfare techniques.

World War II. In the face of hostilities in Europe, the army decided to institute an in-house psychological testing capability and, in 1939, established the Personnel Testing Section of The Adjutant General's Office. This section was responsible for the development of the Army General Classification Test (AGCT), which was administered to more than twelve million men during World War II, and for the development of selection and classification tests for pilots, navigators, and bombardiers for the Army Air Corps. These early efforts at psychometric measurement developed into the field of military psychology (see Watson, 1978, for an insightful overview of the growth of this area).

World War II also saw the mobilization of sociologists and social psychologists in support of the defense effort. Perhaps most visibly, starting in 1941, the research branch of the army's information and education division (which went through at least five changes in name and organization during its existence) did hundreds of surveys and experiments in support of military personnel policy, as a strictly applied research effort. After the war, the professional personnel of the research branch returned to their academic pursuits, one of which was the writing and publication of *Studies in Social Psychology in World War II* (Stouffer and others, 1949a; 1949b; 1950; Hovland, Lumsdaine, and Sheffield, 1949). This project was executed by an ad hoc special committee of the Social Science Research Council, financed by a grant from the Carnegie Corporation, housed at American University, and staffed by former members of the research branch. The applied research effort during the war provided useful information to policy makers and added a new research method to the army personnel managers' tool kit: the social survey. It was the discipline-oriented reanalysis of the data by demobilized civilian social scientists, however, that yielded the conceptual contributions regarding the primary group and the contact hypothesis, as well as the wide range of methodological contributions for which Stouffer's team is noted.

The World War II mobilization of sociologists was not limited to those who served in civilian research roles. Other sociologists served in uniform, many filling operational and strategic intelligence functions and bringing a sociological perspective to the task of analyzing hostile military systems and psychological warfare operations. Again, after demobilization, most of these sociologists returned to academic roles and reported their most interesting findings in traditional academic media (for example, Shils and Janowitz, 1948; Lerner, 1971).

Although the principal sociologists of the research branch left the employment of the army, the branch itself was maintained under a variety of names until 1955 and staffed primarily by nonsociologists. The Personnel Testing Section evolved into the U.S. Army Personnel Research Office (USAPRO), with a broadened mission for behavioral research as the army became increasingly dependent on complex technology that generated problems in the management of the man-machine interface. The dominance of attitude researchers, psychometricians, and human factors engineers in the army's behavioral science research centers gave a decidedly psychological bent to the research program in the postwar years.

Korean War. The Korean War period can be viewed as the dawning of extramural social science contract research sponsored by the defense establishment. The RAND Corporation—established in 1946 with air force support to conduct research primarily in the physical sciences and drawing heavily on the talents of university scientists—entered the social science arena, although economists and political scientists far outnumbered psychologists and sociologists in the organization. The Human Resources Research Office (HumRRO), originally affiliated with George Washington University, was founded in 1951 with army support. Although HumRRO primarily did psychological studies, its work program included more sociological elements, such as Bradbury's studies of communist prisoners of war (Bradbury, Meyers, and Biderman, 1968). The Operations Research Office of Johns Hopkins University conducted psychological research on effective soldiers and units but also moved into the sociological arena with research on the racial integration of the army during the Korean War (Bogart, 1959). The military departments conducted in-house social science research as well, with the air force conducting research on the behavior of American prisoners of war in communist captivity (Biderman, 1963) and the army continuing research on a small scale on the importance of cohesiveness in fighting units, a phenomenon that had been highlighted by research on both American and German troops in World War II (Little, 1964).

Cold War. The defense establishment emerged from the Korean War with a renewed appreciation for the effects of group dynamics on soldier performance and an increased interest in techniques of psychological warfare (which, while psychological in name, have strong and important sociological underpinnings). The former concern led the defense establishment to build financial bridges to one segment of the university-based social science community by supporting the field of small-group research—a field dominated, of course, by psychologists. Research in this area grew tenfold between 1950 and 1960, with over three quarters being performed by academic scholars. Over half of this research was supported by the navy, air force, or army (McGrath and Altman, 1966).

Vietnam War Era. If the decade of the 1950s was characterized by bridge building between the defense establishment and social scientists in universities, the 1960s saw the burning of those bridges. The increasingly unpopular, escalating conflict in Southeast Asia and the student demonstrations that it spawned caused universities to reevaluate their relationships with the armed forces. These reevaluations led in many instances to the removal of ROTC programs from campuses, to the termination of university-based classified research, and to the separation of centers of social science research sponsored by the armed forces from the campuses with which they had been associated.

The Special Operations Research Office (SORO), founded in 1956 as a part of the American University in Washington, D.C., and initially concerned with social science research supporting propaganda efforts directed toward the Soviet bloc, turned its attention in the 1960s to counterinsurgency in Third World nations. SORO became the academic home of Project Camelot, a research effort aimed at attempting to build models to identify the sources of political instability in Third World nations and to evaluate actions that might reestablish political stability (Horowitz, 1967; Deitchman, 1976). The project was seen by its proponents, who tried to enlist an international corps of university-based social scientists to perform the work, as a very basic model-building exercise. Critics in the academic world and in government agencies other than the defense department, however, saw it as an attempt to develop techniques for the support of regimes favorable to American political and economic interests but unpopular in their own nations.

Camelot came under great pressure, resulting in its termination, the reorganization of SORO as the Center for Research on Social Systems (CRESS), and the separation of CRESS from American University. In a similar manner, the Operations Research Office at Johns Hopkins University reorganized as the independent, nonprofit Research Analysis Corporation (RAC) when Johns Hopkins grew unhappy with its military links, and, in 1969, HumRRO was severed from George Washington University.

These reorganizations, producing the independent contract research firms that conducted social science research for the armed forces during the Vietnam War, increased the social and intellectual distance between the social scientists doing government-sponsored research and the academic community and increased the dependence of the defense social science effort on those disciplines that had legitimized and encouraged employment outside the academic world. The distance between sociology as a discipline and the military's applied social science research program was especially great, because, although much of the research program studied sociological problems, very few of the dozens of social scientists employed in the contract research firms were sociologists, either by education or by disciplinary identification. The same situation was true of the armed forces laboratories that conducted in-house research programs or oversaw the contract research: the army's Behavior and Systems Research Laboratory (BESRL), which evolved from USAPRO in the 1960s; the Air Force Human Resource Laboratory (AFHRL); the Division of Psychological Sciences of the Office of Naval Research (ONR); the Air Force Office of Scientific Research (AFOSR); and the Navy Personnel Research and Development Center (NPRDC).

An additional event of the 1960s is worthy of note. In 1960, Robert McNamara left the Ford Motor Company and became Secretary of Defense, bringing to the Pentagon a strong belief in operations research, systems analysis, and other management tools rooted in econometrics and emphasizing those variables, such as cost, that can most easily be quantified. McNamara's researchers omitted from their analyses of the military those variables that were universally regarded as important but were more difficult to measure, such as cohesion, leadership, and esprit de corps. Thus, the late 1960s saw the Office of the Secretary of Defense populated by economists and the military departments drawing heavily on psychologists both in their in-house laboratories and for their outside contractors. Sociologists, to the extent that they participated in the policy and program process, did so from the academy.

The All-Volunteer Force. The economic managerialism of the McNamara years set the stage for the all-volunteer force (Segal, 1981). President Nixon's Commission on an All-Volunteer Armed Force, the Gates Commission, was appointed in 1969 and charged with the development of a comprehensive plan for eliminating conscription.

The deliberations of the Gates Commission were not conducted in an information vacuum. Indeed, probably no policy deliberation in U.S. history has been as informed, or as overinformed, by social science research. In this case, reflecting the managerial orientation of the Office of the Secretary of Defense, the research was done primarily by economists (Segal, forthcoming). In response to opposition to the Vietnam War, criticisms of the draft, and concerns about high draft calls, as well as a 1964 Department of Defense study of the draft, economists had started studying and publishing professional papers on the draft in the mid-1960s. Sociologists were, for the most part, mired in political debates about the war rather than engaged in scholarly analysis.

The economic research focused on labor market factors and attempted to estimate, in economic terms, the cost of military service to those who were drafted (the "conscription tax") and the cost to the nation of recruiting an all-volunteer force at competitive wages. Economists doing staff studies for the Gates Commission found that an all-volunteer force was feasible. Other economists, working under the auspices of a Washington research organization and utilizing the same data, suggested that it was not feasible. This discrepancy may tell us more about economics as a discipline than it tells us about the all-volunteer force, but the optimistic projections of the Gates Commission were used as the policy blueprint for the force, and, through the all-volunteer force era, the feasibility and indeed success of the all-volunteer force concept were defended by economists working for the Office of the Secretary of Defense (Office of the Secretary of Defense, 1978).

Given the policy of maintaining an all-volunteer force, the services themselves, faced with the problem of making the force

work, supported large research programs to deal with such problems as recruitment, retention, attrition, training, drug abuse,
race relations, and job satisfaction. Unlike the Department of Defense research, which was predominantly economic, the research
programs of the services were predominantly psychological, in
staff if not in the nature of the problems.

An overview of the organizations executing the research
program may be instructive. Private research organizations performed almost half the sponsored research. In-house research laboratories carried out over one third. Only about 10 percent was performed in academic institutions. As might be expected, the nature
of the organizations performing the research differed between the
Department of Defense and the individual armed services. The
RAND Corporation, with its heavy emphasis on economic analysis, accounted for 50 percent of the reports written for the Department of Defense. HumRRO, RAC, and Market Facts, Inc., produced over two thirds of the external research reports written for
the army. HumRRO, RAND, and the Western Electric Corporation produced over 80 percent of the policy research for the air
force. Operations Research, Inc., and the University of Michigan
accounted for over one third of the navy's external research program (Snyder and Davis, 1981).

The 1970s saw the growth of in-house research capability,
particularly in the army. In response to a National Research Council (1968) report citing a need for coherence and purpose in the
army's behavioral science research program, an Army Scientific
Advisory Panel (1972) report citing the need for greater focus and
continuity in the program and the minimal qualifications of the
people in contract research organizations executing the extramural
program, and a dismal diagnosis of the military social science program by a second National Research Council (1971) task force,
the army expanded BESRL to the U.S. Army Research Institute
for the Behavioral and Social Sciences (ARI) in 1973 and included
a small sociological research capability. However, the research staff
continued to be dominated by psychologists, and, although the institute was responsible for the army's manpower research program,
not a single demographer or manpower economist was on the professional staff. In 1976, after a major congressional reduction in
funding for research on drug and alcohol abuse and on racial prob-

lems, ARI abolished the division that had housed most of the sociological research, reflecting a perception widely held in the federal government that sociology is only relevant to the study of a limited range of social problems. However, some sociologists remained on the ARI staff.

Current Situation. Although neither sociology as a discipline nor its major professional association has done much to encourage the employment of sociologists in the defense research and policy community, the climate today is favorable for sociological involvement. The optimistic projections of the econometricians who worked for the Gates Commission and for the Office of the Secretary of Defense have not proven valid, bringing about an increasing realization in policy circles that, while economists might contribute to the resolution of some policy issues, they do not have all the answers. Similarly, in the face of declining cohort size, an unfavorable selection ratio, and a major norming error on the version of the mental aptitude test used by the services in the 1970s leading to the recruitment of large numbers of marginal personnel, a more realistic view of the limits of psychometrics is emerging. And declining job satisfaction in all the armed services since the advent of the all-volunteer force, despite the institution of organizational development programs, has demonstrated that industrial psychology does not have all the answers.

Policy makers are focusing increasingly on issues to which sociological knowledge can be brought to bear, such as social-psychological processes of cohesion and leadership and structural and organizational problems of military families and military installations as communities, including the ways in which the military intersects with other social institutions like higher education. Reflecting these concerns, the presence of sociologists in the defense research community is increasingly visible. As of early 1982, military sociologists work at the Army Research Institute, at the Department of Military Psychiatry of the Walter Reed Army Institute of Research, at the Defense Manpower Data Center, and at the Survey Branch of the Soldier Support Center, the current incarnation of the research branch of the Information and Education Division. Sociologists work for many of the defense establishment's largest social science contractors, including the RAND Corporation and Human Sciences Research, Inc., and many other sociologists serve as consultants for these organizations. Sociologists are or have recently been members of the army's Research and Development Advisory Group and the navy's Research Advisory Committee, boards of extramural experts who review the service's research programs.

Sociologists also serve in a variety of advisory and consultative roles to specific defense agencies. Sociologists participated in the research phase of the 1978 Army Training Study (ARTS), a large-scale evaluation of the effectiveness of the army's training system. A rural sociologist was involved in the basing study for the MX missile system, and sociologists are increasingly being used by the Army Corps of Engineers for social impact assessment and, more recently, for the projection of social trends. In addition, sociologists have been deeply involved in research on postservice adjustment problems of Vietnam veterans. These latter roles are generally filled by academically based sociologists, who have also provided considerable advice on the evaluation of the all-volunteer force, the utilization of women in the armed forces, and the potential effects of a new G.I. Bill.

The services differ in the degree to which they utilize sociological information, with the army being the major employer of sociologists, user of sociological consultants and funding source for sociological research. The air force maintains a much lower sociological profile, although a sociologist was employed at the Air Force Office of Scientific Research well before the field became fashionable in the other services, the Department of Behavioral Science and Leadership at the Air Force Academy is headed by a sociologist, and the Air Force Institute of Technology has undertaken a major research effort to test a current sociological theory of military organization, albeit with a team of nonsociologists (Stahl, McNichols, and Manley, 1981). The navy has been the service most resistant to sociological input and indeed is the only service whose academy has nothing resembling a military sociology course. Even there, however, the Division of Psychological Sciences of the Office of Naval Research has been open to research proposals from sociologists.

As noted by Kourvetaris and Dobratz (1977), military sociology still holds a marginal position relative to both the military and sociology. However, it is no more marginal to the former than to the latter; in fact, the relatively few sociologists who work on applied and policy problems in the military seem to have influence well beyond what one would anticipate on the basis of their number.

Lessons Learned

The experience of sociology and of allied social sciences working in the military context is instructive for future applied research, not only in this arena but in other applied realms as well. Some of the lessons learned are worthy of attention.

First, it is important for sociologists to feel it is legitimate to leave the university. One reason for their general exclusion from military studies has been their concentration in institutions of higher education and the concentration of defense research funds outside these institutions. This distribution of funds is not likely to change. A recent report of the Army Science Board (1980, p. 15) on "human issues research" noted that "army needs are unlikely to be met by research funded through traditional academic channels."

Second, disciplinary associations can play a crucial role in defining the conditions under which scholars work in the military research community. While the American Sociological Association has largely confined its role to that of a learned society, the disciplinary associations of psychology and social work have coupled the learned society role with a guild orientation and have drawn on the professional association model characteristic of medicine and law. They have accepted responsibility for professional certification and have fought forcefully and successfully for the recognition of certified members as professionals. Consequently, psychology Ph.D.s who enter the army receive direct commissions as captains, and civilian psychologists who go to work for the army (or any other federal agency) normally have relocation expenses paid. Neither of these conditions is true for sociologists, although the psychologists and sociologists may do essentially the same work.

Third, the growth of applied military sociology is constrained in part by the size of the subfield of military sociology itself. Not all sociologists working on military studies must have a primary specialty in military sociology. Demographers, for example, can project the size of the military age-eligible population without knowing much about the military. For most applications, however, some knowledge of military organization is essential, but few programs offer appropriate training. A survey conducted in 1972 of scholars concerned with national security affairs identified only 9 undergraduate courses and 3 graduate courses in military sociology or the sociology of war in the United States (National Security Program, 1973). A follow-up survey two years later still found fewer than 20 courses on the military being offered in sociology departments (National Security Education Program, 1975). In the late 1960s, only 1 of the 169 departments listed in the American Sociological Association's *Guide to Graduate Departments of Sociology* indicated that the sociology of the military was a departmental specialization. Offerings in the field have increased somewhat, but, in 1975, only 9 of the 216 departments listed in that year's guide indicated that it was possible to specialize in military sociology (Kourvetaris and Dobratz, 1977, p. 7). A plurality, if not a majority, of the military sociologists employed as uniformed members of the services, as civil servants, as employees of contract research organizations, or as consultants have been associated with the four academic departments most closely associated with basic sociological research on the military: the University of Chicago, the University of Maryland, the University of Michigan, and Northwestern University. In terms of the number of Americans coming into contact with it in the course of the life cycle, the military is surpassed, among major institutions, only by the family, the educational system, and the occupational structure, yet it remains one of the smallest subfields in the discipline. Sociology thus "remains relatively out of touch with the mass movement of contemporary international conflict" (Janowitz, 1981, p. 234).

Fourth, if sociology as a discipline wants to encourage participation by sociologists, in the military policy-making process, such participation should be recognized as valuable. Political science associations, regional as well as national, take great pride in pointing to their members who ascend to elected or appointed office. Sociology has less frequently acknowledged the appointment of colleagues to important offices, in part because it happens much less often. A sociologist has been named as deputy assistant secretary of defense for drug and alcohol abuse prevention, and another serves as deputy to the assistant secretary of the army for manpower. They may be the most important sociologists in the Reagan administration, but the discipline has taken no note of them. In recent years, two sociologists have declined appointments as assistant secretary of the army for manpower and reserve affairs, perhaps because of the irrelevance of such an appointment to their sociological career. In the current fiscal and policy environment, however, the declinations are not irrelevant to sociology, since the presence of sociologists in administrative positions increases the opportunities available to the discipline.

Fifth, applied researchers in the military and in other spheres must be afforded publication outlets for their work. Applied psychologists have access to professional journals that, on the one hand, allow them to maintain that part of their professional identity that is rooted in scientific communication with peers and, on the other hand, provide a source of quality control of the research through peer review. Neither of these conditions applies to military sociology. Major sociology journals publish little in the way of research on the military, and the two relatively new journals hospitable to military sociology, although they perform a valuable service, are primarily academic in nature and contribute, as all specialized journals do, to the fragmentation and isolation of subfields from mainstream sociological thinking. As a result, applied military sociologists tend to feel estranged from the discipline. In the absence of peer review and certification, much substandard work is passed off as sociology, negatively affecting the evaluation of the discipline by the user community.

Other lessons need only be noted briefly. Applied sociologists, in this as well as other settings, must learn to communicate in plain English rather than sociological jargon. They must learn the importance of presenting the facts as simply as possible rather than trying to impress and confound the user with fancy methodologies. They must learn to conduct research under real-world constraints and under extreme time pressure. The most carefully executed piece of policy research is useless if the report comes in the day after the policy decision is made. Applied sociologists must be willing to tell the user what the data say, even if the user will not

like the findings. And they must recognize that the results of policy research are potentially consequential for other people. The
costs of erroneous conclusions in a piece of basic research are relatively low: inability to get a paper published or gentle chiding
from one's peers. The costs of error in policy research are reflected
in funds, social institutions, and lives.

References

ARMY SCIENCE BOARD
  1980   *Ad Hoc Study Group Report on Human Issues.* Wash-
          ington, D.C.: Assistant Secretary of the Army for Re-
          search, Development, and Acquisition.
ARMY SCIENTIFIC ADVISORY PANEL
  1972   *Report of the Ad Hoc Working Group on the Modern
          Volunteer Army.* Washington, D.C.: Department of
          the Army.
BIDERMAN, A. D.
  1963   *March to Calumny.* New York: MacMillan.
BOGART, L., ED.
  1959   *Social Research and the Desegregation of the U.S.
          Army.* Chicago: Markham.
BRADBURY, W. C., MEYERS, S. M., AND BIDERMAN, A. D., EDS.
  1968   *Mass Behavior in Battle and Captivity.* Chicago: Uni-
          versity of Chicago Press.
DEITCHMAN, S. J.
  1976   *The Best-Laid Schemes.* Cambridge, Mass.: M.I.T.
          Press.
HOROWITZ, I. L., ED.
  1967   *The Rise and Fall of Project Camelot.* Cambridge,
          Mass.: M.I.T. Press.
HOVLAND, C. I., LUMSDAINE, A. A., AND SHEFFIELD, F. D.
  1949   *Experiments on Mass Communication.* Princeton,
          N.J.: Princeton University Press.
JANOWITZ, M.
  1981   "Review of *1943: The Victory That Never Was.*"
          American Journal of Sociology 87:231–234.
KOURVETARIS, G. A., AND DOBRATZ, B. A.
  1977   "The present state and development of sociology of
          the military." In G. A. Kourvetaris and B. A. Dobratz

(Eds.), *World Perspectives in Sociology of the Military*. New Brunswick, N.J.: Transaction Books.

LASSWELL, H. D.
1927   *Propaganda Technique in the World War*. London: Routledge & Kegan Paul.

LERNER, D.
1971   *Psychological Warfare Against Nazi Germany*. Cambridge, Mass.: M.I.T. Press.

LITTLE, R. W.
1964   "Buddy relations and combat performance." In M. Janowitz (Ed.), *The New Military*. New York: Russell Sage Foundation.

McGRATH, J. E., AND ALTMAN, I.
1966   *Small Group Research*. New York: Holt, Rinehart and Winston.

NATIONAL RESEARCH COUNCIL
1968   *The Behavioral Sciences and the Federal Government*. Washington, D.C.: National Academy of Sciences.
1971   *Behavioral and Social Science Research in the Department of Defense*. Washington, D.C.: National Academy of Sciences.

NATIONAL SECURITY EDUCATION PROGRAM
1975   *Second National Security Study Survey: A Summary of Results*. New York University. (Mimeographed.)

NATIONAL SECURITY PROGRAM
1973   *National Security Studies Survey: A Summary of Results*. New York University. (Mimeographed.)

OFFICE OF THE SECRETARY OF DEFENSE
1978   *America's Volunteers*. Washington, D.C.: Office of the Assistant Secretary for Manpower, Reserve Affairs, and Logistics.

SEGAL, D. R.
1981   "Leadership and management: Organization theory." In J. H. Buck and L. J. Korb (Eds.), *Military Leadership*. Beverly Hills, Calif.: Sage.
forth- "The all-volunteer armed force: Multidisciplinary
coming analysis of an interdisciplinary issue." In E. S. McCrate and M. L. Martin (Eds.), *Servants of Arms*. New York: Free Press.

SHILS, E. A., AND JANOWITZ, M.

1948 "Cohesion and disintegration in the Wehrmacht in World War II." *Public Opinion Quarterly* 12:280–315.

SNYDER, W. P., AND DAVIS, J. A.

1981 "Efficiency and usefulness in policy research: The case of the all-volunteer force." *Public Administration Review* 41:34–46.

STAHL, M. J., McNICHOLS, C. W., AND MANLEY, T. R.

1981 "A longitudinal test of the Moskos institution-occupation model." *Journal of Political and Military Sociology* 9:43–47.

STOUFFER, S. A., AND OTHERS.

1949a *The American Soldier: Adjustment During Army Life.* Princeton, N.J.: Princeton University Press.

1949b *The American Soldier: Combat and its Aftermath.* Princeton, N.J.: Princeton University Press.

1950 *Measurement and Prediction.* Princeton, N.J.: Princeton University Press.

WATSON, P.

1978 *War on the Mind.* New York: Basic Books.

✺ 17 ✺

RESEARCH ON EDUCATIONAL PROGRAMS

Robert A. Dentler

The contributions of sociology to the analysis, development, and continuous reformation of education have been wide-ranging, profound and out of all proportion to the numbers of sociologists who have concentrated on education—a small number relative to the numbers of psychologists, historians, and philosophers. These contributions reach back before Auguste Comte, but the enduring era of workmanship begins with Emile Durkheim and is thus but a century in the making. Durkheim took teacher preparation seriously and set about making a functional analysis of schooling in ways that continue to define the application of sociology today.

We do not know whether that first century, from 1880 to 1980, will become our last. In the event that we have no more than this glorious beginning, we should not examine its periods of development too minutely lest we foreclose on the emergence of

251

the next two hundred years. Too great a self-consciousness in science sometimes creates barriers to new inquiries. We can identify a few milestones along the road from 1880 to 1980, however, without making them into our only monuments.

If Durkheim's educational studies are seen as comprising the first milestone, and if we attend mostly to America thereafter, the second milestone would be that of the generation of educational sociologists from 1910 to 1930. These men and women are shabbily treated in our histories and texts partly because most American sociologists of this period are not well known and partly because they did not join in building a scientific sociology. They also receive scant notice because they left the fold, the fledgling departments of sociology, and entered the mainstream of American public education. They founded schools and departments of education. They were deans and presidents of state normal schools. Some even taught children and immigrants instead of college students. Most unforgivably of all, they were moralistic. They believed in piety, discipline, and civics, and, with other moralizing sociologists of their time, they preached social ethics, eugenics, and social progress. Along the way, however, they built into the separately evolving conventions of educational research a vestibule for social institutional analysis, a small place in schools of education where social issues were examined as distinguished from curriculum and the applied psychology of education.

In the 1930s, a sociology of education began to emerge from the work of the Committee on Human Development at the University of Chicago. The work of Lloyd Warner, Allison Davis, and later Robert Havighurst, among others, showed how social scientific inquiry could have great practical utility. These men built on John Dewey, William Cooley, W. E. DuBois, and Lester Ward and fused theoretical with applied concerns. New York University's School of Education gave a similar importance to applied social research in that period. There, public school teachers became applied sociologists and vice versa, as the quest for solutions to social problems acquired a new science.

Looking back over the years from 1925 to 1950 in educational sociology, Dan Dodson of New York University, one of the pioneers of this era, catalogued many of the practical consequences of the applications of that time (Dodson, 1952). Six years later, Orville Brim (1958) summarized past achievements and charted future directions.[1]

In the last three decades, 1950 to 1980, the milestones have included increasing collaboration with comparative education scholars as the sociology of education went international. The Bureau of Social Science Research at American University was doing federally contracted educational research and evaluations as a regular routine by 1950. After sputnik, federal investments in educational research done by applied sociologists multiplied tenfold between 1960 and 1970. Lee Burchinal entered the U.S. Office of Education and developed both ERIC and concerted research on knowledge exchange. When the Center for Urban Education was funded at $3 million per year in 1965, its staff included many applied sociologists. The Center for the Study of School Organization at Johns Hopkins, while smaller and less applied, became—under the guidance of James S. Coleman, the stimulation of Peter H. Rossi, and the leadership of John McDill and James McPartland—a world-renowned center for the field.

Persisting Themes

Applied sociologists have made a significant contribution to educational research and practice, not because they were geniuses but because the fit between the prevailing content of sociology and the practice of formal education was strategically ideal. What other social institution, after all, is more dependent on population, social organization, and social interaction—the heartland of sociology—than formal education? The contribution has not yet caused a leap of the sort associated with Darwin or Freud, but contemporary educators see their field through sociological lenses, whether they know it or not.

We have transformed the concepts *teaching* and *learning* into *socialization* and *development*; defined the occupation and its environment; defined the input-output relation between social

---

[1] Orville G. Brim, *Sociology and the Field of Education*, Russell Sage Foundation, New York, 1958. Brim opens the current era of the sociology of education, while Dodson gives a history of the last stages of educational sociology.

status and life opportunities; exploded the myths of racial-ethnic superiority; characterized the culture-bound features of knowledge and its diffusion; and reformulated the relation between community and school. In the process, we have transformed most of the ways in which educational research is designed, executed, and interpreted.

In my view, the themes introduced by Durkheim have not changed. Only our strategies of inquiry and the strength of the empirical base have changed. If educational research is done by applied sociologists in the year 2081, as I believe it will be, the themes will persist—socialization, stratification and equity, community, population effects, social and administrative organization, knowledge diffusion, change, interaction and social climate, program evaluation, and macro-system comparison. In the field of educational inquiry, only historiography, psychometrics, and econometrics are left uncovered by this inventory.

Work Role

Applied sociologists who do educational research tend to be employed by one or more of the following organizations: universities, the federal government, state and local educational agencies, the contract research industry, and a few nonprofit foundations, associations, and interest groups. The work is seldom done solo and usually begins and ends as a project. This world overlaps with, but is not organized like, the counterpart world of training design and research, and not many actors from one world migrate to the other.[2]

Another aspect of the ideal fit between applied sociology and educational research is that it can be enacted in virtually every setting. I have done educational research for twenty-five years, and, on nearly every occasion, I felt understood on arrival—understood in the symbolic interactionist sense that the occupational self is neither distanced nor treated as a mysterious anomaly. This ad-

---

[2] Training design relies heavily upon applied psychology and human factors engineering. It is funded mainly by industry and the military. There is every reason to expect that applied sociology will come to share this domain increasingly in the future, perhaps through behavioral organization research.

vantage does not include being liked by everyone, of course, but, whether the setting is a government agency, a community group, a school staff, a meeting with business people, or a field trip to a small village in the rural hinterland, something about my thematic content concerns and my methods is already in place socially before I arrive. In contrast, there are other settings where this role familiarity is absent, where the role of the applied sociologist generates suspicion and hostility. Sharing these settings with us are often those who have reason to expect that our findings will breed social or political controversy or lay a basis for changes that will break established habits or expose to public view the fact that the educational emperor wears no clothes.[3] Our lack of humility in such situations and our readiness to unmask those we consider mistaken or unwise sometimes, unfortunately, corroborates this expectation and thereby reduces our marketability.

Educational research as practiced in North America is eclectic and cross-disciplinary. More and more of it has been done by the contract research industry since 1960 because, there, legitimacy has been given to teaming up with one another to answer the sponsor's question. The teaming up stresses cooperation, not discipline-based pecking orders. With a few exceptions, universities reward individually competitive, single, discipline-based, self-formulated inquiries. By the early 1970s, sociologists on university education faculties began to fail in their quests for promotion and tenure to the extent that they immersed themselves in applied rather than basic research. The judges were often drawn from the ranks of neighboring sociology departments.

Not only is the work role of the applied sociologist in educational research cross-disciplinary and team-centered, but also the sponsors frequently ask questions the sociologist thinks have already been answered. The resulting activity is thus seen as redun-

[3]Those who are suspicious or hostile about educational research done by sociologists in applied settings help to balance the polity. In an open society, we can be glad not only that they are suspiciously pervasive but that their doubts get expressed, because without them our influence would quickly exceed the span of our knowledge. As sociology has matured, however, the humility of its carriers has not always kept pace. As a result, our welcome is often not as deep or as universal as we might wish. Insensitivity to those who practice, and a tendency to unmask the fool with an excess of ego-serving zest, sometimes reduce our marketability.

dant, wasteful, and frustrating. Moreover, since the sociologist is also often subordinate to researchers from other fields, autonomy of inquiry is seriously constrained.

As a result, the applied sociologist in educational research is sometimes viewed by sponsors, clients, respondents, and peers from other fields as feisty, contentious, and balky. My conclusion from long experience is that educators are firmly grounded in the normative—in control, propriety, consensus, and tradition—features that tend to cast the sociologist in an unattractive light. Good energy is then expended in haggling over the formulation of the task, with the applied sociologist feeling constrained by his or her viewpoint to vaunt the merits of reformulation and redirection.

More problematically, the applied sociologist in education is often deemed nonessential, and his or her security is therefore tenuous. The questions asked may concern facets of administration, for instance, that can be handled adequately by someone from public administration research. Or they may concern measurement issues that are well within the grasp of applied psychologists and statisticians. Curriculum and instruction, enrollment projections, and even program evaluation tend to "specialize away" from sociology.

When nutrition education is being studied, all stakeholders agree that a nutritionist is essential. But I do not think that I have encountered a single situation in twenty-five years where anyone present other than myself agreed that the project required a sociologist.[4] In education, we have achieved a combination of high intellectual stature and operational expendability.

By custom, the applied sociologist treats this hazardous status by extending his range of content familiarity. He becomes the increasingly esteemed adjunct whose esteem stems from his earned familiarity with the substances of diverse fields of educational practice. This strategy was especially feasible in the high-growth years from 1958 to 1968, for, at that time, project teams were being formed in every conceivable substantive domain in education.

---

[4]It is equally hard to think of an instance where a sociology faculty designs sociology courses as a committee project and deems it *essential* to include non-sociologists.

On-the-job learning is much less available now than it was even five years ago. But even when it was widely available, no employer advertised for an applied sociologist in education. It is difficult to choose, let alone launch, a career in a field that ostensibly contains no positions.

The work role in question tends to contain a number of other peculiarities. For example, it lacks glamour. Education is not a social subsystem in operation; rather, it is extremely loosely coupled, fragmented, and dependent on other subsystems for its resources. It does not attract those who seek fame, wealth, or political power. Within universities, educational research stands at or close to the bottom of the totem pole of prestige. Within government agencies, it ranks so far below defense, commerce, and other functions as to be a sort of stepchild. In the contract industry, which is symbiotic with the academy and government, educational research—even when it pays the bills—ranks low in technical value. In the heyday of the industry, moreover, educational inquiry was widely regarded as a field that could be entered, at least for brief tours, by gifted generalists who would never have presumed as amateurs to do health, environmental, or foreign area studies with the same self-confidence.

Another peculiarity is that the largest prospective employer in applied educational research and development, the testing industry, comprises a guild of psychologists, statisticians, and educational administrators whose doors have never opened to sociologists. A few of us have entered through the coal chutes and windows, of course, but, once inside, we must continue to mask our identities as sociologists. The doors are closed not because we pose a threat, I think, but because we offer no theory or technology of inquiry that cannot be duplicated from the inside. A "way of thinking" about society is not sufficient.

Some Tentative Solutions

Formal education in America may not be a coherent subsystem, but it does operate through an accessible, well-defined series of establishments. If we put together a list of the associations, institutions, corporations, foundations, government agencies, and interest groups already listed by the National Institute of Education, National Education Association, American Educational Research Association, American Association of School Administrators, to name just a few, we would have not only an ample inventory but also, through cross-classification, a map of most of the stakeholding establishments whose members initiate, sponsor, conduct, and consume educational research. The networks are not enormous in scope or numbers.

Although it may overlook pockets of activity, this map covers ninety percent of the market for research in formal education in America. Not only are inventory maps now unavailable to sociologists, but the persons and groups on the maps do not know where we are. Outreach by sociologists, matched by receptivity by educators would be an essential starting point for market development.

As the public sector shrinks for the remainder of this century, moreover, applied sociologists must be helped to change what they offer. The new challenges are retrenchment, productivity enhancement, and adaptive reorganization at state and local levels. Research on other topics will often be deemed an unaffordable luxury.

Pinched as resources may become, the new challenges for the period from 1982 to 2000 could generate a substantial demand for the application of sociological research to education. Long-standing institutional customs are breaking up, and the pressure to find and test alternatives is building each year. Some sociologists, such as Steve Heyneman of the World Bank, are demonstrating the great potential of the discipline when it is applied to evaluating educational investments in developing countries. Within the United States, educational research by applied sociologists is shifting rapidly from large-scale surveys and program evaluations toward organizational analysis, linkage and network studies, and studies of aspects of the management of retrenchment, for example. Cable television, microprocessors, and related technologies may also call forth new applications. Only a lack of imagination and a rigidity about categories will prevent future contributions from emerging.

The education of applied sociologists in educational research has been poor for the thirty years, with a few exceptions in both the Sunbelt and the Midwest. At most graduate universities, those with a bent for applied educational research either never pursue that interest or fall between the departmental cracks after enrolling.

Fortunately, the failures in these arrangements are not the result of gaps in knowledge or pedagogy but spring instead from the low combined salience of the applied and the educational. What is needed in a doctoral program (and I see little point in master's programs in this specialty) is the basic core of courses and related requirements in the discipline; plus five advanced courses in professional education, to include educational measurement, educational administration research, and curriculum design or evaluation studies; minus an equal number of seminars in nonapplied subspecialities in sociology. Finally, the thesis topic should give priority to practicality rather than originality, and the thesis committee should be interdisciplinary.

We can even set forth with some confidence the skills our graduate should have. These include survey methods, population projection techniques, case-study experience, ethnomethodology or sociolinguistics or interactional analysis, and organizational analysis. Some though not all of these skills should have been developed in the real-life context of educational practice. There are probably at least one hundred major graduate centers with ample capability to arrange such a sequence of preparation with no additional expenditures other than those entailed in cooperative planning. New centers are not needed.

Conclusion

While sociologists entertain ways to make applications a legitimate part of their academic enterprise, educational facilities will continue, out of desperation, to move to eliminate the competition. The 1300 colleges, schools, and departments of education in the United States today are disappearing at a rate that may soon reach 50 a year. As schools of management consolidate their growing hegemony over the production of certified managers and public administrators, so, within the academy in general, the eclipse of the basic social science disciplines will be speeded by the growing separation of the professional schools from collaboration with cognate departments.

Unless sociology faculties build solid bridges across to education faculties and outward toward education and training establishments in this decade, their students will be absorbed at increasing rates into the professional schools, and the very notion of an applied sociology of education will disappear. Our kind of inquiry will persist, but under different labels and auspices. My own sense is that if the bridges between sociology faculties and professional school faculties go unbuilt, the quality of research and its significance to society will be reduced.

The tension between service to the discipline as a science and applications from the science to education is an inevitable and healthy tension. Resolution of it by vaunting the science and discounting the applications could culminate in a disservice to society, for the applied work will live on in other, less competent hands. The reward structures of universities must be differentiated to accord full recognition to those who apply existing knowledge as well as to those who produce new knowledge.

References

BRIM, O. G.
    1958   *Sociology and the Field of Education.* New York: Russell Sage Foundation.
DODSON, D. W.
    1952   "Educational sociology through twenty-five years." *The Journal of Educational Sociology* 26(1):2-6.

✺18✺

RESEARCH ON AGING

Gordon F. Streib

Robert Browning's famous lines, "Grow old along with me! The best is yet to be" is often quoted in gerontological circles because of its "positive-thinking" approach to the process of aging. This nineteenth-century romantic view may be one reason why the field of aging as both a theoretical and an applied area of research has been generally uninteresting to sociologists. Although a few have been working in administration and practice in applied settings, and some have been engaged in sociological research on aging, most sociologists of aging have applied their expertise primarily by offering courses to college students (Streib, 1981a). The discipline in general has devoted its research energies elsewhere, as shown by programs at professional meetings and articles appearing in sociological journals. Sociologists probably reflect the apprehension and bias of the society in general in their aversion to studying the aging process and its consequences.

Some interest has been generated because of the traditional concern of sociologists for minorities, for "victims," for the op-

pressed groups in our society. Inasmuch as the elderly can be defined in these terms, some sociologists have directed their attention to older people and their problems. However, this approach,
which emphasizes only the negative, ignores the broad sociological
aspects of aging as a natural human process, leaving out such important research areas as: the trend towards early retirement
among healthy adults; the relation of the nonworking segment to
the economy; the crisis of Social Security and the intergeneration-
al transfer of payments; the political power of the elderly; the
socioeconomics of our health delivery system; the breakdown of
family support systems and the role of the government in filling
this gap; the migration of the elderly and the formation of new
communities; and the increasing role of bureaucracies in providing
services to our aging population.

Social and Demographic Facts About the Aging

A few demographic and social facts about the elderly in
American society are essential to a discussion of applied sociology
and aging. In 1981, the 25 million Americans who were sixty-five
and older constituted 11 percent of the population (Special Committee on Aging, 1981). In recent years, the demographic patterns
of the elderly have been changing. The decline in fertility rates and
the possibility of zero population growth in the United States and
other developed, industrialized nations mean that these countries
will be societies with an increasing median age and a greater proportion of elderly persons. The net increase in the elderly in the
United States is about 1600 persons per day, or almost 600,000
per year. Demographics alone makes an aging population a focus
of sociological study, for the fastest growing segment of the population is composed of persons over seventy-five.

The heterogenity of the elderly needs to be emphasized, because there is a tendency to concentrate on the deprived groups
and segments in areas of social programs and policy and to overlook the fact that the elderly include all strata and classes, a variety of cultural backgrounds, the healthy and the sick, millionaires
and the destitute. Only about 5 percent of the total older population are in institutions, including nursing homes. In addition,
about 15 percent are home-bound and have very limited mobility.

Retirement is becoming an increasingly important process in American life. One of the highly visible political issues that generated almost unanimous congressional support was the enactment into law of a change in the mandatory retirement rules. The new federal laws permit persons in private employment to work until age seventy and persons in federal employment to work as long as they wish. Despite all the publicity and political concern, this change in the law has had relatively little effect on the lives of most older persons, as less than half of all workers are subject to mandatory retirement regulations. Furthermore, only about 14 percent of older persons desire to work longer (Schulz, 1980).

More important is the overwhelming social fact that most people retire early (Kleiler, 1978). In the past few years, over half the males applying for Social Security have done so before the usual age of sixty-five. Furthermore, employers have found that, when early retirement plans are instituted with some compensatory income, workers are eager to retire early. This set of facts, combined with the demographic reality that the average male who reaches sixty-five has about fourteen years of life expectancy, means that many Americans look forward to a retirement period of twenty to twenty-five years.

The elderly make large demands on the government because of the various entitlement and income transfer programs: Social Security, Medicare, disability, Medicaid, and so on. These claims or demands are likely to increase in the years ahead as the population continues to age.

Another important social trend is the fact that many older persons are active in special interest and pressure groups (Hudson and Binstock, 1976). The aged have become well organized in the past decade. Many people have heard about the Gray Panthers; however, they have a tiny constituency compared to National Retired Teachers Association (NRTA), National Council of Senior Citizens, and particularly the American Association of Retired Persons (AARP), which has a membership of nearly 12 million and over 600 employees (Pratt, 1976). AARP and its collaborating organization NRTA, have lobbyists in many states and in the nation's capital.

Except for the very old, the elderly participate more actively in voting than do younger age groups. Contrary to popular belief, the elderly do not become more conservative politically with age (Glenn, 1974; Hudson and Binstock, 1976).

The medical needs of the elderly increase as they age. The health care cost per capita for persons sixty-five and over was $2,026 in 1979, in comparison to $596 per capita for persons under sixty-five (Special Committee on Aging, 1981). Hospital care was the largest item by far in the health care of older persons, comprising 43 percent of the total expenditures.

The economic situation of the elderly has improved over the past decades. Pampel (1979, p. 139) concluded his thirty-year time series analysis: "However, for the 1970s and 1980s, the results here suggest that stereotypes of worsening plight of the aged are exaggerated."

Many of the problems of old age are essentially the problems of older women: social isolation, fear of crime, low incomes, poor health, and decrease in social networks. Women comprise 74 percent of the nursing home population, a figure not likely to change appreciably in the future, since the life expectancy for women in the United States (average remaining years of life for persons born in 1978) was 7.7 years longer than men, or 77.2 years for women compared to 69.5 for males.

If sociologists are to be effective in applied programs, they should be aware of the importance of employing a multidisciplinary approach. The world of application in aging includes the world of government, politics, economics, and medicine. One cannot be a pure sociologist, whicn is the kind that generally has prestige in academia. In fact, one might offer a proposition: the purity of the discipline is inversely related to the efficacy of applied sociology in the field of aging.

Sociologists interested in applied programs must be willing to cross disciplinary boundaries and must learn something about the basic concepts and ideas of other fields: medicine, biology, psychology, social work, and economics. Obviously, no one can be an expert in a variety of fields, but there must be an openness and a willingness to learn about research advances in other fields and to recognize how these relate to one's sociological specialty.

In particular, sociologists in the field of aging must come to grips with sociobiology (Barlow and Silverberg, 1980). The aims and goals of sociobiologists are subject to much controversy and misunderstanding. For example, they are not trying to pre-empt all science, as some sociologists have charged. Biologists have simply realized that social and cultural factors are extremely important in shaping the lives of people in modern societies, and sociologists need to recognize that there is a residual set of explanations that are biological (Atchley, 1980). We may not know the precise ways in which biological factors (endocrine, genetic, physiological response) manifest themselves in a variety of social contexts. However, one notes in most sociological studies of aging—even the most comprehensive, systematic, and statistically precise—considerable unexplained variance that is probably related to hard-to-measure biological factors.

Critical sociologists often argue that the main problems associated with aging are structural and imply that, if we were to change the structure of society, the problems of aging would be solved (Estes, 1979). Sociologists, as specialists in social factors, are perhaps reluctant to acknowledge underlying, inexorable biological processes and pressures. However, it is increasingly clear that anyone who wishes to be effective in the applied sociology of aging must have some understanding and appreciation of biology and its social implications. In fact, sociologists may be able to acknowledge significant social solutions to biological problems.

Role of Professional Organizations in Aging Research

The American Sociological Association (ASA) and the regional sociological societies have operated primarily as learned societies concerned with promoting and disseminating scholarly ideas and research and engaging in academic discourse. In terms of jobs, the academic marketplace has been emphasized. However, demographic developments resulting in a declining population of young students, the retrenchment of public funds, and concern for new career opportunities outside academia have forced learned societies to become more oriented to nonacademic professional concerns.

American Sociological Association. The ASA Section on Aging—at three years old, one of the youngest sections in the society—attained section status very quickly by obtaining 200 dues-paying members. Within two years, it had attained a membership of 441, and it is now the seventh-largest section in the ASA. The Section on Aging has had a limited sphere of activities: the annual meeting program and a newsletter, which is a vehicle for communication among interested colleagues.

Thus, attention to aging is a recent focus of interest in the society. However, as early as twenty years ago, ASA President Paul Lazarsfeld, in organizing the program for the annual meetings, saw aging as a field that should be included in the discussion of applied sociology. The 1962 program resulted in a 900-page book entitled *The Uses of Sociology* (Lazarsfeld, Sewell, and Wilensky, 1967). For someone who is interested in learning how far we have come in twenty years, this volume is a valuable starting point. The introduction by Lazarsfeld, Sewell and Wilensky gives a thoughtful analysis of the subject, and the specific chapters cover the gamut of applications of sociological knowledge.

In chapter 22, entitled "Aging," Streib and Orbach (1967) consider five areas to be of crucial importance to practitioners in the field of aging: retirement, health, family, housing, and community. Although these areas are still of interest and social importance, new areas in which applied sociologists might make a contribution include law, complex organizations, the sociological aspects of the economics of aging, and the role of voluntary organizations.

Gerontological Society and Applied Sociology. The Gerontological Society of America is another professional organization whose interests and programs overlap with those of sociologists of aging in the ASA. This group has about 5,600 members divided into four sections: biological sciences (430 members); clinical medicine (920 members); behavioral and social sciences (2,440 members); and the section called social research, planning, and practice (1,650 members). The Gerontological Society publishes two journals, *The Journal of Gerontology* and *The Gerontologist.* The structure of the organization and its decision-making processes are governed by the four sections, unlike the American Sociological Association and its sections. This means that educational, research, and service programs have developed within each section as a reflection of the professional initiatives of the membership in that section. The Behavioral and Social Sciences Section and the Social Research, Planning, and Practice Section have been most active in developing applied programs related to the society's members and the older population.

One program developed by the Behavioral and Social Science Section of the Gerontological Society was a summer internship program in which academic gerontologists had an opportunity to spend the summer working in government offices concerned with the planning and delivery of services to older people (Streib, 1981b). Now in its eighth year, this program has sponsored over 100 research fellows and interns who have provided academic expertise of relevance to the ongoing programs of those agencies and offices. For example, one sociologist spent a summer analyzing the structure of the state office on aging and how it related to the federal system and the area offices on aging. Another person developed a detailed methodology for conducting a telephone survey on the energy needs of the elderly. A third person studied how state and federal employment programs discriminated against older workers. Another sociologist studied the intricate relationships between Arizona Indian tribes, the state office on aging, and the federal office on aging. In general, all levels of government administrators have welcomed the input of the summer interns.

Other professional groups such as the Association for Gerontology in Higher Education (AGHE) and the National Council on Aging have also developed applied and educational programs that utilize sociological expertise. Another innovative group, the Western Gerontological Association, has focused on bridging the gap between academic gerontologists, policy makers, and practitioners.

Consortium of Universities as a Training Model. Most institutes, training programs, and centers involved in applied sociology are sponsored by single universities. However, another arrangement deserves attention—the consortium. In the field of the sociology of aging, the Midwest Council on Social Research in Aging (MCSRA) has been an important factor in stimulating conferences, graduate training, and exchange of ideas on academic sociology and on applied programs.

The Midwest Council, a consortium of about a dozen universities, was organized in 1960 to marshal the ideas and research capabilities of nine midwestern universities in preparation for the 1961 White House Conference on Aging. The decision was reached that none of the universities could individually provide the desired expertise and that it would therefore be mutually useful to the universities, their students, and their faculties to work together and to contribute cooperatively to a national effort.

The 1961 White House Conference on Aging passed into history, but the MCSRA has continued. Over the years, MCSRA has received funding from the Aging Program of the National Institute on Child Health and Human Development and from the newly established National Institute on Aging when it was founded in 1976. The MCSRA meets for three seminars per year at which predoctoral students, postdoctoral participants, and the faculty of the cooperating universities exchange ideas, defend thesis proposals, and meet with experts from outside the region in order to inform and challenge the community of scholars interested in the sociology of aging. Over the years, the participating universities have changed slightly, but a core of schools has remained very active throughout the decade. MCSRA has provided a forum for discussion of research and applications not usually provided by a professional meeting of a sociological society. Many persons have received their Ph.D.s because of traineeships supported by MCSRA funds, several postdoctoral scholars have been retrained or stimulated into research on aging, and graduate students from a dozen universities have had the unique opportunity of developing close peer ties with faculty and students of similar interests, and there have been decades of intellectual stimulation, which is rather unique in the sociological community. Since social gerontology has always had links to the applied world, the kinds of research carried out by participants in the council have usually been closely related to program and policy issues.

A consortium such as this might be used as a model for sociologists interested in application to organize themselves on a regional basis in order to create a collegial atmosphere that could result in a more efficacious applied sociology. A regional consortium could also provide interchange between such sections as medical sociology, aging, complex organizations, and family.

Applied Research in Aging

Sociologists interested in working in applied research fields concerned with an aging population must be aware of the developments in both health and economics (Riley, 1979). Some health care providers are becoming increasingly aware that the medical care of the elderly must move beyond the traditional medical fields to encompass the social and legal aspects of health and illness. Effective care of patients must be comprehensive and requires the competencies of professionals in several fields (Reichel, 1978). One area in which sociologists have carried out traditional research is now called social network studies. Networks are informal social structures involving family, kin, friends, and neighbors. There is evidence that these networks are fundamental to the health maintenance of the elderly and pivotal in understanding the nature of the social and the social-psychological processes related to aging.

Other research evidence points to a link between the degree of network connectedness and the mortality of adults. Studies of human populations show that stressful events, such as loss of spouse, may be significant correlates of increased morbidity and mortality. These relationships will undoubtedly need to be specified more precisely to make them efficacious in applied settings, and further sociological study may show more precisely which social-psychological interventions may reduce morbidity and mortality (House and Robbins, 1981).

The need for further studies of how the costs of nursing and hospital care might be lowered without jeopardizing the health and welfare of older and younger patients reflects the multidisciplinary nature of applied research in aging and the need to be aware of everyday realities. The advantages of alternative living arrangements and home care services in comparison to nursing homes and acute care settings need to be explored.

The relation of social factors in drug therapy has been identified as an area requiring research. According to a recent National Institute on Aging report, *Toward Independent Old Age: A National Plan for Research on Aging* (1982, p. 173), "Understanding of the effects of environmental exposure on clinical drug action in the elderly has received scant research attention, but there is suggestive evidence that dietary habits, smoking, and ingestion of alcohol and coffee modify, often unpredictably, drug actions in older persons. Finally, educational programs designed to enlighten practicing physicians and those in training, nurses, pharmacists, and patients themselves about rational approaches to drug therapy are evolving in several centers, but the effectiveness of many of these projects is yet to be demonstrated." The report also emphasizes that there is a need to evaluate the relative importance of social, cognitive, and attitudinal factors in the failure of patients to take prescribed drugs. Applied sociologists are eminently qualified to conduct such research.

Among the exciting and provocative new developments in the aging field is the attention being given to ways to extend health so that the period of disability before death is shortened. Scattered studies indicate that some disabilities of old age can be made easier and possibly reversed. However, of even greater personal and social importance are studies on the prevention of disabilities in the first place. Matilda White Riley and Kathleen Bond (1981) have summarized research on postponing the onset of disability. Drawing on the 1979 Surgeon General's Report, *Health Promotion and Disease Prevention,* Riley and Bond (1981, p. 704) state: "The effects of behavior, social relationships, and life-style are often cumulative, beginning early in life and leading toward the chronic afflictions of later life." Problems of later life—heart disease, chronic bronchitis, emphysema, various cancers—are highly correlated with smoking, and smoking is now generally recognized as an important preventable cause of morbidity and death. Food habits also affect whether persons receive essential nutrients, and deficiencies may contribute in complex ways to heart disease, high blood pressure, and the adult onset of diabetes. Similarly, lack of exercise may be implicated in the increased risk of coronary heart disease.

The challenge for sociologists and other social scientists is to increase our research knowledge and the general public's understanding of how behavioral and social factors control smoking, food consumption, exercise, and the use of both prescription and over-the-counter drugs. Applied sociologists can be important allies with physicians and others in the applied health fields in identifying which intervention strategies are practical and acceptable and which might be started early in life, before the pathology develops.

Career Opportunities

Career opportunities for applied sociologists will rarely be designated by the term *sociologist,* nor will sociological training and experience be called for in job descriptions. Positions are more likely to have titles such as *planner, administrator, director,* or *coordinator,* and often these titles are preceded by the word *assistant.* However, sociologists should not be discouraged by the lack of a specific job title, for they must have the confidence that they can offer skills and knowledge that persons trained in other disciplines may not have. The applied sociologist must integrate insights on the social system with a set of complex, interacting variables that may have to be prioritized for decision making, and the decision making has to be completed in a more limited time frame than the academic sociologist may desire. Furthermore, resources are usually limited and in great demand. Thus, the sociologist must demonstrate the relevance of his or her research.

Traditionally, the sociologist has considered the university as his job setting, but the applied sociologist will find employment in a variety of organizations, such as federal and state government units, area agencies on aging, retirement communities, nursing homes, community service and voluntary organizations, and religious organizations that sponsor programs for the elderly (Riley, Riley, and Johnson, 1969).

In addition, new opportunities are emerging in business, banking, and insurance. One bank in California, for example, has selected a sociologist as vice-president involved in retirement and preretirement planning as it relates to wills and estates. In the life insurance field, sociologists have been involved in research and financial planning for the latter part of the life cycle. Pension consultants to corporations, unions, and public pension funds also need sociological expertise as well as knowledge of economics.

Conclusion

In conclusion, I offer some practical suggestions for sociologists considering applying their knowledge, training, and experience in applied settings. Sociologists interested in working in the aging field must have four basic sets of interests and competencies. The first is the obvious requirement of having expertise in sociological concepts, theories, perspectives, and orientations, as well as skills in methods appropriate for the theoretical issues to be utilized. Second, one should have some training in gerontology that provides an understanding of older persons as a subgroup of the population. The elderly have many similarities to other groups in the society but a wider range of differences than other age cohorts. Third, one must have special skills, either in quantitative or qualitative research techniques or demographic methods or expertise in such fields as administration, health, social organizations, family, and social stratification. Fourth, one must have the flexibility and adaptability to shift one's skills to solve problems that arise in the research or applied setting. Academic sociologists tend to be expert in narrow disciplines, for they are hired to teach courses that have a special focus. This narrow perspective may be prized in the classroom but may be a handicap in the "real world." The problems encountered in serving the elderly involve variables that cut across specialties within sociology.

One must be willing to share one's expert knowledge with decision makers who want answers to factual questions and reasoned opinions based on information, research experience, and professional judgment. Sociologists in the applied field must be able to translate sociological concepts, theories, and jargon into analyses and recommendations that are understandable to the general public. Quality, intellectual clarity, and empirical precision need not be compromised; however, sociologists must come to the heart of an issue with solid information or be able to make inferential suggestions that have a high degree of plausibility.

Informed recommendations and predictions derived from sociological theory are needed, but there must also be awareness of social trends and the political realities of the contemporary world. Sociologists are often reluctant to advise policy makers because they do not have all the facts. They must be willing to take risks and make recommendations based on the best information available.

Sociologists working in aging must separate the roles of observer and advocate. At times, the sociologist will be primarily a surveyor of facts and an analyst providing expertise to make a program or services more effective. At other times, the sociologist may be a partisan advocating a particular activity or course of action. On still other occasions these distinctions may be blurred. In any event, sociologists should know clearly whether they are trying to analyze or advocate. The sociologist, unlike Browning the poet, cannot say "The best is yet to be." He may sometimes say, "The worst is yet to be, because aging is often associated with decline and disability." With an awareness of the complexity of the social aspects of aging, sociologists may carve out important new work roles and help find practical, reasonable, and compassionate solutions to the problems of this important field.

References

ATCHLEY, R. C.
1980 *The Social Forces in Later Life.* (3rd ed.) Belmont, Calif.: Wadsworth.
BARLOW, G. W., AND SILVERBERG, J., EDS.
1980 *Sociobiology: Beyond Nature/Nurture?* Boulder, Colo.: Westview Press.
ESTES, C. L.
1979 *The Aging Enterprise.* San Francisco: Jossey-Bass.
GLENN, N. D.
1974 "Aging and conservatism." *The Annals* 415:176–186.
HOUSE, J. S., AND ROBBINS, C.
1981 "Age, psychosocial stress, and health." In B. B. Hess and K. Bond (Eds.), *Leading Edges: Recent Research on Psychosocial Aging.* Bethesda, Md.: The National Institute on Aging, National Institutes of Health.
HUDSON, R. B., AND BINSTOCK, R. H.
1976 "Political systems and aging." In R. H. Binstock and E. Shanas (Eds.), *Handbook of Aging and the Social Sciences,* New York: Van Nostrand.
KLEILER, F. M.
1978 *Can We Afford Early Retirement?* Baltimore, Md.: Johns Hopkins University Press.
LAZARSFELD, P. F., SEWELL, W. H., AND WILENSKY, H. L., EDS.
1967 *The Uses of Sociology.* New York: Basic Books.
NATIONAL INSTITUTE ON AGING
1982 *Toward An Independent Old Age: A National Plan for Research on Aging.* Bethesda, Md.: U.S. Department of Health and Human Services, National Institutes of Health.
PAMPEL, F. C.
1979 "Changes in the labor-force participation and income of the aged in the United States, 1947–1976." *Social Problems* 27:125–142.

PRATT, H. J.
   1976   *The Gray Lobby.* Chicago: University of Chicago Press.
REICHEL, W., M.D., ED.
   1978   *Clinical Aspects of Aging.* Baltimore, Md.: Williams & Wilkins.
RILEY, M. W., ED.
   1979   *Aging from Birth to Death: Interdisciplinary Perspectives.* Boulder, Colo.: Westview Press.
RILEY, M. W., AND BOND, K.
   1981   "Beyond ageism: Postponing the onset of disability." In B. B. Hess and K. Bond (Eds.), *Leading Edges: Recent Research on Psychosocial Aging.* Bethesda, Md.: The National Institute on Aging, National Institutes of Health.
RILEY, M. W., RILEY, J. W., JR., AND JOHNSON, M. E.
   1969   *Aging and Society.* Vol. 2: *Aging and the Professions.* New York: Russell Sage Foundation.
SCHULZ, J. J.
   1980   *The Economics of Aging.* (2nd ed.) Belmont, Calif.: Wadsworth.
SPECIAL COMMITTEE ON AGING
   1981   *Every Ninth American.* Washington, D.C.: United States Senate.
STREIB, G. F.
   1981a   "Aging comes of age." *Contemporary Sociology* 10: 186–190.
   1981b   *Programs for Older Americans: Evaluations by Academic Gerontologists.* Gainesville, Fla.: University Presses of Florida.
STREIB, G. F., AND ORBACH, H. L.
   1967   "Aging." In P. F. Lazarsfeld, W. H. Sewell, and H. L. Wilensky (Eds.), *The Uses of Sociology.* New York: Basic Books.

☙ 19 ☙

HOUSING AND ENVIRONMENTAL PLANNING

O. Andrew Collver

Since the early days of the discipline, sociologists have contributed in a variety of ways to community planning and management. Concepts from sociological research and theory pervade the fields of housing, transportation, land use planning, urban renewal, school desegregation, new town planning, and environmental impact assessment. Besides doing research and teaching in these areas, sociologists have found employment in the Bureau of the Census, in the land grant colleges dealing with rural community organization, in city planning departments and housing agencies, and in health and welfare planning and administration.

For the most part, this employment has been in the public sector, which today offers few prospects for expanded opportunities. If we wish to increase the number of sociologists involved in community analysis, we should look instead for opportunities in the private sector. The purpose of this chapter is to identify some of the major trends in the community development field and to

describe an approach to the creation of new opportunities in today's political and economic climate.

Current Trends in Community Development

The common denominator of housing and environmental
planning is the neighborhood unit. While the planners' ultimate
goal may be to improve the quality of human life in general, the
intermediate goal is to create more livable neighborhoods with increased housing opportunities and a safe, clean, and esthetically
acceptable environment in which resources are used efficiently, re-
used, and recycled to obtain the maximum human benefit at the
minimum cost in terms of environmental degradation and deple-
tion of nonrenewable resources.

An emphasis on the neighborhood unit in housing and environmental planning is justified because it is at the neighborhood
level that positive and negative effects of physical changes are
most keenly felt and the motivation is strongest to participate in
improvement programs.

In an effort to bring community planning down to the local
level, the U.S. Department of Housing and Urban Development
(HUD) has placed a growing emphasis on neighborhoods and local
communities as planning units. In order to coordinate services and
to plan for the cumulative impact of a number of projects over the
years, HUD favors the designation of neighborhood strategy areas
(NSAs). For purposes of environmental review, all projects, whether in NSAs or not, must be considered in relation to other projects
within the same geographical area. The effect of HUD policies,
then, is to promote the designation of local planning districts,
which may be further subdivided into residential, commercial, and
industrial zones. Parts of any of these land use zones may be designated in addition as low income areas, blighted areas, historic
preservation areas, or flood plains.

Anyone working with housing will surely encounter HUD
programs and policies and consequently find it convenient to use
HUD concepts for planning and review of projects. These concepts
include the preparation of community profiles and retrospective
analyses of the census and other data to develop assessments of the
needs and development potential of each planning area. The HUD

planning process tends to favor thinking in terms of the ecological interdependence of community components. Such thinking, of course, comes naturally to the urban sociologist, who can feel quite at home with the planning, review, and evaluation of projects within this framework.

The following brief review of developments in housing and environmental planning suggests the degree to which these fields have grown closer to the interests and expertise of sociologists.

Emphasis on Conservation and Revitalization. Where formerly the emphasis was on new production, today we see acceptance of a diversity of solutions to housing and environmental problems (Struyk, Marshall and Ozanne, 1978). During the 1970s, rent subsidies combined with funds for rehabilitation of older rental units became an important component of the housing tool kit. Urban homesteading enabled moderate-income families to buy and rehabilitate older houses for owner occupancy. Through adaptive reuse, surplus school buildings were converted to senior citizen housing. Thanks to the environmental movement, plans for use of energy and materials came increasingly to be formulated in terms of conservation, reuse, and recycling. The bicentennial celebration of 1976 called attention to the value of historical buildings in older communities. High costs of new construction further increased the advantages of conserving existing homes. The 1981 tax laws provided additional incentives for investment in existing housing by allowing tax credits for investment in historical structures and rapid depreciation write-offs for low-income housing.

When urban renewal consisted of assembling a large parcel of land in the central city, clearing it, and then building anew, about the only role a sociologist could play was that of critic (Gans, 1968). With the new emphasis on conservation and revitalization, repair and rehabilitation of the social structure of the neighborhood is just as important as the physical repair work. This approach requires social science, to some extent, but also calls for considerable talent in social design and reconstruction. Some of these requirements can be met by the theory and methodology of sociology. The community organizing aspect, however, calls for a different approach—it requires that we regard community structure not only as a natural system to be studied objectively and scientifically but also as an artificial system to be remodeled, repaired, and modified to make it work more effectively.

Broadened Participation. Community development planning has gone through a participation revolution over the past several years. Sunshine laws, the Freedom of Information Act, requirements for public notice, hearings, and public discussion of plans, have opened the decision-making process to a far broader spectrum of views and interests than before. The broadening of participation makes it harder for a small clique of businessmen, engineers, developers, and power brokers to claim a monopoly of expertise and authority for making and implementing plans.

A more direct approach to community participation is the practice of recognizing neighborhood-based nonprofit organizations as legitimate public interest groups, giving them direct grants, and allowing them to implement programs authorized by Congress or by state legislatures (Berger and Neuhaus, 1977). Such groups, if they develop a good working relationship with federal, state, and local government as well as with private foundations and if they establish a respectable record on their first few projects, can become involved in some significant, innovative work.

Shifts in Funding Sources. Over the past two decades, we have seen a gradual erosion of public confidence in the ability of big government to solve our problems with tax money. The message of the taxpayers' revolt, culminating in the Reagan presidency, is that the people themselves can spend their incomes more wisely and constructively than the government. There is now a new emphasis in Washington on private-sector initiatives and voluntarism (Savas, 1982). Institutions are being established that are intended to support the development of private initiatives. Some of these began under the Carter Administration—notably, the Community Reinvestment Act of 1977, which requires that banks reinvest in the communities from which they obtain their deposits, and the National Cooperative Bank, which would, for the first time, provide the kind of financial support for urban cooperatives that has been enjoyed by the successful farmers' coops. The banking industry is undergoing a transformation, the tax structure is changing, and the federal share of funding for housing and community development is being reduced. Although it is still too early to foresee all the implications of these changes, there is clearly abundant opportunity for making innovations at the neighborhood and community level —for example, by creating neighborhood credit unions (Caftel, 1978), consumer and producer coops, and neighborhood development associations. These groups can make deals with banks to satisfy their Community Reinvestment Act obligations, can enter into partnerships with profitable enterprises, and can own and manage property and begin to accumulate capital on behalf of the neighborhood (U.S. Department of Housing and Urban Development, 1979).

Changes in Technology. So far, we have not seen any spectacular changes in the material technology of housing and environmental management. We are, however, seeing a revolution in information technology, both in the type and quantity of information and in the technology of information processing, retrieval, and transmission. The number of variables taken into account in environmental planning and the complexity of analysis have increased apace with data-processing capacity. The participation revolution has raised the demand for data on how projects would affect the various interest groups. The National Environmental Policy Act of 1969 required that planners consider the impacts of projects on the human environment. At first, the engineering establishment overlooked the human side of the act, but gradually they are learning that they are expected to analyze the impacts on people of environmental changes. This analysis requires a knowledge of various occupational and ethnic groups, life-styles, and esthetic tastes—in short, a sociological analysis of the community to be affected by a project.

This growing complexity would not have been possible without the computer and associated data-handling equipment. At first, computers were large and expensive and seemed to be leading, like most technological advancement, toward a monopoly of information by big organizations with large capital budgets. Now, however, the microcomputer industry may make it possible for small neighborhood groups with little capital to be able to operate home computers and have access to some of the same data networks and software that are used by the big corporations. The small computer may give the small neighborhood group the power to use information to its own advantage.

However, the computer alone is not enough to provide intelligence for such groups. They will need good quality information, theory, and analytical models for making sense of the information, as well as software adapted to their particular needs. Among other things, the neighborhood group could make use of: information about the historical trend of the neighborhood life cycle and demography; land use analysis; a cash flow model to tell how the neighborhood is doing economically; and current postings of such information as selling prices of real estate (U.S. Department of Housing and Urban Development, 1980) as an indication of recovery or decline. In addition, the neighborhood group could conduct market analyses to discover opportunities for new enterprises or to advise existing enterprises regarding diversification or expansion plans.

The days of treating one aspect of the community, such as housing, as something separate from other aspects of neighborhood life are drawing to a close. Housing today is treated more in the context of neighborhood revitalization or promotion of economic development. Housing policies will be built increasingly from analytical and diagnostic models of the neighborhood and the larger region. The result will be less doctrinaire promotion of particular programs such as new apartment projects for families. Preference will be given to projects that develop in response to the structure of opportunities available in the particular community.

What Sociology Can Contribute

Although changes in the community development field have opened new opportunities for applied sociology, they do not literally create new jobs. For the most part, sociologists themselves will have to develop their roles under the new conditions. The following are just a few suggestions for tasks that sociologists are prepared to perform in the field of housing and environmental planning.

1. Regional data collection and analysis. Informed decisions about a community or neighborhood should be made in the context of an understanding of the trends of development of the larger region and of the functional relation of the locality

to the larger metropolitan system. This understanding requires demographic data, regional economic models, and so on. Regional data banks are accumulating gradually, and the hardware for storage, retrieval, and processing of the data is rapidly improving. These tools can be useful only to the extent that theory and methodology for analysis and interpretation of large-scale data banks keep pace with their quantitative growth. The social sciences are necessary for the development of analytical models of the dynamics of regional systems.

2. Neighborhood life cycle analysis. Before neighborhood investment decisions are made, it is desirable to know something of the history of the neighborhood and its trend of growth or decline. Heavy investment in rehabilitation of housing that is about to be demolished to make room for expansion of the central business district, for example, would be not only unwise but wasteful. To try to attract middle-class homeowners back to an inner-city neighborhood that lacks such essential elements as architectural charm, good schools, and convenient access to work and recreation would be an exercise in frustration. Sociological analysis of communities can help to point to more feasible futures in line with natural tendencies.

3. Preparation of long-range plans. Even though the urban master plan has been criticized as a lifeless and ineffective document, plans are still needed, if only as a means of communicating common understandings and assumptions. To the extent that such plans can be rationally derived from the stated goals of community leaders and knowledge of the community as a system, the social scientist can contribute to their preparation.

4. Critical review and evaluation of alternative courses of action. Federal and state regulations require impact analysis as part of the planning process. This analysis includes environmental, historical preservation, floodplain, and other reviews that weigh the potential consequences of several alternatives and show why one particular course of action was chosen over others. Social and community impacts have come to be recognized as important factors in these reviews, increasing the need for social scientists on the impact assessment team.

5. Project evaluation. The demand for economy in the use of public funds should help build a strong case for evaluation

showing whether programs have been effective in attaining their stated goals. Sociologists trained in the methodology of evaluation research can help to develop a more rational and scientific approach to the management of community development programs.

6.   Creation of social inventions or alternate structures. The changes in ideology, politics, economics and technology of community development have opened a new frontier for innovation in urban institutions. With a slight change of priorities and assumptions, the sociologist can become a social inventor, moving from the functional analysis of existing institutions to the design of institutions to perform new functions.

Defining Roles for Sociologists

Opportunities in community development abound, and sociologists can make major contributions once their role is clearly defined and accepted by others in the field. However, several prerequisites must be met before this role can be securely established.

First, the sociologist entering the field of community development must remain in contact with and up-to-date in the discipline, with adherence to certain theoretical and methodological perspectives and commitment to applying the discipline's analytical insights. No special theory or methodology, only standard academic sociology, is needed in community development. Of course, one needs to appreciate the contributions of other disciplines in any situation where the activity is problem-oriented rather than theory-oriented, since one cannot deduce a real-life situation from the abstract models of any one discipline.

Second, the sociologist has to establish an image of nonpartisan professional competence in order to obtain acceptance as a legitimate participant in the community development process. A wide discrepancy is likely to exist between the expectations of the academic sociologist and the expectations of others in the field, such as engineers, architects, lawyers, businessmen, and political leaders. In order to establish a working relationship, the sociologist should first demonstrate specific hard skills and tools that will win the confidence of others. Also, a strictly nonpolitical posture is recommended at first, because colleagues in the field are likely to be of a different, generally more conservative political persuasion. Patience is advised with regard to social reform goals, on the assumption that it is better to be in a position to exert steady pressure for reform over the long run than to alienate people by strong advocacy in the beginning.

Third, the choice of a client will have far-reaching consequences for the way in which the sociologist is able to carry out the community development role. Potential clients, including federal, state, and local governments and nonprofit organizations, offer advantages and disadvantages that should be weighed in relation to one's goals.

Finally, having chosen the client, one still must choose from among a variety of ways of relating to the client. One approach is to present oneself as a member of the university faculty or an academic institute or center that has a contract with the client for services. In some instances, the added prestige of university affiliation is an advantage; in others, it only arouses distrust or resentment, especially among local politicians, who seem to feel ill at ease with one who does not have to bear the consequences of unpopular opinions as swiftly and surely as they do. If the sociologist is taking the role of advocate of the interests of a minority group, of course, a cooperative relationship with adversaries is unnecessary.

Another approach is to work as an employee of the client group. Not only can this approach be constraining in relation to intellectual freedom but it also can put one in a position to be used for all manner of tasks that contribute nothing to the advancement of sociology. In some cases, direct employment may not be feasible, such as where local governments require local residency and registration with the majority political party.

Becoming affiliated with a consulting firm has the advantage that the firm is already established and has contracts with clients. A disadvantage, however, is that the services to the client will be brokered by an engineer, architect, or planner and that the sociologist will have little or no direct access to the client. Problems thus tend to become defined in nonsociological terms.

In order to be free of the liabilities of university affiliation, the misdirection that can follow from employee status, and the misrepresentation that occurs when sociological services are sold to the client by a nonsociologist, the ideal solution may be to go into business as a free-lance consultant or to set up a new service or consulting organization in which a sociologist plays a prominent policy role. This alternative affords autonomy and the opportunity to explain one's services directly to clients but also has the highest risk of financial failure.

A New Model

With such thoughts as these in mind, I commented to a lawyer acquaintance in the summer of 1981 that we sociologists seem unable to make social inventions and market them profitably. His answer marked a turning point for me. He pointed out that the physicist is no better able to build a machine than a sociologist is to build an organization. Just as the physicist needs a mechanical or electrical engineer to translate his concepts into a working device, the social scientist should have a lawyer to put social inventions into practice. In his view, the key to successful social engineering is a partnership of law and social science.

The two of us have subsequently collaborated in designing a project to take advantage of trends in the community development field and create a new structure for neighborhood revitalization. This chapter is not the place to discuss details of the plan, but certain elements are pertinent to the present discussion. The plan provides for five types of principal actors: nonprofit neighborhood development corporations representing communities of 5,000 to 10,000 homes; business improvement districts capable of assessing their members for improvements; municipal government; a profit-seeking engineering or construction firm; and what we call an institute for community intelligence. The role of the latter, which will be our responsibility, is to provide the others with the social and economic information they will need in order to carry out their tasks effectively. Our primary task will be to assemble and analyze community data and develop ideas for profitable investments that would promote jobs and income for the neighborhood. The other organizations will be responsible for capitalizing on the opportunities. We hope that our information services will prove productive enough to earn dividends from the economic growth of client neighborhoods and thus become self-supporting.

The proposal would make use of the sophisticated institutions that are used successfully by large businesses. The very corporate enterprise system that has abandoned the older neighborhoods and gone in search of bigger profits elsewhere has also created cooperatives; credit unions with full-service capabilities; the National Cooperative Bank; the Community Reinvestment Act; the neighborhood-based nonprofit business; tax shelter investment possibilities that can be used to advantage on a small scale; and inexpensive small computers that can enormously increase the intelligence capabilities of small enterprises. To complete the picture, the educational system has turned out surpluses of social scientists and lawyers looking for new opportunities.

The model that we are developing, though only one of many possible variations, illustrates the important points that I want to make here. It takes advantage of the shift from federal to local and from public to private funding. To municipal government, it offers help from the private sector in meeting increased expectations for local government services. Instead of complaining about the methods of big business, it turns them to the service of the local neighborhood. It develops a new service, community intelligence, and at the same time creates a clientele with a need for that service. Most important for applied sociology, it places the sociologist in a partnership with a lawyer, whose professional expertise is the ability to take a general concept of what might be done in a community and translate it into articles of incorporation, contracts, municipal ordinances, and other legal documents that implement the idea.

Within the framework thus created, we anticipate a growing market for social data collection and analysis. As federal and state funds and foundation grants diminish, we envision a future in which social research will be accepted as a normal part of doing business by local development organizations that have learned at first hand the advantages of being fully informed as they make their investment decisions.

References

BERGER, P. L., AND NEUHAUS, R. J.
1977   *To Empower People: The Role of Mediating Structures in Public Policy*. Washington, D.C.: American Enterprise Institute for Public Policy Research.

CAFTEL, B. J.

1978   *Community Development Credit Unions: A Self-Help Manual.* Berkeley, Calif.: National Economic Development Law Project.

GANS, H. J.

1968   *People and Plans: Essays on Urban Problems and Solutions.* New York: Basic Books.

SAVAS, E. S.

1982   *Privatizing the Public Sector: How to Shrink Government.* Chatham, N.J.: Chatham House.

STRUYK, R. J., MARSHALL, S. A., AND OZANNE, L. J.

1978   *Housing Policies for the Urban Poor: A Case for Local Diversity in Federal Programs.* Washington, D.C.: The Urban Institute.

U.S. DEPARTMENT OF HOUSING AND URBAN DEVELOPMENT

1979   *Neighborhood-Based Reinvestment Strategies.* Washington, D.C.: U.S. Department of Housing and Urban Development.

1980   *A Guidebook for Using Home Mortgage Disclosure Data for Community Development and Maintenance.* Washington, D.C.: U.S. Department of Housing and Urban Development.

Part Three:
Academic Preparation
for Applied Sociology

INTRODUCTION

Paul D. Reynolds

Most sociologists find it comforting to emphasize the scholarly and scientific aspect of applied sociology—the application of sociological theory and method to practical problems. This conception helps to maintain the image of the sociologist as an independent, detached observer lending his or her skill and knowledge to understanding phenomena in an objective and disinterested way. The implication is that training for such a role may only require a modest shift in the requirements for scholarly training and will allow for a more eclectic academic preparation. The image evoked is that of the applied sociologist as a tenured academic who engages either in consulting or in extrauniversity research projects or who works as a fee-for-service professional, with the option of selecting or rejecting clients and their projects. In either case, the concept of professional autonomy is preserved, consistent with the traditional view of the sociologist as a scientist, scholar, and social commentator. Aloof from the workings of society—the daily competition for resources and influence—he or she can retain a professional distance from the subject matter and maintain a legitimate identification with sociology and sociologists. (Of course, this image is an exaggerated one, and even academic sociologists must compromise—with funding agencies, academic peers, collaborators, university research administrators, and of course, their data sources.)

But the fundamental problem that has focused attention on applied sociology and has led to the compilation of this volume is the current lack of sociological careers for autonomous professionals. Lutterman suggests that the decline in academic positions was clear in the early 1970s; he further comments that federal support for training will be restricted to programs that directly relate sociology to problems of mental health and illness. Training and research support in other federal agencies is becoming increasingly targeted as well. Further, the analysis of Manderscheid and Greenwald in Chapter Three suggests no increase of academic positions for several decades. Hence, the major expansion in career opportunities for current and future graduates will be found mainly in bureaucratic settings, in federal, state, and local agencies, and in private organizations.

This situation leads to quite a different career perspective for applied sociologists. Instead of an autonomous professional providing detached observations and analyses of problems, the applied sociologist, like all professionals in organizations, is becoming involved in and personally committed to the internal processes —decision making, organizational politics, and the like—and the goals and successes of the organization. In short, he or she is becoming a part of the continuing competition for resources and influence that has been the hallmark of most organizational professionals in the past.

Preparation for careers in applied sociology necessarily reflects the dichotomy between the scholarly and practical orientations so aptly expressed by Dynes and Deutscher in the first chapter in this section (Figure 1). In the chapters that follow, Mauksch, Berk, Kornblum, Grusky, Howery, and Lutterman conceive of applied sociology as a redirection of scholarly effort toward practical problems; Dynes and Deutscher alone deal with it explicitly as a new type of career in a distinctive occupational context. Nevertheless, their orientation is implicitly recognized in Howery's discussion on occupational choices of undergraduates and is reflected in Grusky's providing postdoctoral trainees with job-hunting skills.

Training for Applied Sociology

The change of focus to careers in applied sociology may not necessarily result in major differences in the content of training programs. All programs emphasize the breadth of the phenomena and perspectives that comprise sociology. Knowledge of the substance of sociology is required for academic success; a sociological perspective is constantly mentioned as a major contribution to analysis of practical problems (see Dynes and Deutscher, Mauksch).

It may be surprising to find no disagreement in these chapters over the relative merits of quantitative and qualitative research methods. Berk and Kornblum, in their respective chapters, agree that students should know both; they should be able to select the most appropriate research and analytical techniques for the applied problem at hand. Berk assesses the potential training requirements for effective quantitative analysis in the year 2000 as well as the minimum training required to be abreast of present analytical techniques. Kornblum discusses how a student can best become experienced in field observation and prepare for an applied career. Any student with training that reflects the recommendations of Berk and Kornblum would be very well prepared; such strengths are universally recommended for applied programs (see Dynes and Deutscher, Mauksch, Grusky, and Howery). Practical experience is considered critical for both academic and applied training, the latter in the form of field experiences or internship programs on projects with practical objectives.

Training for both academic and applied careers should also include an appreciation of the diverse views as to what constitutes knowledge. Within sociology, there is wide variation in the conception of the boundaries of the field, from attention to structural conditions or social context and concern with individual characteristics or attributes to a focus on individual interpretations and analyses. Knowledge of all these areas is needed to keep track of the objectives and goals reflected in the social science literature and is at the same time useful for knowing how to assist decision makers, for whose attention sociology competes with the perspectives of other disciplines (Dynes and Deutscher, Berk). This host of variations in the criteria for appropriate answers is related to the confidence of decision makers to take action. An applied sociologist that adapts research or analysis to the distinctive intellectual predispositions of decision makers and competing disciplines, even if only to encourage a shift in such predispositions, is likely to be much more effective.

Both academic and applied training should prepare the student to cope with relatively complex, multilevel intellectual structures without becoming confused or overwhelmed. This preparation is the core of any training, and the complexity of the structures varies with the level, the more complex and ambiguous issues being emphasized in graduate programs. Such skills are often acquired as the student specializes in a substantive area, but students in applied programs may go beyond knowledge of specialized areas to consider their implications for practical problems or social policies (see Mauksch).

Despite their substantial similarities, academic training and applied training also differ. Perhaps the most important difference reflects the objective of typical projects encountered by trainees after they graduate. Those in academic, scientific, and scholarly roles focus single-mindedly on achieving the right or best solution to an intellectual problem. In contrast, those in more applied contexts often must accept a trade-off between the importance of a problem and the resources (time, money, personpower) devoted to it (Kornblum). Such pragmatic strategies are seldom covered in academic research or methods training.

A second major difference is the source of problems for attention. Those in academic roles often develop the project goals themselves, or they are developed within the scientific or scholarly community. In contrast, those in applied settings become accustomed to working on problems defined by others—clients, bosses, and the like. Sometimes even the strategy for solutions is selected by others. The skilled applied sociologist will try, through tactful negotiations, to have an impact on both.

The one distinctive substantive feature of some applied programs is knowledge of how decisions are made (Dynes and Deutscher)—acknowledgement of the staff or consulting role of applied sociologists and concern for maximizing their impact.

However, most programs emphasize public policy making, with less attention given to organizational decision making, even though the major potential for expansion of career opportunities is in private organizations.

Finally, the career planning and strategies likely to be most successful in academia differ considerably from those likely to be successful in other work contexts. Unfortunately, most students—regardless of their orientation and training—never receive a full analysis or serious, informal career counseling on these issues. Often the informal advice received is worse than no help at all, as their advisers and mentors provide guidance reflecting career opportunities of decades past. Dynes and Deutscher suggest more attention to such strategic career planning.

One reflection of the sociologist-as-staff-expert perspective is training in job acquisition (mentioned as part of postdoctoral training by Grusky). Applied sociologists seeking nonacademic contexts are in competition with a wide range of professionals—economists, psychologists, and those with training in public health, criminal justice, education, and business, among other areas. The first discipline that comes to mind when decision makers seek staff experts is not usually sociology—unless perhaps they want a survey. Without some assistance and preparation for the competition for jobs, particularly in the private sector, where the Equal Employment Opportunity Commission (EEOC) guidelines need not be followed and most good jobs are located through informal networks, potential applied sociologists can be at a considerable disadvantage. They may take comfort in the fact that no other discipline can bring such expertise to descriptions and explanations of the structures and processes characteristic of social systems. This expertise, the core focus of sociological analysis and knowledge, can be an advantage if presented as relevant to applied issues.

Undergraduate training programs (described by Howery) and graduate and postdoctoral programs (described by Grusky) all involve these basic components. The major differences are the level of sophistication at which the material is approached and the amount of practical experience provided in integrating the many factors involved in applied work—substance, knowledge, and access to the decision-making process. One major aspect of undergraduate training is that virtually all who complete it will represent sociology in nonacademic, or at least non-sociological, contexts (Howery); few undergraduate majors pursue careers as sociologists per se, no matter how the term *sociologist* is defined.

The major difference between the two conceptions of an applied career—autonomous adviser and organizational staff member—may be in the orientation toward their role in the decision-making process. In this regard, the confidence and autonomy of faculty—and the willingness to offer evaluations and commentaries on a wide range of organizational and societal practices—may not be the most appropriate model. Yet it is the only model available to most sociology students. Effectiveness in complex, integrated organizations and agencies with well-established social structures and procedures may require different strategies. Yet these orientations and skills seem to be missing from most applied training programs—programs developed by persons with little experience practicing sociology as members of organizational staff. The many commentaries in Part Two, Chapters Five through Twenty-One, could be most useful in this regard.

Unresolved Issues

The scenario for the future seems clear. Most undergraduates will not be applying sociology directly in their occupational careers; most graduate students will not be able to pursue careers as autonomous professionals. The alternative—reducing the number of graduate students to the needs of academia—is considered undesirable by all concerned. Lutterman describes the disciplinary shift to an emphasis on applied work as a predictable reaction to recessions in academia after the experiences of the 1920s and the economic stagnation of the late 1970s. However, a number of issues seem to remain unresolved, despite the arguments and information presented in Part Three.

Perhaps the most important issue concerns the value of the current applied training program—undergraduate, graduate, and postdoctoral—for helping students pursue applied careers. This issue points directly to the need for the evaluation applied training programs—presumably a speciality of applied sociologists—and, most important, for criteria for determining if the training has been successful. Up to now, most training programs have been developed by academic sociologists, usually faculty members with some experience consulting or working on applied research projects. The common features of the programs described by Grusky and Howery reflect some degree of consensus among academic faculty members. There is considerable merit in trying to expand the base of applied program designers to include applied sociologists in organizational positions. Input from consumers, clients, or supervisors, those that use the products of applied sociologists, could also be of value.

One suggested criterion for evaluating training programs has been the extent to which graduates retain an identification with sociologists and sociology (Dynes and Deutscher). Yet a major measure of success in most organizations is one's incorporation into decision-making processes—one leaves the staff role to occupy a line position. Lawyers, accountants, engineers, economists, and even physicians have been incorporated (or coopted, depending on the perspective) into such responsible positions. Will sociologists consider organizational promotions a failure of applied sociology training? Other disciplines seem to consider this an indication of the value of their selection and educational procedures. If an organizational promotion is a failure, it probably represents a failure of the profession to provide a comfortable postgraduate context for applied sociologists.

This concern leads to another major issue. Will those with applied sociology training continue to be identified as sociologists as they pursue their careers? Are sociologists as a professional group able to provide opportunities for postgraduate training and professional education? A recurring theme among most applied sociologists is the limited advantage of continued contact with their academic peers, partly due to the lack of relevance of the focus of professional associations and partly due to the image of sociology in the society at large. Both issues lead to suggestions directed toward the ASA regarding the incorporation of applied sociologists into the dominant professional association (Berk), suggestions that need not be reviewed again here. Other associations are ready to fill the void if the ASA does not attract practicing applied sociologists.

The most important issues for sociologists as a collective group may be the extent to which the problems and issues pursued by those in applied contexts have an impact on the scholarly agenda of the academic sociologist (Dynes and Deutscher; Mauksch). That is, will those with direct, continuing contact with the problems of society and its major sectors be seen as a credible source of issues for serious attention by nonapplied sociologists? This interchange has occurred frequently in the past—in the practical problems that led to the NORC-North-Hatt occupational prestige research; in the Yankee City studies of community influences on industrial work forces; in the income dynamics study of transitions into and out of poverty status (still supported as basic research); and in the study of school effects on pupil achievement in the Equality of Economic Opportunity research of Coleman and associates. If this interrelationship develops, both segments of the profession will have reason to interact and exchange ideas and analyses. Academic sociology may then be seen by the greater society as attending to concerns of societal significance, which could only improve the general image of sociology and social science. If the interrelationship does not develop, further differentiation into separate professional groups and associations seems inevitable. Both sociology and the new specialty groups that emerge stand to lose from such a trend.

❧ 20 ❧

PERSPECTIVES ON APPLIED
EDUCATIONAL PROGRAMS

Russell R. Dynes
Irwin Deutscher

Discussion of applied sociology and applied educational programs is not new to our discipline. In the first presidential address
given to the ASA, in 1906, Lester F. Ward ends by maintaining
that "Sociology, established as a pure science, is now entering its
applied stage, which is the great practical object for which it
exists." Certainly, such statements give credence to Alvin Gouldner's (1957, p. 102) observation that applied social science "is neither peripheral nor new foliage, but that, on the contrary, it
emerges from the deepest taproots of [our] discipline and has the
most venerable tradition."

More probably, however, the current concern for applied
programs is based less on a sense of tradition than on a sense of
crisis generated in part by what appears to some to be the end of
growth in higher education in the United States. The perception of

the end of growth is of critical importance, since, historically, the primary sociological activity has been academically based. Trying to anticipate the implications of the current crisis in the early 1970s, Dynes (1974, p. 75) remarked: "It is a question of how sociology will survive in a future that will be characterized by a scarcity of resources. This crisis is particularly cogent since perhaps over 75 percent of the present 'converts' to the discipline have not experienced a time when there was any significant scarcity of resources for the field. With only vague remembrances of things past, they may assume that acceptance, support, and all of the necessities of continued institutionalization are automatic."

Our academic marketplace has in fact suffered a severe shakedown during the past decade. Although we continue to encourage young scholars to enter our field and continue to create new Ph.D.s, there no longer appear to be sufficient positions in the academy to employ all our proteges. Thus, for many of those who would earn a livelihood, nonacademic sources of employment are increasingly seen as providing viable career opportunities. What does this shift from university-based research and college teaching to a range of activities lumped together as applied sociology bode for our educational process? With our students entertaining a different distribution of career possibilities, can we or should we continue our traditional educational processes? If we do not, then what do we change in what ways, with what justification? This chapter addresses these questions.

Although our focus here will be on graduate programs, particularly Ph.D. programs, applied sociology has important implications at other educational levels as well. At a time when such concepts as full-time equivalents (FTEs) are a major part of educational planning, departments of sociology seek ways to capitalize on the vocational interests of the current student cohort by adapting the undergraduate curriculum. In days of declining graduate student populations, departments of sociology seek ways to entice and enroll graduate students into new programs, promising new vistas to the students and reduced teaching loads for the faculty. At times, applied programs are discussed in terms that suggest they are a panacea for all our current problems. Although they are not, they deserve careful consideration.

There is a reason, however, for our concentration on graduate schools and graduate curriculum. The graduate curriculum in sociology has undergone considerable standardization. Hill (1975) in connection with his survey of graduate training made in 1971, notes a high degree of similarity across departments, particularly in regard to methodological preparation of students. He observes that this agreement is consistent with an earlier study by Selvin (1963) and seems to be a consequence of disciplinary diffusion supported by patterns of faculty mobility and recruitment. These results suggest that there is probably more consensus on graduate programs than on undergraduate programs. In addition, the understanding of the discipline that evolves during one's graduate years affects one's view of undergraduate education and perhaps the willingness to change and adapt. Because this view of the discipline is so critical and appears to be so widely shared, it is necessary to spend some time outlining the historical groundwork of our discipline. Certain features of the development of sociology may make it somewhat different from other, closely related fields. In turn, those differences may be important as a background for understanding our discussion of application and applied educational programs.

Normative Tradition of Sociology

Every field develops a rationale for its activity that has several functions. As a public justification useful in obtaining social support for the continuation of the activity, the rationale needs to have some credibility if others are not to challenge it openly. Of course, it is also of central importance for those within the field, since it legitimizes their activity and existence. Rationales are more than abstract ideals but represent truths or standards that dominate discussions of graduate education, the content of graduate student socialization, and the evaluation of both intellectual products and the products of graduate-education people.

Rationales develop in particular historical circumstances. The normative groundwork for sociology was defined in a simpler era, and its history may be less complex than those of other disciplines. For example, in its early days, sociology was not overly complicated by diverse cultural origins—it was essentially American and only later claimed European legitimation for indigenous developments. Neither were its founders avocational scholars pursuing knowledge for knowledge's sake, as was true in other intellectual traditions such as ethnology and archeology. The first president of the American Sociological Association, Lester F. Ward, sustained himself as a civil servant in the U.S. Geological Survey while developing the notion that sociology was the "highest landing on the great staircase of education."

A continuing paradox seems to exist within sociology. On the one hand, we have justified ourselves by placing major emphasis on producing knowledge. On the other hand, we have also justified ourselves by emphasizing that the knowledge we produce is useful. Although both justifications have been present from the beginning, one of the justifications has gained ascendancy at one period or another, and the argument has a dialectical quality that resists synthesis.

From the beginning, sociology's home has been in the academy. At the time of its initial institutionalization, the major mission of higher education was to impart knowledge. In that context, there was a limited demand for sociology's knowledge because it was not strongly linked to undergraduate or to professional education. Unlike political science and history, sociology did not develop a strong appeal for undergraduates, nor did it move down into the secondary and elementary school systems. Unlike economics and, to a certain extent, psychology, sociology was considered to have only limited applications to the professions or to other vocations. Thus, although sociology found a home in the academy, its knowledge-imparting functions in undergraduate and, in particular, vocational programs were limited. Consequently, increasing stress was placed on its knowledge-producing functions as the prime justification for its continued support by the academy. As Biderman and Crawford (1968, p. 109) have said, "Sociology arose in graduate school and its 'heart' still remains there. Its major (although sometimes implicit) raison d'etre has been to produce sociology addressed to sociologists who in turn would employ this knowledge to produce more sociology and more sociologists—a logically limitless but economically asymptotic function." Thus, in having a rather circumscribed role within the academy, sociology came to value those conditions that were imposed on it. Its relative purity kept sociology poor, and its relative poverty kept it pure.

Disciplinary purity can best be assured by two conditions—great autonomy within the university for the knowledge producer and problems that are theoretical and hence often nonutilitarian. Institutions able to provide those conditions came to be evaluated as prestigious and thus attractive to faculty members. With the development of tax-supported institutions, these criteria were also used by such institutions as primary measures of self-evaluation. Later, sociologists themselves contributed to the reinforcement of these ideal conditions by ranking them empirically, always assuming that the ranking reflected autonomy and purity of scholarship rather than insularity or irrelevance.

Normative notions about the nature and role of sociology within its academic home are still strong. Although conditions may prevent the implementation of those norms, as during the 1930s and 1940s, such time periods are viewed as atypical or exceptional. On the other hand, periods that reinforce and enhance the norms are viewed as good times. As Dynes (1974, p. 174) has noted, "During the early 1960s, many sociologists began to believe their own myths. Sociologists could get jobs. New departments were opening. Graduate support and research money was readily available. There were pure signs of grace, not mere demographic coincidences."

Good times reinforced and validated the older normative prescriptions. In fact, during the 1960s, conditions were such that graduate students were instructed by their mentors to negotiate in a seller's market for greater autonomy and purity. Having your own research institute (or at least your own computer terminal) and a nonexistent teaching load, were seen as the ideals toward which one strived. Colleagues provided sympathetic support for such career negotiations by quickly awarding tenure, which in turn reinforced the dominant role models available within the academy for graduate students.

An additional factor that makes difficult the discussion of the application of sociology outside the academy relates to the career characteristics of those who are currently determining the direction of graduate programs. Different cohorts have come into sociology with different types of experience. For example, the cohort that appeared during the late 1940s was generally older and usually had several years of experience outside the academic world. On the other hand, new recruits to sociology in the early 1960s often moved from the B.A. immediately into graduate school, in part because they were threatened by the draft. In addition, one might hypothesize that those who were attracted to the field during that period were characterized by a greater distrust of the government and corporate world than even their generally liberal, if not radical, predecessors.

Although sociologists have always talked about the applicability of their discipline, the primary normative tradition within the field has centered about the university as the true home of sociology and about knowledge production as the primary mission of the field. Although the conditions that supported these normative ideals have varied over time, the last twenty years have provided optimal conditions to reinforce those norms. Thus, any discussion, like the one presented in the remainder of this chapter, directed at changing what we have been doing is difficult because it runs counter to a powerful trend.

What Is Applied Sociology?

Although different sociologists have distinctly different notions of what constitutes applied sociology (Rossi, 1980; Whyte, 1982), we use the term to refer to the professional careers of persons trained in sociology who are employed outside academia. At this point, we are satisfied with this crude, residual definition, with only several caveats. Some in academia claim applied sociology as a field of specialization. Others wish to see the job title "sociologist" become usual as an employment description in nonacademic job classifications. (Such a job title exists in the civil service classification. Several years ago, over 600 persons were on the waiting list; during that year, the only two job requests issued were withdrawn before they were filled.) The strategy of trying to make the job title of sociologist standard in nonacademic areas seems to have limited value, since it imposes an academic title on an occupational, functionally organized structure. Sociologists are much more likely to have to adapt to the labor market than is the labor market to the wishes of sociologists. In addition, if such titles became normative, such positions would probably be dead ends, since they would be largely irrelevant to the major goals of the employing organization. All of this may, however, be a matter of timing. Should sociologists demonstrate a capacity to make useful contributions to organizations, such organizations may begin to seek out other sociologists.

Beyond the residual definition, there seem to be common tasks in which sociologists in nonacademic settings are engaged. Those tasks involve informational functions similar to what Wilensky (1967) called organizational intelligence. Although some of the positions may involve pure research, even that research will in some way be considered as input for organizational decision making. More usually, however, such positions involve varied combinations of information seeking (market research, polling, demographic analysis, literature searches, policy analysis, consulting) and project implementation. Sociologists are assumed to know something about the societal content in which all social units—and employing units—must operate, a viewpoint that is useful and perhaps necessary for the continued functioning of the employing organization.

One major thrust for applied educational programs, then, would be to understand the different work worlds. If, in the past, graduate programs have been oriented to the academic world as the primary work setting for sociologists, a realistic direction for change in such programs should be based on a better understanding of the applied work world. We shall return to this point later, but one caution is necessary to facilitate the discussion. Such discussions of application are often couched in terms of a sharp contrast between the ivory tower and the real world. We have worked a considerable time in the so-called ivory tower and have seen little ivory and only a few towers. At the same time, we have spent all our lives in the real world, including the time spent in the academy. Such distinctions are pejorative as well as epistemologically incorrect—the academy is as real and as authentic as other work settings. Understanding the different work settings is more important than judging their reality.

Modifications Needed in Current Graduate Programs

The applied future of sociology suggests some directions for graduate training: some are intensifications of old problems; others might involve some reorientation. All graduate programs are centered on theory and method. By and large, theory involves understanding the sociological viewpoint and is taught in a variety of ways. Since the aim is to make the student think sociologically, the student is surrounded with others—faculty and students—who think sociologically—an approach that may in fact present a major barrier to multidisciplinary and interdisciplinary courses in graduate schools. This aim is the rationale behind course sequences, choice of thesis and dissertation topics, and so on. We know a great deal about how to produce the sociological viewpoint, but we have never seriously considered how it can be sustained in an environment in which it is not constantly reinforced. Many graduate faculty have difficulty seeing this as a problem, since their sociological viewpoint is constantly reinforced by contact with peers and by self-selected isolation. In this respect, we have something to learn from those who maintain their sociological imagination in small colleges and multidisciplinary research settings, for example. Perhaps we need to recapture David Riesman's metaphor of the inner-directed person, whose sense of self was applicable in a variety of situations.

Another, more critical reason for emphasizing a sociological viewpoint is that several studies of sociologists in applied positions suggest that they are seldom employed for their sociological knowledge. Lyson and Squires (1981, p. 5), in studying employers using the *ASA Employment Bulletin*, stated: "However, available evidence indicated that most employers are seeking individuals skilled in the techniques of research methods and statistics and that knowledge in substantive areas of sociology is of secondary concern. If such is the case, then the range of nonacademic employment opportunities open to sociologists is open to Ph.D.s in other social sciences as well." Hence, our current usefulness in the nonacademic market may have little to do with sociology.

On the brighter side, however, this evidence suggests that our research skills and techniques are marketable—not particularly surprising, since the Ph.D. has usually been defined as a research degree. Much of the graduate curriculum is oriented toward learning research skills and ultimately producing an original piece of research publishable in scholarly journals. Around that requirement, a number of norms have evolved that define what is appropriate research. These criteria are at the center of the value system conveyed during graduate school socialization, and, although these criteria are sometimes breeched in the academy for pragmatic reasons, their value is seldom challenged. On the other hand, the conditions upholding these criteria are seldom found outside academia. When confronted with this fact, we often assert that we need to have ideals to guide us in such settings, but it is simpler for graduates to try to avoid such settings in their employment search. When they cannot be avoided, low job satisfaction frequently occurs, in part because the graduates feel they are negatively sanctioned by their academic peers and mentors.

Current graduate research training tends to emphasize the knowledge production norms shown in the left-hand column in Table 1 as generalized truths applicable to all situations, not just

Table 1. Normative Conditions for Knowledge Production.

In Academic Settings	In Applied Settings
Knowledge problem set by scholar in terms of discipline	Knowledge problem set by organization in terms of information need
Scope of problem unlimited by norms of academic freedom	Scope of problem limited by organizational interests
Scope of problem should be only limited by disciplinary boundaries	Scope of problem should be multidisciplinary or multiorganizational unit
Apprentice model aimed at producing entrepreneur; supplemented by colleague support	Team model based on multidisciplinary contributions; isolation from disciplinary colleague support
Time frame set by the problem, usually unlimited	Time frame set by organization, usually restricted
Emphasis on creating data and conducting extensive analysis	Emphasis on finding data and conducting limited analysis
Emphasis on reporting in disciplinary journals	Emphasis on verbal and written reports to diverse audiences
Status rewards for following disciplinary and professional norms	Status rewards for following organizational norms

academic ones. They are taught as a part of the abstract research process. Research courses also give little attention to the operations of academic research centers or commercial research contractors. If they are used as examples, they are often used negatively, as illustrations of how compromised they are. And if they are defended, they are often defended in terms of how close they come to the ideal conditions.

Possibly, of course, the difference between the norms in academic and applied settings will eventually result in modifications in our conceptualization of ideal norms, particularly as more and more sociologists become involved in applied settings. Deutscher (1981, p. 169), in discussing some of the difficulties encountered in evaluation research, suggests the following:

> It occurs to me that perhaps the rules of basic research are in need of reformulation themselves, rather than modification for applied and policy purposes. I think that what I had to say about objectivity and reactivity may be as relevant to basic research as applied research—they are self-delusions of the basic researcher. I do not deny the desirability of measurement and operationalization. I argue only that we must sometimes do what needs to be done even though measurement is not feasible . . . This suggests that graduate education may be dysfunctional for both basic and applied research. A more moderate suggestion is that if, in fact, the things we learn during our graduate education need sometimes to be unlearned when conducting evaluation research, then there are implications for graduate education.

In addition to modifying the core of the graduate program, other directions may need to be encouraged:

1. Students should be encouraged to engage in more interdisciplinary work. This direction is difficult, since graduate departments are often more concerned with ensuring that students become familiar with sociological specialties than with educating them in other fields. At least one argument against such concern is that persons are more likely, at some later point, to follow up a specialty within their own field than to gain knowledge of other disciplines.
2. More understanding is needed of the policy process and of its relation to knowledge production. Other fields have preempted

this concern, or we have simply failed to understand the process. One of the few benefits of scarce resources might be to force our attention again to understanding the process in a multidisciplinary setting.

3. More understanding is needed of the diverse settings in which intellectual work takes place. This is not a plea for specialization in the sociology of work but a suggestion that students become aware of the limited literature dealing with actual research settings (see Hammond, 1964; Horowitz, 1969). The literature is sparse simply because it is not professionally rewarded and is often only written by those who are professionally (and perhaps personally) secure.

4. Because we urge sensitivity to the interdisciplinary settings and perspectives the applied sociologist is likely to encounter, such sociologists must also have a firm grasp on their own disciplinary perspective. They must be able to pull their weight in an interdisciplinary setting or one where there is no peer support. To do this, they need to provide a clear sociological perspective rather than reiterating other disciplinary orientations. As we mentioned earlier, other social sciences also produce technically competent young scholars. Such competence, although necessary, is not sufficient justification for the employment of sociologists in applied settings.

In sum, numerous questions about what to teach need to be addressed when we consider preparing students for careers outside the academy. We need to understand that these will in fact be careers and not just interim jobs. We need to reconsider our traditional requirements for specialized capacities, for a grasp on sociological theory, for mastery of research methods, and for an original dissertation. Do the relative values attributed to such requirements shift as we move toward applied education? Do we need to abandon traditional requirements and invent new ones? Although some sociologists will do research in applied settings, others will engage in different activities. Is there a difference between educating sociologists for academic research and educating them for applied research? Can emphasis on research of any kind turn out to be a useless facet in the education of some applied researchers?

Our academic faculties have the responsibility for wrestling with such questions—a somber thought that we will consider after first considering the student selection process.

Changes in the Selection and Processing of Graduate Students

Most graduate faculty members argue that, beyond their own intellectual examples, a key element in the success of any graduate program resides in the quality of graduate students. How to ensure the recruitment of such quality is the focus of continual discussion and becomes less clear-cut the longer one has been involved in the process.

In our observation, the selection process has become increasingly dependent over the years on narrow academic qualifications. The ease of using grade point ratios and scores on Graduate Record Exams (GREs) overcomes our usual skepticism toward aggregate measures of complex life experiences. This pattern, which has now been well institutionalized, may be at the root of our problem in adapting to nonacademic situations. Perhaps high GRE scores are also highly correlated with rigidity. In this light, we might wish to look more carefully at the criteria we use in the selection process and give greater weight to certain experiential dimensions. For example, it might be better to refuse to admit anyone to graduate school who cannot give evidence of three years of experience outside academia. Further, it might be better not to admit anyone who does not currently have a job and to admit only those who will continue to work part-time. It might even be better not to admit anyone who majored in sociology as an undergraduate. Some of these suggestions will be easy to implement in the future. With the decline in monies for graduate student support, an increasing number of students will have to depend on other sources of income to complete their graduate education. Although some will view this situation as detrimental to good education, it is also useful to remember that such were the conditions under which most older cohorts of sociologists earned their degrees.

The experiential dimension could also be obtained in ways other than the selection process. With the decline in resources, one of the obvious directions is to experiment with external training programs—forms of predoctoral and postdoctoral internships or fellowships. In the past, such programs have been devalued unless they could closely reproduce the academic milieu. Although such programs are usually seen as threatening to academic autonomy, they could provide important links for application. Sociologists in applied settings could supervise such students and, in the process, maintain contact with the academy themselves. This approach would also tend to systemize more effectively the adaptations necessary to translate academic norms into applied situations. Setting up such programs would require the graduate faculty to explore the range of possibilities and thereby perhaps learn more about applying sociology. This type of linkage between the academic and the practical worlds is not without precedent.

We do not underestimate the difficulties of developing such programs. We will have to convince others of our utility, something we have difficulty doing even to ourselves. And we may have great difficulty treating such internships as an integral part of graduate programs rather than as an economic aberration. For example, where would an internship fit into the graduate program? As a primary source of dissertation data molded to academic norms? In lieu of the dissertation? Would all the experience have to be retranslated into the academic context? Would it be done in addition to the usual academic requirements? We have no easy answers for these questions, except to suggest that other fields, particularly in the physical and biological sciences, have been doing such things for years without any threat to their academic respectability.

Changes in Faculty Attitudes and Behavior

Focusing exclusively on graduate students and graduate curricula as the key to change is simplistic, because we would have the same graduate faculty members teaching them. The situation is analogous to leaving sex education to the unmarried clergy.

Earlier, it was hypothesized that those individuals who entered the field of sociology in the last twenty years or so have had less contact with other work settings than previous cohorts of graduates. Since they missed that experience, mechanisms should be developed to allow them to receive it. Perhaps the internship and fellowship notion would be as applicable to faculty as to graduate students. Perhaps sabbaticals and research leaves should be implemented only in nonacademic contexts. Perhaps research seminars should be jointly taught with someone in a research setting outside the university. Perhaps we need to experiment with split academic positions so that individuals can maintain positions in other institutional sectors. For example, the recent innovation at the Massachusetts Institute of Technology relating to genetic engineering allows faculty to work with a company half-time and maintain faculty status. We might wish to consider the models and precedents established in other fields. The attitudes of most faculty members may be our major barrier to adaptation within the academy. These attitudes create and then reinforce particular reward structures that tend to give low priority and, in most instances, negative sanctions to applied activity. In tenure decisions, applied work is usually used as a reason for lack of standard academic publications. Applied work may have some tenure currency if it involves obtaining grants that add to university resources or if the researcher is adept at exploiting the grant for publications in academic journals. Whether the funding agency is satisfied with the work is largely irrelevant. Extensive involvement in applied work is most often seen as a measure of marginality within the academy. Major exceptions are senior faculty who have made academic reputations (and have tenure) and are therefore allowed to engage in applied work, in much the same way that other eccentricities generally imputed to older professors are tolerated. Another anomaly is that of recent past presidents of the ASA who have achieved their distinction and spent most of their careers in applied sociology. It is not clear how well we understand our own history in this respect. The historical revisionist might discover that we have a distorted image of our past.

Certainly, one of the consequences of the lack of continued growth of higher education will be a rethinking of tenure, particularly since it has been transformed over the years from an issue of intellectual autonomy into a matter of job security. Hopefully, in that rethinking process, the resolution of the issue will not involve an increasing withdrawal of the academy from a concern with applied problems. In fact, the reward structure we have described is perhaps peculiar to sociology, although more generally applicable to the social sciences. Other areas of the university have quite comfortably incorporated applied contributions into their reward and tenure structure, suggesting that the ability of a field to deal with applied problems is perhaps a measure of disciplinary maturity rather than a lack of disciplinary purity.

Focusing on the current faculty is more likely to provide solutions to the applied problem than to build hope on future cohorts of graduate students. If one looks carefully at manpower projections, one can say, in paraphrase of Pogo's dictum, "We have met the sociologists of the future and they are us." But there are other reasons for this focus. Just as the Ph.D. is not a terminal disease, neither is it a vaccination that will protect one for all time in all situations. For a number of years, like car manufacturers, we have been concerned only with production and not with maintenance costs. We have concentrated our efforts on increasing graduate student support in order to sustain our academic efforts, assuming that quality terminal education would satisfy career needs. Since the graduate experience generally constitutes less than one tenth of one's career time, however, it is strange that we should give it 100 percent of our attention and most of our declining resources.

With some creative imagination, we might be able to include other educational opportunities when the appropriate time arises. What do we do with our lives after we have tenure? Is there life after retirement? How do we help fellow sociologists explore interests in new specializations or in other disciplines? How do we help individuals moving out of academia into other work settings? Do they have to be taught to write again? How do they learn to adapt to a routine eight-to-five schedule without regarding it as punishment? Do they have to learn to talk to others in a common language? Perhaps our knowledge, which draws on reintegration programs in other areas of the society, can help us design a program for ourselves. To seek such opportunities is not a confession of personal failure. Interests and opportunities change. New skills are needed for new understandings. The Ph.D. should not be considered as a permanent claim on a restricted status but one stage in a long, continuous educational process. By definition, those engaged in knowledge production should also be involved in learning. Again, we might look around the campus for already existing models. Many other fields have short courses, summer institutes, and a variety of other formats that assist in the development of specific skills. Many professional associations have taken the lead in such activities, and the thriving commercial market for continuing education suggests that much of the innovative thinking is going on outside the academy.

In brief, sociology will be better able to focus on applied problems if such understandings can be communicated by faculty members who have had applied experience themselves. Applied sociology must be seen as one important element in the total role of sociologist rather than as an area of specialization. Such specialization implies that the rest of sociology is nonapplicable and separates the production and the application of knowledge, a separation that is ultimately destructive of both.

The major focus of applied education programs, then, needs to be directed toward faculty, particularly existing graduate faculty. To ask future graduate cohorts to do what we have been unable to do is not sound educational philosophy but passing the buck.

References

BIDERMAN, A. D., AND CRAWFORD, E. T.
1968   *The Political Economics of Social Research: The Case of Sociology.* Washington, D.C.: Bureau of Social Research.
DEUTSCHER, I.
1981   "Social needs vs. market demands." *Sociological Focus,* 14:161–172.
DYNES, R. R.
1974   "Sociology as a religious movement: Thoughts on its institutionalization in the United States." *The American Sociologist* 9:169–174.
GOULDNER, A.
1957   "Theoretical requirements of the applied social sciences." *American Sociological Review* 22:92–102.
HAMMOND, P.
1964   *Sociologists at Work: Essays on the Craft of Social Research.* New York: Basic Books.

HILL, R.
   1975   "Report on a survey of graduate training." In N. J.
          Demerath, O. Larsen, and K. Schuessler (Eds.), *Social
          Policy and Sociology.* New York: Academic Press.
HOROWITZ, I. L., ED.
   1969   *Sociological Self-Images: A Collective Self-Portrait.*
          Beverly Hills, Calif.: Sage.
LYSON, T., AND SQUIRES, G. D.
   1981   "Sociologists in nonacademic settings: A survey of em-
          ployers." Unpublished paper. Available from T. Lyson
          at Clemson University, Clemson, S.C. 29631.
ROSSI, P. H.
   1980   "The presidential address: The challenge and opportu-
          nities of applied social research." *American Sociologi-
          cal Review* 45:889-904.
SELVIN, H. C.
   1963   "The teaching of sociological methodology in the
          United States of America." *International Social Sci-
          ence Journal* 15(4):2-20.
SIBLEY, E.
   1963   *The Education of Sociologists in the United States.*
          New York: Russell Sage Foundation.
WARD, L. F.
   1907   "The establishment of sociology." In American Socio-
          logical Society, *Papers and Proceedings, first annual
          meeting, American Sociological Society.* Chicago: Uni-
          versity of Chicago Press.
WHYTE, W. F.
   1982   "Social inventions for solving human problems."
          American Sociological Review 47:1-15.
WILENSKY, H. L.
   1967   *Organizational Intelligence: Knowledge and Policy in
          Government and Industry.* New York: Basic Books.

❦21❦

TEACHING APPLIED SOCIOLOGY: OPPORTUNITIES AND OBSTACLES

Hans O. Mauksch

Concern with the application of sociology has motivated sociologists from the earliest days of the discipline, particularly in the United States. Among its founders were many who saw in sociology a potential for improving the human condition and for ameliorating human misery. The distinction between applied and pure sociology would probably not have been meaningful in those early days, when the application of sociology did not suggest distinctive knowledge and specialized skills.

As part of its thrust to be accepted as a pure science, sociology, like other disciplines, increasingly accorded prestige, priority, and rewards to the pursuit of conceptual and theoretical issues, with little regard to their application. This climate, pervasive even today throughout many academic sociology departments—particularly at research universities—places great value on purely academic careers and considers careers in applied settings less worthy and somewhat suspect.

Although such subcultural norms still prevail, significant

312

changes have occurred in the last ten years. Applied sociology has claimed the attention of the profession, has been identified as a means of attracting students, and has caught the imagination of sociological researchers and theorists, who have devoted significant efforts to conceptualizing the questions raised by the rediscovery of the discipline's applied potential.

This chapter will focus on applied sociology in the undergraduate setting. However, some of the issues raised are relevant to all facets of applied sociology. In developing these observations, I have drawn on the lessons learned from participating for seven years in the ASA Projects On Teaching Undergraduate Sociology and its successor organization, the ASA Teaching Services Program. Being involved in an enterprise that seeks to serve sociology faculty members from all corners of the United States has provided valuable opportunities to become familiar with various types of undergraduate programs. Approximately 140 sociology departments in liberal arts colleges, community colleges, and universities have been visited by volunteers of the ASA projects' Teaching Resources Group. During these seven years, more than 2,000 different sociologists have attended workshops.

Curiosity, interest, or a desire to follow current trends characterizes the attitudes at a large number of undergraduate sociology programs. Some of the opportunities associated with the development of application-oriented programs will be discussed in this chapter, as will some of the hurdles and pitfalls that serve as obstacles to the development of quality and long-range success.

Like all new ideas, the idea of applied sociology evokes various images among its users. There is a real need to clarify the taxonomy of applied sociology and to agree on some definitions that can be used to communicate effectively and consistently among knowledge producers, knowledge disseminators, and knowledge users. An understanding of the real nature of applied sociology is less important than an understanding of the meanings and precise definitions of the various approaches to applied sociology and their promise for the discipline.

Meanings of Applied Sociology

In one sense, applied sociology refers to technique and methodology. Unlike the inquiry model governing pure research, applied sociology starts with the definition and exploration of a real problem or mission. Where pure sociology, like all pure science, seeks to test hypotheses and propositions and thus abstracts from reality, applied sociology confronts the methodological requirement to translate complex, pluralistic situations into sociologically manageable questions. Furthermore, the methodology of applied sociology includes several models that deserve full development in the literature and in the laboratory: the research model of problem solving, the research model of formulating and testing action options, and the research model of evaluation. The literature on evaluation methodology is probably better developed than literature on the other models.

In some quarters, applied sociology is identified with substantive knowledge. The numerous domains of social life in which sociologists have accumulated data and expertise include many applied fields—for example, health, energy, agriculture, and social welfare. While these three examples are uniformly labeled applied sociology, substantive knowledge in the equally applied specialties of criminology, the family, and race and ethnic relations has been accepted as part of the core areas of sociology. This difference in the labeling of specialty areas and their assignment to either the core or the periphery of the discipline has more significant implications for the history and sociology of sociology than for logical and consistent taxonomy. Applied sociology, with its substantive connotation, implies the ethnography of a specific social domain, with particular emphasis on the special and unique knowledge associated with that field. Special methodological or political considerations are part of this image. The give-and-take of knowledge between the special field and the core of sociology varies among these fields.

As suggested earlier, applied sociology is also disciplinary politics. Recognizing the drift of vocational orientations among undergraduate students and responding to dropping enrollments, departments of sociology have chosen applied curriculum content and the label of an applied, career-related curriculum as hopeful means of attracting and keeping students. Another political dimension, particularly observed at state colleges and small universities, involves a pervasive drift in which professionally oriented and practice-oriented curricula such as management, public administration, and social work absorb sociological content. These disciplines offer under their egis undergraduate courses that frequently cover subject matter previously the property of the sociology department. The full process of applied sociology in undergraduate colleges cannot be adequately appreciated if one does not recognize that the choice of applied sociology may possibly be a fundamental shift in the philosophy of sociology curricula. What previously, in its search for purity, was typically structured as a defended disciplinary fortress may be moving, in the curricular and student-hour wars, toward a progammatic and symbolic offensive, with applied sociology serving as the weapon of choice.

These observations should not be interpreted as critical comments. On the contrary, genuine appreciation of the trend in undergraduate education toward applied sociology content must avoid the myth that intellectual issues are the only legitimate justification for new scientific or pedagogical development. The world of the undergraduate college is a complex and competitive social system. A discipline that does not recognize that social change and academic planning must include a delicate balance between science, pedagogy, and politics may not fare well.

In addition to the perspectives previously suggested, the development of applied sociology should also be examined as cultural change. As suggested earlier, sociology, unlike chemistry and psychology, has no tradition of practice and is characterized by a strong adherence to the academic value system, which attributes worthiness and success to academic rather than applied careers. The norms of sociology can be accused of harboring values that give applied sociology a diminished status and a diluted sociological identity—at times, with a sense that application equals apostasy. If applied sociology is to be intellectually, pedagogically, and politically successful, acceptance by the discipline of the legitimacy and potential excitement of applied work must be part of the informal culture of the graduate school and of the elite structure of the discipline. In this way, applied sociology may come to have legitimacy among both undergraduate faculty members and undergraduate programs. To accomplish a change in social and cultural context, several issues have to be confronted, issues that may be more consequential in fostering success on the undergraduate scene than the mere development of new courses, new labels, and new tricks.

Potential Obstacles

The first issue to be confronted is directly related to the subculture of the sociological community in academia. Applied sociology must be identified by faculty and experienced by students as an integral and important part of the total sociological enterprise, and all vestiges of taint and extraneousness must be eliminated. Overcoming the potential obstacles identified in the following paragraphs will contribute to achieving a disciplinary unity in which the boundary between pure and applied becomes irrelevant. Essentially, the argument presented in this chapter is not confined to the development of specific areas of innovation in the undergraduate curriculum; rather, it links effectiveness of applied sociology development with the capacity for accomplishing structural and attitudinal changes in the total context of sociological teaching.

The second issue to be confronted when considering applied sociology programs relates to the epistomological bases of pure and applied knowledge. Is applied sociology a body of knowledge distinct from the core of the discipline? Conversely, does applied sociology represent a continuum that, on the one hand, is firmly anchored in the utilization of the fundamentals and theories of sociology and, on the other hand, extends to include detailed work within specific sociological practice fields and laboratories? If the second formulation is accepted—and this chapter argues that position—the development of an applied sociology program must be a total faculty concern and not just the business of those who teach the so-called applied courses. If application of knowledge has its roots in the core concepts of the discipline, the teaching of these core concepts must include the various uses of basic knowledge. Teaching theory as a basis for the pursuit of intellectual questions must be balanced with demonstrations showing that theory is the intellectual core of sociological application to real-life concerns.

A third issue that deserves to be introduced here has intellectual, pedagogical, and political implications. The aforementioned issue of the unity of knowledge and science becomes complicated by the prevailing notion that the applied sociologist draws on the knowledge system of his or her discipline in pursuing an applied career but that applied sociology has little, if anything, to contribute to the advancement of the discipline. This notion of one-sided benefits is paralleled by the pattern of alienation of applied sociologists from disciplinary affairs and organizations. These patterns are clearly based on erroneous perceptions. A major challenge to the undergraduate program lies in developing a climate in which the applied setting, with all its special properties, serves as a legitimate laboratory where the propositions of the discipline can be tested or modified and where new questions relevant to basic knowledge can be discovered and formulated. In the proper circumstances, this reciprocity and intellectual interdependence can become a major contribution of the development of applied sociology. This contribution is particularly significant for sociology, which, according to student responses, is frequently experienced as an aggregate of rather diverse and disconnected courses with little sense of progression and increased sophistication throughout the undergraduate years (Mauksch, 1981).

The issue of course and substance reciprocity has a number of ideological and logistical implications. Full acceptance of this issue implies a challenge to the excessive distinctions made between pure and basic research. Perhaps the development of pride and the commitment to quality among applied sociology students should be linked to the principle that the better the research, the smaller the distance between pure and applied research. Genuine acceptance of the notion that excellence can be a cohesive force provides one of the crucial conditions for success of an applied program. Applied courses and their subject matter must be integral components of the departmental repertoire. Faculty teaching applied courses must be fully integrated in the departmental community.

Like all the issues presented thus far, the fourth issue to be considered overlaps and interrelates with the other three. Each department and program must come to grips with the kind of image that the applied program elicits among students. The previously urged continuity between the core of sociology and the applied program has different implications when seen in the context of public image. Sociology has not been noteworthy for its success in developing among its undergraduate majors a sense of identity with the discipline. Of real concern is the phenomenon of applied areas that splinter into separate fields. Criminal justice, which, in many institutions, started as an applied sociology program, has be-

come a distinct curriculum with diminished intellectual and professional identity with sociology. Examples of this pattern, whereby new programs are jettisoned into new and distinct identities,
abound. A cooperative, cohesive curriculum environment in which
the learner is socialized into a sociological identity with the conviction that the applied program is intellectually and methodo-
logically linked to sociology might, for students and faculty alike,
counteract the tendency for programs to seek independence.

Opportunities

Based on these discussions, the undergraduate program
should include three kinds of courses. Before these three components are described, however, it is worth repeating that the undergraduate faculty offering an applied program should candidly confront its own philosophy and values and determine whether, as an
entire faculty, it is willing and able to accept the applied program
as a serious, intellectually challenging, and respectable component
of the sociology enterprise. Next, the faculty needs to translate beliefs into social structure and avoid stigmatizing those who teach
applied courses. Organizationally, the applied program is the responsibility of the entire faculty.

In turning to the three curriculum components, one should
remember the assertion that applied sociology must have its roots
in the core of the discipline. Thus, the first component of the applied curriculum is the common core that identifies the discipline
and its central concepts. Theory, methodology, and the courses
offering the major intellectual areas of sociological concern must
be seen as a component of the applied curriculum and as the basic
experience that provides programmatic unity for all sociology majors, no matter what their program options.

Serving as a component of the applied curriculum has implications for the teaching of core courses. In an era when sociology
embraces the option of application, its core courses must demonstrate the compatibility of sociological knowledge as pure science
and sociological knowledge as a basis for application. Whether in a
course in social psychology, demography, social organization, or
any other of the staples of the undergraduate curriculum, the applied capability must not be seen as a special innovation, a fad, or

a desecration of scientific purity. This premise applies to theory and, most certainly, to research methods.

The second component of the curriculum consists of the many substantive areas in which special applied sociological knowledge has already been achieved. Many of these fields, ranging from health, criminal justice, and community management to policy and impact evaluation, have been developed in the undergraduate curriculum as separate courses with hardly a sense of the sociological unity and similarities among them. Although these fields of practice and policy are indeed profoundly different, and although some sociologists have become highly specialized in just one of these areas, a genuinely sophisticated applied curriculum must offer opportunities for cross-specialty learning in order to remind sociologists of the unity of their discipline.

A comparative and synthesis-oriented approach to the teaching of specialty areas significantly strengthens the quality of the sociology being taught.. Intimate knowledge of the occupational stresses of nurses and physicians or of the patterns of communication between prisoners and prison guards is a necessary but not sufficient preparation for the sophisticated practitioner of applied sociology. The design of these specialty courses must be seen as a matrix in which one axis is defined by the substantive, specialized properties of the field and the other axis—common to all specialty courses—consists of fundamental sociological concepts such as power, class, and role strain. The organization of apparently diverse areas into matrices of common analysis will help the student and the researcher achieve comparative analyses and apply sociological ideas derived in one applied area to other areas. Hughes (1971) has called the ability to transfer concepts from fields of discovery to apparently different areas of sociological inquiry one of the significant tools of the sociologist. Considerable literature, expertise, and laboratory opportunities for these specialty courses can be identified in many departments. The development of a sophisticated, comparative, and unifying sociology has yet to be achieved.

The third curriculum component consists of courses and other learning experiences that address the special issues of conceptualization, methodology, and technique in the applied arena. Perhaps the most formidable challenge to those who are at the forefront of the undergraduate and graduate sociological enterprise is to develop and package a body of knowledge that prepares students intellectually for the process of application. In his writings on the application of sociology, Lazarsfeld (Lazarsfeld and Reitz, 1975) recognizes and emphasizes the need for a methodology of application and acknowledges the high level of sophistication required to tackle this task. Translating a real problem into a researchable construct and subsequently converting research results into relevant, practicable, and comprehensible policy options requires theoretical and methodological models for which sociology has offered ad hoc rather than generic approaches.

It is important to emphasize the complexity and breadth of this third curriculum component. To select the sociology from complex situations that, like all reality, do not pay heed to academic departmentalization requires competence and intimate familiarity with the epistemology of the discipline. At the same time, the application of any discipline to the solution or explanation of real issues requires familiarity with the ethical, cultural, and political context within which sociology is to be practiced.

Conclusion

This chapter has argued for certain preconditions as requirements for successful undergraduate applied sociology programs. A significant part of the argument is the insistence on favorable and respectful cultural conditions within the sociology department that endeavors to offer such programs. Further, sociological identity must not be lost; on the contrary, it should be a formal and informal curriculum emphasis. The most idealistic and challenging point made here concerns the need for sociological sophistication and continuity in applied sociology offerings. This chapter is a plea for protecting and enhancing the sociology in applied sociology. By no means does this challenge imply a lessening of the importance of substantively competent specialists in selected topical areas. On the whole, a model for an applied curriculum combines the appeal of identifiable, vocationally relevant topical areas with the achievement of a sociological identity and a repertoire of sociological skills.

References

HUGHES, E. C.

1971   *The Sociological Eye: Selected Papers on Work, Self, and the Study of Society.* Hawthorne, N.Y.: Aldine.

LAZARSFELD, P., AND REITZ, J. G.

1975   *An Introduction to Applied Sociology.* New York: Elsevier.

MAUKSCH, H. O.

1981   "Social change and learning outcomes: A planned approach." In G. Loacker and E. G. Palola (Eds.), *New Directions for Experiential Learning: Clarifying Learning Outcomes in the Liberal Arts,* no. 12. San Francisco: Jossey-Bass.

❧ 22 ❧

UNDERGRADUATE EDUCATION

Carla B. Howery

When the first president of the American Sociological Association (ASA), Lester Frank Ward, described the discipline of sociology seventy-six years ago, he divided it into three categories: dynamic sociology, pure sociology, and applied sociology (Ward, 1906). Students may feel that *dynamic* and *pure* sociology are often dormant in their courses, but *applied* sociology is being explicitly reintroduced (or relabelled) in their undergraduate curricula.

There are several explanations for the increased interest in applied sociology training on the part of students and faculty. The student culture of the 1960s pushed for relevance and for concern with social problems; their successors in large numbers now bail out of the liberal arts and opt for vocational and professional degrees, increasingly choosing to come to college primarily for occupational training.[1] Faculty in liberal arts departments, including sociology, feel the pinch of retrenchment in academic jobs and the decline in student enrollments. Applied sociology programs are seen as one strategy for holding and expanding the market for sociology, given its intrinsic interest for students, and for teaching marketable skills.

This chapter bypasses the question of whether applied sociology cheapens or enriches the discipline. While the value of applied sociology as an intellectual and academic endeavor continues to be widely debated, programs of applied sociology do exist and are being further expanded and developed. The point of departure here is that a need exists *ipso facto* for sociologists to familiarize themselves with such programs. Furthermore, effective teaching and curriculum development are generic activities; efforts that occur as part of the implementation of an applied program may benefit a department's entire undergraduate program.

In this chapter, I intend to describe relevant issues about undergraduate sociology curricula; identify reasonable instructional goals for an undergraduate clientele; illustrate the alternative forms of applied sociology programs in place at various institutions; show how the various programmatic emphases relate to jobs for undergraduates; comment on the internship or field experience component of many of most applied sociology programs; and make suggestions for program development and curriculum assessment for departments considering development of an applied program. Case examples are taken from materials submitted by departments about their bachelor's level applied sociology programs in response to a mail survey to 100 departments in March 1982 and from presentations at the ASA Workshop on Directions in Applied Sociology, held in December 1981 in Washington, D.C.[2] Altogether, information was available on thirty-four programs (see the appendix at the end of this chapter for a complete listing). According to inquiries received at the ASA Executive Office, the greatest interest in applied sociology programs at this time seems to come from four-year schools, both liberal arts colleges and state universities, without a graduate program.

Undergraduate Curriculum: The Nature of the Beast

Ideally, a department's curriculum is a statement of its collective instructional goals and can be said to represent a contract with its students. The diversity and dissension in the discipline of sociology is reflected in most departmental curricula. In 1971,

Bates and Reid examined undergraduate curricula to draw inferences about the core of sociology as it was presented to students.
They found that the "lack of consensus on requirements, the
diversity, and, in many instances, the marginality of courses required convey the idea that it makes little difference what the student takes so long as he accumulates enough credit hours" (Bates
and Reid, 1971, p. 248). Course sequencing, another measure of
systematic curriculum planning, is notably absent in sociology, in
contrast to other fields. This confusion has led Frederick Campbell, guest editor of a special issue of *The American Sociologist* on
curriculum, to compare the typical sociology undergraduate curriculum to a beast that once lived on large herds of undergraduate
students but has now stopped hunting and seems bound for ex-
tinction. "This beast should occupy the principal niche in our
undergraduate program, but, as it is, it contributes little and be-
longs in the basement." The beast is little "more than just a collection of courses that people are moved to offer" (Campbell,
1980, p. 2).

The disarray is accelerated as some departments try hur-
riedly to add an applied curriculum. Mauksch (1981, p. 3) warns
against curriculum revisions motivated by "the search for a formula which will attract students, increase enrollments, and enable
the sociology catalogue to compete with other offerings for the
1980s. Applied sociology, from this perspective, can be viewed as
a packaging device, as a sexy addition to the old virtues, and as a
way by which manipulations of labels may give the appearance of
changing content and message." Such actions may revive the beast
temporarily but probably will not sustain it in the long run.

But just as there is some beauty in all beasts, there are good
reasons for arguing that the undergraduate level is the most strategic place for departments to start the development of applied
curricula. First, the terminal B.A. student has always been "applied" in that he or she has not sought employment in academic
sociology. The current attention to providing jobs after college has
several positive ramifications: departments are thinking about
ways to assist undergraduate students with job placement, and
existing curriculum and course requirements are being examined
and repackaged with potential improvement in the patterning and
grouping of courses for students. One effect of developing an ap-

plied program will be the placement of students in internships and subsequently in jobs where their learned sociology skills will be made visible. Sociology may be better understood and more generally appreciated by employers, legislators, and the general public than it has been in the past. Although this impact may be overstated, the demonstrated utility of sociology may come primarily from undergraduate majors as they pursue their internships and postcollege work roles.

Second, sociologists argue within academia for the discipline's importance to the liberal arts and its relevance to professional degree programs. We assert that nurses should take courses in marriage and the family and that a course in formal organizations is essential for business majors. Apparently, we believe that sociology applies to jobs for our majors and for students with other career aspirations.

One example of an applied program for majors is at the University of Wisconsin, Whitewater. The department has not elected to offer a program of new courses in applied sociology within its department. Instead, its *Handbook for Sociology Students* lists specific course offerings appropriate to each of twenty-one career options for sociology majors and suggests courses for minors in complementary fields. A student interested in business would major in sociology, with courses in organizations, work, and occupations, and minor in business, with courses in management, business statistics, and organizational behavior from other departments. Sociology is the major field, inculcating a liberal arts outlook, but with departmental guidance training in professional skills is also carefully included from the satellite curricula around the university (course work in police science and counseling). The integrity of the sociology curriculum is maintained, and students with an interest in the substance of sociology are not lured away by professional programs. University of Wisconsin, Whitewater sociology enrollments have remained steadily high over the last decade.

At Western Washington University, the sociology department puts its applied emphasis into the sociology services courses for *nonmajors* (Simpson, 1981). Western Washington University has a demographic research laboratory in place and uses this base to emphasize research skills for undergraduate students. The involvement of students in small-scale group research projects has the added benefit of counteracting student passivity, so often a problem in service courses. Structuring assignments in this way shows students that sociology is not simply "doing good" but that it is also a goal-oriented approach to knowledge. Thus, the department conceptualizes the difference between social work and applied sociology in this way: social work applies knowledge to practical problems and needs; applied sociology increases knowledge in a context of value-oriented goals. The same view is held for those in and aspiring to careers in other occupations and professions. For these groups, the department contends, "we can teach the many who engage in de facto applied sociology how to do it better" (Simpson, 1981, p. 21).

Note that neither of these programs has opted to put aside the liberal arts orientation of the sociology major. The first impulse of a department might be to change the major from basic to applied. These two schools and other departments with such programs advise against this approach as intellectually debilitating, difficult to implement, and not very successful in addressing student interests.

A third reason for starting applied sociology at the undergraduate level is that curriculum revisions may be the easiest to implement. Many graduate-level courses are the exclusive domain of a particular professor, reflecting his or her research interests and closely linked to his or her idiosyncrasies. Undergraduate courses are more often the collective property of a department, sometimes doled out haphazardly or with mild coercion to ensure that all offerings are covered. If undergraduate courses belong to the group rather than to individuals, they may be more easily modified. The blunt reality is that faculty jobs rest on enrollments in undergraduate courses. Departments realize that, to some extent, they rise and fall collectively according to how they are perceived on the undergraduate student grapevine. They can cultivate their image by offering new courses, working with other departments and with college advisers, organizing a sociology club, teaching effectively, attending to service courses, and so on.

A case can be made that departments are motivated by the carrot as well as the stick to make curriculum changes and try innovative teaching methods including an applied emphasis. Bradshaw and McPherron (1978) surveyed departments in universities, four-year colleges, and community colleges about their course offerings, pedagogical techniques, and attitudes toward sociology's contribution to their school. Respondents showed a desire to innovate and to teach more effectively. Many felt strongly that sociology is central to the liberal arts and to students' basic skills development, especially to the ability to analyze a problem and think critically. This orientation could facilitate the incorporation of applied sociology experiences in the curriculum. A department's motivation is further enhanced by student demand and the perennial question, What can I do with a B.A. in sociology? Administrators too are not only watching enrollment trends but are also asking departments to justify existing courses, to make explicit their contributions to the university, and to show efforts to respond to student interests and a new student clientele. Community colleges are the fastest-growing sector of higher education, attracting the older, returning student who attends school part-time and has a keen interest in higher education coupled with grounded ideas about career plans. A similar student body is growing in state universities. An applied sociology emphasis is attractive to these students.

Lastly, the job market may be dismal for Ph.D. sociologists looking for academic careers, but it is still a fairly open field for the B.A. liberal arts graduate. Sociology skills are useful in a range of entry-level jobs for which advanced degrees are not required. Although the overall number of jobs in the public sector is not keeping pace with the number of liberal arts graduates at all degree levels, there are some positive signs for the B.A. sociologist. Manderscheid and Greenwald (1981) predict some increase in employment for sociologists in state and local governments, the very places where students are likely to have interned in an applied sociology field experience. Students, the department, and public-sector agencies and offices are familiar with one another, and the match of education and jobs is likely to be more harmonious.

Instructional Goals for an Undergraduate Curriculum

Olsen and DeMartini (1981, p. 2) define applied sociology as "sociological knowledge and action oriented toward intentional social change to achieve desired goals." For the B.A., M.A., Ph.D., or postdoctoral student, then, this orientation uses the concepts and theories of sociology, appropriate methodology, and a sensitivity to the policy process to connect practical knowledge and social change (Dorn, 1982). The basic difference between each level of student training is the sophistication of the material.

For the B.A. student, this definition of applied sociology is operationalized in three general ways: a set of specific skills (for example, research training, writing skills, and so on) in which the student is deliberately trained; substantive concentration in sociology specialties (for example, criminology, family, or urban studies) that are built into the curriculum; and job-hunting advice and assistance. All these elements may be present to some degree in an existing sociology program. The process of making these features explicit and coordinated is one of the benefits of implementing an applied program. If a department can collectively agree upon its goals for training students in applied sociology, this intentionality of purpose may have a positive spill over into the department's entire teaching mission. In short, a department should not focus so much on overhauling its program, but making it clear, cohesive, and linked to learning goals.

The average applied sociology program requirements consist of one or two theory courses, one or two research methods and statistics courses with an emphasis on certain methodologies (for example, impact assessment, evaluation research, secondary data analysis, construction of social indicators), basic computing skills, and practice in evaluating research as a consumer as well as a producer of data. Most B.A. programs offer electives in the substantive fields of sociology (for example, marriage and the family, criminal justice), with several of these courses taken in one area forming a concentration. Lastly, a course in applied sociology is offered as a capstone to the major to provide an overview of the policy-making process, to sensitize students to ethical dilemmas in social action, to offer career advice, and to monitor the practicum or internship experience (Dorn, 1982). As described, except for the seminar in applied sociology, this curriculum outline resembles that of a regular major and lends support to Mauksch's view that applied sociology programs are really "a matter of organization of subject matter and communication rather than content" (Mauksch, 1981, p. 4).

Given this basic curricular framework, we shift to a look at outcomes. What can the B.A. student who completes this program really do? In my view, it is reasonable to expect the student, when confronted with a tangible social problem, to be able to: place the issue in a social-structural, nonpsychological context; correctly use theories of the middle range and relevant concepts in describing the phenomenon; identify relevant data needed for informed social action; construct a research design and be able to follow through its steps or critique the research process of others and the validity of its findings; analyze research results and make clear recommendations to appropriate audiences; identify aspects of the policy-making process that affect social change; and write clearly, using accepted style, grammar, and vocabulary.[3] The student who performs these behavioral objectives would have an impressive set of skills relevant to a number of employment settings. A functional résumé could reflect these abilities. Although the want ads do not usually contain a listing entitled, "Sociologist Wanted," the *Dictionary of Occupational Titles* lists literally hundreds of jobs for which the B.A. sociologist has good general preparation.

If a department accepts this or another set of behavioral objectives, measurement strategies should be devised to assess students' performance toward these goals. Traditional objective tests will not be the most valid measures of many of these objectives (see Boros and Adamek, 1981).

Some critics of applied sociology programs argue that the substance of the discipline is pushed aside in favor of a grab bag of research and computer skills. This criticism seems to be least valid for undergraduates, who are drawn to the field for its substance and who, on average, are exposed to eight or more content courses. Graduate programs seem much more likely to emphasize methodology and to attempt to prepare their students for competition with degree-holders in business and computer science as well as in other social sciences. Bachelor's-level students cannot be expected to have much methodological sophistication or experience and generally do not conduct primary research, except as part of a team. For example, at the University of Massachusetts–Amherst, according to an unpublished program statement, the undergraduate traineeship in social research and analysis "does not attempt to train its majors to design, conduct, and analyze their own research but to hone their research skills vocabulary, sophistication, and all-around savvy to the point where they can perform admirably in 'senior research assistant' positions" relevant to a number of roles in the public and private research sectors. The regular sociology B.A. is augmented with four core courses in research methods and statistical analysis and an independent research project.

Alternative Undergraduate Programs

Departments that offer "applied sociology" show a wide range of curricular definitions of the term. A department might only offer a single, separate course in applied sociology as an elective, with or without prerequisites. Or several courses can be grouped as a track within the B.A. sociology major. Requiring several courses within a single substantive area (for example, criminal justice or gerontology) may be the applied component, as this concentration prepares a student for work in a particular job specialty. Interdisciplinary programs, for example, may result in a degree in applied social science, counseling, or policy analysis and usually include standard courses in sociology as well as cross-listed courses especially developed for the program. Another common option is to offer or require an internship experience as the embodiment of the applied curriculum. These field experiences can occur in a wide range of placements in the community. In some cases, an on-campus research and consulting center offers practicums for students. These alternative forms will be examined in turn.

Single Course. At the University of Virginia, a single course in applied sociology is offered, with introductory sociology as the prerequisite. In an unpublished program statement, the three-credit course is described as follows: "A review of the uses of sociology in practical affairs, providing theory and data for public policy, institutional reform, social action programs, and social inventions and contributing to architectural design, industrial engineering, community planning, and innovative legislation."

Applied Sociology in Regular Courses. At Dowling College, a small liberal arts school with high enrollment in business and other career-oriented programs and a small sociology-anthropology faculty, field experiences are incorporated within regular courses (Seperson, 1981). Although no applied program per se is in place, the department offers an applied emphasis within its regular major; most students who take sociology courses have a fieldwork experience of some kind, whether it is interviewing for a research project or making qualitative observations about some aspect of campus life. A reorientation of assignments in current courses might be a way to begin testing faculty and student interest in applied sociology, as well as a way to optimally use scarce resources.

Applied Sociology Track. Concentrations within the regular sociology major take two general forms: intensive work in a particular substantive area and training in applied social research. The typical B.A.-level applied program provides substantive and theoretical information on a particular topic. Concentrations in criminal justice are the most common, with other programs offered in marriage and the family, human services and counseling, legal studies, organizations and administrations, medical sociology, and urban studies.

An examination of sample programs indicates that departments have maximized their strengths by offering concentrations in areas with faculty depth. At East Carolina University in North Carolina, three tracks are available for the B.A. or M.A. student: maritime studies, medical studies, and marriage counseling. Each track involves some work experience in an internship setting, usually with some salary for the student. Although the East Carolina program does not offer training in many substantive areas, it reflects three subfields where several faculty are currently doing research, writing, and teaching. Valdosta State College in Georgia has a B.A. degree with concentrations in anthropology, general sociology, social services, research, and criminology, as well as a B.S. degree in criminal justice with special work in law enforcement, organization and administration or corrections, probation, and parole. Many of the programs listed in the appendix to this chapter have similar programs at the M.A. level, with comparable courses at a higher level of sophistication.

Montclair State College in New Jersey offers a minor in applied sociology with emphasis on either helping professions and institutions or community organization and social policy. Another option is applied research, which is training in skills rather than a substantive specialty. Rutgers University has a certification in applied social research, with thirty hours of course work for all the

B.A. requirements and an internship for a field research project. Policy analysis and evaluation is the thrust of the program at the University of Nebraska, Lincoln, an interdisciplinary program in the social sciences. Undergraduates at the Australian National University are trained in social policy, applied research, and social change, with a required project report from an internship. In many cases, these special concentrations in a substantive area or applied research are noted on the diploma, a form of credentialing that is useful in job hunting.

The Department of Sociology at the University of Illinois, Chicago Circle has created a collective résumé listing the skills it expects graduates with a major from that department to have. This résumé is useful for orienting the department to its collective responsibility for student learning goals, for communicating to employers what skills to expect from a student, and for providing a learning contract for students. When departments offer a degree with a special title, such a collective résumé is useful for operationalizing the student's abilities in terms understandable to all these audiences.

A special degree results from some applied programs with a single, topical focus. At the University of Houston, Clear Lake City, the B.A. degree is in community and organizational behavior; West Virginia University is beginning a program in social justice; California State College, Bakersfield offers an internship program in community sociology; and the University of California, Irvine offers an undergraduate applied program in applied ecology. These curricula reflect the interests and strengths of the respective faculties.

Field Experience. Practical experience of one of three basic types seems to be an integral part of many of these applied programs:

1. Internship: an off campus experience under the supervision of a field placement adviser on location. For the B.A. student, the supervision is usually not from a sociologist; the student usually carries out a project for the placement and learns about that setting. Students should not replace regular employees or be assigned routine clerical tasks.
2. Practicum: on or off campus, students work with a practitioner, preferably at a job level similar to one they might assume on

completion of their undergraduate degree. At Middle Tennessee State University, students work with faculty on a research project, such as a recent study on youth diversion programs. At Illinois State University, junior-year majors work with a faculty member on a project in their practicum; in the senior year, they work independently in their own placement site, with supervision from faculty and agency personnel.

3. University consulting and research centers: on campus, students assist faculty in conducting research—in-house for the institution, by contract from bidders, or as a service to the community. Faculty members can control the field experience of the student and better coordinate it with course work. At Illinois State University, faculty members get release time to do community research and students are involved from the proposal writing stage through project write-up. Anne Arundel Community College in Maryland has one of the most exciting examples of a research center in place: the Center for the Study of Local Issues (Park and others, 1981). Using personnel on loan from the federal government's Intergovernmental Personnel Act, the college set up an independent research center and now supports itself through contract research to the local community. The center provides an important service to the area and probably opens a few doors for jobs for its students as well. The sociology faculty working in the center argue that substantive sociology can be taught by the use of research methods. Phenomena are in need of explanation, and, within a specified time frame, the center staff and students pursue this task.

Over half of all undergraduate departments offer internships for undergraduates (Satariano and Rogers, 1979), and sociology departments plan to increase their use of field experience more than any other teaching technique (Bradshaw and McPherron, 1978).

Career Counseling Programs

Sociology has always had an applied side, as Rossi (1980) reminds us. Curricular change to applied sociology may not imply a change in courses and content as much as in assisting students in job-hunting strategies and career planning. Dorn (1982, p. 16) suggests that one goal of an applied program is the "establishment of a vehicle by which students are linked with the career placement center on campus and introduced to sociologists who have experience working in applied settings who can serve as role models." He further notes that the 1982 ASA Code of Ethics states that departments of sociology have an ethical obligation to assist students in finding employment. The campus career center is particularly helpful in teaching job-hunting skills, such as résumé writing, interviewing, and skills assessment, as well as in offering concrete job leads in the local community. The effectiveness of these centers is significantly enhanced if the sociology department has communicated directly with the staff to explain the components of the sociology major and to suggest possible career options.

The sociology department itself may choose to offer a credit or noncredit course in job hunting. At the University of Illinois, Chicago Circle, students are given course credit for working on a research project to assess the job market. Research skills are used to address the student's own questions about what jobs are available in their metropolitan area. The University of Wisconsin, Whitewater offers a seminar in career development for sociology majors containing tangible advice on job hunting and other topics, such as ethical issues in applied research.

Other suggestions for assisting students in making the connection between their skills and possible jobs include: guest presentations from applied sociologists (especially alumni) in classes throughout the curriculum; establishment of a sociology club for undergraduates, with some program time devoted to job-hunting topics; coordination with the placement service and career counseling staff of workshops that might particularly help liberal arts majors; sponsorship of undergraduate research conferences to give students practice in written and oral communication of their work (some departments have annual research conferences for undergraduates; for a listing of such conferences, see the *ASA Teaching Newsletter,* February-March, 1982); a departmental handbook on career opportunities for the various tracks and emphases offered by the department; awareness and use of other written career materials, such as *Embarking on a Career with an Undergraduate Sociology Major* (Huber, 1982); and participation in career-day events for graduates of all majors and in similar events in local high schools, where incoming students might be attracted to sociology.

Training in Job-Related Skills

Training students in specific skills can occur within any of the curricular arrangements for applied sociology. In the sample programs, five groups of skills seem to be emphasized. Although these same skills could be developed within a standard major, the applied emphasis is usually more skill-oriented because departments are likely to identify instructional outcomes; employers indicate what skills they seek; skills are needed for internships and are further developed in the field; and the job title "sociologist" is only marginally connected to actual job openings requiring a presentation of oneself in terms of skills. The categories of skills most prevalent in applied programs are:

- Quantitative research skills, including evaluation research (measuring an effect usually during or after it has occurred), impact or needs assessment (projecting effects), research design and instrument construction, and data analysis, particularly of secondary data.
- Problem-solving skills, including qualitative indicators, problem framing, case-study analysis, and identification of relevant variables.
- Counseling skills, or social intervention at the individual, group, or community levels, including training in clinical sociology, social casework and group work, and administration of social services. (The Clinical Sociology Association offers a syllabi set of instructional resources for such courses; it is available from David Kallen, Michigan State University, Department of Pediatrics and Human Development, East Lansing, Michigan 48824, or from the Teaching Resources Center of ASA, as of January 1983.)
- Special substantive knowledge and skills concerning particular policies and trends in the areas of children and families, gerontology, urban and community work, medical and legal institutions, and the criminal justice system.
- Skills in oral and written communication, to include public

speaking, translating of social science information to a lay audience, clear and concise writing, and interviewing. Dowling College terms this competency sociological journalism.

Internship Component

Elective or required internships seem to be a central feature of most of the applied sociology programs that go beyond a single course and have similar goals. The objectives of a field experience program include the following:

- To link theoretical material, perspectives, and ideas to the practical concerns of concrete examples.
- To provide students an opportunity to test abilities and attitudes toward particular vocational or career possibilities for the future.
- To prepare students for employment.
- To give students experiences that will aid them in course selection and motivate them toward academic achievement in future course work.
- To increase retention at the undergraduate level.
- To provide students with opportunities to earn a salary while pursuing educational goals.
- To provide opportunities for productive and creative service to public and private, profit-making and nonprofit-making organizations (use for others' benefit of the information and perspectives gained in college work).
- To provide opportunities for community agencies, businesses, and governmental units to receive special or temporary assistance from students with the motivations and the developing skills they need.
- To establish additional means of communication between the members of the university population and the public.

A department should collectively discuss and set priorities for these or other objectives in order to make the complex tasks of identifying placement sites and measuring student learning in internships easier. For example, if career testing is a high priority, internships should be modeled on apprenticeships, with the stu-

dent working closely with an agency supervisor who has a job similar to or at a slightly higher level than one the student might reasonably expect to take. Goals of community service might suggest
establishment of a campus research and consulting center. Linkage
of class work with practice could be accomplished with a field experience seminar—an ongoing course to help students reflect on
their internships and receive academic credit in sociology (Howery, 1982).

Five sets of issues merit particular attention and careful
forethought before a department initiates an internship program:

- Goals. What are the educational goals of the internship, and,
  therefore, what modal type of experience does the department
  want a student to have? What skills can be developed in these
  settings?
- Identification of sites. Which sites will further the educational
  goals of the department? How are these contacts made? Do faculty members have existing contacts within the community? In
  smaller towns, are there a sufficient number of sites? Will the
  field site supervisors be willing to provide an educational experience for students and invest in supervisory time? (For some
  suggestions, see Hill, 1982.)
- Coordination with field supervisors, the department, and students. Can a learning contract be developed to serve the needs
  of all three parties? How are responsibilities for supervision to
  be divided? What are the options if the contract is not followed
  by any of the three parties? Texas Christian University has prepared booklets outlining the expectations for the placement
  site and the student to clarify these issues.
- Evaluation of student learning. How are learning goals assessed?
  In what manner and for what types of work are sociology credits granted? (For a sample contract, see Hill, 1982, and Ali and
  Stanton, 1982.)
- Faculty and departmental commitment. How many faculty
  members will be involved? What professional rewards will be
  granted? Is the administration supportive? A word of caution:
  most departments greatly underestimate the faculty time involved in the establishment and management of a field experience program. If programs are to meet educational objectives,

they require careful faculty supervision. A general estimate of time seems to be the equivalent of a full-time faculty load for one person with full responsibility for supervision of thirty students.

The assignment of one faculty member to be in charge of the field experience program has both assets and drawbacks. The strength of the arrangement is that an individual can develop internship sites over time and nurture their maintenance through personal relationships with the field site supervisors. If academic supervision is a responsibility rotated among the faculty, careful records must be kept about the idiosyncrasies of the placements, and extensive socialization must occur with the transition from one academic supervisor to another. In general, if one faculty member is in charge of placements, he or she should not be selected from untenured, junior ranks, a situation likely to occur because the task is not particularly sought after by most faculty. To assign a junior faculty member, however competent, to internship supervision while at the same time binding him or her to traditional faculty norms for productivity is a set-up for role strain, since the faculty supervisor is unlikely to be as productive as junior colleagues with regular teaching loads. The University of Kentucky has addressed this problem by using different criteria for the tenure decision on the field adviser. Another disadvantage of the one faculty member approach to fieldwork supervision is that it can reflect or create weak commitment on the part of other faculty members to the program or curriculum in applied sociology. Applied sociology is personalized rather than collectively shared. Since most departments seem predisposed to choose a single faculty supervisor, some of these drawbacks should be considered.

A set of faculty supervisors can be designated to correspond to the concentrations or tracks in the applied program. At the University of Maryland, faculty members oversee the three field experience focuses—social service, organizational internships, and research internships—and several faculty members are identified as potential managers for each of the tracks. Therefore, no one faculty member has the task for a long time, yet coordination between faculty and supervisors is maintained.

A third supervisory model involves the use of a civil servant

or administrative assistant (often with a B.A. in sociology) to handle part of the supervisory tasks of fieldwork. He or she bears responsibility for most paperwork surrounding the internship and
often for job-advising assistance. Some or all faculty members are
used for substantive supervision and for granting credit in sociology, essentially on an independent study basis. This approach reduces the burden on any one faculty member and offers students
a choice of faculty members with different substantive specialties.
The arrangement is particularly effective if faculty members are
rewarded for supervision of independent study projects. For example, a department could relieve a faculty member from a committee assignment for supervision of every ten internships. Or the
number of students supervised is recorded in personnel information used in merit raises and promotion and tenure decisions.

Faculty members are also rewarded for their important efforts when a field experience seminar is the mechanism for granting credit and supervising students in the field. The seminar is part
of the faculty member's course load and part of the departmental
curriculum. If the number of students interested in fieldwork is
rather small (less than twenty annually), this approach is advantageous and feasible.

The least desirable alternative is ad hoc advising by some or
all faculty members with no faculty rewards. Students may choose
faculty advisers but must take the initiative to find their placement, propose a project, and take their chances that the experience will be fruitful. Needless to say, simply having an experience
does not necessarily connect with any desired educational goals.
Quite a bit of material is available about the mechanics of internship supervision (see, for example, Ali and Stanton, 1982; Yelon
and Duley, 1978; Davis, Duley, and Alexander, 1977; and Hill,
1982). The National Society for Internships and Experiential Education is the organization to consult first.[4]

Two more comments about internships and applied curricula are in order. The first guideline concerns course sequencing.
DeMartini (1980) suggests that, in applied settings, students first
confront the collection of information or data or encounter a
problem or issue that requires a response. Sociological concepts
are brought to bear to understand the data, information, or problem, and then closure is sought, taking into account the political

realities of the particular issue. This typical pattern should be mirrored in the applied sociology curriculum. Students should first take courses in methodology and philosophy of science, followed by the sequence in theory, including middle-range theories and concepts associated with particular substantive specialties. Lastly, the issues of policy making and application of social science for intentional social change should be covered either in a field experience seminar or in a course called applied sociology. This point of view suggests that the internship be placed near the end of the student's work for the B.A. degree.

Another observation about B.A.-level internships reinforces the placement of the field experience in the senior year. Many placements are reluctant to take undergraduate interns because supervisory costs outweigh the benefits of the students' contributions. The more skills students have already developed, the more significant the contribution they will be able to make. If learning goals are carefully articulated in the curriculum, they can be communicated to people at the field sites, who can then expect students to be able to assist them in specific ways. An internship in the student's senior year has the potential of turning into a job or at least into job leads. An internship placement may well be the single most significant assistance departments can give a student for job seeking, as studies of alumni and their current positions document.[5]

Conclusion

Applied sociology programs require carefully articulated learning goals. Changes in both the organization and content of the curriculum can be minor or major, as these goals dictate. Although such changes are not an easy remedy for departmental neglect of curricula and students, they do appeal to students and can address faculty concerns for the integrity of sociology and the liberal arts and for declining enrollments. The process of curriculum revision may well have payoffs for the entire curriculum as a collective product of a department's mission for its students. Students graduating in sociology may be better equipped to get jobs using their identifiable skills in theory and method and are thus important disseminators of information about our discipline. Ward's identification in 1906 of applied sociology as a vital part of the discipline may best be embodied in the 1980s in our undergraduates.

Appendix: Sample Undergraduate Programs in Applied Sociology

University of Akron
Akron, OH 44325
Tracks: criminology; urban
planning and social research; and family

*Anne Arundel Community College
Arnold, MD 21012
Contact: Betty Jean Park

Australian National University
Canberra, Australia 2600
Contact: Owen Dent

University of California, Irvine
Irvine, CA 92717
Contact: Ellen Greenberger

University of California, Northridge
Northridge, CA 91324
Contact: Bernard Thorsell
Tracks: criminal justice and social control; medical sociology; counseling and interviewing in work settings; and social welfare

California State College, Bakersfield
Bakersfield, CA 93309
Contact: Joseph Julian

University of Delaware
Dover, DE 19901
Tracks: pregraduate school; social welfare; urban studies; health services; and sociology teaching at the high school level

DePaul University
Chicago, IL 60614
Contact: Roberta Garner
Tracks: social services; legal studies; law and society; juvenile justice; and community and urban studies (some tracks include internships)

*Dowling College
Oakdale, NY 11769
Contact: Susanne Bleiberg Seperson

East Carolina University
Greenville, NC 27834
Contacts: John Maiolo, David Knox, and Marty Zusman

University of Houston, Clear Lake City
Houston, TX 77058
Contact: Peter Bishop

*A paper on this program was presented at the ASA Workshop on Directions in Applied Sociology, December 1981, Washington, D.C.

University of Illinois, Chicago
Circle
Chicago, IL 60680
Contact: Kathleen Crittenden

Illinois State University
Normal, IL 61761
Contact: Roy Treadway and
Vernon Pohlman

Iowa State University
Ames, IA 50011
Tracks: corrections and criminal justice; social work; and
public service and administration

*University of Maryland
College Park, MD 20742
Contact: Barbara Altman

University of Massachusetts,
Amherst
Amherst, MA 01003
Contact: James Wright

Middle Tennessee State Univer-
sity
Murfreesboro, TN 37132
Contact: Donald Schneller

Montclair State College
Upper Montclair, NJ 07043
Contact: Len Rubin

University of Nebraska,
Lincoln
Lincoln, NE 68588
Contact: Alan Booth

University of New Hampshire
Durham, NH 03824
Contact: Sally Ward

University of North Carolina,
Chapel Hill
Chapel Hill, NC 27514
Contact: Duncan MacRae

Northern Arizona University
Flagstaff, AZ 86011
Contact: Florence Karlstrom
Tracks: corrections; social plan-
ning; and social work

Northern Kentucky University
Highland Heights, KY 41076
Contact: Ralph Peterson
Tracks: minorities; corrections;
consumer affairs and business; gerontology; medical;
and community service
agencies

University of Pittsburgh
Pittsburgh, PA 15260
Contact: Patrick Doreian

Purdue University
West Lafayette, IN 47907
Contact: Gaye Mathews
Tracks: criminology and cor-
rections; and social work

Rutgers University
New Brunswick, NH 08903

---

*A paper on this program was presented at the ASA Workshop on Di-
rections in Applied Sociology, December 1981, Washington, D.C.

University of Texas, Dallas
Richardson, TX 75080
Contact: Phillip Armour
Tracks: sociology; urban
  studies; law and society;
  and political economy

Valdosta State College
Valdosta, GA 31601
Contact: Louie Brown

University of Virginia
Charlottesville, VA 22903
Contact: Theodore Caplow

Virginia Commonwealth University
Richmond, VA 23284
Contact: Allan Schwartzbaum
Tracks: industrial relations;
  health care organization; data
  analysis; law, deviance, and
  social control; urban studies;
  learning social behavior; socialization; policy dimensions
  of social and cultural change;
  and family relations

Virginia Polytechnic Institute
  and State University
Blacksburg, VA 24061
Tracks: probation and parole;
  juvenile delinquency; corrections; mental health; and
  gerontology

West Virginia University
Morgantown, WV 26506

*Western Washington University
Bellingham, WA 98225
Contact: Carl Simpson

University of Wisconsin, White-
  water
Whitewater, WI 53190
Contact: Charles S. Green III

Notes

1. *The Chronicle of Higher Education* in 1980 conducted a survey of freshman characteristics and attitudes and found that 77 percent of freshmen cited "to be able to get a better job" as a "very important reason" in deciding to go to college. 74.6 percent responded "to learn more about things" and 34.4 percent said "to become a more cultured person" was very important.

2. Over half of the departments (N = 363) listed in the 1982 *Guide to Graduate Studies,* published by the American So-

*A paper on this program was presented at the ASA Workshop on Directions in Applied Sociology, December 1981, Washington, D.C.

ciological Association, indicate a concentration of courses in applied sociology for *graduate* students. Based on the assumption that they might also offer a program for undergraduates, eighty departments were randomly sampled and sent a questionnaire inquiring about the program at the B.A. level. An additional twenty undergraduate departments, who were thought to offer an applied concentration, were sent questionnaires. Nonresponse could indicate that no such program was currently in place in a department. Thirty-four departments responded to this nonrepresentative survey, from which the illustrations in this chapter are drawn.

3. The University of Maryland requires a writing course for all students and the Department of Sociology's applied sociology program incorporates this requirement into its program, reinforcing it with writing practice in several other courses. An alumni survey at Loyola University showed writing skills to be extremely important to alumni looking back on their B.A. degrees (Nyden, 1982).

4. The National Society for Internships and Experiential Education (NSIEE) offers a number of services relevant to sociologists involved in applied sociology programs and internship supervision. Its newsletter, *Experiential Education,* is published bimonthly and is a benefit of membership. NSIEE holds an annual national conference and many regional training sessions for professional development of faculty as well as agency personnel. NSIEE's Peer Assistance Network in Experiential Learning (PANEL) offers a phone referral service. Callers using the toll-free number for questions about experiential education will be referred to a local volunteer peer assistant who is knowledgeable on the topic; information on print resources is also provided. The phone number is 800-424-2933 (in Washington, D.C., Alaska, or Hawaii, it is 202-331-1516). The organization's publication list is lengthy and includes a *Directory of Washington Internships* and a *Directory of Undergraduate Internships.* A new publication is "Integrating the Community and the Classroom: A Sample of Postsecondary Courses" ($15.00), which includes eighty-six course descriptions in the humanities and social sciences and sample syllabi, learning contracts, and evaluation forms. To receive a publication list and order blank, or to inquire further about NSIEE, write: NSIEE, 1735 I Street N.W., Suite 601, Washington, D.C. 20006.

5. Six examples of alumni surveys are:

Malnig, L. R., and Morrow, S. L. *What Can I Do with a Major In . . . ?* Jersey City, N.J.: St. Peter's College, 1975.

Routh, L. R. "Increasing faculty involvement." *Journal of College Placement,* 1977, 37(3):36-39. Reports on the University of Northern Iowa.

Nyden, P. "A survey of alumni majors in sociology." In C. B. Howery (Ed.), *Teaching Applied Sociology: A Resource Book.* Washington, D.C.: Teaching Resources Center, American Sociological Association, 1982. Reports on Loyola University, Chicago.

Elder, J. "Report on a Decade of Majors in Sociology." Unpublished manuscript. Reports on graduates of the University of Wisconsin-Madison.

Collins, M. "The Sociology B.A.: Educational and Occupational Attainment and Program Evaluation." M.A. thesis, University of Maryland.

Ruggiero, J. Alumni Survey at Providence College.

References

ALI, K., AND STANTON, F.
1982   *The Experienced Hand: A Student Manual for Making the Most of an Internship.* Cranston, R.I.: Carroll Press.

BATES, A., AND REID, S. T.
1971   "The sociology major in accredited colleges and universities." *The American Sociologist* 6:243-249.

BOROS, A., AND ADAMEK, R. H.
1981   "Developing applied sociology programs." *Teaching Sociology* 8(4):387-399.

BRADSHAW, T., AND McPHERRON, S.
1978   *Data Report: Issues and Resources in the Undergraduate Curriculum.* Washington, D.C.: Teaching Resources Center, American Sociological Association.

CAMPBELL, F. L.
1980   "A note from the special editor." *The American Sociologist* 15:2-5.

DAVIS, R. H., DULEY, J., AND ALEXANDER, L. T.
1977   *Field Experience.* East Lansing: Michigan State University Press.

DeMARTINI, J. R.
1980   "Constraints to the development of curricula in applied sociology." *The American Sociologist* 15:138–145.

DORN, D. S.
1982   "Setting educational goals for an applied sociology program." In C. B. Howery (Ed.), *Teaching Applied Sociology: A Resource Book.* Washington, D.C.: Teaching Resources Center, American Sociological Association.

HILL, D.
1982   "Identifying, supervising, and evaluating internships." In C. B. Howery (Ed.), *Teaching Applied Sociology: A Resource Book.* Washington, D.C.: Teaching Resources Center, American Sociological Association.

HOWERY, C. B.
1982   "Field experience seminar." In C. B. Howery (Ed.), *Teaching Applied Sociology: A Resource Book.* Washington, D.C.: Teaching Resources Center, American Sociological Association.

HUBER, B. J.
1982   *Embarking on a Career with an Undergraduate Sociology Major.* Washington, D.C.: American Sociological Association.

MANDERSCHEID, R. W., AND GREENWALD, M.
1981   "Supply and demand of sociologists in 1990." Paper presented at the ASA Workshop on Directions in Applied Sociology, Washington, D.C., December.

MAUKSCH, H. O.
1981   "The teaching of applied sociology: Opportunities and obstacles." Paper presented at the ASA Workshop on Directions in Applied Sociology, Washington, D.C., December.

NYDEN, P.
1982   "A survey of alumni majors in sociology." In C. B. Howery (Ed.), *Teaching Applied Sociology: A Resource*

Book. Washington, D.C.: Teaching Resources Center, American Sociological Association.

OLSEN, M. E., AND DeMARTINI, J. R.
1981   "Predoctoral and postdoctoral training in applied sociology." Paper presented at the ASA Workshop on Directions in Applied Sociology, Washington, D.C., December.

PARK, B. J., AND OTHERS.
1981   "The Center for the Study of Local Issues: A vehicle for applied sociology." Paper presented at the ASA Workshop on Directions in Applied Sociology, Washington, D.C., December.

ROSSI, P. H.
1980   "The presidential address: The challenge and opportunities of applied social research." *American Sociological Review* 45:889-904.

SATARIANO, W., AND ROGERS, S.
1979   "Undergraduate internships: Problems and prospects." *Teaching Sociology* 6(4):355-372.

SEPERSON, S. B.
1981   "Applied sociology at Dowling College." Paper presented at the ASA Workshop on Directions in Applied Sociology, Washington, D.C., December.

SIMPSON, C.
1981   "Illustrative undergraduate programs: Applied sociology at Western Washington University." Paper presented at the ASA Workshop on Directions in Applied Sociology, Washington, D.C., December.

WARD, L. F.
1906   *Applied Sociology.* Boston: Ginn.

YELON, S. L., AND DULEY, J.
1978   *Efficient Evaluation of Individual Performance in Field Placement.* East Lansing: Michigan State University Press.

23

GRADUATE AND POSTDOCTORAL EDUCATION

Oscar Grusky

Like the biobehavioral and biomedical sciences, which have increasingly undertaken postdoctoral training over the years with positive consequences for their scientific development, the social sciences and applied sociology in particular have begun to offer extended technical training, including postdoctoral training programs, especially in health-related applied social science fields. As competition for jobs increases and academic-sector opportunities

Note: This paper was prepared with the partial support of the National Institute of Mental Health (USPHS NIMH-14583), although this agency is not responsible for the views presented. I am grateful for the assistance and the helpful advice of Alexander Boros, Howard Freeman, James Greenley, Robert Groves, Kenneth Lutterman, Marvin Olsen, Paul Reynolds, William Zumeta, and several of my former and current postdoctoral colleagues: Paul Benson, Dean Gerstein, James Holstein, Kathleen Tierney, and Steve Vandewater. Finally, I wish to thank Peter Coggeshall and Herbert R. Pahl of the National Research Council, National Academy of Sciences.

decline, new graduate programs in the applied fields are also emerging (Manderscheid and Greenwald, 1981) as interesting adaptations to anticipated and actual market conditions. By describing and analyzing both postdoctoral and graduate programs, this chapter will contribute to an increased understanding of future prospects for the applied sociology profession.

Postdoctoral Training

Postdoctoral teaching is comparatively new to the social sciences, and, because so few scholars currently engage in it on a significant scale, its complexity and importance are easily overlooked. Yet it promises to be increasingly important in the future, as sociology follows in the footsteps of the physical and natural sciences, medical education, and, to some extent, clinical psychology.

As of 1980-81, the National Institute of Mental Health (NIMH) supported twenty-eight mental health-related research training programs involving postdoctoral scholars. Six of these are exclusively devoted to training postdoctoral fellows (the rest have predoctoral trainees as well); of the six, the program at the University of California, Los Angeles, (UCLA) is the only one in sociology alone. The other five are in psychiatry (Harvard); education, anthropology, and psychiatry (Harvard); psychology and National Opinion Research Center (Chicago); social work and sociology (Rutgers); and psychiatry, public health, and sociology (Wisconsin)). This section of the chapter, which draws heavily on my experiences as director of the UCLA program since 1976, describes some of the special characteristics, satisfactions, and problems of postdoctoral teaching.

Ambiguity of the Postdoctoral Role

Postdoctoral fellows in applied sociology simultaneously confront three sets of role expectations: as students, as supervised researchers, and as junior faculty members. As students, they typically take formal courses originally created for graduate students, sometimes for credit and sometimes as auditors. In the role of supervised researcher, they are assigned responsibilities for library and field research, data analysis, extramural grant proposal preparation, and other duties. Finally, as junior faculty members with the title of adjunct assistant professor, they often teach, initiate, and conduct their own research projects and attend to various departmentally assigned tasks. Because of this complex mixture of responsibilities and statuses, postdoctoral fellows often find their role troublesome and confusing. Trainees are frequently treated as if they were graduate students, even though they hold a faculty title. In addition, they are often handled administratively by the universities' graduate divisions, which also handle predoctoral students. In part because of these ambiguities, problems of control and lack of prestige plague these appointments. At issue is the appropriate balance among the three components of the postdoctoral role.

The postdoctoral fellow has temporary, transitional status and performs work also performed by research assistants, research associates, instructors, visiting scholars, and professors. A National Research Council study (National Academy of Sciences, 1969, p. 42) defines postdoctoral fellows as "appointments of a temporary nature at the postdoctoral level that are intended to offer an opportunity for continued education and experience in research, usually, though not necessarily, under the supervision of a senior mentor. The appointee may have a research doctorate (for example, Ph.D., Sc.D.) or professional doctorate (for example, M.D., D.V.M.) or other qualifications which are considered equivalent in the circumstances." Berelson (1962) points out that postdoctoral fellows typically do not have standard programs of study, usually engage in research (but may teach a little), and may be indistinguishable on the job from research associates and other trainees. Postdoctoral fellows are generally funded either from awards the fellow has personally received or from a professor's research grant. At UCLA, a distinction is made between the postdoctoral fellow, who is funded, and a visiting scholar, who is not.

Postdoctoral Education in the
Social and Behavioral Sciences

The 1969 review of postdoctoral study in the United States, published under the title *The Invisible University,* was definitive up to that time. Its theme was that postdoctoral education, although of fundamental importance to higher education and the advancement of knowledge, emerged quietly and without either a rationale or an overall plan and that its strategic contributions have therefore gone generally unrecognized by educators. This lack of recognition of the contributions of postdoctoral study to research and instruction and the special problems it generates in major universities remains to this day.

The National Academy of Sciences and the Rockefeller Foundation were responsible for inaugurating the first large-scale postdoctoral fellowship training program in science, which, between 1919 and 1949, awarded 1,359 postdoctoral fellowships. Rand's (1951) influential study of the remarkable accomplishments of this group stimulated further support. He reported that they had been awarded three Nobel prizes and that sixty-five had been elected to the prestigious National Academy of Sciences. One of the earliest postdoctoral fellowship programs in the humanities and social sciences was initiated by the Guggenheim Foundation. Eleven percent of the first 246 Guggenheim awards made between 1925 and 1939 were for postdoctoral work in sociology. In 1944, Congress passed the Public Health Services Act and large-scale support for postdoctoral training began in earnest shortly thereafter. From 1963 to 1966, an average of over 6,000 postdoctoral awards were made each year in all fields. Of course, only a small proportion were in the social or behavioral sciences. Table 1 summarizes some recent findings regarding behavioral science postdoctoral appointments from 1972 to 1977. First, the table documents a steady growth in behavioral science postdoctoral awards, which, in nonclinical areas (anthropology, sociology, and nonclinical psychology), increased from 124 in 1972 to 379 in 1977. Second, it shows that the proportion of nonclinical Ph.D.s taking postdoctoral positions has increased from 17.6 percent in 1972 to 23.4 percent in 1977. The National Research Council study (National Academy of Sciences, 1978, p. 72) notes that "behavioral scientists who took postdoctoral training within one year of earning a doctorate made up about 13 percent of the total number of 1971-1975 behavioral science Ph.D. recipients in both the academic and nonacademic sectors. Furthermore, over half in each employment setting indicated that the postdoctoral appointment was taken either . . . [to gain] research experience or to switch

Table 1. Current Trends in Supply/Demand Indicators for Behavioral Science Ph.D.s.[a]

	1972	1975	1976	1977	Average Annual Growth Rate (in percent)	Average Annual Change
Supply indicators:						
Nonclinical:					*(1972-77)*	*(1972-77)*
Ph.D. production	2,213	2,580	2,709	2,746	4.4	107
Postdoctoral appointments[b]	*389*	*515*	*580*	*644*	*10.6*	*51*
Clinical:						
Ph.D. production	902	1,118	1,262	1,305	7.7	81
Postdoctoral appointments[b]	*124*	*247*	*313*	*379*	*25.0*	*51*
Demand indicators:						
Behavioral sciences R & D expenditures in colleges and universities (in 1967 dollars)	$99.8 mil.	$94.5 mil.	$83.0 mil.	NA	*(1972-76)* −4.5	*(1972-76)* $−4.2 mil.
Labor force:[b]						
Ph.D.s employed in nonclinical behavioral fields:					*(1972-77)*	*(1972-77)*
Total	18,472	23,682	25,170	26,657	7.6	1,637
Academic (excluding postdoctorals)	14,443	18,433	19,269	20,105	6.8	1,132
Business	1,173	1,651	1,770	1,888	10.0	143
Government	977	1,289	1,888	1,651	11.1	135
Other (including self-employed and postdoctorals)	*1,699*	*1,936*	*2,151*	*2,365*	*6.8*	*133*
Unemployed and seeking	180	373	510	648	29.2	94
Ph.D.s employed in clinical behavioral fields:						
Total	10,511	14,729	16,138	17,547	10.8	1,407
Academic (excluding postdoctorals)	4,159	5,064	5,248	5,432	5.5	255
Business	1,297	2,383	2,969	3,554	22.3	451
Government	1,135	1,222	1,313	1,405	4.4	54
Other (including self-employed and postdoctorals)	*3,873*	*5,995*	*6,536*	*7,077*	*12.8*	*641*
Unemployed and seeking	47	65	72	79	10.9	6

Behavioral science enrollments:					(1972-76)	(1972-76)
First-year graduate	22,604	25,081	26,270	NA	3.8	917
Estimated total graduate						
nonclinical	31,033	34,368	35,385	NA	3.3	1,088
clinical	10,852	14,669	16,411	NA	10.9	1,390
Estimated nonclinical undergraduate[c]	682,002	673,197	754,138	NA	2.5	18,034
Total nonclinical graduate and undergraduate	713,035	707,565	789,523	NA	2.6	19,122

[a]In this table, clinical behavioral fields include clinical and school psychology, counseling, and guidance; nonclinical behavioral fields include anthropology, sociology, and nonclinical psychology.

[b]Labor force and postdoctoral estimates have been revised from those shown in the committee's 1977 report.

[c]Estimated by the formula $U_i = (A_{i+2}/B_{i+2})C_i$, where U_i = behavioral science undergraduate enrollments in year i; A_{i+2} = behavioral science bachelor's degrees awarded in year $i+2$; B_{i+2} = total bachelor's degrees awarded in year $i+2$; C_i = total undergraduate enrollments in year i.

Source: National Academy of Sciences, National Research Council, 1978, p. 62.

fields. About one fifth of the respondents in each sector indicated that the absence of employment opportunities led them to take postdoctoral appointments."

Postdoctoral Training at UCLA

Table 2 presents the distribution of postdoctoral enrollments at UCLA by specialty from 1977 to 1980. Data on earlier

Table 2. UCLA Postdoctoral Enrollments by Field, 1977–1980.

	1979-80	1978-79	1977-78
Nonmedical professional schools	74	72	75
College of Fine Arts	1	2	6
College of Letters and Science			
Humanities division	42	35	8
Life sciences division[a]	104	103	92
Physical sciences division	92	73	86
Social sciences division:			
Political science	0	0	0
Anthropology	2	2	0
Geography	0	0	0
Economics	2	4	8
History	7	8	6
Sociology	11	9	6
Other, general campus	27	14	22
Health sciences	205	169	176
School of Medicine, other divisions	146	118	121
TOTAL ENROLLED	713	609	606

[a]Includes psychology.
Note: Data were provided by the Fellowship and Assistantship Section, Graduate Division, UCLA.

postdoctoral enrollments was described to me as unreliable. Worse yet, the UCLA definition of postdoctoral scholar is unclear. A Guggenheim recipient (who generally has a permanent or semipermanent academic post) obviously differs significantly in career path and use of the postdoctoral experience from the recent Ph.D. who receives an NIMH award. Although information was available only for a three-year period (thereby making extrapolation hazardous) and the exact definition of postdoctoral fellow is unclear, the trend suggests the likelihood of an increase in the future, since the number has risen steadily since 1977. Of course, the current reduction in federal research spending may reverse this trend. Table 2 shows that about half of all postdoctoral fellows at UCLA specialize in the health sciences. The next largest group, constituting about one third of all postdoctoral fellows, is found in the life sciences and in the physical sciences. Within the College of Letters and Sciences, the smallest number of fellows is found in the social sciences—remarkably, even fewer than in the humanities. Even though the numbers are exceedingly small, a detailed breakdown by discipline is shown for the social sciences to highlight two facts. First, mainly because of sociology's training program, department enrollments at UCLA have registered consistent gains (from six in 1977-78 to eleven in 1979-80); second, in the most recent year for which data are available, sociology accounted for no less than half of all postdoctoral enrollments in the social sciences division.

UCLA Training Program. This two-year program in mental health evaluation research is primarily for Ph.D.s in sociology, although one Ph.D. in social science and one in education and sociology have been appointed. Research methods training is stressed in the first year, with more program flexibility and substantive training encouraged in the second. Trainees take required courses on evaluation and statistical methods and on the sociology of mental illness and health and may take additional course work in other areas as desired. Scholars undergo a lengthy evaluation internship in a community mental health facility, for which they are remunerated. Unlike most postdoctoral fellows, they teach and are paid for this service as well (Zumeta, 1981). The program seeks to strengthen trainee qualifications for both academic and nonacademic mental health posts. As of July 1, 1981, seventeen scholars have undergone training in the program or are currently enrolled. In order to ensure broad faculty participation in the selection process, we use a two-step review of applicants. Primary responsibility for evaluation of candidates is vested in a steering committee consisting of the program director and four sociology faculty members. Once candidates are selected, their materials are independently reviewed by the department's elected executive committee. Trainees are simultaneously appointed postdoctoral fellows and adjunct assistant professors of sociology.

The basic purpose of evaluation research is to provide "a

firm assessment—an assessment where the results would be un-
changed if done by another group or if replicated by the same
evaluators" (Rossi, Freeman, and Wright, 1979). Evaluation training enables students to be aware of the specific problems involved
in appraising the appropriateness of program changes, in developing new programs and policies, in improving interventions, and in
testing hypotheses or professional practices. Although each of
UCLA's instructional and research programs contributes to mental
health evaluation training, the social policy and organizations
fields play particularly important roles, sharing major responsibility
for the program with specialists in mental illness and methodology. The key objective of the UCLA program is to provide advanced specialized evaluation research training in mental health to
better prepare Ph.D.s to engage in evaluation research as needed
by federal, state, local, or private mental health agencies and to
perform basic research and teaching of significance to the mental
health field.

Five commonsense principles guided the program's development. First, we felt that the program must reflect current faculty
strength and resources, particularly in the policy, methods, organizations, and mental illness fields. Second, in view of the declining
job market for Ph.D.s in academic settings, we insisted that the
program prepare trainees for both academic and nonacademic
positions. Qualified personnel are needed not only to do evaluation research in mental health settings but also to train others for
these tasks. Third, we felt that the program should provide individualized, rigorous methodological training. Accordingly, the
trainees' own specific methods backgrounds and needs had to be
considered in planning each program. Fourth, the program was designed to coordinate the trainee's particular research and instructional interests with the program's formal structure and included
a broad range of special emphases to complement and strengthen
areas not previously stressed in the trainee's career. Any area that
promised to enhance mental health or evaluation training could
provide a training focus. Fifth and finally, the program sought to
use three types of interpersonal relationships for didactic purposes: relationships between trainees; relationships between
trainees and predoctoral students (this relationship was not
stressed, since the program had no predoctoral trainees, although

such contacts were used); and, most critical of all, relationships between trainees and faculty.

Effective training of postdoctoral students involved more than simply transmitting present research technology and theory. Careful application to significant research programs and participation in actual evaluation research was needed. All these concerns pointed toward a balanced and eclectic curriculum. Good applied sociology training integrates the traditional academic commitment to scholarship, depth, ideas, and theory with concern for problems of implementation, utilization, and methodological and analytical skills and interests. Methods are stressed in the first year because design and data analysis skills are seen as critical for effective work in applied settings.

Core Curriculum. The two-year program offers intensive methodological training that is at once broad and fundamental and integrates six major types of professional training: regression and multivariate analysis, evaluation methods training, supervised on-the-job research and evaluation experience, training in theories of mental health, training in organizational theory as applied to mental health settings, and teaching experience in the field of mental health and mental illness.

Two major required courses are taken in the first year, a seminar in evaluation research that introduces the student to the methodological and political aspects of evaluation and a quantitative methods course that presents students with advanced training mainly in advanced multiple regression and multivariate analysis techniques. In addition, all trainees take a special seminar that serves as a coordinating center for program research and evaluation activities and as a sounding board for new research and evaluation work currently in a preliminary stage. Typically, new trainees present their recent work and guest speakers present their current ideas. Since the course is the only one all postdoctoral fellows take concurrently for two years, it serves an essential integrative and informational function.

Links with Community Mental Health Agencies. Since hands-on evaluation training is a key component of the training program, new associations with a number of community mental health agencies have been developed, and trainees have worked under faculty supervision as evaluation consultants in a variety of settings. These connections not only provide agencies with sorely needed program evaluation assistance at low cost (in return for the opportunity for trainees to obtain needed evaluation research experience) but also show those agencies that the university is concerned with community needs. As one community mental health official put it: "This is the first time UCLA has shown any interest in us." It is significant that this facility was located far from UCLA in a predominantly minority community. Unlike many consultant arrangements, ours is typically long-term, frequently lasting for four years or longer. In addition to assisting these agencies in meeting their standard evaluation needs, the UCLA program has spawned a variety of new mental health research projects, including studies of patients' rights in state mental hospitals, an evaluation of delivery system effectiveness, a study of linkages between family entry characteristics and treatment course, and the development of new approaches to community needs assessment.

Postdoctoral fellows also work closely with faculty on a broad range of federally funded research projects, such as studies of family coalition formation, ethnographic study of an urban after-care center, the efficacy of nosocomial infection control, and the effects of patient participation on health care utilization and costs.

Job Placement. One of the developing strengths of the program is its placement program, which is facilitated by a rigorous selection process that accepts only first-rate candidates. Each trainee is given individualized and practical placement advice, and trainee career preferences, potential weaknesses, and career strengths are discussed at regular intervals.

The trainee is made aware of training needs in his or her first year and, in the second year, is given extensive preparation for the job market. At the end of the first year, the director and the trainee develop a plan that takes into consideration the trainee's job preferences and strengths, arrangements for trips to national and regional professional meetings, and participation in activities of key nonsociology professional organizations (such as the American Public Health Association). If the trainee has strong regional affiliations, participation in regional association meetings might be stressed. In addition, the trainee is advised and supervised in the preparation of a curriculum vita for nonacademic positions. For example, technical and job-related skills are stressed, and educational background is given less prominence. Preparation for academic positions includes advice on methods and style of the presentation of papers and on factors relevant to the personal interview process. Few trainees have previously received advice regarding job hunting either in academic or nonacademic settings—in fact, few have been advised by their mentors on any aspects of the job search process, including such mundane concerns as proper vita preparation.

Table 3 presents an overview of the three career paths followed by UCLA program graduates. First, we have placed trainees in posts at Columbia University, the University of Connecticut, the University of Virginia, Tulane University, and the University of Maryland, College Park. These persons teach and do research in applied sociology, mainly in mental health, evaluation research, and deviancy. Second, schools of public health, social work, criminology, and social policy represent a relatively new academic area of placement for applied sociologists. One postdoctoral fellow was placed in the School of Social Work at Michigan State University, where he was given responsibility for graduate evaluation research and policy training, and another joined the Arizona State University School of Criminology. Third, nonacademic posts are more varied and may include positions with research firms such as RAND Corporation, System Development Corporation, Mathematica, and Abt as well as soft money positions with ongoing health or mental health research projects. For example, one graduate took a post with the Oakland-based Race, Crime, and Social Policy Center; another has a post in the evaluation section of a Veterans Administration Hospital adjoining UCLA; a third is research associate on an NIMH-funded mental health research project at the same hospital; a fourth is senior research associate with the National Academy of Sciences; and a fifth recently took a position with the United States General Accounting Office's Institute for Program Evaluation.

Variations in Social Science Postdoctoral Training

Twenty-two NIMH mental health–relevant postdoctoral research programs train both predoctoral and postdoctoral scholars. Many of these programs were originally designed as predoctoral training programs, with their postdoctoral training component

Table 3. Overview of Career Paths of UCLA Postdoctoral Fellows.

Fellow	Ph.D.-Granting University	Main Dissertation Area	Academic, Sociology	Academic, Other	Policy/Research/ Government
				Career Path	
A	State University of New York, Stony Brook	Social psychology			X
B	University of California, Berkeley	Urban	X		
C	Harvard University	Theory			X
D	University of Michigan	Social psychology		X	
E	University of Massachusetts, Amherst	Methods	X		
F	University of California, San Francisco	Theory/medical	X		
G	Florida State University	Deviance			X[a]
H	University of Wisconsin	Social psychology	X		
I	University of Notre Dame	Urban/race relations			X[a]
J	University of Chicago	Urban/race relations			X
K	University of California, Santa Barbara	Criminology		X	

[a]G's first position was an academic sociology post, but she is now in a research/policy slot. I took a research/policy position on a temporary basis and may return to an academic (other) post.

grafted on in response to the National Research Council recommendations (National Academy of Sciences, 1975, 1976, 1977, 1981) for an increase in postdoctoral and a decrease in predoctoral support. This recommendation stemmed from the anticipated glut of Ph.D.s in the social sciences. The 1976 National Research Council report proposed a gradual shift in training emphasis in the social and behavioral sciences "from a program of predominantly predoctoral support to one of predominantly postdoctoral support, with a ratio, ultimately, of 30 percent predoctoral/70 percent postdoctoral awards," and urged a focus on research "in innovative areas of behavioral research, such as research in health and behavior" (1976, p. 55). However, the postdoctoral program sector is less well established and more fluid than is the predoctoral sector, since most social scientists have little previous experience training postdoctoral fellows. Predoctoral training is considerably more institutionalized than postdoctoral training in mixed programs. In some cases, in fact, the concept of postdoctoral training may be seen as a simple extension of predoctoral training. As a consequence, some postdoctoral fellows complain about being treated in a demanding fashion. They do essentially the same type of work as research assistants, from whom they are differentiated only by a slightly higher placement on the publication hierarchy. Another major source of complaint is the postdoctoral fellow's uncertain job future.

As noted earlier, six current NIMH training programs are devoted exclusively to postdoctoral instruction. Concentration on postdoctoral training alone permits a strong commitment to a single purpose. Postdoctoral training also requires less supervision than predoctoral training. Since postdoctoral fellows have typically obtained the Ph.D. from another institution, they have more varied experiences to offer a department and therefore can be more easily integrated into its research and instructional programs. Specialization in postdoctoral training also permits the hiring of postdoctoral fellows with relatively similar interests. A group of such fellows has greater influence and can have its training needs expressed more effectively than a single postdoctoral fellow attached to a professor's research team. One disadvantage of such specialization, however, is that it may reduce postdoctoral–predoctoral research contacts.

Four of the six NIMH mental health-related, exclusively postdoctoral training programs are interdisciplinary. Of the single-discipline programs, one is in social psychiatry and the other is in sociology. Although interdisciplinary programs profit from a mix of scholars and instructors, they may face unique communication problems. First, each field has its own specialized jargon, and translation takes time. Since postdoctoral fellows lead busy lives, they may wish to avoid having to learn a new jargon. Second, disciplinary differences and communication difficulties discourage interaction among fellows. Anthropology postdoctoral fellows may be more inclined to talk to other anthropologists, with whom they already have much in common, than to psychology or sociology fellows.

Third, interdisciplinary programs may encounter greater difficulties placing their graduates. Even though the program director and his staff may have an excellent network of contacts in their own discipline, their network probably does not extend to neighboring fields. Hence, postdoctoral fellows in a different field could experience serious placement problems and feel unjustly treated. The history of interdisciplinary programs in universities—for example, social relations at Harvard, social psychology at the University of Michigan, and social ecology at the University of California, Irvine—suggests that special placement difficulties for program graduates are especially serious in an academic environment, which is highly segregated according to discipline. Harvard's social relations and Michigan's social psychology program did not prosper for very long and the Irvine program is a marginal one. In contrast, the professional school academic market and the nonacademic market put far less emphasis on disciplinary boundaries.

Since sociology and other social science faculty members have so little experience with nonacademic employment, they are typically ill equipped to train students in this area. Naturally, they encourage their best students to enter the academy. Academic systems are reproductive institutions, continually churning out Ph.D.s in the mold of their tutors. Applied sociologists-in-the-making, however, do not have the same number of highly visible and prestigious role models available to them.

A major problem faced both by trainees and by those administering postdoctoral training programs is control. Postdoctoral fellows see their program participation as a means of producing publications that will enhance their visibility and hence their access to academic jobs. Such fellows are restless when program requirements are extensive and threaten to reduce time available for personal research. Thus, a structured program creates conflict between the personal and program goals of the postdoctoral fellow, who may see program goals as interfering rather than helping his or her career. The program faculty, on the other hand, views trainees who fail to follow program requirements as recalcitrant and ungrateful. In their eyes, since a structured program was devised for the trainee's benefit, and since the trainee agreed to participate, reluctance or lack of enthusiasm is considered inappropriate. If the program is an interdisciplinary one and the director is in a different field, the postdoctoral fellow's control is weakened even more. Tension and dissatisfaction between program staff members and fellows can result.

Another problem is time. Trainees usually have only a one- or two-year period to settle into a new environment, make contacts with faculty, conduct their research, publish, fulfill program requirements, and find a new position—a busy schedule requiring a frenetic pace. Likewise, program directors and staff members experience time pressures. Whereas predoctoral students usually accept faculty authority quite placidly, postdoctoral trainees are typically more mature, energetic, questioning, and demanding and are consequently seen by faculty as more difficult to handle. The director and staff members are involved in recruiting, selecting new candidates, administering the program, advising trainees on research programs (and often on their personal problems as well), and assisting them in finding jobs. In addition, undergraduates and graduate students must be taught and one's own research program conducted.

Hence, the pace of the director and of program faculty members is also frenetic, and, if postdocs are viewed as difficult to control, their attractiveness declines, interaction is less frequent and less positive, and the scene is set for potentially difficult interpersonal exchanges. Generally kept submerged, these tensions quickly surface in times of stress—for example, when drastic program budget cuts (especially the elimination of institutional training costs) seem imminent, as in the spring of 1981.

Recommendations for Postdoctoral Programs

The following recommendations and observations summarize my experiences with postdoctoral programs:

First, interdisciplinary substantive and methodological training is an essential ingredient of a good postdoctoral program, because most research problems transcend disciplinary boundaries. The benefits of interdisciplinary work can be obtained by means of a variety of administrative arrangements, each with its own advantages and disadvantages. One technique is to create a program by assembling staff members and trainees from different disciplines. For example, Greenley's program at the University of Wisconsin utilizes a staff from psychiatry, public health, and sociology and has trainees who have taken their Ph.D.s in anthropology, sociology, and psychiatry.

The UCLA program takes another approach. Although it is administratively based in sociology and takes mainly sociology Ph.D.s, a core of faculty advisers in other fields plays an active role in the training process, and a close working relationship has been established with the Department of Psychiatry at the Neuropsychiatric Institute. The department has even developed a special seminar for the trainees reviewing their clinical treatment programs in depth, and several postdoctoral fellows have engaged or are engaged in research projects with department members. Other key working relationships involve representatives from the schools of public health, law, medicine, and education. In addition, trainees routinely work with psychologists and social workers during their community agency consultantships.

Second, a carefully structured postdoctoral training program (as compared to an ad hoc individualized faculty-postdoctoral arrangement) enhances the chances of systematic training and decreases the likelihood of exploitation. Working under the direct supervision of a good faculty researcher can provide useful training and, at the same time, numerous possibilities for mistreatment. Being treated as a glorified research assistant is both unrewarding and demeaning. If a major unresolvable difference of opinion arises between the principal investigator and the postdoctoral fellow, the latter can experience a crushing blow to his career. In general, the more research autonomy trainees are permitted, the better their training is likely to be, providing they have mastered the fundamental research and design skills in their area. An important advantage of a structured program is that it is likely to give high priority to the training needs of the postdoctoral fellow.

Third, a one-year postdoctoral training program is typically too short. So much time must be taken up getting settled, finding a place to live, learning the ins and outs of the laboratory, department, computing center, university, and community that too little time remains for actual training. A minimum of two years' training is desirable.

Fourth, except under unusual circumstances, postdoctoral training programs should exclude recent Ph.D.s from their own university. Postdoctoral trainees profit from exposure to an entirely new set of surroundings, curricula, and research programs. Also, if they stay in the same university, mentors will have difficulty relating to them as colleagues instead of students, making it all the more difficult for trainees themselves to accept their postdoctoral status. In addition, by training Ph.D.s from other universities, postdoctoral programs encourage the spread of ideas. These programs are especially important for stimulating innovation in light of the decline in opportunities for hiring new assistant professors.

Graduate Training

Even though graduate training has for many years been the center of the discipline's pedagogical interest, applied sociology programs are a relatively new development. Although degree-granting programs are relatively scarce, many colleges and universities offer courses in applied sociology. A count of universities in the *Guide to Graduate Departments of Sociology* shows that 44.3 percent (107 of 241 departments) listed such courses in 1979, and 45.8 percent (116 of 253 departments) listed them in 1981. Five graduate programs granting degrees in applied sociology were described in detail at the 1981 ASA Workshop in Applied Sociology. Three were M.A. programs (University of Michigan, Kent State University, and University of Oklahoma), and two offered both the M.A. and the Ph.D. (University of Minnesota and Washington

State University). These five programs, of course, do not exhaust the types of programs available now or in the past. The University of Pittsburgh, for example, established an M.A. program in applied sociology and then disestablished it for two reasons. First, it was thought that the technical skills of the sociologist could not provide a competitive edge and, second, it was concluded "that the level of professional skill actually required for competent, autonomous work in applied sociology or applied social science is considerably higher than that attainable in a one- or even two-year master of arts program" (Fisher, Holzner, and Dunn, 1981, p. 14). These considerations have not deterred the University of Central Florida in Orlando from recently establishing a new two-year applied M.A. program housed in the department of applied sociology.

The five illustrative programs are quite varied. Michigan's M.A. program is narrowly occupation-oriented, training persons, for example, for survey sampler and analyst positions, whereas Kent State's and Oklahoma's M.A. programs are more general, preparing their graduates for a broader and more diffuse range of posts, such as counselor or administrator. Both Ph.D. programs (Minnesota and Washington State) train generalists who will hopefully maintain a distinctive sociological approach either in academic or nonacademic settings.

University of Michigan

This eighteen- to twenty-four-month program, begun in fall 1981, provides preparation for such positions as survey sampler, analyst, statistician, population analyst, and demographer (Groves, 1981) and trains researchers for public and private survey organizations and for agencies that use demographic methods. The program capitalizes on the university's internationally known Institute for Social Research and Survey Research Center. The program began in 1981 with four to six students. All students take two semesters of statistics and the two-semester Detroit Area Study sequence, which provides hands-on training in all aspects of survey research. The program has three tracks: survey research, sampling, and population studies. For the survey research track, students take a survey-sampling course, a research design course, two cognate field courses, and one course in two of three areas: social organization, social psychology, and populations studies. For the survey-sampling track, students take two additional courses in survey sampling and sampling techniques; for the population studies track, a substantive course in population studies and a course in demographic analysis are required. Most students obtain practical experience by working on research projects under faculty supervision. Students also participate in an informal seminar that deals with such topics as interviewer supervision, research budgeting, and questionnaire formatting. Those completing the program are awarded an M.A. in applied social research. The program director, Robert M. Groves (1982), reports that the first group of graduates "has been able to find jobs in good organizations," that is, those that have need for competent technicians.

Kent State University

The Kent State University applied sociology M.A. program, initiated in 1969, may be the oldest in the nation (Boros, 1981) and is probably the largest. The program, which has graduated about six students each year since its inception, consists of three parts: an introduction to research methods, current theory, and statistics; required courses in human services and applied sociology, combined with a summer field experience practicum and an internship; and a set of electives. The human services course surveys various agency problems and acquaints students with agency function by means of guest speakers and field trips. The applied sociology course teaches applied methods, program design techniques, grant proposal writing, and in-service training methods. The eight-week fieldwork experience involves helping an agency deal with what it has defined as a problem. The intern submits a technical report to the agency at the end of the eight-week stint, and the agency sends the course coordinator a written evaluation of the report. The applied sociology practicum, taken in the summer during the fieldwork experience, meets at different internship sites each week in order to familiarize students with a variety of agencies and expand their applied experiences beyond their own projects. In lieu of an M.A. thesis, students prepare a detailed written report on their internship experience, which is defended in an oral examination.

Most graduates end up as counselors or administrators in education, mental health, business, or social or medical services agencies. Only a small percentage go on to Ph.D. programs or maintain their identity as professional sociologists.

University of Oklahoma

In fall 1980, the University of Oklahoma, with NIMH funding, initiated a two-year M.A. program in applied sociology. The purpose of the program was to provide training for persons "to assess the mental health needs of urban minority groups and to design and evaluate agency programs aimed at satisfying these needs" (Grasmick, Zurcher, and Sandefur, 1981, p. 2). Because of Oklahoma's substantial Indian population, the program emphasizes the problems of urban Indians. NIMH support was assured for three years, and the university has agreed to assume the costs of maintaining the program after that start-up period. Even though the program primarily prepares experts in needs assessment and evaluation research, its structure is basically similar to an M.A. curriculum in general sociology. Accordingly, no new courses have been created. Program students take courses in social research methods, urban sociology, applied sociology, ethnic studies, population analysis, statistics, social planning, advanced research methods, and theory. In addition, students take two electives, undertake a summer internship, and complete two field projects, one of which involves participation in the Oklahoma City Survey (which is modelled to some extent after the Detroit Area Study training program) and the other of which consists of a mini internship in a mental health or human services agency. Most students develop their M.A. thesis from their participation in the city survey. The first student cohort had four full-time and one part-time student. The program staff reports a high level of student commitment and performance levels equal to or greater than those of regular nonprogram students.

University of Minnesota

The University of Minnesota has had both an M.A. and a Ph.D. program with an applied sociology emphasis since 1979 (Reynolds, 1981). Like most major graduate training centers, Minnesota has stressed its doctoral training and deemphasized training at the master's level. The M.A. program, called the Policy Research and Evaluation Program, has been offered for about eight years but has attracted only five students. Students in the program must take five of the six seminars required for all doctoral students (a three-seminar set in methods and statistics and a seminar each in social psychology and social organization) and a course on research and social policy. One of the three seminars on methods and statistics must be on evaluation research. For the thesis option, students take three nonsociology courses, usually in an applied field; for the nonthesis option, they take six courses outside the department, complete an internship, and prepare two papers. All students must take a final oral examination.

The applied sociology Ph.D. program, called the applied-emphasis doctorate, was initiated in fall 1980 as part of the regular Ph.D. offering. From one third to over one half of the entering graduate cohort, or between eight and fourteen students, plans to specialize in this area. Program students must take the five required seminars noted above plus a sixth in social theory, a two-seminar sequence on designing and supervising research projects and on professional presentations of social science, and three courses in an applied discipline, such as public health, law, or business. The student must also demonstrate research experience in an applied context. The program coordinator assists in placing students in internship positions and supervises their performance. Finally, students must submit an acceptable Ph.D. dissertation that may or may not emphasize applied issues.

The Ph.D. program has apparently stirred the enthusiasm of Minnesota graduate students. An applied sociology symposium held in May 1981 attracted over one hundred persons, and many others had to be turned away. The main program problems are inadequate faculty resources and an insufficient number of suitable internships.

Washington State University

Washington State University offers predoctoral and postdoctoral programs in applied sociology and social policy that are less structured than most of the others we have described. In the Ph.D. program, students select applied sociology as one of their two areas of specialization, after completing required courses in theory, methods, and statistics. For the applied specialty, they must take at least nine hours of graduate course work selected from among courses in sociology and public policy, evaluation research, social impact assessment, social policy analysis, and intentional social change, and they must satisfactorily complete a written comprehensive examination in applied sociology that deals with theory, research, and action as related to applied work. In their other substantive specialty, students must also complete at least nine hours of course work and pass a comprehensive written examination covering that area (Olsen and DeMartini, 1981).

If a student decides to specialize in the applied area, he or she is assigned a faculty advisor who recommends appropriate courses. Students are also strongly advised to participate in a one- or two-semester internship providing practical experience in research design, data collection, analysis, write-up and consultation and are required to write a dissertation.

The postdoctoral program is even more flexible and individualized. The postdoctoral fellow may or may not audit courses, typically works closely with a faculty member on a research project, and completes a lengthy internship in the field, involving greater autonomy and responsibility than are afforded predoctoral students.

Overview

One of the chief problems training programs face at undergraduate, graduate, and postdoctoral levels is the development of an applied sociology core. Applied sociology may be seen as a specialization with a particular set of questions that differentiate it from other fields or as a distinctive methodological specialty. If it is the former, then the central questions of the field must be specified; if the latter—and that approach seems to be implied in Rossi's (1980) stress on quantitative training (although he also acknowledges the importance of qualitative work)—then the methodology should be clarified.

Without systematic evidence, it is not clear whether new applied sociology programs are more or less numerous than other types of programs. Organizational theory tells us little about why new programs form or about the conditions that induce or inhibit their creation. The population ecologists stress the importance of survival and would presumably claim that market forces operating through differential selection affect the rate of development of new programs in the applied area (Aldrich and Fish, 1982). Other, more individualistic approaches stress managerial decisions and strategy formulation. Neither perspective explains why certain types of universities produce new programs and others do not or why some persons rather than others are inclined to start programs.

Nevertheless, I anticipate, for a number of reasons, that only a limited number of viable applied programs will emerge in the near future. First, the prestige of the applied field is low. Rossi (1980, p. 889), for example, has noted that applied sociology is "decidedly below basic or theoretical work in the hierarchy of preference, prestige, and esteem." The Michigan program deals with the prestige problem in three ways: by limiting its applied training to the M.A. level rather than offering the more prestigious Ph.D.; by making the training narrowly occupational (survey sampler, survey statistician, population analyst, and so on); and by not awarding fellowship support to students in the program. Not one of the top ten graduate schools in sociology has established a Ph.D. program in applied social research.

Second, since sociology is so diverse and its fields so poorly delimited, any single area has difficulty assembling a sufficient number of persons to create and maintain a strong program. Small departments, even those of high prestige, are particularly unable to bring together the critical mass of faculty needed to establish new programs. Not surprisingly, none of the prestigious private schools, such as Harvard, Yale, or the University of Chicago, have applied programs. Interdisciplinary programs face special problems of their own, such as the intrinsic strength of departments, the discipline-based character of the environment, and higher program start-up costs.

Third, since relatively few sociologists have managed programs, obtained research grants, or worked collaboratively on programs, they may lack the practical organizational, entrepreneurial, and managerial experience without which new ventures are prone to fail.

Fourth, sociologists rarely have extensive community contacts. In recent years, the methodological emphasis has been on data analysis rather than on data-gathering. Such an emphasis is compatible with university reward structures, which focus on publication. The academic is wiser to spend his or her time reanalyzing available data sets than to collect new information, a procedure that is more expensive, tedious, and time-consuming. In any case, an effective applied program requires placements in commercial or public agencies, and developing these contacts requires energy and time.

Fifth, rewards for instructing graduate students may be declining for a number of reasons. The proportion of outstanding students seeking a sociological career is diminishing. As a result, teachers must exert greater effort and anticipate less intellectual gain. And it is frustrating to train students with high potential when they are unable to obtain the jobs they and the instructor think they deserve.

However, the organizational need to survive is a powerful one and may simply outmuscle the combined strength of these negative factors. Plummeting enrollments and diminishing research and job opportunities may compel academics to devise applied programs. Moreover, despite the obstacles, wise academics will perceive the benefits for basic as well as applied work that may derive from applied programs.

Conclusion

Most of the problems of postdoctoral and graduate instruction relate to the newness and corresponding low level of institutionalization of programs, the diverse technologies of the social science disciplines, the inexperience of academics in training persons for nonacademic posts, and the lack of entrepreneurial and managerial skills and attitudes. Students in letters and science graduate programs around the nation are becoming increasingly alienated and bitter because their social position and career expectations do not compare favorably with those of their mentors. Whereas their professors typically have jobs, tenure, and a future in sociology, they have scant hope of attaining any of these precious rewards (Manderscheid and Greenwald, 1981). Little wonder students easily become embittered and demoralized.

Postdoctoral and graduate training programs share certain types of problems, such as obtaining adequate resources, gaining departmental acceptance, managing programs, locating community agency internships, and placing graduates. But they have their differences as well. Postdoctoral programs are more prestigious and substantially more expensive and are therefore more dependent on outside funding. They are also generally smaller than other programs in a department or university and, because of their expense, have smaller growth potential. Accordingly, they are perceived to be less threatening to existing programs.

Postdoctoral and graduate training programs in applied sociology can serve the important function of helping students cope with an increasingly competitive job situation by giving them marketable skills. Postdoctoral programs not only reduce pressure on the academic and nonacademic job market over the short term by extending the educational period, but, more significant for the long term, they equip the trainee with skills either not available or not taken advantage of during the predoctoral experience. Postdoctoral fellows and graduate students can learn new methods, refine those they already have, develop new substantive interests, and refine those that have fallen into disuse. They can also learn basic, essential skills such as clear and effective writing, accounting, preparation of grant proposals, vita preparation, managerial skills and tools (such as management information systems), and self-presentation in teaching and research situations. They can develop their personal and professional contacts, meet and learn from established researchers and teachers, and learn from other postdoctoral trainees and from undergraduate and graduate students as well.[1]

At the same time, both types of programs provide new and exciting opportunities for sociology faculty and their institutions, particularly by affording greater contact with and knowledge about the community. Applied programs can encourage development of new data collection techniques and can help discover and make available new data sources. Basic and applied research both profit directly from the intimate knowledge derived from field experience. Applied postdoctoral and graduate programs, if they are to have any value at all, must further ties with the community, where hands-on training begins and future job opportunities lie.

These programs can also have significant positive impacts on a department's research and instructional programs. Particularly now, when new assistant professor positions are scarce, bright, young Ph.D.s bring to the university a sorely needed vigor and reservoir of ideas. At UCLA, postdoctoral fellows have worked closely with faculty in ethnomethodology, evaluation research, organizations, stratification, medical sociology, social psychology, family medicine, education, public health, law, and psychiatry. They have stimulated the development of new undergraduate and graduate courses in mental health and medical sociology and new interdisciplinary research programs, in addition to strengthening existing courses and programs. When a faculty member suddenly takes ill or gets a grant at the last minute and seeks to go on leave, the department can rely on a pool of highly qualified postdoctoral fellows to fill in for him. Finally, of course, a good postdoctoral or graduate program can bring a university national visibility.

The enormous benefits that postdoctoral and graduate programs in applied social research can offer the social sciences may have become apparent just when their future is most clouded and uncertain. The current climate is unfavorable, if not hostile, to social and behavioral sciences training. Nevertheless, the promise of these programs is so great that every effort should be made to strengthen existing programs and develop needed new ones.

Note

1. Obviously, a great many researchable questions on the educational impact of graduate and postdoctoral programs remain to be systematically explored. Here is an illustrative list: To what extent do postdoctoral programs affect the quality and quantity of research output? How do postdoctoral programs affect the quality of graduate programs? Do faculty members gravitate away from graduate students in favor of postgraduate teaching? Do postdoctoral programs take other resources, such as space and computer funds, away from graduate programs? To what extent are Ph.D.s aware of opportunities for postdoctoral training? How do they assess these opportunities? Does taking a postdoctoral position enhance the chance of securing a better job—that is, better than one would have obtained as a new Ph.D.? A few of these questions have been addressed for biochemists (McGinnis, Allison, and Long, 1982).

References

ALDRICH, H., AND FISH, D.
1981   "Origins of organizational forms: Births, deaths, and transformations." Paper presented at the Social Science Research Council Conference on Organizational Indicators of Social Change, Washington, D.C.
BERELSON, B.
1962   "Postdoctoral Work in American Universities." *Journal of Higher Education* 33(3):119-130.
BOROS, A.
1981   "Objectives and products of the Kent State University M.A. Applied Sociology Program." Paper presented at the ASA Workshop on Directions in Applied Sociology, Washington, D.C., December.
FISHER, E., HOLZNER, B., AND DUNN, W.
1981   "Bringing social science to bear on practical problems: The University of Pittsburgh Program for the Study of Knowledge Use." Paper presented at the ASA Workshop on Directions in Applied Sociology, Washington, D.C., December.
GRASMICK, H., ZURCHER, L., AND SANDEFUR, G.
1981   "University of Oklahoma program." Paper presented at the ASA Workshop on Directions in Applied Sociology, Washington, D.C., December.
GROVES, R. M.
1981   "The University of Michigan Master's Program in Applied Social Research." Paper presented at the ASA Workshop on Directions in Applied Sociology, Washington, D.C., December.
1982   Personal communication. March 24, 1982.
McGINNIS, R., ALLISON, P. D., AND LONG, J. S.
1982   "Postdoctoral training in bioscience: Allocation and outcomes." *Social Forces* 60(3):701-722.
MANDERSCHEID, R. W., AND GREENWALD, M.
1981   "Supply and demand of sociologists in 1990." Paper presented at the ASA Workshop on Directions in Applied Sociology, Washington, D.C., December.

NATIONAL ACADEMY OF SCIENCES, NATIONAL RESEARCH COUNCIL.

1969   *The Invisible University: Postdoctoral Education in the United States.* Washington, D.C.: National Academy of Sciences.

1975-1979   "Personnel needs and training for biomedical and behavioral research." Annual reports of the Committee on a Study of National Needs for Biomedical and Behavioral Research Personnel, Washington, D.C.

1981   *Postdoctoral Appointments and Disappointments.* Washington, D.C.: National Academy Press.

OLSEN, M., AND DeMARTINI, J. R.

1981   "Predoctoral and postdoctoral training in applied sociology at Washington State University." Paper presented at the ASA Workshop on Directions in Applied Sociology, Washington, D.C., December.

RAND, M. J.

1951   "The national research fellowships." *Scientific Monthly* 73(2):71-80.

REYNOLDS, P. D.

1981   "Applied graduate sociology programs at the University of Minnesota." Paper presented at the ASA Workshop on Directions in Applied Sociology, Washington, D.C., December.

ROSSI, P. H.

1980   "The presidential address: The challenge and opportunities of applied social research." *American Sociological Review* 45:889-904.

ROSSI, P. H., FREEMAN, H. E., WRIGHT, S. R.

1979   *Evaluation: A Systematic Approach.* Beverly Hills, Calif.: Sage.

ZUMETA, W.

1981   *The Changing Role of Postdoctoral Education in the United States.* Los Angeles: Higher Education Research Institute.

🎍24🎍

TRAINING IN QUANTITATIVE METHODS

Richard A. Berk

Few would dispute that, over the next few decades, quantitative techniques will play a significant role in the applied research undertaken by sociologists. Therefore, sociologists engaged in applied research will need a minimum of quantitative skills simply to read the literature, as well as—if current trends are a fair indicator —substantial training in measurement, research design, data reduction, and data analysis. Assuming also that much applied work will be initiated by individuals who have not yet reached graduate school or who do not currently possess the requisite skills, the quality of training in quantitative methods will clearly have an enormous impact on the effectiveness of applied sociology.

In this chapter, I discuss training in quantitative methods, with particular emphasis on the quantitative skills needed by sociologists wishing to do applied research. The chapter begins by defining the enterprise of applied sociological research, moves to a projection of the technical skills that will be required in the years to come, and then dwells at some length on how to train for this future. The chapter does not aim to present a broad overview of applied sociological research or of training for such research in general. Rather, it focuses on the narrower issue of future training in quantitative methods for sociologists who want to use their research skills to address practical problems.

Some Definitions

Any discussion of training for applied, quantitative, sociological research must begin with a few brief definitions. What do we mean by *quantitative*? By *applied*? By *sociological*?

First, at the risk of trespassing on carefully protected preserves, I must say that I find the often-cited categorical distinction between quantitative and qualitative research to be grossly overstated. To begin with, both traditions develop and employ taxonomies (for example, Mezzich and Solomon, 1980) as the basis of any analysis; both require conceptual pigeonholes to which symbols (either mathematical or verbal) are attached. Indeed, in many instances, both use the same conceptual categories (for example, Bittner, 1980; Berk and Loseke, 1981). Similarly, qualitative and quantitative approaches both routinely make ordinal statements: things are bigger or smaller, more or less, longer or shorter, and the like. Both traditions also commonly employ cardinal numbers, with simple integer counts as perhaps the best example. In short, I fail to see any fundamental difference in the nature of the measurement approaches applied.

I find it just as difficult to make categorical distinctions between the research designs used. Since both traditions require the observation of variability, only two kinds of designs are possible: over cross-sectional units (for example, persons) and over time (for example, weeks). I also have yet to find a qualitative study that is not accurately characterized as one or another kind of quasi-experimental design (Campbell and Stanley, 1963; Cook and Campbell, 1979). Certainly, there are differences in emphasis; but there may well be fewer distinctions than at first seem apparent.

Third, both traditions concern themselves with the role of stochastic error; that is, both are quite properly worried about being misled by chance. The fact that, in qualitative work, the so-called confidence intervals are informally constructed does not mean that chance is neglected. No self-respecting field worker would build an analysis on a few isolated events, in part because these events may not reflect anything systematic about the phenomenon under scrutiny.

For these and other reasons (Rossi and Berk, 1981), the differences center primarily around points of emphasis. For example, qualitative researchers may find that generalizations are more easily undertaken through replications: Does the phenomenon recur in a wide variety of settings, at different times of the day, and with many different participants (see, for example, McCall and Simmons, 1969, chaps. 5 and 6; Schatzman and Straus, 1973; Lofland, 1971; Georges and Jones, 1980)? Survey researchers may find it more convenient to develop generalizations through probability samples from some population of interest (see, for example, Kish, 1967). Both are fully aware that it is important to move substantially beyond the data at hand using different approaches in response to different kinds of opportunities and constraints. For example, the participant observation may avoid structured questionnaires because the behavior in question is best measured through observation (for example, the ways people line up for public events such as rock concerts), and generalization through sampling may be constrained by a lack of a sampling frame. In contrast, if one is interested in the kinds of households that give their teenagers an allowance, it would be terribly expensive to observe the transfer of money. An item or two on a questionnaire delivered over the telephone would almost certainly suffice. And, as a result of the telephone questionnaire approach, statistical generalization may well be possible. These observations initiate an implicit theme that will reappear in various forms throughout the discussion that follows: empirical research is a difficult problem-solving endeavor that requires a full arsenal of social science weapons. An ideological commitment to only a portion can only undermine the quality of the ultimate product.

With the differences in emphasis clearly stated, it is possible to speak about quantitative approaches in a meaningful way—but still as a matter of degree. I will use the term *quantitative* to describe social science research methods that make explicit and substantial use of mathematical tools. The question of where qualitative ends and quantitative begins I will leave to methodologists with talmudic leanings, but, by *mathematical,* I mean the full array of techniques offered by that discipline—not, for example, just calculus or just differential equations.

Definitions of applied research can also lead one into a conceptual swamp. Even among researchers with similar perspectives and styles, definitions of applied research may well vary (compare, for example, Berk and Rossi, 1976; Berk, 1977, 1981; Rossi, 1980). For present purposes, I will define applied research as empirical work that uses social science theory and method solely as a means to an end. No conscious effort is made to address intellectual themes in the discipline per se, although there may be implications for those themes (Rossi, 1980). For example, in a recent monograph, some colleagues and I (Berk and others, 1981) report an evaluation of the effectiveness of water conservation programs initiated in California during the drought of 1976 and 1977. Although we necessarily drew on major research traditions in social psychology, sociology, and economics (for example, the dilemma of the commons), we did not begin the research with the goal of addressing those traditions. Rather, they served as a means by which to understand why conservation programs succeeded or failed. We did not set out to test theories about the household production function in microeconomics, for instance, but built on what theoretical insights it might provide. In short, basic research is primarily focused on questions posed by the concepts, traditions, and theories of the discipline. Applied research responds to research agendas developed with little concern about whether important questions within the discipline are being answered. The many implications that follow from this difference are discussed elsewhere (Berk, 1981) and need not be considered here. We will use the term *applied research* simply to indicate that social science tools are being used to address empirical questions not posed by the social science disciplines themselves.

Perhaps the most difficult question is what one means by *sociological.* I usually fall back on the old saw that sociology is the study of groups or other collections of people, but, when pushed, I do not feel that really fundamental differences exist between sociology and the other social sciences studying human groups (that is, social psychology, economics, political science, and anthropology). Equally important, I will soon argue that applied social research building on sociological traditions must also draw on the full array of related disciplines. Again, applied research is a problem-solving activity in which one uses whatever tools are available.

Training for What?

Perhaps the most important initial observation about appropriate quantitative training for applied sociology is that there is not one kind of training but several, which owe their distinctiveness to the following questions: Are we training for the immediate or distant future? Are we training from scratch or retooling? and, Are we training consumers or producers of applied research?

With respect to the time frame, I will distinguish between the year 1985 and the year 2000, although I am really doing nothing more than separating the long run from the short run. With respect to the foundation on which to build, I will distinguish between new graduate students and individuals who, having finished an advanced degree, find it impractical to invest full-time in the enhancement of their human capital (allowing, in practice, for part-time commitments to either employment or schooling). Finally, with respect to consumers or producers of applied research, I will focus primarily on the producers, since training consumers seems primarily to be a matter for undergraduate course work or course work in graduate schools of law, business, planning, and the like. Applied research training in graduate departments of sociology should be aimed at the education of persons who will actually be doing applied research. Not to diminish the importance of undergraduate education, especially in teaching an appreciation of applied social research; however, a discussion of how to train applied research consumers in quantitative methods is beyond the purview of this chapter. (Curious readers might look at any of the following texts: Katzer, Cook, and Crouch, 1978; Horowitz and Ferleger, 1980; and Hastings, 1979.)

Training for the Year 2000

The year 2000 may seem a long way off, but the students we train today will just be reaching their prime twenty years from now, and our training in quantitative methods must anticipate the skills they will require. In fact, too many sociology departments

are training students in obsolete technology, and only a handful
are really teaching the state of the art.

Part of the problem no doubt lies with the students we recruit, who rarely have any mathematics beyond the high school
level. While the overall return to basics may eventually improve
the background of students applying to graduate school, the vast
majority of our applicants will probably still not have strong
mathematical training. Perhaps more important, most departments
of sociology lack the personnel to offer a rich program in quantitative methods on a regular basis. With a modest (and often
shrinking) number of faculty positions, sociology departments
find it difficult to allocate staff to training in quantitative methods. A wide variety of courses must be offered and, to the degree
that the body-count evaluation of course offerings continues,
other, more popular kinds of courses are likely to dominate the
curriculum. Moreover, too many departments have apparently
been reluctant to send their students elsewhere in the university
for training, despite the fact that most universities have virtually
all the necessary courses. Whether or not this reluctance is a symp-
tom of a more general narrowness that has come to characterize
much of sociology, it is absolutely fatal for training in quantitative
methods. In any case, I will return later in this chapter to the importance of drawing from other departments.

What Might the Future Hold?

If we are to train for the year 2000, we must at least have
some informed hunches about the kinds of skills that will be required. What follows, then, are some speculations about the sorts
of quantitative procedures that will be commonly used in applied
research twenty years from now. At the same time, no claim to
prescience is made; these forecasts are but one attempt to make
the necessary projections to help guide our training programs.

Computing Capacity. Computational power will no longer
be a significant obstacle for applied quantitative research in the
year 2000. (For recent discussions, see Boardman, 1982; Abelson,
1982; Branscomb, 1982; Birnbaum, 1982.) Computers for data
analysis will be small, fast, and cheap. Departments of sociology
(or even individual researchers) will routinely have their own com-

puters designed for social science applications with many times the power currently available on most university mainframes. A combination of new developments in electronics, specialized processors (for example, designed solely for statistical computations), numerical analysis, and efficient algorithms will create computational possibilities that are, in effect, limitless. Indeed, one could imagine a desktop computer designed primarily to solve sets of nonlinear simultaneous equations that would allow researchers to undertake general purpose, maximum likelihood estimation with the same ease with which they now calculate square roots.

Computers of the future will also be extremely "friendly." Simple English commands will suffice for even very complicated procedures, and virtually all communication will be interactive, including a wide variety of error checks and help commands to enable even first-time users to proceed without difficulty.

With efficient, dedicated computers, disks and tapes will serve primarily as backup storage facilities; data will be kept resident, which in turn will reduce costs and increase speed still further. In short, advances in computer technology will allow for "deskilling"; applied quantitative researchers will no longer need to be part-time computer programmers to get their work done.

Data Collection. Equally stunning advances will be made in the ways we elicit and collect data. Thanks to significant developments in cognitive psychology, we will generate far more accurate data from individuals. We will know, for instance, how to arrange survey items to minimize response sets. (For a sense of the current state of the art, see, for example, Dillman, 1978; Bradburn and Sudman, 1979; Labaw, 1980.) We will also be able to capitalize on a wide variety of technological fixes. For example, computer-assisted interviewing is already revolutionizing the way telephone interviews are conducted. In the near future, one can imagine respondents carrying small, computerized radio transmitters allowing researchers to contact them to determine the activities in which they are engaged. In the more distant future, it will be possible to monitor subjects so closely that their activities may be easily recorded without any explicit researcher–respondent interaction (for example, speech will be digitized and directly coded).

Coupled with these advances for the recording of individual behavior will be the standardization and wide availability of official data that has been routinely collected. For example, the time may well come when all police departments record their arrest data in the same fashion and make that data available through a central clearinghouse. Moreover, there may well be data collection personnel in police departments who are committed to the accuracy of the official data and are able to improve data quality. In any case, as we learn more about organizational behavior, the sources of measurement error in official data will be better understood, and correct procedures will be more readily available. Finally, technological innovations will also have an enormous impact on official data. For instance, computerized dispatching in some police departments is already keeping an ongoing record of how long police take to respond to different kinds of calls.

Just as the quality of social science measurement will improve, so will our aspirations. Even as our measurement abilities now approach those of the natural sciences, we will also aspire to their levels of precision, not just because of our own ambitions but also because of the demands of applied social science users. With millions of dollars riding on an important policy decision, measurement error of plus or minus 10 percent will not be ignored. In short, concern for accurate measurement will not decline; in this realm, at least, "deskilling" will not occur.

Data Reduction. Important advances will no doubt also be made in classification, clustering, and scaling techniques (for example, Mezzich and Solomon, 1980). These enhancements will include improved statistical justifications for the procedures, better criteria for making what are now tough judgment calls (for example, for the number of clusters), and more efficient algorithms. Since networking techniques (for example, Leinhardt, 1977) rest on clustering algorithms, I expect to see commensurate improvements. However, despite the current excitement surrounding network analysis in sociology, its eventual impact in applied quantitative work may well be rather modest without some fundamental statistical and conceptual breakthroughs. The many problems that will have to be solved include: how to model group boundaries as other than all or nothing relationships; how to describe network characteristics with summary statistics making descriptive and inferential sense; and how to integrate function into structure.

Research Design. In addition, the current cross-fertilization of research designs among the social sciences will continue. Randomized experiments are now commonly embedded within sample surveys (for example, Berk and Rossi, 1977; Garrett, 1978), and sample surveys are likewise commonly embedded in randomized experiments (for example, Keeley and others, 1978).

Viewed more generally, there is a growing concern in statistics with optimal research design, in which research designs from a variety of social science traditions are rationalized and combined to obtain information in the most efficient manner (for example, Morris, Newhouse, and Archibald, 1980). To take a simple example, in the usual linear regression model, multicollinearity at the very least degrades statistical power, and, as multicollinearity increases, the determinant of the regressor cross-product matrix approaches zero. Thus, cross-product matrices with larger determinants are preferable to cross-product matrices with smaller determinants, implying that, in designing an experiment, one form of optimality might rest on maximizing the determinant of the design cross-product matrix. Such notions have been around for years (for example, Wald, 1953; Keiffer, 1958) and are now bearing fruit.

Certainly, methodological integration will continue, and probability sampling, randomized experiments, and quasi-experimental procedures will ultimately be organized into a general data collection model from which efficient special cases can be derived. Indeed, at some point, the designing of research will be computerized to such an extent that an applied researcher will be able to specify certain parameters to be estimated, the likely characteristics of those parameters (for example, the mean and variance), a number of practical restrictions (for example, the sampling frame only contains households, whereas the individual is the desired unit), and a budget constraint. The optimal data collection design will then be produced (see, for example, Welch, 1982; Cook and Nachtsheim, 1982).

Operations Research Techniques. By the year 2000, I expect to see a significant influx of methods from operations research. In brief, operations research concentrates on optimization in ways that are far more general and flexible than comparable approaches in economics. This breadth and flexibility follows from a style of work emphasizing how things should be done rather than how they are actually done. Thus, it is common to find powerful analyses of how computers should process sequences of instructions to minimize CPU time (for example, Coffman, 1976) or of how much inventory factories should keep on hand (Hillier and Lieberman, 1980, chap. 12).

Operations research techniques typically rest on powerful mathematical technology, including linear and nonlinear programming (for example, Koo, 1977), that can provide instructive benchmarks for actual performance. For example, before completing a study of whether courts are processing cases efficiently (for example, Goldman, 1980), one might build a model of how courts might work in principle if certain processing criteria were being optimized (subject to constraints). I have always considered it strange that more sociologists studying formal organizations, for instance, have not drawn on concepts and models from the operator's research literature.

Statistical Procedures from the Natural Sciences. I also anticipate a growing influence from statistical procedures developed originally for applications in the natural and health sciences. For instance, impact evaluations commonly use time to failure as one important outcome measure. Thus, most evaluations of efforts to reduce recidivism (for example, Rossi, Berk, and Lenihan, 1980) treat the number of weeks to a new arrest as a significant performance indicator. A variety of powerful statistical techniques have been developed by biometricians precisely for failure measures of this kind (for example, Kalbfleisch and Prentice, 1980), but these procedures have rarely been used outside health-related fields.

Statistical Model for Causal Analysis. The pieces of a very general statistical model for causal analysis already exist and will surely be assembled in the next twenty years. One piece, which can be thought of as the substantive component of the model, represents the causal process of a substantive phenomenon under study. The systematic part of the usual regression equation is a simple example. This substantive component will be quite general and allow for multiple equations, reciprocal causation, complicated lag structures, and nonlinear functional forms. Starting with this very general formulation, a wide array of special cases will be produced simply by placing constraints on the general form. Readers familiar with statistical procedures for multiple-equation models will readily see that I am only suggesting modest extrapolations from procedures that already exist. Readers familiar with evaluation research terminology will also recognize that the substantive component speaks directly to the question of internal validity (Cook and Campbell, 1979).

Another piece of the general causal model is meant to capture the measurement process producing the observed data. Here, I am suggesting little beyond the kinds of measurement models developed by Jöreskog and his colleagues (Jöreskog and Sörbom, 1979) and found in the LISREL computer program. However, I anticipate that more complicated error structures will be included. That is, the observed indicators will be a function of underlying, unobserved factors and stochastic error with the possibility of nominal indicators (Muthén and Christofferson, forthcoming), intrinsically nonlinear relationships, nonnormal error structures, and the like. Readers familiar with evaluation research terminology will see that this component addresses the question of construct validity (Cook and Campbell, 1979).

Yet another component responds to the stochastic disturbances appended to the substantive causal structure. In the usual regression case, this is simply the error term. However, here the disturbance structure will be more flexible, allowing for unequal variances and nonindependence both within and across equations. Moreover, normality need not be assumed. In evaluation research terms, this component speaks to the issue of statistical conclusion validity (Cook and Campbell, 1979).

Finally, the model will include a component characterizing the way the data were sampled in order to generalize the work of Heckman (1979) and others so that problems with sample selection bias can be directly addressed. Moreover, special cases of censoring or truncation lead directly into probit and Tobit formulations that are still computed as stand-alone problems. Again, in evaluation research terminology, the last component considers the problem of external validity (Cook and Campbell, 1979).

The four-component model will provide at least the following options. Bayesians will be able to specify prior distributions for one or more of the parameters of interest. That is, the model will be applicable from either a classical or Bayesian perspective (Zellner, 1971). My own projection is that, within the next twenty years, Bayesian estimation will come to dominate quantitative techniques in applied social science. However, similar claims have been wrong in the past. Researchers who wish to avoid the Bayesian approach as well as fixed parameters will be able to estimate models with stochastic parameters (Swamy, 1971). The model will also allow researchers to weight observations in a manner consistent with the growing tradition of robust estimation (Huber, 1981). The robust estimators will be accompanied by diagnostics to help determine when conventional approaches may be misleading (Belsley, Kuh, and Welsch, 1980).

The four-component model will surely support a number of different approaches to estimation. Given the enormous computing power available, I suspect that maximum likelihood techniques will be the most popular. Maximum likelihood approaches have, under quite general conditions, known properties; provide a single way to think about estimation; and are asymptotically optimal by the usual statistical criteria. However, thanks to jackknife or related techniques, estimators not yet subsumed under a maximum likelihood approach will nevertheless be applied (Mosteller and Tukey, 1977). In addition, to the degree that useful approximations can be found for what have proved to be inherently intractable combinatorial problems (Coffman, 1976), nonparametric (that is, distribution-free) estimators, even for complicated causal models, will still play an important role. In summary, by the year 2000, a general-purpose statistical package will be available that will include the ability to address all of today's concerns and far more, within a single broad framework. Because of constraints placed on the model's overall structure, special cases will materialize. (Although I also expect far greater use of graphic techniques, I fail to see any important implications for training. Computers will do the plotting from very simple instructions, and the graphs will be easy to read.)

Implications for Training from Scratch

Although the future will hardly be a brave new world, it will be a world with important implications for the way we train students today. What follows, then, is a discussion of training for the long run, organized according to the kinds of skills that will have to be learned.

Mathematics. For new graduate students in applied quantitative methods, substantially more mathematics will be required than is offered in most graduate programs, with matrix algebra and calculus through differential equations as the probable minimum. (Note that I am addressing the needs of applied researchers; sociologists who wish to claim quantitative methods as their specialty will require still more mathematics, such as courses in numerical analysis.) However, if possible, instructors of these courses should emphasize the logic of the mathematics and its social science applications, with far less attention to computational procedures. Once students learn the chain rule in their first calculus class, for example, computation skills need not be fine-tuned. In most later applications, machines will do the computing. Ideally, a mathematics sequence should be designed for the social sciences that would include numerous applications. Readers interested in obtaining a more detailed sense of the kind of sequence I have in mind might take a close look at the excellent text by A. C. Chiang (1974), who addresses most of the important topics that could be covered in more depth in such a series. It is also important to stress that the envisioned sequence is but a foundation on which students will build later in their careers.

The student will also need a serious mathematics-statistics sequence through multivariate models. Every major university offers such courses. The first semester covers the kind of material found, for example, in Mood, Graybill, and Boes (1974); the second semester moves on to the level presented, for example, in Anderson (1958). With this background, the student is then prepared to advance to more specialized courses, depending on interest and available offerings. For example, at least a semester of econometrics at the level of the classic text by Johnston (1972) and a semester of psychometrics at the level of the equally superb text by Lord and Novick (1968) would prove extremely instructive. Also at about this point, two courses in research design should be taken, one covering both probability and nonprobability sampling (Cochran, 1977; Sudman, 1976), the other covering randomized and nonrandomized experiments (Cox, 1958; Campbell and Stanley, 1963).

Computer Science. The importance of courses in computer science is less clear. Although it might be useful in the long run to become acquainted with a single, relatively low-level language to get a sense of how computers think, most of the languages used in practice will be of an increasingly high level (for example, the programming language used within SAS). Similarly, although it might be interesting in the long run to know something of how computer algorithms are designed in order to appreciate the numerical analysis problems surmounted, the kinds of difficulties for which such knowledge would be helpful (for example, rounding errors in matrix inversion routines; see Searle and Hausman, 1970) will typically require the sophistication of a specialist. Finally, knowledge of the physical characteristics of computers beyond what can be learned in a wide variety of popular treatments (Crowley, 1967) is almost certainly unnecessary. In contrast, a course providing an overview of emerging applications would be extremely useful, especially as technological fixes for measurement problems are developed. In any case, the training task in this area is gradually being simplified.

Although all the courses suggested thus far should emphasize applications, there is no substitute for hands-on experience with real data. Indeed, hands-on experience plays such a vital role that I often find it instructive to distinguish between courses in statistics and courses in data analysis. The former focus on formal theory and on how things should work in principle. The latter focus on what happens when the formal theory is applied to data that contain many unknown factors and from which a "story" needs to be extracted. For example, diagnosing multicollinearity involves difficult judgment calls that require considerable practice (Belsley, Kuh, and Welsch, 1980). Likewise, it is one thing to know the formal meaning of parameter estimates and quite another to know what the parameters mean for the "story" being constructed from the data.

Research Practicum. These observations suggest that a research practicum is an essential part of any training program in quantitative methods for applied research. From my experience, the practicum can be effectively organized in several different ways; however, students are more motivated and get a better feel for the ways in which research really unfolds when, over an entire academic year, a legitimate study (rather than a class exercise) is undertaken from start to finish. One year, for instance, my class (cotaught with Marilynn Brewer, formally of the psychology department at the University of California, Santa Barbara) evaluated the effectiveness of local water conservation efforts (Berk and others, 1980). Other projects have included an impact assessment of campus efforts to reduce the number of bicycle accidents (Jurik, Johnson, and Kreb, 1978) and a study of campus definitions of sexual harassment.

I have also tried, with somewhat less success, to allow students to define their own applied research projects. Among the most important problems are that it is extremely difficult for the instructor to remain sufficiently informed about each project to provide proper guidance and that the small scale on which individual students operate is rather unrealistic. Also, far less interaction takes place among the students, thereby reducing the extent to which they learn from each other. Since the practicum has always included students from several disciplines, this loss is not a small one. In any case, the start-to-finish format carries students through a review of the literature, a formulation of the problem, questions of measurement and research design, data collection, file construction, data analysis, and report writing. A great many things are learned, but, most important in the context of this discussion, students have the experience of transforming classroom skills into practical skills. For example, they quickly become facile with statistical software such as SAS and BMD.

As students become familiar during the practicum with the kinds of data they will ultimately have to analyze, they discover that they will have to learn additional statistical skills. The problem, of course, is that, beyond a general background in statistics, econometrics, and psychometrics are a large number of special purpose procedures designed for particular kinds of analytical situations. Among the more important procedures are confirmatory factor analyses (Jöreskog and Sörbom, 1979), techniques for pooled cross-sectional and time series data (Kmenta, 1971), Box-Jenkins time series models (Box and Jenkins, 1976), and procedures for nominal endogenous variables (Hanushek and Jackson, 1977, chap. 7; Pindyck and Rubinfeld, 1981). Selected material of this sort can often be introduced as part of the practicum, although students must be rather sophisticated for a piecemeal strategy to succeed. More likely, regular courses will have to be offered at least once over a two- or three-year period.

Additional Courses. Beyond the research practicum, it may be useful to add a course in which students read at least two applied studies on each of several applied problems (for example, two studies on compensatory education, two studies on health care delivery, and so on) and then produce written comparisons and critiques of the research methods used. Each year, several anthologies of the best articles in evaluation research and policy analysis are published, and, from these, one can usually find several studies on each of a wide array of problems: housing, labor-force participation, health care, criminal justice, energy use, the environment, and many more. In addition, material can be found in a growing number of applied social science journals, including *Evaluation Review, The Journal of Human Resources,* and *Policy Analysis.* Whether used as a text or as a reference, these anthologies provide plenty of material for students to consider. At each class meeting, students, having presumably completed their written critiques, come to class prepared for what is often a lively discussion. Such courses can be made even more exciting if occasionally one or more of the authors of the studies under scrutiny can be brought to the campus (or even to the class) for a lecture or seminar. However, such classes, no matter how well run, are no substitute for the research practicum.

With the possible exception of the research practicum and the course in great readings, the program I have suggested for the applied quantitative sociologist differs little from the program for the more traditional quantitative sociologist. Indeed, I feel rather strongly that the curriculum outlined above should be part of the training offered by all serious departments of sociology—although many of the courses would be housed in other departments. Most of the offerings constitute no more than the quantitative training found in good economics departments. An important question, therefore, is whether other material with an applied bent should be required. Given the essential role of firsthand experience in all applied social science, I favor asking students to do master's theses and dissertations with substantial applied content. At the very least, the policy implications of important findings should be thoroughly discussed.

Of course, I am focusing only on training in quantitative methods. Clearly, a number of other topics need to be included in training for applied research. With all of these requirements, training from scratch for the year 2000 will entail several years of study roughly equivalent to the more traditional Ph.D. Retooling for the year 2000—discussed later in this chapter—ultimately requires the same level of expertise, although perhaps attained through different means.

Question of Feasibility

How feasible is this training program? To begin with, no one sociology department has the skills and resources to provide all the courses suggested, and there is no reason why it should—plenty of superior expertise already exists elsewhere on campus. Indeed, the majority of courses should probably be taught by persons who invent and transmit these skills for a living. Moreover, for at least some of the more standard skills, the computer-assisted instruction of the future will reduce the need for traditional courses. Instead, sociology departments will have to invest resources in special purpose applied statistics courses (perhaps), in courses in data analysis, in the research practicum, in the course in great readings, and in supervision of applied masters theses and dissertations—hardly a significant drain on departmental resources.

Yet instituting a program for applied researchers will certainly have its costs. First, in an era when the number of graduate students in sociology is declining, the applied quantitative program might well draw students who would have ordinarily pursued more traditional sociological curricula. Academics can always find something to quarrel about, and it would be a rare department indeed that could avoid an acrimonious struggle over a dwindling number of graduate students.

Second, many departments, while sympathetic to applied research, are hostile to any further incursions by quantitative methods. In some locales, these feelings are so pervasive and so strong that the kind of training program I have suggested would not even be seriously discussed. Nevertheless, some departments might discuss this type of program anyway. An enormous amount of time might be spent in an organizational effort that would ultimately fail. In other locales, efforts to institute such a program would further split the department into opposing camps. The costs of such schisms are well known.

Finally, graduate training in sociology seems to produce in

graduate students all kinds of anxieties, misperceptions, and suspi-
cions, and the current job market has surely made things worse.
Initiation of a major new training program in quantitative methods
would almost certainly cause significant backlash. Some factions
would argue, with some validity, that their graduate program in sociology is being threatened by technocrats. Other factions, again
with some validity, would charge that young sociologists are learning skills only then to sell them to the highest bidder—and we all
know who has the resources to buy those skills. Reasoned rejoin-
ders can be made to such charges, and applied programs can be designed that provide effective safeguards against technological sub-
version and auction-block sociology. Nevertheless, some consterna-
tion can be expected from faculty and students alike.

Implications for Retooling

    In the context of the goals just described, retooling sociolo-
gists who are already out in the world presents a very difficult set
of problems. Ideally, of course, retooling for the year 2000 should
include much the same courses and research experiences as training from scratch, However, the necessary organizational structures
are not fully available. A standard two-year postdoctoral position
would almost certainly be insufficient, unless the retooling sociologist already had a solid background in the relevant mathematics,
statistics, or both. In other words, sociologists well trained in the
fundamentals would be able to retool within two years. For others, the task could prove to be impossible.
    A postdoctoral position, then, needs to be coupled with
substantial preparatory work. A few individuals may be able to
work through the appropriate texts over a period of several years.
A growing number of mathematics texts, for example, are designed with social science applications in mind and written for
self-instruction (for instance, Searle and Hausman, 1970; Green,
1976; Coughlin, 1976; Chiang, 1974; Zill, 1979). What these
books lack can often be found in publications such as the Schaum
Outline Series (McGraw-Hill). Similarly, applied statistics texts
have improved dramatically of late, and one can now find rather
difficult material written in an accessible manner. Indeed, a little
matrix algebra at about the level found in Johnston's econometrics

text (1972, chap. 4) makes a surprising amount of material immediately available. With the equivalent of a semester's introduction to differential and integral calculus, rather advanced treatments can be productively used. In short, a serious self-instruction effort can succeed.

As a complement to self-instruction, informal study groups can be enormously effective. I have seen study groups address with great success both mathematical and statistical material. However, some arrangements work better than others, and, at the very least, the group must meet at least once per week, must have a discussion leader at each session responsible for summarizing the material, must rotate the discussion leader role so that all members of the group carry this burden equally, and must do written exercises.

Yet another genuine possibility is to audit the necessary courses as they are offered. In my experience, a surprisingly large number of university faculty members will not object (many will actually be flattered) to having colleagues attend their courses. I have also frequently found faculty members who will help with class assignments and even grade homework. It has always seemed strange to me that we do not do a better job of learning from each other.

Finally, there is always the option of formally registering for courses, if not at one's home institution, at least at a neighboring one. Again, the mathematical and statistical material is hardly arcane and is routinely available, even at small liberal arts colleges. For individuals who feel that they need the structure provided by a traditional classroom environment, this "night school" option is clearly the best solution. Moreover, were some of the relevant courses organized into a master's degree program, the "night school" approach would have the added potential of formal certification. However, it is probably not possible to retool, let alone train, for the year 2000 by relying primarily on master's level programs—too much material is involved. On the other hand, master's programs have considerable promise as way stations to the ultimate destination. A master's degree in applied mathematics for social scientists is one example. A master's degree in applied statistics for social scientists is another. Some universities already come very close to having such programs, and, with some minor tinkering, an extremely useful training experience could be offered.

In summary, retooling for the year 2000 will take a major commitment made all the more difficult by the need to piece together a program. Of course, some sociologists already have many of the necessary skills, and their path will be easier. But, even for those fortunate few, the task of retooling should not be minimized.

Training for the Year 1985

We should be in the business of training for the future. Although this point may seem obvious, it contradicts much current practice. At the same time, however, the year 2000 is some time off, and applied quantitative work will be done in the interim. Two related questions follow, based on the earlier distinction between training and retooling: How do we train students to function effectively in the interim? and, What can we do in the context of retooling that will improve the quality of applied quantitative work here and now?

Training for the Short Run

First, because current computing power limits the kinds of analytical procedures that can be used, efforts must be made to teach procedures that may be suboptimal but are the best available under current circumstances. For example, many maximum likelihood estimators can be prohibitively expensive to compute. Therefore, one may have to settle for an estimator that is asymptotically consistent but somewhat less than fully efficient. Greene (1981), for instance, has developed a simple adjustment to the usual least squares estimates that approximates maximum likelihood Tobit procedures. Unfortunately, some special assumptions are required that are not normally associated with Tobit procedures.

The need for such suboptimal procedures will necessarily mean that instructors will have to cover a variety of approaches to given problems, with a careful discussion of the trade-offs. To illustrate, although the linear probability model is formally inappropriate for a binary endogenous variable when there is theoretical reason to prefer some S-shaped functional form (for example, the cumulative normal), the model will usually not give terribly misleading results except for the marginal impact of regressors as the equation's predicted values approach either the upper boundary of 1.0 or the lower boundary of 0.0. The critical caveat, however, is the word *usually*. Depending on how the regressors are distributed, the misspecified functional form can lead to substantial distortions (Pindyck and Rubinfeld, 1981, 275-280). Future applied quantitative work will probably be characterized by easy access to general statistical procedures that can be readily conceptualized within a single broad formulation and allow one to apply an optimal procedure for a particular analytical problem. In the short run, however, we will commonly be saddled with approximations that follow from disparate concepts and must be presented to students with a host of caveats.

Second, since there is still surprisingly little communication across the social sciences, somewhat different technical languages have flourished. For example, where sociologists are likely to talk about independent variables, economists will talk about exogenous variables or regressors. Where psychologists talk about analysis of variance, economists may talk about regression with nominal regressors. Where economists often present empirical results from regression equations in terms of elasticities, sociologists and psychologists almost never report elasticities. Applied sociology means drawing heavily on work in other disciplines; consequently, differences in technical languages need to be explained to students.

Third, sociology has some language difficulties of its own. Part of the problem is that quantitative technology from outsiders has entered the discipline in a piecemeal fashion and out of phase with broader developments. Thus, the ways in which sociologists apply multiple regression and the language used to describe the results are a hybrid of influences from statistics, psychology, and economics. For example, the size of causal effects is still commonly talked about in terms of the amount of variance explained. (For a related critique of the use of standardized regression coefficients, see Hanushek and Jackson, 1977). Similarly, one frequently reads research reports in which, through significance tests, one regression coefficient is deemed more significant than another. In short, training for the here and now will require teaching students how to wade through current confusions in the discipline.

Fourth, quantitative training will have to provide experience working with a number of statistical packages that run on different kinds of operating systems and are accessed through different media (for example, terminals with different keyboards). In addition, at least a reading familiarity with simple FORTRAN, PL1, or the most popular language used locally can come in handy. One is still commonly subjected to computer programs written by paraprofessional programmers. A reading knowledge of FORTRAN, for example, will significantly help to reduce the chances of victimization.

In summary, both basic and applied quantitative work in sociology are currently in a state of flux. Training for the short run will mean helping students live with this disorganized state of affairs and still accomplish professional applied work. For such a difficult pedagogical task, instructors need more than a sound technical background; they also require a good familiarity with the way quantitative sociology is typically done. In other words, instructors will have to help students make sense of quantitative work in sociology and not just in the abstract—one reason why the discipline cannot delegate all training in quantitative methods to other departments.

Retooling for the Short Run

Retooling for the here and now raises all the complications just described, and more. To the degree that self-instruction alone will not suffice, one must again face the problem of designing organizational forms in which learning can occur. All of the possibilities already described need to be considered, with special attention given to master's level programs. As long as such programs are clearly understood to be, at their best, only way stations or short-term solutions, they possess great potential. The way station variant is clear enough: the teaching of fundamentals, with an eye toward uses in applied sociology. The stopgap variant is more difficult to describe because different people need different gaps stopped; individuals come to these programs with disparate backgrounds, aspirations, and immediate needs (for example, for market research or program evaluation). This issue raises the question of priorities, to which I will return later in this section.

Role of Professional Organizations. Although the American

Sociological Association and its spin-off professional organizations too often seem to be suffering from terminal torpor, it is perhaps in training that some contribution might be made. To begin with, The American Sociological Association should retain its practice of offering didactic seminars at its annual meetings, with more offerings than in the past in quantitative methods. Yet, although didactic seminars can be instrumental in exposing individuals to new ways of thinking, they are far too brief to serve as effective retooling devices. A more intensive experience is required, and the annual meetings might include several all-day seminars or several shorter seminars spaced over more than one day. The Methodology Section of the ASA, for instance, has had some success with an all-day workshop the day before the regular sessions begin. In each case, specialists in some quantitative technique, often invited from outside the discipline, have directed a rather demanding, all-day meeting. Sometimes preparatory readings were to be done, and all the workshops were rich in practical examples, handouts, and displays.

There are other settings in which the American Sociological Association or other professional bodies (for example, the Social Science Research Council) could help provide the opportunity for learning quantitative skills. For instance, summer workshops lasting as long as two months have had a lasting impact on participants. Thus, for three years, the Social and Demographic Research Institute of the University of Massachusetts offered a summer curriculum in evaluation research, funded by the Center for the Study of Metropolitan Problems at NIMH, that exposed well over 150 graduate students, faculty members, and practitioners to a rich diet of statistics, research design, and more substantive issues in program evaluation. Analagous efforts in survey research have been held for many years at the University of Michigan's Survey Research Center. These models can be adapted for the kinds of skills described here. The key, of course, will be to find ways to support such activities at a time when social science is under attack.

One possibility would be for the American Sociological Association or some other organization to interest selected universities or even private enterprise in offering summer courses of study with a promise of partial subsidy for the first few years until the program was supporting itself through tuition. Indeed, a number of private organizations already exist that routinely offer short seminars and workshops in the application of statistical techniques. Perhaps all that is needed is evidence of an untapped market. This information, in turn, could be collected through a survey of the membership or by counts of the attendence at ASA-sponsored activities for applied research.

Should these efforts fail to involve universities or free enterprise in quantitative training programs, the ASA itself could bear the organizational burden by offering its own institutes and providing some subsidies for costs not covered by tuition. Although the ASA has neither the personnel nor the structure to get into the training business, this approach might provide a short-term response to an important need in the profession.

A related kind of support might be provided should the ASA be prepared to assume the role of broker. For example, although internships for students are commonly designed, internships for faculty have, to my knowledge, not been tried. The ASA could thus link interested members to government agencies, private organizations, and universities where internships might be established.

To illustrate, it might well be possible for an ASA member to take a position in a high-quality research firm with the understanding that he or she will work as a visiting research associate on projects where applied quantitative skills may be learned. For these efforts, the visiting research associate might be paid a modest salary or be expected to work part of the day on assigned tasks, with the rest of the day spent observing how applied research is done. Alternatively, the internship might be organized less formally; much like a postdoctoral fellow at a university, the visiting research associate might be apprenticed to an experienced applied researcher. Again, perhaps a part-time salary could be provided by the research firm. Of course, for these kinds of arrangements to work, the intern must be prepared to assume the apprentice role, and the sponsoring organization must not exploit the apprentice's labor; a meaningful learning experience must be provided over a substantial portion of the internship period.

If it proves too difficult to get ASA members to places where retooling can occur, the ASA might sponsor traveling presentations bringing the desired material to sociology departments around the country. One could imagine, for example, a two person touring group: one statistician with expertise in Box-Jenkins time series procedures and one sociologist with expertise in the application of Box-Jenkins techniques. Over the course of an academic year, the pair might put on presentations in a half-dozen different departments. Should the ASA not want to pay for such tours, it might instead serve as a clearinghouse where members could find out about traveling presentations that were available. Expenses and honoraria would then be the responsibility of each department.

In retooling activities, the profession will have to be especially creative, not just because of the near absence of arrangements in which retooling can occur but also because of the diversity of retooling needs. Some sociologists may require just a brief refresher, whereas others may have a lot of hard homework to do. In addition, since retooling inevitably requires choices as to the techniques to be learned and the depth in which to learn them, a large number of different programs must be made available. Individuals need to be able to find just the experiences that best suit their particular retooling needs. Finally, the American Sociological Association has its organizational competitors. For example, the Evaluation Research Society is but a few years old and already boasts many members, its own newsletter, its own journal, and a well-attended annual meeting. On a more traditional front, the American Statistical Association routinely sponsors a wide variety of training experiences not only for its members but for outsiders as well. Indeed, a director of continuing education has recently been authorized to develop and coordinate retooling activities. If the American Sociological Association chooses not to respond to the legitimate needs of members with applied orientations, a number of alternative organizations are clearly available.

Retooling Priorities. With all of this said, the critical question of priorities remains. For the here and now, what are the most important quantitative skills to acquire? Unfortunately, for several reasons, it is impossible to provide a compelling argument for any particular ranking. First, the many styles of applied quantitative research require different kinds and levels of skills. For example, when randomized experiments are used, relatively modest statistical techniques will usually suffice to extract the experimental effects. However, the moment one tries to model the ways in which the experimental manipulation worked, the statistical procedures become much more demanding (Rossi, Berk, and Lenihan, 1980; Berk and others, 1980).

Second, in order to establish priorities, one must first determine the base level of existing skills. Although central tendencies might be approximated, the variance is surely enormous. Moreover, the sociologists who decide to retool in quantitative methods will almost certainly not be a random sample of the profession as a whole.

Third, whatever the priorities, expertise must be assembled to offer a wide variety of retooling experiences. It is not at all clear what kinds of expertise can be easily marshaled—as usual, the best people will no doubt be those who are least available—or whether they can be marshaled at all. And priorities depend on viable options.

Fourth, who determines the priorities? On the one hand, perhaps priorities should be established by the suppliers, by the experts in the material to be conveyed. Although these individuals need not reside in academe, there is a good chance that, if they control the agenda, fundamentals will dominate training. Few would argue that, in principle, fundamentals are bad, but time and money are limited, and much useful applied research can be done without the in-depth background that might otherwise be desirable. Thus, applied researchers or their sponsoring organizations should perhaps be the ones to establish priorities. Presumably, they know which skills are needed. The problem, of course, is that demand solutions require that the buyers have sufficient information to choose in their best interests. Most buyers may not be so fortunate, and one risks lowest-common-denominator or faddish training programs that may actually make things worse. Obviously, the solution is to establish priorities from both the supply and demand sides, but we have yet to develop a forum that would make this solution possible.

Despite these and other drawbacks, I see no harm in stating my views about what the priorities should be. Simply put, the floor for sociologists doing applied quantitative research should be an ability to intelligently handle applications of the general linear model at the level described in the better introductory econometrics texts (for example, Hanushek and Jackson, 1977; Pindyck and Rubinfeld, 1981). Practically speaking, this minimum will involve analysis of variance, analysis of covariance, and multiple regression. The floor should also include expertise in applied sampling corresponding to Sudman's excellent volume (1976) and in experiments and quasi experiments consistent with the classical Campbell and Stanley monograph (1963). Finally, familiarity with measurement issues should at least be at the level found in many popular methods texts. This basic expertise represents an absolute minimum—researchers who undertake applied work with these skills will sometimes be in over their heads. Therefore, a keen sensitivity to potential problems should be developed; work may then be halted until help can be obtained. A feel for when something is wrong is the sixth sense required if applied researchers are to avoid embarrassments (or worse). As long as fundamental errors do not slip by, one is not likely to get into serious trouble. But once errors become part of any final product, they are extremely difficult to correct without completely undermining one's credibility.

Conclusion

Several broad conclusions follow from the material discussed in this chapter. First, it is probably fair to say that, in far too many sociology departments, students are being trained in obsolete quantitative procedures. Thus, unless improvements are made, quantitative training for applied research will be establishing itself on a shaky foundation. Second, we must make a clear distinction between short-term and long-term training needs. We must train for the year 2000 while recognizing that applied sociology will be undertaken during the interim. Third, we should provide both for the training of new graduate students and the retooling of practicing sociologists. Although, in principle, both should ultimately be comfortable with the same quantitative techniques, the organizational forms in which the learning can occur are likely to differ. Moreover, if retooling is going to be properly achieved, provision must be made for a wide variety of experiences that may be mixed and matched as needs arise. Fourth, the American Sociological Association and other professional organizations can serve a

number of important functions in facilitating both training and retooling, from making modest enhancements in the program of the
annual meetings to constructing and offering summer institutes.
Finally, it is important to emphasize again that I have been addressing only quantitative training for applied sociologists, not
training for specialists in quantitative methods or other kinds of
training that applied sociologist should have. Qualitative methods,
social science theory, and a rich background in several substantive
literatures have an important place in applied research. We should
be training sociologists who happen to do applied work, not statisticians, computer scientists, or operations researchers.

References

ABELSON, P. H.
    1982   "The revolution in computers and electronics." *Science*
            215(4534):751-753.
ANDERSON, T. W.
    1958   *An Introduction to Multivariate Statistical Analysis.*
            New York: Wiley.
BELSLEY, D. A., KUH, E., AND WELSCH, R. E.
    1980   *Regression Diagnostics.* New York: Wiley.
BERK, R. A.
    1977   "Discretionary methodological decisions in applied re-
            search." *Sociological Methods and Research* 5:317-344.
    1981   "On the compatibility of applied and basic sociological
            research: An effort in marriage counseling." *The Amer-
            ican Sociologist* 16(4):204-211.
BERK, R. A., COOLEY, T. F., LaCIVITA, C. J., PARKER, J., SREDL, K.,
AND BREWER, M.
    1980   "Reducing consumption in periods of acute scarcity:
            The case of water." *Social Science Research* 9:99-120.
BERK, R. A., COOLEY, T. F., LaCIVITA, C. J., AND SREDL, K.
    1981   *Water Shortage: Lessons in Water Conservation For the
            Great California Drought, 1976-1977.* Cambridge,
            Mass.: Abt Books.
BERK, R. A., LENIHAN, K., AND ROSSI, P. H.
    1980   "Crime and poverty: Some experimental evidence for
            ex-offenders." *The American Sociological Review* 45:
            766-786.

BERK, R. A., AND ROSSI, P. H.

1976   "Doing good or worse: Evaluation research politically reexamined." *Social Problems* 23:337-349.

1977   *Prison Reform and State Elite.* Boston: Ballinger.

BERK, S. F., AND LOSEKE, D. R.

1981   " 'Handling' family violence: Situational determinants of police arrest in domestic disturbances." *Law and Society Review* 15:317-346.

BIRNBAUM, J. S.

1982   "Computers: A survey of trends and limitations." *Science* 215(4534):760-765.

BITTNER, E.

1980   *The Functions of Police in Modern Society.* Cambridge, Mass.: Oelgeschlager, Gunn, and Hain.

BOARDMAN, T. J.

1982   "The future of statistical computing for desktop computers." *The American Statistician* 36(1):49-59.

BOX, G. E. P., AND JENKINS, G. M.

1976   *Time Series Analysis: Forecasting and Control.* (Rev. ed.) San Francisco: Holden Day.

BRADBURN, N. M., AND SUDMAN, S.

1979   *Improving Interview Method and Questionnaire Design.* San Francisco: Jossey-Bass.

BRANSCOMB, L. M.

1982   "Electronics and computers: An overview." *Science* 215(4534):755-760.

CAMPBELL, D. T., AND STANLEY, J. C.

1963   *Experimental and Quasi-Experimental Designs for Research.* Chicago: Rand McNally.

CHIANG, A. C.

1974   *Fundamental Methods of Mathematical Economics.* (2nd ed.) New York: McGraw-Hill.

COCHRAN, W. G.

1977   *Sampling Techniques.* (3rd ed.) New York: Wiley.

COFFMAN, E. G., JR., ED.

1976   *Computer and Job/Shop Scheduling Theory.* New York: Wiley.

COOK, R. D., AND NACHTSHEIM, C. J.

1982   "Model robust, linear optimal designs." *Technometrics* 24(1):49-54.

COOK, T. D., AND CAMPBELL, D. T.
1979   *Quasi Experimentation: Design and Analysis Issues for Field Settings.* Chicago: Rand McNally.
COUGHLIN, R. F.
1976   *Applied Calculus.* Boston: Allyn & Bacon.
COX, D. R.
1958   *Planning of Experiments.* New York: Wiley.
CROWLEY, T. H.
1967   *Understanding Computers.* New York: McGraw-Hill.
DILLMAN, D. A.
1978   *Mail and Telephone Surveys: The Total Design Method.* New York: Wiley.
GARRETT, K.
1978   "Defining the seriousness of child abuse." *Medical Anthropology* 2(1):1–48.
GEORGES, R. A., AND JONES, M. O.
1980   *People Studying People.* Berkeley: University of California Press.
GOLDMAN, J.
1980   *Ineffective Justice: Evaluating the Preappeal Conference.* Beverly Hills, Calif.: Sage.
GREEN, P. E.
1976   *Mathematical Tools for Applied Multivariate Analysis.* New York: Academic Press.
GREENE, W. H.
1981   "On the asymptotic bias of the ordinary least squares estimator." *Econometrician* 49:505–514.
HANUSHEK, E. A., AND JACKSON, J. E.
1977   *Statistical Methods for Social Scientists.* New York: Academic Press.
HASTINGS, W. M.
1979   *How to Think about Social Problems.* New York: Oxford University Press.
HECKMAN, J. J.
1979   "Sample bias as a specification error." *Econometrica* 47:153–162.
HILLIER, F. S., AND LEIBERMAN, G. J.
1980   *Introduction to Operations Research.* San Francisco: Holden Day.

HOROWITZ, L., AND FERLEGER, L.
1980   *Statistics for Social Change.* Boston: South End Press.
HUBER, P. J.
1981   *Robust Statistics.* New York: Wiley.
JOHNSTON, J.
1972   *Econometrics Methods.* New York: McGraw-Hill.
JÖRESKOG, D., AND SÖRBOM, D.
1979   *Advances in Factor Analysis and Structural Equation Models.* Cambridge, Mass.: Abt Books.
JURIK, N. M., JOHNSON, T. R., AND KREB, A. R.
1978   "The wheels of misfortune: A time series analysis of bicycle accidents on a college campus." *Evaluation Quarterly* 2:608-619.
KALBFLEISCH, J. D., AND PRENTICE, R. L.
1980   *The Statistical Analysis of Failure Time Data.* New York: Wiley.
KATZER, J., COOK, K. W., AND CROUCH, W. W.
1978   *Evaluating Information.* Reading, Mass.: Addison-Wesley.
KEELEY, M. C., AND OTHERS.
1978   "The estimation of labor supply models using experimental data." *The American Economics Review* 88: 873-887.
KEIFFER, J.
1958   "On the nonrandomized optimality and randomized nonoptionality of symmetrical designs." *Annals of Mathematical Statistics* 29(4):675-699.
KISH, L.
1967   *Survey Sampling.* New York: Wiley.
KMENTA, J.
1971   *Elements of Econometrics.* New York: MacMillan.
KOO, D.
1977   *Elements of Optimization with Applications in Economics and Business.* New York: Springer-Verlag.
LABAW, P.
1980   *Advanced Questionnaire Design.* Cambridge, Mass.: Abt Books.
LEINHARDT, S., ED.
1977   *Social Network.* New York: Academic Press.

LOFLAND, J.
1971   Analyzing Social Settings. Belmont, Calif.: Wadsworth.
LORD, F. M., AND NOVICK, M. R.
1968   Statistical Theories of Mental Test Scores. Reading,
       Mass.: Addison-Wesley.
McCALL, G. J., AND SIMMONS, J. L.
1969   Issues in Participant Observation. Reading, Mass.: Ad-
       dison-Wesley.
McKELVEY, R. D., AND ZAVONIA, W.
1975   "A statistical model for the analysis of ordinal level de-
       partment variables." Journal of Mathematical Sociol-
       ogy 4:103–120.
MANSKI, C. F.
1981   "Structural models for discrete data: The analysis of
       discrete choice." In S. Leinhardt (Ed.), Sociological
       Methodology. San Francisco: Jossey-Bass.
MEZZICH, J. E., AND SOLOMON, H.
1980   Taxonomy and Behavioral Science. New York: Aca-
       demic Press.
MOOD, A. M., GRAYBILL, F. A., AND BOES, D. C.
1974   Introduction to the Theory of Statistics. (3rd ed.)
       New York: McGraw-Hill.
MORRIS, C. N., NEWHOUSE, J. P., AND ARCHIBALD, R. W.
1980   "On the theory and practice of obtaining unbiased
       and efficient samples in social surveys." In E. W.
       Stromsdorfer and G. Farkus (Eds.), Evaluation Stud-
       ies Review Annual. Vol. 5. Beverly Hills, Calif.: Sage.
MOSTELLER, F., AND TUKEY, J. W.
1977   Data Analysis and Regression. Reading, Mass.: Addi-
       son-Wesley.
MUTHÉN, B. AND CHRISTOFFERSON, A.
forth- "Simultaneous factor analysis of dichotomous vari-
coming ables in several groups." Psychometrica.
PINDYCK, R. S., AND RUBINFELD, D. L.
1981   Econometric Models and Economic Forecasts. (2nd
       ed.) New York: McGraw-Hill.
ROSSI, P. H.
1980   "The challenge and opportunities of applied social re-
       search." The American Sociological Review 45:889–
       904.

ROSSI, P. H., AND BERK, R. A.
1981   "An overview of evaluation strategies and procedures."
         Human Organization 40(4):287–299.
ROSSI, P. H., BERK, R. A., AND LENIHAN, K.
1980   *Money, Work, and Crime: Experimental Evidence.*
         New York: Academic Press.
SCHATZMAN, L., AND STRAUS, A. L.
1973   *Field Research.* Englewood Cliffs, N.J.: Prentice-Hall.
SEARLE, S. R., AND HAUSMAN, W. H.
1970   *Matrix Algebra for Business and Economics.* New
         York: Wiley.
SUDMAN, S.
1976   *Applied Sampling.* New York: Academic Press.
SWAMY, P. A. V. B.
1971   *Statistical Inference in Random Coefficient Models.*
         New York: Springer-Verlag.
WALD, A.
1953   "On the efficient design of statistical investigations."
         Annals of Mathematical Statistics 14(1):134–140.
WELCH, W. J.
1982   "Branch-and-bound search for experimental designs
         based on D optimality and other criteria." *Techno-
         metrics* 24(1):41–48.
ZELLNER, A.
1971   *An Introduction to Bayesian Inference in Economics.*
         New York: Wiley.
ZILL, D. G.
1979   *A First Course in Differential Equations.* Boston: Prin-
         dle, Weber, and Schmidt.

❧ 25 ❧

TRAINING IN QUALITATIVE METHODS

William Kornblum

The scholar who would pursue a career in applied sociology is best advised to develop an eclectic knowledge of social scientific method and theory. The presentation of numbers plays a prominent role in situations in which our skills and insights can be most persuasive. As an ethnographer, however, I believe that participant observation promises the most useful understanding of social processes. Qualitative methods are also generally of vital importance in developing quantitative research instruments, but, in most applications of our work, the sociologist cannot rely on qualitative methods alone. Skills in survey research techniques, demographic analysis, historiography, and economic data analysis are often the calling card that allows the participant observer to remain involved in a given process of social change. These methods also represent the side of social research on which our daily bread is most often buttered.

In addition to methodological eclecticism, the best training

410

in qualitative methods seems to involve mentors who have maintained a long-standing commitment to efforts at direct social change. The applied sociologist must develop and sustain relationships with individuals in the research setting who are dealing with practical problems. The research agenda grows out of this relationship. An action agenda may follow from the research, and very often the applied sociologist has an important role there too (for example, as expert witness, field organizer, or planning consultant). In contrast, the traditional academic sociologist is likely to start with a given theoretical issue and a favorite set of methodologies suited to the substantive issue. Once the data are collected from a given population, he or she is generally not committed to the population other than to publish research results.

Many sociologists have had opportunities to work in situations in which their research has had immediate applications for decision making. But relatively few of our colleagues maintain day-to-day professional relationships with those who use their research. The participant observer requires mentors who are able to give significant assistance with field placements and who understand the time commitments necessary for high-quality field research. Mentors who meet these criteria tend to be involved themselves with persons outside the university in long-term efforts at social change.

The final point on which this chapter is organized pertains to the best dissertation research strategies for the student interested in an eventual career in applied sociology. As tenured positions in the social sciences continue to diminish, the sociologist with at least one foot in an applied field appears best equipped to find work both inside and outside the academy. This, in turn, suggests that one should begin to develop practical expertise early in one's professional career. One of the best means to this end is to encourage dissertations that are good sociology and at the same time give the researcher a reputation for expertise in an area of social life where his or her knowledge and techniques are valued. At my own university and most others I am familiar with, students whose dissertations are highly abstract and addressed strictly to problems of the sociological literature are finding placement quite difficult. Students whose work becomes a reference for persons in an applied field of research or in the social action arena, however, find placement easier, though by no means assured. Before citing examples for these three organizing themes—methodological eclecticism, the choice of a mentor with a commitment to the applied field, and the career value of applied research—let me briefly review the sociological experiences that led me to develop these themes.

For the past ten years, since leaving graduate school, I have practiced a version of applied sociology in my attempts to use sociological research to further the aims of persons seeking far-reaching changes in their organizations. This self-definition began when my life with steelworkers led me to become involved with a major union insurgency that reached one climax in the International Union Elections of 1977 (Kornblum, 1974). While continuing to maintain an involvement with steelworkers and their movements, I encountered other opportunities to develop applied research strategies. In 1973, in the midst of a great deal of research and organizing with the steelworkers, I was recruited by sociologists in the U.S. Department of Interior to work as a research sociologist for the National Park Service. There, the assignment was to conduct research related to the needs of the Park Service in the North Atlantic states. Part of the assignment was to develop a cooperative research unit to carry out planning studies, organizational consulting, environmental impact analysis, public involvement in planning efforts, and bureaucratic in-fighting over scarce government resources.

My unit for the Department of Interior Park Service has conducted studies from Assateague Island, Virginia, to Cape Cod, Massachusetts. Our major contribution has been to organize much of the research and planning strategies for the development of urban national parks, a movement that, like so many others that have attracted sociologists, is now being heavily attacked.

Increasing expertise in the field of urban ecology and large-scale urban revitalization efforts resulted in an offer from the Ford Foundation in 1978 to conduct a study of Manhattan's blighted West Forty-Second Street "bright light zone." The Ford Foundation report that resulted from this study is now used as a basic resource on West Forty-Second Street and has resulted in continuing involvement for me and those who have worked with me in plans to redevelop New York City's de facto "combat zone." This ongoing research also resulted in an invitation from the U.S. Department of Labor and the Ford Foundation to conduct a comparative community study of low-income youth and their efforts to find income and survive in an extremely tight labor market.

All of these projects require continued consulting and additional research. Although my training at the University of Chicago under Morris Janowitz and Gerald Suttles best prepared me for pure ethnographic research, I have had to conduct a substantial number of surveys in connection with these projects. However reluctant I have been to conduct survey research, my clients generally demand numerical data and are happiest when given numbers not otherwise available to them. For a qualitative sociologist, this lesson has been a difficult one and is related to a central issue of this chapter, the relationship between field research and survey research in applied sociology.

Qualitative Research and Surveys in Applied Sociology

The big business in sociology, of course, is polling and survey research. Even though our survey methods have been coopted by many other practitioners, most large-scale applied sociological research continues to be based on extensive sample surveys. In New York City, where I practice my art and craft, survey sociologists are employed in many of the dominant corporations. The major television networks employ small survey research staffs; the advertising and market research firms will hire survey sociologists but generally demand marketing backgrounds as well; and the major social research corporations, such as the Manpower Demonstration and Research Corporation (MDRC), like to scatter among their econometricians a few sociologists with abilities in sampling and data-base management. Cuts in social programs have eliminated the jobs of many sociologists, who have found somewhat more marginal positions in agencies where they conduct program evaluation, most often relying on combinations of quantitative and qualitative methods. Now the recent attacks on educational and social welfare programs have brought hard times for sociologists employed in the larger research firms. Mathematica, Abt Associates, and MDRC, the top three companies in the field of quantitative survey methods for policy analysis and evaluation, were in charge of much of the extensive polling and evaluation research for the U.S. Department of Labor's manpower programs. As Comprehensive Employment and Training Act (CETA) and the other manpower legislation are gutted, the demand for sociologists who can work on complex, national-level surveys is drastically diminishing. Similar decreases in large-scale social research have occurred in other areas of social welfare funding.

The types of surveys and other quantitative research that field researchers most often conduct are less dependent on large-scale public funding. We are generally called on to develop new information on narrower issues very often limited to a particular community within a given city. Those of us who prefer qualitative research but can also design and carry out surveys are sometimes able to continue working even when our more specialized colleagues have lost their grants. The demand for new information about society and social processes is not destroyed by the short-term myopia of the present federal administration. The trick is to be able to conduct a modest survey—based, for example, on mailback questionnaires or telephone interviews and combined with insightful qualitative material—for under $25,000. If this is done two or three times in the interest of causes that you believe in and that you can help through the production of new knowledge, then after that the work will continue coming in, or will at least be easier to compete for.

For the participant observer in applied research, the survey is frequently a means toward acceptance in the field. In our research on Forty-Second Street, for example, the Ford Foundation and other groups interested in the development potential of this most urban neighborhood wanted an insider's view of the street. We were asked to report on patterns of public use by time of day and week, on the structure and functioning of street markets for drugs, sex, and pornography, on the populations of homeless people who frequent the street, on crime and police work, and on the larger public's perception of the street as an entertainment zone. And, as is so often the case in applied research, the clients wanted the research delivered in a short time. We were given four months to complete the entire project so that our report could assist in efforts to plan for investments and, conversely, so that our research effort could not in any way be used as an excuse for delay of decisions. Since my colleagues Terry Williams, Vernon Boggs,

Jennifer Hunt, Charles Winick, and I had already been doing field-work in the area, we began with a firm base of qualitative data about life on the street. But we needed extensive quantitative data on pedestrian traffic flows, and we had to develop a brief survey that would compare how people in the metropolitan region viewed this problematic section of Times Square in comparison with other entertainment zones in the city.

High-quality ethnographic research could not have been written within the deadline, nor would it have convinced our more technically minded clients that we knew what we were talking about. The insertion of some basic quantitative observations about who uses the street, broken down by time of day, sex, race, and age, as well as a short survey that tapped public opinion about the area made the presentation of our qualitative material much stronger. A chapter in the report by historian Stanley Buder was also of immense value in rounding out the research monograph by showing how present conditions on West Forty-Second Street evolved over better than half a century of market processes in mid-town Manhattan.

Since the study was completed, in 1978, my colleagues and I have had a steady source of additional small grants and consulting opportunities, both related to West Forty-Second Street and to similar areas in other cities. Most important, the holistic approach taken in the initial project has made it possible for us to continue participant observation in previously foreclosed areas of Times Square politics and finance.

Demographer Philip Houser has frequently summed up the overall point I am making: "Remember," he told his classes in more or less these words, "that well-chosen and succinctly presented demographic variables can form the spine around which you build your analysis based on other types of data." Wise as this advice has proven to be, the question remains as to what constitutes appropriate training in qualitative methods.

Mentors and Qualitative Methods

The essential methods of qualitative research in the social sciences have not changed appreciably over the past two generations. One needs to write field notes, keep a diary of more personal experiences in the research, and develop life histories. More

specific methods, such as the coding of economic transfers, focused interviews, photography, and oral history, are very often of
immense value and can be learned during graduate years, but they
are not universally applicable. Not having mastered them before
one begins long-term research in no way precludes developing a
familiarity with these and other new techniques once one has left
the university.

All these techniques of data gathering are merely the most
superficial aspect of qualitative research. Interpretation of what
one is observing and experiencing is a far greater challenge, as are
the personal adjustments one makes during the course of field research. Both the difficulties in interpreting qualitative data and the
processes of access, commitment, and exit are areas of this kind of
research that are definitely eased in a didactic relationship in
which the mentor has had extensive experience in ethnographic research. One needs to work with people who think of themselves as
field researchers. They may not always be immersed in field research themselves, but they must have "made their mark" previously in this research style.

It is also extremely helpful to learn qualitative methods on
the graduate level at a university where this style of research is
valued. Too often, one feels like a second-class citizen, even with a
fine mentor, if the latter must struggle to convince a reluctant faculty that a dissertation lacking beta coefficients has scientific
merit.

Field Research Seminar. Problems with interpretation of
participant observation data are often best solved in a research
seminar where the fieldworker is able to present periodic progress
reports. The lone ethnographer often gets mired in a maze of details, many of which deal with idiosyncratic aspects of personal or
group behavior. The fieldwork seminar is an opportunity to present material to colleagues who are not intimately familiar with
the field situation. They can often help pinpoint the processes or
relationships which appear to be new contributions to empirical
fact or theory. Thus, at the University of Chicago, Gerald Suttles's
field research seminar typically meets in students' apartments in
the evening. Long hours are devoted each week to an individual
student's research. Those who have finished the seminar and are
involved in longer-term field research continue in the seminar and

periodically have the opportunity to develop ideas about their research findings.

Many of the best qualitative studies in the American social scientific literature have been produced out of seminars that brought field researchers together in a common effort at participant observation and interpretation. *Tally's Corner,* for example, was originally Elliot Liebow's dissertation produced out of the research project "Child Rearing Practices Among Low-Income Families in the District of Columbia" under the direction of Hylan Lewis (Liebow, 1967). A skilled field researcher, Lewis had learned his craft at the University of Chicago as part of the famous community studies of industrialization in the South under the direction of John Gillin. Lewis was used to guiding student research in a collegial setting and developed the same approach to field research training in the Washington, D.C., project. In his appendix to *Tally's Corner,* Liebow mentions that his field research took a problematic turn at the outset when he became involved with one of his street-corner men in a court case. As the case developed, Liebow consulted with Lewis at every step to determine how much he should become committed to taking a role in the court proceedings. In later phases of his research, he used opportunities to speak in Lewis's research seminar to refine his conclusions on the basis of collegial criticism. Many other examples could be cited. A field research seminar is the cornerstone of good training in qualitative methods.

Perhaps the foremost goal of the qualitative research seminar is to give students a chance to learn for themselves if they enjoy and have a talent for field research. I strongly believe in arranging field placements or organizing field observation exercises before requiring extensive reading in the methodological literature about qualitative research. When students are asked to begin writing field notes, their first questions are usually about how to determine what to record from the rich array of possible observations. Of course, these questions have no easy answers. Selections from the original research literature are helpful for making the student aware of the various levels of social interaction he or she might focus on. Erving Goffman's *The Presentation of Self in Everyday Life* (1959) is particularly valuable for dealing with micro levels of interaction and with the symbolic content of mundane behavior.

Clifford Geertz's *Peddlers and Princes* (1968) is a brilliant example of comparative institutional analysis that also helps teach students how to incorporate field research materials gracefully into finished writing. *Reflections on Community Studies* (1964), edited by Arthur Vidich, Joseph Bensman, and Maurice Stein, is an excellent discussion of the craft of field research and also has good material for a discussion of the natural history of the fieldworker's involvement in the research setting. The key to this seminar's success, however, is continual production of field notes by students and commentary on those notes by the instructor and other students. As the student becomes more familiar with the field setting and as salient issues begin to emerge, he or she stops being confused about what to record. Students who have good intuitive abilities begin to become more conscious of the systematic aspects of field research. Indeed, they often become so immersed in the research that one has to remind them to continue making progress toward completing the overall graduate program. On the other hand, students who have little of the capacity for empathy and gentle self-assertion required by career field researchers tend to limit the scope of their involvement with this research style.

Mentors and Direct Social Change. These comments on mentors and methods have not dealt specifically with applications of the sociological method to direct social change. Many of the best field research mentors are not particularly interested in this issue. For example, Gerald Suttles, a brilliant sociologist and an excellent field methods teacher, generally directs his work at larger questions of social theory rather than at smaller-scale processes of social change. The emphasis in his teaching, which is exemplary of the best ethnographic training in sociology, is on the contribution of empirical fact to sociological theory rather than to direct action. Most commonly, therefore, the student who wishes to work in an applied field will need to assemble a committee that includes one or more experienced field methods practitioners and another researcher who is involved in direct applications of social research.

In some relatively uncommon cases, the same talents and experiences are found in one person. William F. Whyte at the Cornell New York School of Industrial and Labor Relations, Kai D. Erickson at Yale, and Joan Moore of the University of Wisconsin at Milwaukee are examples of ethnographers whose work is applied to immediate problems of social change. After a brilliant career of research and teaching in the field of work and organizations, Whyte remains totally dedicated to the application of his research to advances in the organization of work. Along with Joseph Blasi of Harvard, Whyte took the lead in formulating and lobbying for passage of legislation that became the 1980 Small Business Employee Ownership Act. Kai Erickson's incisive analysis of the traumatic impact of community destruction helped victims of the 1972 Buffalo Creek disaster win $13.5 million in damages from the coal company that had so dominated and destroyed their lives. Joan Moore's work with the Chicano community of East Los Angeles, described in her book *Homeboys* (1978), was instrumental in helping former prison inmates in that community develop a strong community organization that eventually helped many individuals move from crime into more constructive careers as political leaders and community activists. Of course, there are others whose work combines sound academic research with the best applied results, but the three mentioned here are good examples of mentors that one would seek for qualitative research in applied sociology.

Environmental Research and Activism. Sociologists who work in applied fields and are in a position to arrange field placements are often tucked away in professional schools in large universities. Frequently they have only limited contact with academic doctoral programs, partly because of the nature of their daily work and partly because of the academic sociologists' lack of interest in colleagues whose work is applied to practical outcomes. For these reasons, the person seeking a mentor for work in an applied area of research often needs to explore university programs that are not part of the standard doctoral program. A good example of this situation is a career in environmental research and activism. Suppose a young social scientist seeking a career in academic and applied research or simply in applied research wishes to work on environmental issues. To be even more specific, suppose our hypothetical student wishes to work with environmentalists who are seeking to prevent the large-scale industrial development of Western wilderness areas. How would that person go about developing a career in applied sociology, and where would it be possible to get the kind of training and experience that would allow for entry into this field?

In my opinion, two universities offer the training and field experience necessary to prepare one for applied research on environmental causes: the University of Washington and Yale University. Both have extremely strong academic programs in sociology where one can get the kind of eclectic training in social scientific methods discussed earlier and where one can find master teachers in the field of qualitative methods. But, more important for the purposes of a person seeking to develop a career in applied environmental sociology, both Yale and the University of Washington have schools of forestry, with sociologists who have developed channels into exactly the kinds of research our hypothetical student wishes to develop. Donald Field at the University of Washington and William Burch at Yale are both professors in forestry programs; both have, to my knowledge, somewhat limited contact with sociology programs on their campuses, but both have colleagues in those departments who have collaborated with them and who would certainly be more than happy to direct the motivated student to them. Field at the University of Washington is probably the most knowledgeable sociologist in the United States on issues pertaining to the uses of social research in the management of forest and wilderness recreation areas. He is both a professor in the School of Forestry of the University of Washington and the chief scientist for the National Park Service (U.S. Department of Interior) for the Pacific Northwest, a region of the nation where forestry issues are of primary importance. On the other coast, in the unlikely setting of an Ivy League university, Yale's Burch is the dean of sociologists who do research on social behavior in wilderness and recreation areas. He has worked on more critical public planning issues than I can even begin to review here, and he is the author of some of the best general writing in the American sociological literature on the human uses of nature. Field and Burch are also the prime movers in developing a national network of former students and sympathetic collaborators who devote their professional lives to applied research in environmental affairs. Both of these applied sociologists are best known in environmental and rural sociological circles, but, for our hypothetical student seeking a career with a group like the Conservation Foundation or the National Resources Defense Council or any of the more regional environmentalist associations, these scholars are the best mentors in this country.

The unadvised student with skills in qualitative methods who seeks a career in environmental affairs would have to carefully research this field in order to realize the importance of my assessment of these two applied sociologists. The same caution applies to many other applied fields, especially to those in nonurban environments. Extremely rewarding careers are available in less developed regions for sociologists familiar with farming, forestry, and housing construction. The disposition of the American Sociological Association to allow and encourage the development of special fields within the larger discipline has done much to assure the existence of journals and newsletters where one can learn about practitioners like Burch and Field, but perhaps more needs to be done to inform the profession in general about the existence of applied sociology networks.

Developing Expertise in Applied Fields
Through the Dissertation

My comments on desirable mentors and the necessity to select them strategically leads to the relationship between the doctoral dissertation and a career in applied sociology. Obviously, the selection of a mentor and the subject matter of the dissertation are closely related. But my argument here is that the dissertation itself needs to satisfy a number of sometimes mutually exclusive conditions if it is to qualify the writer for a career in applied sociology. I am alluding to the common problem that, in academic sociology, dissertation research is expected to make a contribution to the sociological literature. Aspects of the dissertation that might appeal to an audience of practitioners are generally sacrificed in favor of conventions of sociological research and publication.

I do not argue that norms of sociological research and dissertation writing be altered to accommodate an applied market for our work. On the contrary, the student who seeks a doctorate in sociology should be ready to satisfy the requirements of scientific scholarship as they are practiced in a given department. But the student is free to find departments with mentors who can support both the applied and academic aspects of field research and can encourage dissertations that span the gap between academic and applied sociology. These two aspects need not be in conflict if the dissertation committee does not insist that sociological theory must outweigh the practical applications of the research. A few examples from my experience may help to illustrate the kinds of research at issue. I begin with a dissertation project that has not yet been undertaken simply to show how many important subjects central to the sociological enterprise are available for the ambitious student.

For the past few years, I have been attempting to find a student who would embark on a dissertation about mass transit in New York City. A dissertation based on insightful field research in the subways would be a publishable study, and, more important, would very likely assure its author employment in academic or applied work or both. The number of social scientists who have real expertise on the way people run and use subway systems is extremely small. The field is dominated by engineers. In consequence, there is an unmet demand for research on labor management relations and productivity, on safety and the perception of safety by passengers, on the politics of financing improvements in older subway systems, and on many more issues that lend themselves to social research. No single student could adequately deal with all these problems in one dissertation, but, in a holistic account of how a subway system operated, one could develop the basis for an ever-improving store of knowledge and experience in this important field. But no student has come forward to tackle this ambitious project, for which, I should add, the contacts for field placement are well established.

One reason I have not found a student to take on this fieldwork is that it appears to require too great a commitment of time and energy—at least three years of intensive research both in the field and in the various technical libraries. Most students cannot imagine how they would support themselves during that time. If I could offer a job placement rather than the more nebulous contacts for field research interviews and exploration, someone might be able to begin the project and see what develops. Unfortunately, such research does not usually begin this way—rather, the student needs to have personal and intellectual reasons for beginning. After the research has begun, and assuming that this beginning has resulted in a steadily expanding number of contacts in the field and in the networks of persons working in the applied area, the student could probably be placed, at that time in an actual job from which the field research could be conducted. Of course, such placement is not assured, but then other funding possibilities exist including local foundations and the Metropolitan Transit Authority itself. In short, the student who wishes to conduct field research in an applied area of social science needs to develop a personal strategy, in consultation with advisers, for supporting a growing commitment to that research.

Too often, students gravitate to areas of research with immediate support. In other cases, students choose topics that reduce the length of time required to complete the dissertation. But the latter strategy often leaves the student with a rather pedestrian thesis that offers only limited entry into the shrinking academic job market and holds no interest outside the narrowing circle of university and college sociology departments. As a result, too many topics that could lead to careers in applied sociology, such as the fate of our beleaguered mass transit systems, go begging.

As a more positive example, let us consider the case of a student who is engaged in an applied sociology dissertation that also requires extensive field research. The student is Michael Jacobson; the subject is arson. To carry out his work, Jacobson, a graduate student at the City University of New York (CUNY), landed a job as a researcher with the Arson Strike Force of New York City, the agency responsible for much of the local research and policy development in this area. Arson is the terrible scourge of older inner city communities. Every day in New York City, this crime accounts for death and loss of property, yet no research even approaches the status of a definitive study on this topic, either in New York or in any other city. Jacobson's thesis could fill that present void. As one of the principal proposal writers and researchers for the Arson Strike Force, Jacobson has had the opportunity to compile citywide comparative statistics on the incidence of arson; he has interviewed most of the fire department and insurance company experts on the subject and has had the opportunity to develop and evaluate indicators of blocks within the city that are at risk and therefore demand special attention from the fire department. His thesis will deal with all of these issues and more. Thus, he would probably be able to continue working with the city if he chose to and, at the same time, he would probably be in an extremely competitive position for jobs, not only in sociology departments, but also in urban studies programs, public administration departments, criminology programs, and professional academies. His thesis spans the seemingly mutually exclusive worlds of academic research and applied knowledge. At my university, we seek to produce more young scholars with dissertations like this one.

Dissertation topics are available that will facilitate careers in applied research. One needs mainly to think about the kind of work and the types of causes to which one wishes to devote oneself. Yet some may consider my review of this approach to sociological careers to be overly sanguine. Some students have followed my advice and still find it difficult to land good jobs in the field of their choice, especially in public policy and social change, which are prime targets for cuts in public spending. Since those fields encompass most areas of commonwealth with the exception of the military, careers in applied sociology, even along the lines argued for here, may not seem promising. However true this view may be in the short run, students in our experience who have carried out dissertations in applied fields either secure employment during the course of their dissertation research or make enough contacts along the way to the dissertation that they have less trouble competing on the labor market for decent jobs than do students who depend entirely on the academic network for their opportunities.

A more serious problem of the style of applied research developed here concerns disciplinary boundaries. Who is this applied sociologist as an intellectual and as a social scientist? And how does this kind of emphasis in training bear on the future of sociology as a science? Many sociologists will argue that emphasis on applied sociology must weaken the scientific basis of sociology and perhaps make it indistinguishable from social work or public administration. I contend, of course, that the opposite is true: the more sociologists contribute their special skills in participant observation and other research methods to institution building in vital areas of society, the more respect the field will gain and the more investment will be made in its academic departments. Conversely, the less we stress the applications of our work in favor of producing research and students with Ph.D.s who are limited to careers in the academy, the more vulnerable will sociology be to declines in academic enrollment and to cuts in funded research. Morris Janowitz's extremely useful concept of institution building is a convenient heading for this argument. Much of the argument presented in this chapter can be summarized by assessing what sociologists with the kind of training advocated here can contribute to the continual growth of society—that is, to institution building.

Conclusion: Applied Sociology and Institution Building

Three broad positions have been presented in this chapter. The first is that an applied sociologist with skills in qualitative methods needs to master other research methods, particularly the techniques of small-scale survey research and quantitative analysis, for the sake of survival as a practitioner and continued access to field research situations. The second point is that the student who wishes training as a field researcher in an applied subject must seek mentors who themselves have experience as fieldworkers and, wherever possible, have experience in applied work. The third point is that emphasis should be placed, during the dissertation phase of training, on developing practical expertise in the field of research which can be translated into applied work in the future. Each of these points is based on my experience as an applied sociologist and as a mentor at the CUNY Graduate School and other universities.

The argument that students with talent in ethnography also need to develop skills as survey researchers (and as photographers, policy analysts, and so on) raises further questions about how the typical graduate curriculum might be revised to accommodate this demand. Here, we need to evaluate our graduate programs to see how much practical research experience our students can accumulate during their graduate training. Graduate students routinely study statistics and the general linear model; they learn to handle large data sets; they clean tapes and construct path diagrams. But how many receive training in all phases of social research from initial fieldwork through questionnaire design, data collection in the field, coding and analysis, report writing and the presentation of results to the client? Of the many models available in university curricula for accomplishing this practical level of training, one of the best I have encountered is the human ecology training program developed first by Ernest Burgess and later by Donald Bogue at the University of Chicago Community and Family Study Center. In that year-long training course, students were taught all phases of applied research, including some often-neglected but extremely helpful ways of incorporating demographic methods into non-demographic research. Bogue's training program was more thorough on the quantitative than on the qualitative methods, but the great strength of this Chicago School program was its practicality. Emphasis was placed on how to incorporate each technique into one's ongoing research. Care was taken to demonstrate to students how best to present data to the public so that the data could be understood by as wide an audience as possible without sacrificing scientific validity. A program seeking to strengthen its training for applied sociologists, no matter what their methodological preferences, should consult the Burgess-Bogue model.

On a more theoretical level, the concept of institution building in society as developed by Morris Janowitz (1976), is a helpful approach for teaching Applied Qualitative Methods. Institution building refers to the intentional work of citizens who attempt to alter and improve the organizations in which they participate. These organizations are concrete examples of activity in a given institutional sector of society (for example, the U.S. Army is an organization within the nation's military institution).

The institution-building perspective recognizes that society is enacted. Even organizations that function within the marketplace are built by their creators, the entrepreneurs. This sociologically pragmatic view of modern society recognizes that the entrepreneurial function is by no means limited to economic organizations. There is potential in society for the elaboration of an extremely wide range of social organizations within institutions that carry out many of the vital functions of society. The current reaction against intentional social change is merely another indication that much learning needs to occur as active citizens work to improve society. As sociologists, we need to be more concerned about holding our own in academic employment. If some of our students drop out to become dedicated to lives of activism, our field will be better off for their contributions and for their feelings that social science education helped them pursue their goals.

References

GEERTZ, C.
  1968   *Peddlers and Princes.* Chicago: University of Chicago
          Press.
GOFFMAN, E.
  1959   *The Presentation of Self in Everyday Life.* Garden
          City, N.Y.: Doubleday.
JANOWITZ, M.
  1976   *Social Control of the Welfare State.* Chicago: University of Chicago Press.
KORNBLUM, W.
  1974   *Blue Collar Community.* Chicago: University of Chicago Press.
LIEBOW, E.
  1967   *Tally's Corner.* Boston: Little, Brown.
MOORE, J.
  1978   *Homeboys: Gangs, Drugs, and Prison in the Barrios of
          Los Angeles.* Philadelphia: Temple University Press.
VIDICH, A., BENSMAN, J., AND STEIN, M.
  1964   *Reflections on Community Studies.* New York: Wiley.

❧ 26 ❧

CHANGING OPPORTUNITIES IN APPLIED SOCIOLOGY EDUCATION

Kenneth G. Lutterman

The education of sociologists has been and continues to be influenced by American social conditions and by our unique heritage as a nation. Much of the early emphasis in sociology, as evidenced by the work of E. A. Ross at Wisconsin and of the Chicago School, concerned applied social problems. Although the purpose of this chapter is not to do a historical analysis of the sociology of sociology, we can only understand current and prospective trends in the education of sociologists if we see them in a historical context.

Historical Perspective

In its earliest days, sociology in America had a strong concern for applied problems. The Chicago School—Robert E. Park,

Note: The statements and opinions expressed in this chapter are those of the individual author and do not necessarily reflect the policy or position of the National Institute of Mental Health.

Ernest W. Burgess, and Louis Wirth—was concerned with the social ecology of cities and the distribution of crime, delinquency, mental illness, suicide, drug and alcohol use, and deviant behavior. How could the variations in rates be explained? The flow of immigrant populations through the zones of the city and the effects of urbanism as a way of life on individual persons and families were of both theoretical and practical concern to sociologists at the University of Chicago.

The issue of race and racism has long been central to American society and to sociology. Sociological concern has ranged from legitimating racial differences in the early 1900s, at the time of the "yellow peril" and exclusionary immigration policies, to analyzing barriers to equality in education, housing, jobs, income, and health care. The range of positions and the kinds of research sociologists have done have been closely related to the wider problems of our society. In the early 1900s, the problems of unemployment and the cultural differences between the new immigrants, especially Asians, and those already here were reflected in Giddings' "conciousness of kind" and Sumner's emphasis on the stability of "folkways," which could be used to legitimate the status quo in race relations. But the Nazi threat to democracy, with its racism and genocide, altered our perception of minorities. Blacks and Asians fought and died for our freedom and desegregation slowly began to occur in the armed forces, housing, schools, and employment. As these changes were occurring, sociologists became more and more involved in fostering, legitimating, and researching the equalization of opportunity for all races.

In the last two decades, sociologists, especially female sociologists, have been analyzing the sexism of work, of academia, of health care, and of the legal system. In spite of the success of the suffragettes, the academic success of women students, and the contributions of women to the labor force during World War II, research on the issue of sexual discrimination did not flourish until women in our society generally, and women sociologists especially, demanded that their concerns be addressed. Women's issues did not become a focus of concern in sociology until women had entered graduate training in sociology in substantial numbers.

Economic Factors. The development of sociology and the training of sociologists have been directly linked to U.S. economic history. The prosperity of the twenties and the expansion of education meant a rapid increase in job opportunities for sociologists and a flowering of sociological research. As Robert E. L. Faris (1945) points out, the twenties also saw a large increase in the funding of research, with support from individuals, foundations, and, in some cases, government agencies. W. I. Thomas and Florian Znaniecki's *The Polish Peasant in Europe and America* (1927) was funded by an individual, Helen Culver, and the large cooperative research directed by William F. Ogburn for *Recent Social Trends* (Ogburn and Gilfillan, 1933) was supported by a substantial grant from the Rockefeller Foundation. In addition, the Social Science Research Council helped in the training of sociologists by providing predoctoral and postdoctoral fellowships. But Faris (1945, p. 551) observes that this rapid growth had some negative effects on the training of sociologists:

> This prosperity that did so much to promote sociology and sociological research came perhaps too suddenly in the decade following the first World War, and the abruptness of the process of expansion produced some undesirable conditions. The demand for professors in colleges that were adding to their sociology offerings rose more swiftly than the supply of adequately trained persons. The result was that many poorly qualified persons came into the field, and some who were scarcely qualified in any way. Graduate students in unmanageable numbers flooded some of the larger universities, and many found employment on college faculties before their training was completed. Thus, a heterogeneous and somewhat undigestible mass was taken into the profession of sociology. The result is that teaching and research became necessarily uneven in quality.

But the Depression, with its widespread unemployment, ended the boom in higher education and depressed the job market for sociologists. Although some found work in the many government agencies established by the New Deal, the thirties were a time of retrenchment. Social class, poverty, and comparative analyses of capitalism, communism, and socialism became issues of substantive concern to sociologists. Racism also became a salient issue, as the Ku Klux Klan flourished and blacks and so-called foreigners became the victims, the scapegoats, the groups that provided "racial superiority" to even the poorest of white Americans.

World War II brought dramatic changes. Women were recruited for war jobs that had been all male; Rosie the Riveter and women who helped build ships were celebrated. Men fought and died for freedom against the racism of the Nazis and the Japanese. In spite of the internment of American citizens of Japanese heritage and the segregation of blacks in the armed forces, war propaganda articulated a rhetoric of freedom, democracy, and equality that led to change. Sociologists and psychologists focused attention on the nature of prejudice and discrimination, on the recent, largely twentieth-century origin of segregation and Jim Crow, on the structural basis of prejudice in the army and in housing, and on the authoritarian personality. The war effort also brought social science to the nation's attention through the use of screening tests that discovered the enormous number of young men with health problems, especially mental health problems, that precluded their service in the armed forces. Sociologists worked on problems of morale, intergroup relations, productivity, psychological warfare, and such practical questions as, Why did 75 percent of the men engaged in combat not fire at the enemy?

Postwar Expansion. Following World War II, the nation responded to the unemployment that characterized the Depression by passing the GI Bill. The need for trained personnel was recognized, and the value of education was clear to all. Colleges and universities expanded rapidly. The expansion of enrollments created a demand for teachers. The economic growth of the forties and fifties, the postwar baby boom, the rapid expansion of new colleges and universities by state governments, as well as the increase in elementary and secondary school students who needed teachers and the increase in the proportion of high school students going on to college created a large demand for college and university faculty members. In many ways, the two decades following World War II were similar to the period after World War I and had similar effects on the training of sociologists.

The war had revealed many of the hidden needs of our society and had also demonstrated our ability as a nation to mobilize resources to handle problems. The draft had revealed that large numbers of young men were unable to serve in the nation's armed forces because of poor physical and mental health and that many were illiterate or poorly educated. The draft and the war turned a local and state concern into a national concern. Similarly, the very success of the national effort in fighting the war suggested that the nation could address other societal needs. The success of the Manhattan Project demonstrated the power of research. In 1946 and subsequent years, Congress greatly increased the funding of medical research through the National Institutes of Health (NIH) extramural grants program and through additional specific disease programs and institutes. In 1946, the National Mental Health Act was passed, and, in 1949, the National Institute of Mental Health (NIMH) was established to do research to promote mental health and the treatment and prevention of mental illness. In 1950, Congress established the National Science Foundation (NSF) to support research largely in the physical and biological sciences.

In the fifties, it became clear that the development of knowledge in the behavioral sciences required support for basic research as well as for "targeted" or applied research. Some hoped that NIMH would become the National Institute for Mental Health and Behavioral Sciences and vie with NSF for this national responsibility. Because it was recognized that so little was known in the behavioral sciences, and because this basic knowledge was seen as essential for progress in understanding specific problems in mental health and illness, NIMH supported a relatively broad range of behavioral science research. In fact, in many years NIMH provided as much or more funding of research by sociologists than did NSF. The expansion of colleges and universities and of support for research created a tremendous demand for teachers and researchers in sociology as well as other fields. In the fifties and sixties, "the abruptness of the process of expansion produced some undesirable conditions" (Faris, 1945, p. 551), just as it had in the twenties.

The need to improve the training of researchers was evident in the quality of research applications, and, in 1957, NIMH began a program of support for research training in the behavioral sciences. Better quantitative and research training became the focus of the program. Support was provided to students to enable them to pursue their education and be involved in research full-time. Support was also provided to hire the faculty needed for a strong research training program and to provide the faculty with the time and resources necessary to work closely with trainees. Initially, the Social Sciences Section of NIMH focused on training in medical sociology, anthropology, and social psychology, but it quickly became evident that broader support of the social sciences was needed to produce the kinds of researchers and knowledge needed to understand mental health and mental illness.

By 1969, the Social Sciences Section was supporting 77 research training grants, which in turn supported 626 trainees—over 600 of them predoctoral students—at a cost of $5.2 million. Forty-three grants were in departments of sociology and focused on such areas as medical sociology, deviant behavior, methodology, complex organization, socialization, family, social change, racism, social psychology, evaluation research, urban problems, and demography. Seventeen were multidisciplinary, focusing on organizational behavior, social psychology, social psychiatry, urban problems, and evaluation research. Other programs focused on anthropology and cultural change, economics and human resources, and political science and urban conflict.

Although the Office of Education and the National Science Foundation also provided support for graduate work, the NIMH and NIH programs were unique in their emphasis on improving the quality of research training. The peer review of training grant applications, with site visits to the programs to talk with students and faculty, implicitly established national standards of quality in graduate training and facilitated communication between departments. The emphasis on training for research careers also directed attention to the recruitment of students and to their training in research design and in quantitative and qualitative research methodology.

Flux in Supply and Demand Through the Sixties. While the academic demand for sociologists was strong through the sixties and early seventies, the demographic effects of the baby boom could be seen in the decrease in demand for elementary and secondary school teachers. But, just as schools of education had their own impetus to train far more teachers than the market could use, graduate departments of sociology had their own impetus to train graduate students. Whereas NIMH was primarily concerned with improving the quality of research training by supporting a small number of excellent trainees, the marketplace for doing research in 1970 was the university—over 88 percent of Ph.D. sociologists were employed in educational institutions.

In order to get a better estimate of the future need for sociologists and to make better use of resources, Robert McGinnis was funded by NIMH in the early 1970s to estimate the supply and demand for professional sociologists in the United States. His projections, using a logistical growth model, indicated that there would be a substantial oversupply. He estimated that the 470 Ph.D.s produced in 1970 who went into the labor force were seven times the number needed for replacement. Even with drastically reduced growth rates, he projected production in 1980 would exceed replacement needs by a factor of 5.4 (McGinnis and Solomon, 1973, p. 60). With these kinds of estimates as a backdrop and with little evidence that graduate departments were concerned about the oversupply that they were creating for a limited academic marketplace, NIMH funded a conference of training program directors in December 1972 that focused on the relation of sociology to social policy and on the training of sociologists for this kind of research in and out of academia. Earlier, NIMH-supported conferences had focused on improved methods of training (1971), on training in quantitative and qualitative methods (1969), and on organizational aspects of graduate training (1967). Whereas the earlier conferences focused on basic methodological aspects of research training, the 1972 conference explicitly discussed issues of training for applied research and the application of research to issues of social concern (Demerath, Larson, and Schwessler, 1975). Although McGinnis's projections were discussed and Harrison White's *Chains of Opportunity* (1970) was cited, there appeared to be no practical way to deal with the issue of supply and demand and little interest in training sociologists for nonacademic positions. In order to encourage graduate departments to consider the possible implications and alternatives to the projected oversupply in sociology and anthropology, NIMH funded a grant to support further research on the extent of the problem and on alternatives. Roy D'Andrate and Eugene Hamel did a detailed analysis of present and projected supply and demand in anthropology, but the Executive Office of the American Sociological Association decided that sociology departments were well aware of the issues and that no further research was needed. Funds for similar research in sociology were denied.

Trends Toward Applied Sociology

In 1969 and 1970, federal funding of graduate education by the Office of Education, Social and Rehabilitation Service (SRS), National Aeronautical and Space Administration (NASA), and NSF was drastically reduced or phased out. Phase-out for NIH and NIMH research training was also proposed in 1970 by the Office of Management and Budget (OMB), but Councillor to the President Patrick Moynihan intervened, and a two-year hold was provided for a study of the need for continued research training support in health and mental health. In 1973, President Nixon again proposed to phase out all research training over a four-year period and impounded the funds that Congress appropriated. Following a court order, the funds were later released. But Congress decided that it needed better information on the need for research training and, in passing the National Research Act of 1974, requested that the National Research Council do a study to "establish (a) the nation's overall need for biomedical and behavioral research personnel, (b) the subject areas in which such personnel are needed and the number of such personnel needed in each such area, and (c) the kinds and extent of training which should be provided such personnel" (Commission on Human Resources, 1981, p. iii).

While the study was being done, Congress continued to support research training in health and mental health. The Committee on a Study of National Needs for Biomedical and Behavioral Research Personnel has issued six reports strongly recommending that support for research training be continued at a stable level. They have also identified some fields, such as epidemiology, as shortage areas and have recommended a progressive shift in support from predoctoral to postdoctoral training in the behavioral sciences, with a 70 percent/30 percent postdoctoral/predoctoral ratio recommended by 1981. However, the transition from predoctoral to postdoctoral programs has moved slowly (to 34.9 percent postdoctoral in 1980) and has occurred largely as a result of a sharp decline in predoctoral support (63 percent decrease since 1975). Although the committee recommended stable funding of training, funding by the Alcohol, Drug Abuse and Mental Health Administration (ADAMHA) declined by 23 percent in real dollars between 1976 and 1980 and has declined further since 1980 (Commission on Human Resources, 1981).

The NIMH Social Sciences Section did implement the recommended shift toward postdoctoral training. In 1973, 77 programs provided support for 567 trainees, almost all of them predoctoral, at a cost of $5.1 million. In 1980, funding had been reduced to $3.3 million and support was provided to 99 postdoctoral trainees in 33 programs. Beginning in 1972, the Social Sciences Section placed an explicit emphasis on training for research careers in applied settings such as community mental health centers and state, federal, and private research settings. A major concern of the seventies was the delivery of mental health services and the evaluation of service programs. By 1980, about half the programs concerned services research and evaluation research and involved training for applied settings. Faculty members with experience in applied research are hard to find, and often departments are unenthusiastic or hostile to developing training programs with an applied focus. It is much easier and less threatening to deal with disciplinary problems rather than the problems of the client; it is simpler to reproduce one's self and to continue the "pyramidal sales scheme" than to train students to work in applied settings. Unlike schools of public health and public policy, sociology departments generally lack strong ties to agencies or other nonacademic research settings. Thus, it is difficult to place students as interns, to supervise their research, and to help them find jobs in nonacademic settings. In addition, intellectual snobbery often dictates what kinds of research are important and worthwhile, and applied research is usually seen as less respectable, unless perhaps performed by a Paul Lazarsfeld, a James Coleman, or a Peter Rossi.

The most recent trend in federal support of social science research and research training at NIMH is to require that it be explicitly focused on mental health and mental illness (from announcement of National Research Service Awards, NIMH, August 1981), which substantially narrows the substantive areas of sociological research and research training that are eligible for support. Research and research training focusing on theoretical, methodological, and statistical issues in mental health services continue to be a major area of support. Services research includes: assessment of costs and financing; assessment of factors influencing the supply and use of facilities and services; interactions between general health and mental health services systems that influence the care of persons with mental disorders; assessment of the need for mental health services; applications of research data to the planning, coordination, and implementation of cost-effective mental health services systems; and evaluation of mental health services systems through assessment of appropriateness and quality of care, systems impact, and client outcome.

Research in these areas almost inevitably requires multidisciplinary cooperation; consequently, multidisciplinary research training is strongly encouraged. One of the best examples of multidisciplinary research is the large-scale epidemiologic research being done at five sites and involving sociologists, psychiatrists, psychologists, epidemiologists, and statisticians in the use of survey techniques with standardized interview schedules to diagnose mental disorders in the general population and in institutions. It has taken about thirty years to apply survey methods, psychometrics, and diagnostic procedures to the problem of the incidence and prevalence of specific mental disorders in the population. Such focused research is directed by sociologists at three of the five sites—Jerome Myers at Yale, Lee Robins at Washington University, St. Louis, and Richard Hough at the University of California, Los Angeles (UCLA). Postdoctoral training for this kind of research is occurring at UCLA, Yale, and elsewhere and is the kind of training which provides sufficient depth to pursue applied research careers in mental health.

Recent Role of Sociology in Instituting Social Change

An important trend in the seventies has been the application of sociological and economic methods to the study of institutional racism and sexism. Lawyers and courts have used sociological methods to assess equality of opportunity in schools, politics, and employment. This concern has been recognized by the ASA in the appointment of persons in the executive office with specific responsibilities for minorities and women. NSF, NIH, NIMH, and the Ford Foundation have all provided support to minorities to reduce the past pattern of institutional racism in the profession. Although the Ford Foundation has ended its predoctoral support, it has replaced it with a small postdoctoral program. As a result of the efforts of N. J. Demerath III, ASA executive officer, and Mary Harper of NIMH, the NIMH-supported Minority Fellowship Program was initiated in sociology in 1970 and was later extended to other disciplines. A research training program focusing on the problems of women began in 1980 at the City University of New York. But, in spite of the passage of the Equal Pay Act and explicit antidiscrimination laws, the empirical study of institutional racism at the organizational level, such as at American Telephone and Telegraph, has proceeded very slowly.

Since very few sociologists are employed in industry, the funding of sociological research and the size of the cohort of students in colleges and universities are critical determinants of the demand for sociologists. However, reliable data on the source and amount of funding of sociological research are extremely difficult to obtain. The amounts and sources of funds are critical because they condition research opportunities and substantive directions of research as well as job opportunities. But there is still no on-going system for collecting and monitoring research funding, even though the flow of funds is the bloodstream of sociological research. Preliminary data for fiscal year 1980 provide a crude, though perhaps inaccurate, estimate of the source of most federal funding for sociological research (unpublished data from NSF and SRS, May 1981):

Source of Funding	Millions
Health and Human Services	$34.9
Justice	8.1
Agriculture	5.4
NSF	4.8
Transportation	4.7
Agency for International Development	3.6

These amounts are only rough estimates and may be seriously in error, but they do indicate a need for further research on who is funding what kinds of sociological research and on who is doing the research.

Summary

In summary, the education of sociologists has been strongly influenced by the prosperity following World War I and World War II and by the Depressions of the thirties and the eighties. The emphasis on methodological and statistical training has been most evident in the past twenty years. In the periods of prosperity, the range of research concerns has been very broad, but, as funds have decreased, there has been an increase in the demand for relevance and for research that focuses directly on the problems of concern to the funding agency. Although the current academic market has been saturated and the future is bleak at least until 1990 (when many of the sociologists who earned their degrees in the forties and fifties will be retiring), departments have been slow to implement educational programs for nonacademic research settings. The ASA Workshop on Directions in Applied Sociology, from which much of the material in this volume emerged, represents one hopeful sign of change.

References

COMMISSION ON HUMAN RESOURCES
  1981   *Personnel Needs and Training for Biomedical and Behavioral Research: The 1981 Report of the Committee on a Study of National Needs for Biomedical and Behavioral Research Personnel, Commission on Human Resources, National Research Council.* Washington, D.C.: National Academy Press.
DEMERATH, N. J., III, LARSON, O., AND SCHWESSLER, K. F., EDS.
  1975   *Social Policy and Sociology.* New York: Academic Press.
FARIS, R. E. L.
  1945   "American sociology." In G. Gurvitch and W. E. Moore (Eds.), *Twentieth Century Sociology.* New York: The Philosophical Library.

McGINNIS, R. AND SOLOMON, L.

1973   "Employment prospects for Ph.D. sociologists during the seventies." *The American Sociologist* 8:60.

OGBURN, W. F. AND GILFILLAN, S. C.

1933   *Recent Social Trends.* New York: McGraw.

THOMAS, W. I. AND ZNANIECKI, F.

1927   *The Polish Peasant in Europe and America.* New York: Knopf.

WHITE, H. C.

1970   *Chains of Opportunity: Systems Models of Mobility in Organizations.* Cambridge, Mass.: Harvard University Press.

Part Four:
Summing Up

✕ 27 ✕

THE COURSE OF APPLIED
SOCIOLOGY: PAST AND FUTURE

Albert E. Gollin

The workshop on applied sociology[1] that led to this book is only the most recent of a series of attempts to confront the persistent tensions—between knowledge and action, between theory and practice, and, more generally, between academic and applied aspects of the discipline—that have characterized American sociology since its inception. The inclusion of "practical sociologists" as members was a question debated—and answered affirmatively—at the 1905 organizational meeting of the American Sociological Society. Even so, a few doubts apparently persisted in the minds of at least some among the practical sociologists in the society, who requested that the statement of purpose in the draft constitution make explicit that such persons could be included as members. The issue was finessed by assurances that the wording was broadly inclusive and did not require such specification (Rhoades, 1981). But the legitimacy of applied sociology and its practitioners has remained a contested issue, as a selective review of our history will document.

History of Applied Sociology: Some Interpretive Notes

The search for scientific legitimacy led many sociologists in the early decades of the society to want to put as much distance as possible between its historical roots in social reform and its aspiration to status as an academic discipline. Several proposals, for example, were presented at the 1931 annual meeting for the purpose of changing the society's public image from one of a "religious, moral, and social reform organization" to one of a "scientific society" and of "prun[ing] the society of its excrescences and . . . intensify[ing] its scientific activities." To achieve these goals, tighter control of membership and limitations on programs and publications were urged. But such initiatives toward scientific purification were countered by a concurrent, lively interest in applying sociological knowledge to the social problems of the Depression and in taking up the research opportunities presented by the New Deal. The research committee appointed to broker this dispute noted in a report in 1932 that the proposed changes would hinder the society's function of promoting sociological research and would, moreover, encourage others (presumably nonsociologists) to address the issues posed by the Depression, with an eventual loss of opportunity for and control over sociological work (Rhoades 1981, pp. 25-28).

The twin orientations reflected in these early debates—inward toward the development of sociology as a scientific discipline and outward toward its engagement with problems of the wider society—have continued to influence the course of the discipline and the programs of its professional association. Several objectives were being sought simultaneously during this and subsequent periods: to strengthen sociology's academic legitimacy and multiply opportunities for teaching and research on campuses; to widen the range of job opportunities outside academia, as the Depression and then World War II restricted hiring by colleges; and to enhance public recognition of sociology's contributions to knowledge and practical affairs as a means of defending and promoting the wider professional interests of sociologists. These objectives fluctuated in importance over the ensuing decades.

By the 1950s, the battle for academic respectability had largely been won, and sociology entered a period of sustained differentiation in subject matter, theoretical tendencies, and method-

ological approaches. In time, this differentiation intensified the
stresses and conflicts within individual departments and across the
face of the discipline over styles of sociological work. The concern
with sociology's practical applications became more deeply politicized, with most of the criticism of applied sociology in the period
from World War II to the mid-1960s coming not from the "scientific center," worried about the diversion of discipline-building
energies caused by involvement with public- or private-sector concerns, but from the "qualitative left," sociologists concerned with
the conservative stance and trivial or inhumane uses of an increasingly potent social science (Lynd, 1939, 1940; Mills, 1959; Gouldner, 1965).

On occasion, these tensions were expressed in especially re-
vealing ways. In 1960, Paul Lazarsfeld, as president-elect of the
American Sociological Association, was given the opportunity to
propose a theme for its 1962 meetings. In line with his long-standing belief in the analysis of case studies as a basis for theoretical
and methodological advance and, I suspect, as a direct challenge to
those who viewed his interest in applied work critically, he proposed a theme that could be variously entitled "Sociology in Action" or "Applied Sociology." The Executive Council of ASA
found the topic "a bit undignified" and changed the title to "The
Uses of Sociology." Moreover, Lazarsfeld had to formulate a special justification that session chairpersons could use in soliciting
papers, in which the value of this theme as a means of answering
doubters or critics of sociology was stressed (Lazarsfeld and Reitz,
1975, pp. 30-31). The whole effort was beset with difficulties, the
most significant of which were the problems most authors of papers
had in identifying concrete applications of sociological ideas or
findings. Eventually, an ASA-sponsored book on the topic appeared (Lazarsfeld, Sewell, and Wilensky, 1967); despite Lazarsfeld's own disappointment with the outcome (Pasanella, 1979),
many of the essays deserve careful study, not only for what they
tell us about sociology in the 1950s and early 1960s but also for
their detailed appraisals of work in various specialty areas or fields
of application.

A decade later, in 1972, another ill-starred effort was made
to build bridges between the discipline and the practical demands
of social policy. In the intervening years, the issue of relevance had

shaken and galvanized academic sociology as well as other social science disciplines. Domestically, a long agenda of unmet economic, social, and political needs was posing insistent questions whose urgency was underscored by protest, conflict, and a wave of urban disorders. Internationally, the Cold War had heated up; confrontations in Berlin, Cuba, and then increasingly in Southeast Asia produced waves of campus antiwar mobilizations in which sociologists often took leading roles. These issues and the heightened visibility of individual sociologists as scholars or activists contributed to an accelerated growth of students and academic programs.

As in earlier times of societal stress—depression, industrial or racial strife, war, urban disorders—sociology's claims of relevant skills in diagnosis and problem solving won for it increasing public interest and support. Federal funding for research and training that was explicitly applied in orientation grew significantly in this period. But demands for accountability accompanied this quickening flow of resources. The case for increased federal financial support had to be made and remade, and a stream of advocacy or stock-taking reports issued forth in response to this need (President's Science Advisory Committee, 1962; U.S. Congress, 1967; National Research Council, 1968, 1969; National Science Foundation, 1969; Lyons, 1969; Orlans, 1969).

As an offshoot of this trend, sociologists in departments with graduate training programs supported by the National Institute of Mental Health (NIMH) were brought together late in 1972 at a conference held under the auspices of the American Sociological Association. The conference was convened partly in response to pressures "to demonstrate the relevance of their work for the public good. Still another consideration was that federal funding agencies appeared to have more interest in research with some practical value than in research with theoretical value alone" (Schuessler, 1975, p. 4). Papers and commentaries were presented on a restricted set of problems in areas that fell within NIMH's mandate, all of which were devoted to explicating the links between sociology and social policy. Just as a decade earlier, however, the claims of relevance were hard to document. The reasons for sociology's limited contributions to social policy in these and other areas were pinpointed with greater clarity and in greater volume than were the contributions themselves.

Apart from its solidly negative conclusions, another noteworthy feature of this gathering is that not a single sociologist
working in an applied setting was invited to attend. To fill the
void, a paper by Nelson Foote, presented a year later, that sharply
rebuts such conclusions was reprinted in the book of conference
papers. (By that time, Foote had returned to academic life after a
lengthy career in industry as an applied sociologist; see Foote,
1974.) To be sure, many of the tensions felt by representatives of
both the academic and applied sides of sociology were registered
during the course of the proceedings (cf. Demerath, 1975). But,
unlike Lazarsfeld, who had made an effort in 1962 to include the
perspectives of sociological practitioners, believing that they
would probably be better able to identify and analyze instances of
use, the conference organizers saw no need to go beyond a roster
of academic sociologists interested in graduate training issues and
programs. Once again, the official disciplinary perspective on the
question of sociological applications was dominated by the experiences and concerns of academic sociologists.

The foregoing sketch of key events in the organizational history of sociology's involvement with issues of application can
serve to set the 1981 workshop sharply apart from its precursors.
Many of its features were similar to those observed at earlier conferences—reports of worsening academic job shortages, questions
about the relevance of graduate training, a concern with the practical applicability of sociology. This time, however, the issues were
discussed by both academic and applied sociologists, and the latter
were recognized as strategic resources in dealing with the issues
raised, a recognition unique in the history of the discipline. That
this important advance is, nevertheless, only one step toward the
fuller integration of sociological practitioners will presently become clearer.

A Personal View from the Applied Side

My personal history as recounted provides further useful
background for the rest of my remarks, along with the organizational history I've just discussed. Like many in attendance at the
1981 workshop and like numerous other sociologists who have received professional training in the field, I *chose* to become an ap-

plied sociologist in the early 1950s, when academic career vistas
seemed limitless. My initial interest in sociology, which stemmed
from an engagement with political and social issues during my college years, was strengthened by service in the U.S. Army during
the Korean War—a conflict in many ways as unpopular and socially corrosive as Vietnam, but one that mercifully lasted only
three years. I chose to attend Columbia University's sociology department primarily because of the reputation of Robert Lynd. My
training at Columbia, however, blunted my social concerns for a
time, while sharpening my admiration for the intellectual and professional virtuosity of its faculty during the "golden era" Lazarsfeld, Merton, Hyman, Goode, Lipset, Zetterberg, and many others,
including Lynd and C. Wright Mills. Moreover, those were the
Eisenhower years, a rather bleak and unpromising era for social
change.

As a graduate student at Columbia, I first became exposed
to the pariah status of applied research in the estimation of some
academic sociologists, epitomized by the frictions between a segment of the sociology department (and other social science departments) and the Bureau of Applied Social Research (BASR), in
which faculty, staff, and students were all implicated. Even though
my own attitude toward the bureau was initially unsympathetic,
the depth of the schism and hostilities seemed to me excessive—as
often a matter of mutual envy as of intellectual, political, or professional differences. Such tensions between academics and the
staff of affiliated research institutes straining toward autonomy
were (and are) not unusual. But that schism, a microcosm of differences pervading the discipline as a whole, was a source of an-
guish and unresolvable tension for many graduate students at
Columbia and for BASR staff members. Partly as a result, a significant number of talented individuals were scarred or lost to sociology in the struggle to define their sociological identity. I was one
of the lucky ones: identified early as a promising Ph.D. candidate,
I was able to circulate freely and maintain some distance from the
combat zone.

In time, my interest in the craft of social research led me to
join the BASR staff and gave me the chance to work with and
learn from Bernard Berelson, Allen Barton, and many other talented, ambitious sociologists. Since then, for the past two decades,

I have pursued a career in applied research, with a growing portion of my time and efforts devoted to management or administrative tasks as project budgets have grown larger and research designs have become ever more difficult to implement. The conduct of research often led to opportunities to consult for a variety of agencies and groups in the community, an experience that occurred so frequently that it became difficult to see these as neatly distinguishable roles for applied sociologists, except perhaps for analytical purposes. The experience of doing applied sociological work is both more varied and more seamless in its daily realities than has often been described.

I will resist the joys of telling war stories of life in the front lines of applied sociology. However, when I speak to groups of graduate students or individuals about careers in applied sociology —bearing witness that one can indeed do sociology and retain one's sociological identity—among the themes I try to stress by providing examples are the professional and personal benefits of such careers[2] and the opportunities to make contributions to the discipline. These benefits and opportunities figure prominently in many of the chapters in this book dealing with careers in applied sociology. I applaud their appearance here because I believe that they have been insufficiently recognized and publicized in the past. Under current and foreseeable circumstances, for young sociologists to persist in the belief that only an academic career can be gratifying and professionally respectable is as unwarrantedly depressing or arrogant as it is dysfunctional for the future of the discipline. Equally, those who have the responsibility for training future sociologists should question (if they have not already) whether their obligation to our discipline is best met by adhering to practices that I have elsewhere called academic cloning: socializing students to be just like themselves in their scholarly career aspirations and professional values.[3]

During my career, like many others who have worked in applied settings, I discovered that one's sociological identity depends heavily on interaction with colleagues in work settings and local sociological associations. This interaction had an especially reinforcing effect in Washington, D.C., where I worked for fourteen years at the Bureau of Social Science Research. The District of Columbia Sociological Society is among the oldest of ASA's affiliates, and, over the years, its membership has been drawn heavily from the ranks of government and other applied sociologists. Holding membership and office in that society brought me into contact with many practicing sociologists, including some (for example, Stuart Rice, Paul Glick, Conrad Tauber, Melvin Kohn) whose professional achievements made the notion that nonacademic careers are second-best seem all the more ludicrous. The importance of such professional contacts and relationships in reinforcing one's earlier professional socialization and sociological identity cannot be overemphasized. (Riley, 1967). Lacking such contacts or supportive work colleagues, one can become caught up in a disengagement process. Isolated at work, and finding inadequate recognition from the discipline, one stops attending meetings or reading professionals journals, and, in time, even membership in the American Sociological Association comes to seem pointless. Often, as several workshop participants noted, other organizations appear to hold out greater promise as reference groups in helping one maintain a professional identity.

My understanding of the tensions between academic and applied sociology has been deepened over the years by linkages with the former through my wife and friends on various campuses and especially by my work as chairperson of the ASA's ad hoc Committee on Expanding Employment Opportunities (ExEO) from 1976-1979. That committee, which succeeded the ad hoc Committee on Employment that had been chaired for five years by John W. Riley, Jr., was asked to canvass the prospects for nonacademic employment in light of the crisis of a large and growing surplus of trained sociologists. The ExEO Committee did its work well, issuing two reports containing a wide variety of recommendations for concrete steps the discipline could take, locally and nationally, in its own self-interest (Gollin, 1977, 1978). Our efforts proved to be largely ineffective, however, as the executive councils of ASA ignored or seemed unable to act on our recommendations.

The dilemmas presented by the need to reorient the discipline's prevailing values and academic self-image seemed especially nettlesome for the Council, a judgment that was further strengthened by my subsequent experiences as chairperson of the Eastern Sociological Society's Committee on the Profession and of ASA's Section on Sociological Practice. Seen in retrospect, perhaps the efforts of the ExEO Committee did chip away successfully at the problem. The vigorous initiatives taken by its successor committee, chaired by Howard Freeman, and the support of key ASA Executive Office staff members and of two successive ASA presidents, Peter Rossi and William Foote Whyte, have led to some progress. The worsening state of the job market has also maintained the pressure for change. But the historic fault lines and tensions within the discipline remain. Sometimes academic and applied sociology seem to resemble two factions within the Mother Church: the mainstream academic faction, which still controls the pulpit and bestows the symbols of grace, and the applied faction, schismatic and growing more assertive in its assigned status as deviants. Those with even a smattering of knowledge of religious organizations can readily identify the dangers posed by such a situation.

Future of Applied Sociology: Prospects and Problems

The historical record offers both constraining and liberating lessons, of course, and, in the present context, is best consulted only briefly, since the prospects for the applied side of sociology are of primary concern. In the comments that follow, I touch on some of the more pressing issues that will affect our attempts to formulate an organized response to the crises and opportunities that confront us.

What Is Applied Sociology?

The first issue that should be raised is definitional: What is applied sociology? In the past, answers have been proposed initially in terms of a set of broader distinctions that often reflect the intraprofessional tensions or biases noted earlier. Basic versus applied, discipline-oriented versus policy-oriented, autonomous versus field-induced, are all polarities concerned primarily with the applied researcher role; the preferred element in each pair has often been easy to identify. (No one has ever used the adjective "mere" to modify the first term in these pairings.) In their keynote chapter in this volume, Rossi and Whyte, like Merton (1949) or Angell (1967), to name just two earlier analysts, go beyond these analytical pairings by specifying a range of roles in which sociological ideas, tools of inquiry, and findings can be used.

Their distinctions gain added value in this context by the testimony provided in the chapters written by applied sociologists themselves. When defined in this manner, the commonalities of interest among knowledge producers, knowledge consumers, and strategic intermediaries in the utilization process become clearer. A careful reading of these chapters will identify several strategies for defining occupational roles that offer fruitful points of departure both in establishing specifications for training programs and in identifying nontraditional or latent job opportunities for sociologists.

As always, whatever the typology, the problem of goals soon arises in discussions of applied sociology: Who sets them and thus shapes the resulting activities and interactions? Indeed, Angell (1967, p. 725) has used this as the key element in his definition: "When sociology is not an end in itself but becomes a means to some other end, it is applied sociology." Others have similarly stressed the goals or ends of applied work, an approach that leads to deceptively clear-cut definitions because it often fails to take into account the continuous process of negotiation between individuals and employing organizations that significantly shapes the direction of work and alters organizational or subunit goals. In addition, such definitions almost invariably lead to (if they do not embody) normative issues. Angell, for example, contrasts what he terms the "high calling" of scientific discipline building with the more mundane or morally questionable activities that define applied work. This easy, invidious assumption—that the direction and ultimate value of sociological work, for sociology or society, are isomorphic with its settings and sources of support—embedded as it is in definitional or normative distinctions long prevalent in sociology, has caused much bitterness or anger among sociological practitioners and has been a prime source of the tensions that have long surrounded sociological practice.

Illustrations of such indignant sentiments appeared occasionally during the workshop. Carolyn Dexter and Henry Steadman (1981, p. 3), past chairpersons of ASA's Section on Sociological Practice, bluntly questioned, in a paper presented on behalf of that section, the purposes of the workshop in light of the record of the past: "Is there any role within the ASA for sociologists in divergent work settings? Do ASA concerns go only so far as locating a sufficient number of placements for sociologists-in-training to ensure the continuance of courses staffed by sociologists? Is this conference a self-serving vehicle for the academy, or is there a genuine concern for the status of sociology in nonacademic settings?"

Sections in the ASA, some of which are heavily populated with applied sociologists, do not seem to be more sensitive to their needs than the association generally. Cynthia Cook (1981, p. 2) commenting from her perspective as a member of the community section and other sections, made a point that I have heard made more than once: "Section activities . . . bear little relation to the needs of applied sociologists . . . . Precisely because of [their] concern with enhancing the professional image of their members, which for social scientists has often meant taking a 'hands-off' attitude toward applied research, the sections may have inadvertently helped to create an atmosphere in which the applied sociologist feels like a second-class citizen. The ASA sections have in fact tended to become rather rigidly structured communities in their own right, with internal stratification systems in which status and power have been very largely based on academic achievement."

Finally, Cecile Strugnell (1980) has recently completed one of the few sociological studies of the process of entry into careers in applied sociology. Her informants evidenced a strong sense of their marginality and alienation relative to their academic training centers, sociology in general, and its professional associations. It is not surprising that sociological practitioners, like other people, respond with anger to status indignities or to questioning of professional morals. What is perhaps surprising is that so many remain willing to assist the discipline of sociology—which has largely neglected their needs and rejected their participation—in its current troubles.

A close reading of the literature and extended personal experience support the conclusion that ideal types and stereotypes abound in contemporary perceptions and appraisals of applied sociology. The "scientific goals" posture does not stand up on close examination as a justification for denigrating beliefs and attitudes, since most sociologists are transmitters of scientific knowledge rather than producers through primary research. Rossi (1980) has recently made the case that, even considered solely from the standpoint of its contributions to sociological knowledge, theory, and methods, applied sociological research has played an indispensable role in the discipline's progress. Thus, on substantive grounds as well as out of elementary considerations of individual dignity and collective welfare, it is certainly time to bring academic and applied sociologists closer together in a common effort to improve the quality and social value of all types of sociological work.

It is interesting to note that the feeling is not confined to applied practitioners. As Mauksch (1981) notes in his workshop paper, faculty at small colleges often feel left out and experience a "pervasive sense of distance between those who teach and those who produce knowledge." He makes the related point that "the health of our discipline begs for a narrowing of this gap" and warns that greater concern for sociological practice should not be allowed to lead to the establishment of "a new elite."

Assessing the Needs of the Marketplace

One of the ways in which the gap between academic and applied sociologists can be narrowed is exemplified in the workshop papers devoted to existing training programs for careers in applied sociology. A salient element in the development of many was the prior assessment of the needs of the marketplace and consultation with practitioners and employers about skill requirements. The papers on roles and activities in various applied settings provide a highly pertinent counterpoint to this main theme in that a relatively small number of technical, professional, and interpersonal skills were commonly identified as critical or advantageous for job seeking in an increasingly competitive era. Such forms of collaboration need to be institutionalized by individual graduate training centers in their own regions through networks of mutual aid and information sharing. The two-way character of these relationships can be ensured by providing practitioners opportunities for refresher course work, seminar participation, and access to other campus-based benefits. Simply asking former students who are now working in applied settings for their help may yield surprisingly good results. In most cases, I suspect, it will be the first communication that such former graduates have received from their departments since being awarded their degrees. In the process, mutual stereotypes are certain to undergo a good deal of useful reality testing.

Improving Sociology's Image

Applied sociology and the discipline as a whole will benefit from improvements in the image and reputation of sociology, not simply through clever public relations but through the building of support based on demonstrable achievements. As we have seen, in the past, these achievements have proven elusive to document. In part, the problem arises from what Merton (1949, p. 164) has called "an interlocking system, in which social status and utilization interact endlessly. Not only does utilization affect esteem, but esteem affects utilization. The higher the social standing of a discipline, the more likely it will recruit able talents, the greater the measure of its financial support, and the greater its actual accomplishments." And, as Biderman (1969, p. 130) added, "Sociology not only will become more influential as it becomes more scientific. It will become more scientific because it becomes more influential."

Several modes of entry into this interlocking system can be used to bring about improvements. One that I would stress in particular is the quality of sociological practitioners, on whose successes much depends, as they help build the reputation of the discipline by their performance in public and private work settings where the label *sociologist* often elicits blank stares. Perhaps, had there been less of a stigma attached to such careers in the past, more of the most able among us would have entered them, and the way would now be easier for others to follow. Economic necessity is inexorably altering patterns in the flow of talent, and the stock of highly qualified sociologists working in diverse applied settings is increasing appreciably even in the face of the currently uncertain job market.

A note of caution must be introduced at this point. New Ph.D.s are unlikely to represent our strongest suit in opening up or consolidating opportunities in applied settings and enhancing the reputation of the discipline. A recent employer survey confirmed the handicaps of inexperience: lack of sophistication, difficulty in communicating with nonsociologists, and limited knowledge outside the field of sociology (Lyson and Squires, 1981). Underlying these drawbacks are not only the relative lack of worldly experience of sociologists who now complete their graduate training at younger ages but also the variable caliber of those entering the field. For the short term, the ranks of applied sociologists who can be counted on to improve the reputation of the discipline are likely to be swelled by the cohort of older, more experienced sociologists being forced to leave academic life, at great personal cost, by the tenuring-out process. Special efforts are called for to assist such persons to make the transition, not only because they should be able to look to their professional association for help but also because their success in new careers as practitioners can serve the collective interest. Demerath (1981, p. 89) has claimed that "we have not always put our best foot forward, tending to leave applied work to those unable to crack the academic club"—a comment that reminds me of Groucho Marx's jibe about clubs that would accept him as a member. As should be obvious by now, I emphatically disagree with the accuracy of the generalization. But, to the extent that it persists as a shared belief, it will dim the appeal of applied sociological careers and may thereby restrict the contributions that sector can make to the reputation of the discipline—hence my argument for the salience of applied sociological work in shaping the future of sociology itself.

Another road that must be followed in securing the financial support needed to foster accomplishments is, of course, the political route. Here too, past strife within sociology and in sister disciplines has cost us lost opportunities. As Prewitt (1982, p. 15) has observed, "The seemingly endless discussion among social scientists in search of a definition of 'basic' and 'applied' research had little bearing on the involvement of government mission agencies in their purchase of policy evaluation studies. But it was the procurement policies of the federal government, not scholarly discussions, which transformed parts of our disciplines in the 1960s and 1970s."

What was given can as readily be taken away without the need for consultation or negotiation. Prewitt linked the identification of the need for a national policy for the social sciences with the political presence that has only recently been achieved in Washington by the Consortium of Social Science Associations, in which sociology is represented. In the conduct of information and lobbying campaigns, sociologists who work in government or have had experience in the national policy arena comprise a strategic resource, one that has only occasionally been recognized and tapped. Moreover, in the past, those in positions of strategic importance in channeling funds for research, training, or social experiments have looked in vain for political support or evidence that would strengthen the case for such allocations (Lutterman, 1975). We need to learn to be able to respond effectively to such appeals through our professional associations and political networks. Here again, the skills of applied sociologists can be of material assistance to the discipline as a whole.

Popularizing Sociological Analysis

Beyond such institutional activities, we must also reconsider and change our pattern of talking largely to one another. The importance of popularizing sociological analysis and applying it to policy issues in building public esteem should not be overlooked. We need to encourage and reward such activity by those among us with the flair for it, rather than denigrating it or viewing it as a form of pandering. As Etzioni (1967, p. 833) noted with regard to peace research, "as a discipline, sociology does not encourage, or at least does not train for, the sociologist-intellectual pairing of roles . . . . Today, in the age of specialization, more and more sociologists feel that . . . the only way [to] face a policy problem is through the lenses of theory and methodology."

To the degree that this diagnosis is still valid and writing to influence a wider audience is discouraged, the field is left open for Vance Packard, Gail Sheehy, Alvin Toffler, and others. Whatever the merits of pop sociology as currently produced, it does little to increase public esteem or the discipline's social relevance. Social analysis or criticism as other types of applied sociological work need not be confined to national issues or carried out only for those most able to pay.[4] The gadfly role, played with sophistication and the use of the full range of analytical tools, is still available as a mode of sociological practice. From such efforts, we can learn much about the power of sociological ideas and the flexibility of social institutions or arrangements and can add other kinds of accomplishments to our record.

In his chapter in this volume on military sociology, Segal makes a compelling case for the need to recognize and reward achievements by sociologists everywhere. Loomis and Loomis (1967) and Dentler in his chapter in this volume gently chide us for turning our backs on important sources of our discipline's growth by neglecting those who built reputations for sociology in fields such as rural and educational sociology. We lose out by neglecting sociologists who achieve eminence or prominence in the society at large. By becoming more outward-looking in our activities and reward patterns, sociology can avoid the sin of creeping parochialism. Moreover, the excesses of self-doubt and self-criticism that stem from too prolonged a gaze into the academic looking glass can also be minimized by expanding our view. In defining merit almost exclusively in terms of excellence in scholarship, we lose some of the energies that a more diversified set of reward criteria might bring to our collective life and forgo opportunities for successfully soliciting greater public attention to the accomplishments of those we single out, thereby building esteem for the discipline. Our aspirations and failures in this realm are long-standing (for example, Rhoades, 1981).

Ethical Issues

Ethical issues are never far from the surface in discussions about applied sociology. Even though no workshop paper specifically addressed the topic, it quickly emerged in a variety of contexts. As we have seen, definitions of applied sociology often go beyond cognitive distinctions and incorporate political or moral dimensions. Angell's paper cited earlier represents a laudable attempt to squarely confront the "peculiar ethical problems of the applied sociologist." In his view, these "stem mainly from the fact that he has two masters, his profession and his employer, whereas a pure [sic] sociologist has only his profession" (1967, pp. 739–40). He ends his analysis with a stirring appeal to applied sociologists to order their ethical priorities so that the claims of their employers come last. One envies the person who inhabits a moral universe that encourages such clear-cut advice, even if, as the author admits, following such advice might well lead to the loss of one's means of livelihood.

But ethical considerations are critical at various times for most sociological practitioners, and they should be able to count on their professional association to provide guidance. The ASA's recently adopted (1982) code of ethics offers them precious little. Only one short paragraph addresses the concerns of those working outside academic settings, and the only issue specifically noted is that of possible constraints on research and publication. This concern will seem quixotic to many applied sociologists for whom such issues are experienced mainly as practical problems (that is, finding the extra time, money, or energy) or as irrelevant because scholarly publication outlets are not hospitable to reports about their types of work. A relevant code of ethics for practitioners must take account of the work worlds they actually inhabit and not some idealized conception. One hopes that, in the future, several applied sociologists will be asked to help in this vital task.

Certification and Licensure

One issue that is of concern to a growing number of sociological practitioners and is closely linked with the issue of professional ethics is certification and licensure, a matter that the association has shied away from, with the sole exception of the field of social psychology (Rhoades, 1981). The issue is complex and controversial even among those most directly affected by it (Behavior Today, 1981; Roos, 1981). At stake are the disadvantages experienced by clinical and consulting sociologists who lack a formal certificate or license to practice that has been awarded by some authorized agency. These disadvantages can take a number of forms, symbolic or substantive; currently, one of the more vexing is difficulties in receiving third-party insurance payments. The problems are most readily apparent in fields such as health or social services, but they can crop up in a wide range of applied settings. Segal points out, for example that sociologists in the military can experience unequal treatment while performing the same duties as someone who possesses recognized credentials.

What has this concrete problem to do with professional ethics? It is the same issue—that of the social control of professional conduct—approached from the other side. If we cannot define and recognize sociological competencies in a manner that permits applied sociologists to compete on equal terms with others in providing a variety of professional services to clients, then we cannot reasonably expect them to seek out our community and loyally adhere to its ethical code. As it now stands, adherence is a matter of individual conscience; no credible enforcement mechanism exists. But the code's existence provides reinforcement for one's earlier professional socialization and can play an independent role in encouraging high standards of conduct for all those who voluntarily commit themselves to it.

The issue of certification and licensure highlights the need to have both positive and negative sanctions available in reinforcing scientific and professional standards. To those who view the ASA primarily as a learned society, this issue will seem remote from their interests and largely irrelevant to the future of sociology. To many sociological practitioners, however, it goes to the heart of their expectations about the role of a professional association in defending or advancing their interests. So far, attempts to deal with the issue have been inconclusive. If the ASA is not successful in grappling with it, those who are disadvantaged by a lack of appropriate credentials are likely to look elsewhere for the professional support they need. The prospect of their loss should encourage ASA to intensify its efforts to seek a solution.

Intellectual Challenge of Applied Work

Although much of the renewed interest in sociology in applied settings has arisen as a response to the academic employment crisis first definitively identified by Allan Cartter a decade ago (Cartter, 1971),[5] the justification for sociological concern with practical applications as a scientific problem is equally compelling. Drawing on the experiences of social scientists in World War II, Merton (1949, p. 167) called for a program of "applied social research on applied social research" as a means of understanding the social context within which ideas and findings gain support and acquire policy relevance. Since then, but particularly in the past two decades, a wide variety of efforts have been undertaken to understand the process whereby scientific knowledge gains acceptance and influence.

In part, this activity has reflected the concern of applied social scientists to understand why their efforts have so often failed to bear fruit. Coping with such negativism by converting it to positive use was one of the key elements underlying Lazarsfeld's early identification of the utilization process as strategic for the future progress of the discipline (Lazarsfeld and Reitz, 1975; Weiss, 1978; Pasanella, 1979). He was proposing, in effect, an attempt at intellectual jiujitsu: to grapple with one's opponent and ultimately prevail by turning the opposing force to one's own advantage. Every applied sociologist has at some time encountered this need in daily work, faced as he or she often is with misunderstanding, indifference, or even hostility to sociological insights and conclusions. But it has also been experienced by every academic sociologist who has sought to demonstrate the power and relevance of the sociological perspective to students.

The deflation of the expectations that several decades of well-funded experience have produced can be traced by comparing the titles of works dealing with the topic, which ranged from the studied "relation of knowledge to action" (Millikan, 1959) to the hortatory "knowledge into action" (National Science Foundation, 1969) and finally to "knowledge and policy: the uncertain connection" (Weiss, 1978). As many have noted, we have been victimized in the past by our own ambitions and have also mistaken the urgent calls for help from others as confirmation of our ability to respond effectively. Now, when questions about the relevance of the social sciences previously raised from several points on the political spectrum have been fused into a systematic assault on the basis for its federal funding from the political right, the utmost clarity is called for in current assessments of our scientific abilities and professional interests (Prewitt, 1982). From this standpoint, the uses of sociology remains a topic of great urgency.

In my view, analysis of the process of social science utilization can best be approached with middle-range aspirations. Progress in our time will not be achieved by theoretical enterprises that approximate attempts to identify the role of rationality in human affairs but rather by more limited efforts to develop a theory of advice. We need a better understanding of the contexts and situational patterning of problems; conditions that sustain effective consultation between practitioners and clients on such problems; and the social (usually political and organizational) factors that affect the fate of proposed solutions. Lazarsfeld's formulations of the problems of "translation" (from problem to research strategy) and "gap" (between recommendation and outcome), as codified into several subtle variations by Weiss (1978), point the way to the creation of a more flexibly useful theory of advice, as does Foote's identification of "recipes" as a fruitful way of defining the kinds of assistance that practitioners should optimally seek to provide (Foote, 1981).

Almost thirty years ago, writing in an era of expansion for sociology, Everett Hughes warned us of the perils of the growing scholasticism of the discipline and of a narrow professionalism that hampers interdisciplinary traffic and collaborative work (Hughes, 1958). Many of the trends and problems that I have commented on are, in a sense, footnotes to that prescient analysis. The sociology of the next few decades is not likely to repeat the patterns of our recent past, if that history is properly understood and its lessons are taken to heart. In the pursuit of that understanding, the experience and talents of sociologists of all types—academic sociologists, applied sociologists, and those who move between the two settings—represent our principal intellectual resources.

Notes

1. It is easy to provoke a heated debate by expressing a preference for one or another term to describe sociology outside of academic settings and sociologists who work in them. To forestall terminological quarrels, I shall be deliberately eclectic and use a variety of terms interchangeably to characterize each of the two.

2. This workshop's proceedings add appreciably to the skimpy literature previously available. One key study, also ASA-sponsored, was conducted in the mid 1970s by Panian and DeFleur (1975). More recently, Dentler (1981) added a novel essay to the literature on the problematics of sociological practice, in which the often-proclaimed disadvantages are transvalued into attractive benefits.

3. Such dysfunctional perspectives can crop up in surprising places. Take engineering for example, which has long been considered to be practical in its essence. Not so, when seen from the perspective of one distinguished engineer. In a letter in the *New York Times Magazine,* July 16, 1981, William F. Schreiber of MIT said: "At the most prestigious universities, promotion and tenure go

largely to the 'innovators' and to the writers of papers, the more theoretical the better. Let a faculty member devote himself to teaching his students how to design things that work and he will eventually be looking for a job elsewhere. This attitude, of course, spreads to students who shape their careers after those of their mentors. As a result, much of the practical technical work of the country gets done by the graduates of lesser institutions, with predictable results" (p. 78).

4. This point of view was espoused by a group of humanist sociologists at the workshop, who issued a statement on "Applied Sociology for Whom?" In it they noted the dominance of "models of doing applied sociology . . . in the service of powerful clients. . . . Specifically underrepresented were examples of applied research done in the service of the powerless."

5. Irwin Deutscher has introduced a useful note of skepticism about the accuracy and policy relevance of such projections as a basis for reorienting academic programs (Deutscher, 1981).

References

ANGELL, R. C.
    1967 "The ethical problems of applied sociology." In P. F. Lazarsfeld, W. H. Sewell, and H. L. Wilensky (Eds.), *The Uses of Sociology*. New York: Basic Books.
BEHAVIOR TODAY
    1981 "Some challenges confronting sociologists in therapeutic practice." *Behavior Today* (July 20):1-3.
BIDERMAN, A. D.
    1969 "On the influence, affluence, and congruence of phenomena in the social sciences." *The American Sociologist* 4:128-130.
CARTTER, A. M.
    1971 "Scientific manpower for 1970-1985." *Science* 172:132-140.
COOK, C. C.
    1981 "Academic and applied sociologists and the process of community change." Paper prepared for ASA Workshop on Directions in Applied Sociology, Washington, D.C., December.

DEMERATH, N. J., III
1975 "Epilogue." In N. J. Demerath III, O. Larsen, and K. F. Schuessler (Eds.), *Social Policy and Sociology.* New York: Academic Press.
1981 "ASAying the future: The profession vs. the discipline." *The American Sociologist* 16:87-90.

DENTLER, R. A.
1981 "The positive pleasures of sociological practice." Paper presented to the Section on Sociological Practice, annual meeting of the American Sociological Association, Toronto.

DEUTSCHER, I.
1981 "Social needs vs. market demands." *Sociological Focus* 14:161-172.

DEXTER, C. R., AND STEADMAN, H. J.
1981 "Addressing the needs of sociologists in diverse work places." Paper prepared for the ASA Workshop on Directions in Applied Sociology, Washington, D.C., December.

ETZIONI, A.
1967 "Nonconventional uses of sociology as illustrated by peace research." In P. F. Lazarsfeld, W. H. Sewell, and H. L. Wilensky (Eds.), *The Uses of Sociology.* New York: Basic Books.

FOOTE, N. N.
1974 "Putting sociologists to work." *The American Sociologist* 9:125-134.
1981 "The theory of sociological practice." Paper presented to the Section on Sociological Practice, annual meeting of the American Sociological Association, Toronto.

GOLLIN, A. E.
1977 "ASA committee makes recommendations for expanding employment opportunities." *ASA Footnotes* 5:1, 8.
1978 "Comment on Paul Kay's 'The Myth of Nonacademic Employment . . .' " *The American Sociologist* 13:224-226.

GOULDNER, A.
1965 "Explorations in applied social science." In A. Gouldner and S. M. Miller (Eds.), *Applied Sociology: Opportunities and Problems.* New York: Free Press.

HUGHES, E. C.

1958   "Professional and career problems of sociology." In
        E. C. Hughes, *Men and Their Work*. Glencoe, Ill.: Free
        Press. (Originally published as a separate essay, 1954.)

LAZARSFELD, P. F., AND REITZ, J. G.

1975   *An Introduction to Applied Sociology*. New York:
        Elsevier.

LAZARSFELD, P. F., SEWELL, W. H., AND WILENSKY, H. L. (EDS.)

1967   *The Uses of Sociology*. New York: Basic Books.

LOOMIS, C. P., AND LOOMIS, Z. K.

1967   "Rural sociology." In P. F. Lazarsfeld, W. H. Sewell,
        and H. L. Wilensky (Eds.), *The Uses of Sociology*.
        New York: Basic Books.

LUTTERMAN, K. G.

1975   "Research training from the perspective of government
        funding." In N. J. Demerath III, O. Larsen, and K. F.
        Schuessler (Eds.), *Social Policy and Sociology*. New
        York: Academic Press.

LYND, R. S.

1939   *Knowledge for What? The Place of Social Science in
        American Culture*. Princeton, N.J.: Princeton Univer-
        sity Press.

1940   "Democracy in reverse." *Public Opinion Quarterly* 4:
        218-220.

LYONS, G. M.

1969   *The Uneasy Partnership: Social Science and the Fed-
        eral Government in the Twentieth Century*. New York:
        Russell Sage Foundation.

LYSON, T. A., AND SQUIRES, G. D.

1981   "Sociologists in nonacademic settings: A survey of em-
        ployers." Unpublished paper, Department of Agricul-
        tural Economics and Rural Sociology, Clemson Univer-
        sity, Clemson, S.C.

MAUKSCH, H. O.

1981   "The teaching of applied sociology: Opportunities and
        obstacles." Paper prepared for ASA Workshop on Di-
        rections in Applied Sociology, Washington, D.C., De-
        cember.

MERTON, R. K.
1949 "The role of applied social science in the formation of policy: A research memorandum." *Philosophy of Science* 16:161–181.

MILLIKAN, M. F.
1959 "Inquiry and policy: The relation of knowledge to action." In D. Lerner (Ed.), *The Human Meaning of the Social Sciences.* New York: Meridian.

MILLS, C. W.
1959 *The Sociological Imagination.* New York: Oxford University Press.

NATIONAL RESEARCH COUNCIL
1968 *The Behavioral Sciences and the Federal Government.* Washington, D.C.: National Academy of Sciences.

1969 *The Behavioral and Social Sciences: Outlook and Needs: Report of the Behavioral and Social Sciences Survey Committee.* Englewood Cliffs, N.J.: Prentice-Hall.

NATIONAL SCIENCE FOUNDATION
1969 *Knowledge into Action: Improving the Nation's Use of the Social Sciences: Report of the Special Commission on the Social Sciences.* Washington, D.C.: National Science Foundation.

ORLANS, H.
1969 *Making Social Research Useful to Government.* Reprint 155. Washington, D.C.: Brookings Institution.

PANIAN, S. K., AND DeFLEUR, M. L.
1975 *Sociologists in Nonacademic Employment.* Washington, D.C.: American Sociological Association.

PASANELLA, A. K.
1979 "The evolution of a thesis: Utilization of social research as a sociological problem." In R. K. Merton, J. S. Coleman, and P. H. Rossi (Eds.), *Qualitative and Quantitative Social Research.* New York: Free Press.

PRESIDENT'S SCIENCE ADVISORY COMMITTEE
1962 *Strengthening the Behavioral Sciences: Report of the Life Sciences Panel.* Washington, D.C.: U.S. Government Printing Office.

PREWITT, K.
1982   "Annual report of the president." In *Social Science Research Council Annual Report, 1980-1981.* New York: Social Science Research Council.

RHOADES, L. J.
1981   *A History of the American Sociological Association, 1905-1980.* Washington, D.C.: American Sociological Association.

RILEY, J. W., JR.
1967   "The sociologist in the nonacademic setting." In P. F. Lazarsfeld, W. H. Sewell, and H. L. Wilensky (Eds.), *The Uses of Sociology.* New York: Basic Books.

ROOS, P. D.
1981   "Certification in sociology." *The Applied Sociologist Bulletin* 2 (December):4-5.

ROSSI, P. H.
1980   "The presidential address: The challenges and opportunities of applied social research." *American Sociological Review* 45:889-904.

SCHUESSLER, K. F.
1975   "Prologue." In N. J. Demerath III, O. Larsen, and K. F. Schuessler (Eds.), *Social Policy and Sociology.* New York: Academic Press.

STRUGNELL, C. P.
1980   "Pathways out of academia: Careers of sociologists in nonacademic settings." Unpublished doctoral dissertation, Department of Sociology, Northeastern University.

U.S. CONGRESS, HOUSE OF REPRESENTATIVES
1967   *The Use of Social Research in Federal Domestic Programs.* (4 vols.) Washington, D.C.: U.S. Government Printing Office.

WEISS, C. H.
1978   "Improving the linkage between social research and public policy." In L. E. Lynn, Jr. (Ed.), *Knowledge and Policy: The Uncertain Connection.* Washington, D.C.: National Academy of Sciences.

APPENDIX

Committee on Applied Sociology 1982

Howard E. Freeman, Chair
Edna Bonacich
John W. Evans
William H. Friedland
Ronald W. Manderscheid

Philip Monchar
Marvin E. Olsen
Adrian Tiemann
Barbara R. Williams
Robin M. Williams, Jr.

Panelists, Discussants, and Organizers

Barbara M. Altman
Richard A. Berk
Joseph R. Blasi
Alex Boros
Francis G. Caro
David B. Chandler
Christopher Chase-Dunn
Hugh F. Cline
Roberta S. Cohen
O. Andrew Collver
Cynthia Cook
Herbert L. Costner
Harold J. Counihan
Marvin J. Cummins
Joseph R. DeMartini

Robert A. Dentler
Irwin Deutscher
L. Carroll DeWeese III
Ragwinder K. Dhindsa
William N. Dunn
Russell R. Dynes
Evelyn M. Fisher
Howard E. Freeman
Geoffrey Gibson
Jean Giles-Sims
Albert E. Gollin
Harold G. Grasmick
Charles S. Green III
Mathew Greenwald
Robert Groves

467

Oscar Grusky
Lawrence D. Haber
Allen Haney
Burkart Holzner
Jan Howard
Carla B. Howery
Paul L. Johnson
William Kornblum
Otto Larson
Kenneth G. Lutterman
Ronald W. Manderscheid
Hans O. Mauksch
Christopher Meek
Philip Monchar
Marvin E. Olsen
Betty Jean Park
David J. Pittman
Paul D. Reynolds
Ray Rist
Peter H. Rossi
Richard G. Salem
Gary Sandefur

David R. Segal
Susanne Bleiberg Seperson
Carl Simpson
A. Emerson Smith
Marian A. Solomon
Robert C. Sorensen
Daphne Spain
Henry J. Steadman
Stephen F. Steele
Peter J. Stein
Phyllis Stewart
Gordon F. Streib
Seymour Sudman
Barry S. Tuchfeld
Ruth Wallace
William Foote Whyte
Doris Wilkinson
Barbara R. Williams
Rosemary Yancik
Margaret A. Zahn
Louis A. Zurcher

Participants

Seth Arkush
Henry M. Barlow
Robert Bendiksen
Sheila Kishler Bennett
Jill F. Bernstein
Clifford M. Black
William R. Brown
Pamela S. Cain
Steven B. Caldwell
Paul Cantrell
Ida J. Cook
Kathleen S. Crittenden
Peter David
Ann Davis

Dean Dorn
Robert J. Dotzler
Paula J. Dubeck
Susan Brown Eve
Coralie Farlee
Jim Fendrich
Leonard Fontana
Thomas R. Ford
Kazimierz Frieske
Jan Fritz
Norman Goodman
Judith Gordon
Sue Gordon
Charlotte K. Gotwald

Jeffrey Hadden
Richard N. Harris *Penn?*
Cecile E. Harrison
Michael Hennessy
Marvin R. Hershiser
Barbara Heyns
Denny E. Hill
Harold S. Himmelfarb
Frank Howell
Allen W. Imershein
C. Lincoln Johnson
Doyle P. Johnson
David E. Jorgenson
Caroline L. Kaufmann
Robert F. Kelly
William E. Knox *UNCG*
Mitchell Koza
J. Robert Larson
Daniel Lichter
Marilyn Little
Alwyn M. Louden
McKee J. McClendon
Sharon M. McPherron
Duncan MacRae, Jr.
Jay Meddin
Baila Miller
Marilyn Moretti
Stephen D. Nelson
Philip W. Nyden
Jon Olson
Susan A. Ostrander
Ann L. Paterson
Robert Perrucci
Wilhelmina E. Perry
James Pitts

David Popenoe
Tom Rice
David L. Rogers
Josephine A. Ruggiero
Terrence Russell
Inger J. Sagatun
Stanley L. Saxton
Janet Schofield
Maureen Searle
John E. Seem
Mady Wechsler Segal
Robert Seufert
Sharon B. Shaw
Brian Sherman
Herschel Shosteck
Margaret H. Stein
Charles S. Stevens
Sandra Adkisson Tausend
Arthur Vidich
Theodore C. Wagenaar
Sally K. Ward
Mark Warr
W. David Watts
Ellen Weed
Karl E. Weick
Richard H. Wells
Louise C. Weston
JoAnne L. Willette
Yolanda A. Willis
Rosemary Wade Wilson ←
Sue Wilson
Michael Wise
Thomas C. Wyatt
Jim Zuiches

NAME INDEX

SUBJECT INDEX

A

Abt Associates, 359, 413
Academic freedom, in federal agencies, 224-225
Adjutant General's Office, Personnel Testing Section of, 237, 238
Advertising. *See* Consumer and advertising research
Aging, research on: analysis of, 261-274; career opportunities in, 270-271; consortium for, 267-268; findings in, 268-270; future of, 271-273; as multidisciplinary, 264-265; professional organization role in, 265-268; and social and demographic facts, 262-265
Air Force Academy, Department of Behavioral Science and Leadership at, 244
Air Force Human Resource Laboratory (AFHRL), 240
Air Force Institute of Technology, 244
Air Force Office of Scientific Research (AFOSR), 240, 244
Akron, University of, undergraduate education at, 341
Alcohol, Drug Abuse, and Mental Health Administration (ADAMHA), 436
American Association for Public

Opinion Research (AAPOR), 94, 104-105
American Association of Retired Persons (AARP), 263
American Association of School Administrators, 258
American Dental Association, 186, 218
American Educational Research Association, 258
American Hospital Association (AHA), 217, 218, 220, 221
American Medical Association (AMA), 217, 218, 220
American Public Health Association (APHA), 222, 232, 358
American Sociological Association (ASA): and applied sociology, 124-126, 293, 442, 444, 445, 449, 459, 461; Code of Ethics of, 334, 458; Committee on Expanding Employment Opportunities (ExEO) of, 449-450; Committee on Professional Opportunities in Applied Sociology of, xxi, 52; and employment, 4, 62, 177, 434-435; Methodology Section of, 399; as professional organization, 1, 97, 143, 144, 222, 232, 245, 246, 308, 343-344, 421, 437; Projects on Teaching Undergraduate Sociology of, 313; and retooling in quan-

titative methods, 398-399, 400-401, 403-404; Section on Aging of, 265-266; Section on Sociological Practice of, 449, 451-452; Teaching Resources Center of, 335; Teaching Services Program of, 313; Workshop on Directions in Applied Sociology of, xxiv, 6, 38, 61, 323, 341n, 342n, 343n, 365, 439

American Telephone and Telegraph, 438

American University: Bureau of Social Science Research at, 253; and military studies, 237, 239, 240

Analytic studies, in applied social research, 8-9

Anne Arundel Community College: Center for the Study of Local Issues at, 333; and undergraduate education at, 333, 341

Applied social research: characteristics of, 8-9; concept of, 380; doing good through, 24-25; organizational context of, 13; and policy relevance, 17

Applied sociology: and aging research, 261-274; analysis of, 5-31; applied focus of, 67-70; and assessing marketplace needs for, 453; basic sociology distinct from, 2, 6, 15-16; benefits of, xxv-xxvi; centrality of, 7; certification and licensure for, 458-459; in community development, 275-286; concept of, 300-301, 313-315, 327, 450-453; consequences of trends in, xxiv-xxv; consumer and advertising research as, 189-199; corporate marketing as, 172-188; course of, past and future, 442-466; data specialist function of, 72-73, 74; disciplinary perspective of, 38-40; distinctive features of, 12-26; educational research as, 251-260; ethical issues in, 457-458; evaluation research in, 77-93; future of, 450-459; generic knowledge for, 20-22; and goals, 451; government policy research as, 128-137; health serv-

ice administration as, 152-164; in health services research, 215-233; history of, 443-446; in housing and environmental planning, 275-286; human services planning as, 106-117; improved settings for, 232-233; intellectual challenge of, 459-461; introduction to, xxi-xxvi, 1-4, 65-76; irony and paradox in, 74-75; issues in, ix; in law and criminal justice, 200-214; legislative consultation as, 138-151; logic of, 42-43; low status of, xxii-xxiii; marketing of, 195-196; in military studies, 234-250; models of, theory in, 38-41; personal view of, 446-450; political function of, 75; and professional associations, 124-126; programmer's perspective on, 40-41; prospects for, 26-29; reconnaissance function of, 66, 69-70, 73, 74; research orientation of, 66-67, 69; roles in, 29-30; satisfactions in, 67; settings for, 65-286; social and demographic analysis as, 118-127; social research in industry as, 165-171; socialization for, 448-449; specialized knowledge for, 22-24; status of, 1-63; survey research as, 94-105; theory's role in, 32-50; tradition of, 70-72; training for, 15, 16-17, 19, 287-440; training trend toward, 435-437; trends in, xxiii-xxiv, 5-6, 26-27; varieties of, 7-12; as vocation, 72-74. *See also* Sociology

Arizona State University, postdoctoral trainee at, 359

Army Corps of Engineers, 244

Army General Classification Test (AGCT), 237

Army Research Institute for the Behavioral and Social Sciences (ARI), 242-243

Army Science Board, 245, 248

Army Scientific Advisory Panel, 242, 248

Army Training Study (ARTS), 244

analysis of, 215-233; disadvantages of settings for, 220-222; improvement strategies for, 229-233; intramural, 223; peer review in, 220-221; policy impact of, 219, 225; settings for, 216-229
Hospital Corporation of America, 217
Housing and environmental planning. *See* Community development
Houston, Clear Lake City, University of, undergraduate education at, 332, 341
Human Resources Research Office (HumRRO), 238, 240, 242
Human Sciences Research, Inc., 243
Human services planning: analysis of, 106-117; areas in, 107-112; citizen participation in, 110; design and implementation in, 111; needs assessment in, 107-108; resources allocation in, 109-110; resources analysis in, 108-109; and sociological theory, 112-113; values and objectivity issues in, 114-115

I

Illinois, Chicago Circle, University of, undergraduate education at, 332, 334, 342
Illinois, University of, survey research training at, 99
Illinois State University, undergraduate education at, 333, 342
Indiana, University of, survey research training at, 99
Industrial Cooperative Association, 141
Industry, social research in, 165-171
Institution building, and qualitative methods, 425-426
Interdisciplinary approach: in aging research, 264-265; and applied sociology, 17-19, 28; in clinical sociology, 18; in educational research, 255; in graduate education, 304, 305, 371; in health service administration, 160-162; in law and criminal justice, 208-209; in postdoctoral training, 362, 364; in

social engineering, 18; in training, 437
Intergovernmental Personnel Act, 223, 333
Internships: and alumni, 340, 345; issues in, 337-338; in undergraduate education, 332-333, 336-340
Interviewing, in consumer and advertising research, 191-192
Iowa State University, undergraduate education at, 342

J

Johns Hopkins University: Center for the Study of School Organization at, 253; and military studies, 238, 240
Johnson Foundation, Robert Wood, 217
Journals: for aging research, 266; for evaluation research, 78; and military studies, 247; for quantitative methods, 392; for survey research, 104-105

K

Kaiser Family Foundation, 217
Kellogg Foundation, W. K., 217
Kennedy administration, 27
Kent State University, graduate training at, 365, 366, 367-368
Kentucky, University of, undergraduate education at, 338
Knowledge: for applied sociology, 20-24; boundaries of, 289-290, 303-304, 316-317, 424-425

L

Law, and sociology, 284-285
Law and criminal justice: academic and professional responses to, 206; analysis of, 200-214; and clinical sociology, 209-210; and community mediation movement, 205-206; corrections programs in, 202-203, 204; current situation in, 201-204; evaluation research in,